Lecture Notes in Computer Science 10615

Commenced Publication in 1973
Founding and Former Series Editors:
Gerhard Goos, Juris Hartmanis, and Jan van Leeuwen

Editorial Board

More information about this series at http://www.springer.com/series/7410

Robert Krimmer · Melanie Volkamer
Nadja Braun Binder · Norbert Kersting
Olivier Pereira · Carsten Schürmann (Eds.)

Electronic Voting

Second International Joint Conference, E-Vote-ID 2017
Bregenz, Austria, October 24–27, 2017
Proceedings

 Springer

Editors
Robert Krimmer ⓘ
Tallinn University of Technology
Tallinn
Estonia

Norbert Kersting
University of Münster
Münster
Germany

Melanie Volkamer ⓘ
Technische Universität Darmstadt
Darmstadt
Germany

Olivier Pereira
Université Catholique de Louvain
Louvain
Belgium

Nadja Braun Binder ⓘ
German Research Institute for Public
    Administration
Speyer
Germany

Carsten Schürmann ⓘ
IT University of Copenhagen
Copenhagen
Denmark

ISSN 0302-9743   ISSN 1611-3349   (electronic)
Lecture Notes in Computer Science
ISBN 978-3-319-68686-8   ISBN 978-3-319-68687-5   (eBook)
DOI 10.1007/978-3-319-68687-5

Library of Congress Control Number: 2017955783

LNCS Sublibrary: SL4 – Security and Cryptology

Printed on acid-free paper

This Springer imprint is published by Springer Nature
The registered company is Springer International Publishing AG
The registered company address is: Gewerbestrasse 11, 6330 Cham, Switzerland

Preface

This volume contains papers presented at E-Vote-ID 2017: International Joint Conference on Electronic Voting held during October 24–27, 2017 in Bregenz, Austria. The current edition represents the Second International Joint Conference on Electronic Voting (E-Vote-ID), after the merging of EVOTE and Vote-ID.

Together with last year's conference, more than 800 experts from over 35 countries over the last 13 years have attended the conference series. Thus, the conference continues as one of the major events in the field of electronic voting providing ample room for interdisciplinary and open discussion of all issues relating to electronic voting.

This year, too, the conference consisted of:

- Security, Usability and Technical Issues Track
- Administrative, Legal, Political, and Social Issues Track
- Election and Practical Experiences Track
- PhD Colloquium (on the day before the conference)

This year's edition, E-VOTE-ID 2017, received 48 submissions, with each of them being reviewed by three to four Program Committee members, using a double blind-review process. As a result, 16 papers were accepted for this issue, representing 33% of the submitted proposals. The selected papers cover a wide range of topics connected with electronic voting including experiences and revisions of the real uses of e-voting systems and corresponding processes in elections. Beside the accepted papers, the volume contains three invited papers from the conference keynote speakers.

Special thanks go to the members of the international Program Committee for their hard work in reviewing, discussing, and shepherding papers. They ensured the high quality of these proceedings with their knowledge and experience.

We also would like to thank the German Informatics Society (Gesellschaft für Informatik) with its ECOM working group for their partnership over several years. A big thank you goes also to the Swiss Federal Chancellery for their continued support.

October 2017

Robert Krimmer
Melanie Volkamer
Nadja Braun Binder
Norbert Kersting
Olivier Pereira
Carsten Schürmann

Organization

Program Committee

Roberto Araujo	Universidade Federal do Pará (UFPA), Brazil
Frank Bannister	Trinity College Dublin, Ireland
Jordi Barrat i Esteve	eVoting Legal Lab, Spain
Josh Benaloh	Microsoft Research, USA
David Bismark	Votato, Sweden
Nadja Braun Binder	FÖV Speyer, Germany
Christian Bull	The Norwegian Ministry of Local Government and Regional Development, Norway
Susanne Caarls	Seconded National Expert Public Administration Reform in Greece at European Commission, Greece
Gianpiero Catozzi	UNDP, Belgium
Veronique Cortier	CNRS, Loria, France
Ardita Driza Maurer	Zentrum für Demokratie Aarau/Zurich University, Switzerland
Aleksander Essex	Western University, Canada
David Galindo	University of Birmingham, UK
J. Paul Gibson	Mines Telecom, France
Kristian Gjøsteen	Norwegian University of Science and Technology, Norway
Rajeev Gore	The Australian National University, Australia
Ruediger Grimm	University of Koblenz, Germany
Rolf Haenni	Bern University of Applied Sciences, Switzerland
Tarmo Kalvet	Ragnar Nurkse School of Innovation and Governance, Tallinn University of Technology, Estonia
Norbert Kersting	University of Münster, Germany
Aggelos Kiayias	National and Kapodistrian University of Athens, Greece
Shin Kim	Hallym University, Korea
Robert Krimmer	Tallinn University of Technology, Ragnar Nurkse School of Innovation and Governance, Estonia
Ralf Kuesters	University of Stuttgart, Germany
Oksana Kulyk	TU Darmstadt, Germany
Steven Martin	OSCE/ODIHR, Poland
Ronan McDermott	Mcdis, Switzerland
Juan Manuel Mecinas Montiel	CIDE, Mexico
Hannu Nurmi	University of Turku, Finland
Jon Pammett	Carleton University, Canada
Olivier Pereira	Universite catholique de Louvain, Belgium

Contents

X   Contents

Election Security and Economics:
It's All About Eve

David Basin[1]([⊠]), Hans Gersbach[2], Akaki Mamageishvili[2],
Lara Schmid[1], and Oriol Tejada[2]

[1] Institute of Information Security, ETH Zurich, Zurich, Switzerland
basin@inf.ethz.ch
[2] Chair of Macroeconomics: Innovation and Policy, ETH Zurich,
Zurich, Switzerland

Abstract. A system's security must be understood with respect to the capabilities and behaviors of an adversary Eve. It is often assumed in security analysis that Eve acts as maliciously as possible. From an economic perspective, Eve tries to maximize her utility in a game with other participants. The game's rules are determined by the system and its security mechanisms, but Eve can invent new ways of interacting with participants. We show that Eve can be used as an interface to explore the interplay between security and economics in the domain of elections. Through examples, we illustrate how reasoning from both disciplines may be combined to explicate Eve's motives and capabilities and how this analysis could be used for reasoning about the security and performance of elections. We also point to future research directions at the intersection of these disciplines.

1 Introduction

Election security is an important societal problem as attacks on elections put democracy at risk. When establishing that an election system is secure, one must reason about the adversarial environment in which the system is used. This requires specifying the capabilities of the adversary, henceforth called Eve.

In the security community, one provides an adversary model that specifies Eve's capabilities and assumes she will exploit these capabilities, independent of the costs. For election security, one typically assumes the existence of reasonably strong adversaries when designing the system, for example adversaries that may compromise the client's platform but not the voting server or the postal channel. Such assumptions are usually made without detailed economic justifications. In economics, one considers what Eve is rationally motivated to do and one looks at the entire range of sophisticated mechanisms available to her to exploit the humans that use the system. For example, a wealthy adversary might try to buy votes in elections, with adverse consequence; see e.g. [14]. Moreover, economists may consider the scenario where a majority of citizens base their voting decisions on false assumptions about their decisions' effects, with adverse long-term societal consequences [6].

© Springer International Publishing AG 2017
R. Krimmer et al. (Eds.): E-Vote-ID 2017, LNCS 10615, pp. 1–20, 2017.
DOI: 10.1007/978-3-319-68687-5_1

In this paper, we outline these two perspectives of Eve. We show that the perspective used in one discipline can sharpen the assumptions, models, and results used in the other discipline. Hence, both disciplines together can best ensure election security and the quality of election outcomes.

First, security analysis is central to economic models of elections since these models always depend implicitly on security properties such as integrity or coercion resistance, as we will illustrate in this paper. Hence, trust in an election's outcome depends on whether such security properties can be proven to hold. Moreover, when harmful adversarial behavior cannot be ruled out, an analysis of the adversary's capabilities provides a guide to constructing economic models involving these adversaries. One can then calculate the expected election outcome in the presence of the modeled adversary.

Second, economic analysis is important for security analysis in order to determine what a rational adversary will do. On the one hand, Eve may never undertake certain actions and thus these actions can be omitted from the security analysis. On the other hand, Eve may invent entirely new games to interact with a system's participants, which can undermine the system's security properties. This may necessitate modeling Eve or other participants differently in the security analysis. We illustrate this with two examples in this paper. In the first example, we show that the use of decoy ballots, which are fake ballots that are introduced to avoid vote buying, are much less secure than assumed so far. In the second example, we explain why the authenticity of voting-related information must be considered to be a central security property since, otherwise, an adversary could spoof a trusted information source and send biased information to voters, which could lead to undesirable voting outcomes.

Most research in security analysis and economics has been carried out independently. In recent times, research straddling these two disciplines has emerged. For example, malware researchers [8,25] have investigated the behavior of real-life adversaries and how this behavior relates to their economic goals. Other researchers [1,11,15] have modeled (coercible) users and security providers as rational agents and used this to investigate the adequacy of different security measures. Game-theoretic models have been employed [24,27] to analyze the security of physical environments, such as airports and harbors, and to determine the best strategies to protect them against adversaries. Recently, researchers in elections have started investigating this interplay too, for example, in the context of vote buying [18]. We see our work in line with this trend, explicating the interplay between security and economics and highlighting Eve's use as an interface between these disciplines.

We proceed as follows. In Sect. 2, we review how (voting) protocols are generally formalized in information security and economics, highlighting Eve's special role. In Sect. 3, we describe two voting protocols, a simple voting protocol and Chaum's [9] *random sample elections*, which we use in Sects. 4 and 5 to illustrate how information security researchers and economists analyze voting protocols and to investigate the interplay between these two disciplines. Finally, in Sect. 6, we draw conclusions and provide a perspective on the scope and some of the challenges of this important interdisciplinary research area.

2 General Approaches

2.1 Information Security

To analyze a system in information security, one must specify the system P, the adversary (alias "Eve") A, and the desired security properties $Prop$. The system's security is established by proving an assertion of the form $P, A \vDash Prop$, which states that all possible system behaviors satisfy the property $Prop$, when P is executed in an environment with the adversary A. When the system is distributed, such as (voting) protocols are, this essentially means that all possible behaviors arising from agents executing the protocol, operating in parallel with the adversary, satisfy the property $Prop$. Rigorously establishing this requires precise specifications of P, A, and $Prop$ and constructing proofs, ideally, using theorem provers or model checkers. For security protocols, the specifications are often given using symbolic models, and proofs are constructed using model checkers like ProVerif [7] or Tamarin [17,20]. See [4] for more on this.

We now further describe P, A, and $Prop$, focusing on the distributed setting. Here, P specifies the protocol that honest agents follow. For example, P is defined by *role specifications* that describe the behavior of honest agents in terms of which messages they send and receive and in which order. The protocol's execution semantics is defined by all possible interleavings of instantiated roles, also interleaved with actions of the adversary A.

A property $Prop$ is intended to hold in every possible execution of the protocol. What $Prop$ specifies depends on the system under consideration. For voting protocols, we are typically interested in the following properties. *Integrity* demands that information, e.g., votes, cannot be changed by an unauthorized entity. *Verifiability* additionally stipulates that integrity can be verifiably established, e.g., by individuals who check that their own votes are recorded as cast (*individual verifiability*) or that all votes are counted as recorded (*universal verifiability*). *Secrecy* and *privacy* guarantee that it is indistinguishable who voted for what. Finally, *coercion resistance* states that a voter cannot prove to an adversary how he voted, even if he actively collaborates with the adversary.

Eve, the adversary A, is the focus of this paper. We emphasize that a system's security can only be analyzed meaningfully with respect to a class of adversaries. For example, a system P that keeps data secret ($Prop$) in the face of a network adversary A, may be insecure against a stronger adversary with physical access to the system, who can perform side channel attacks or even remove and copy the hard disk. For security protocols, a popular adversary is the *Dolev-Yao* adversary [10], who has full control over the network. This adversary can read and change everything sent over the network, and can also send messages herself. Furthermore, this adversary can compromise agents and learn their secrets. We will consider a number of other adversaries shortly in the context of voting.

2.2 Economics

Economic models of collective decision mechanisms help to analyze the design and goals thereof. In particular, they can be used to establish if a given voting protocol is based on principles of liberal democracies and whether it yields welfare gains.

Game-theoretical models, in particular, are best suited for assessing the properties of collective decision mechanisms. These models aim to explain the strategic interaction between agents with opposing interests and to discern why some agents may opt for particular behaviors. A game-theoretical model of a collective decision mechanism demands that we specify the following elements:

1. The player set *(Who)*: who are the agents that can participate in the game?
2. The game rules *(How)*: what is each agent allowed to do and what information is available to him when he takes his decisions?
3. The strategy set *(What)*: what strategies are available to the agents, where a strategy describes what the agent does in each game situation?
4. Utilities *(Why)*: what does each player want to achieve in such a game?

Each player aims to maximize his (expected) utility, given his observations about other players' past actions and his predictions about past and future actions. Given a game, one looks for its *equilibria*, i.e., for the situations where no player has an incentive to change his decision given the (expected) decisions of the remaining players. These equilibria are predictions about the outcome of collective decisions, and can be investigated with respect to the quality and costs of the game's outcome. Most game-theoretical models do not assume the existence of an adversary that can influence the outcome of the collective decision. There is however a strand of literature that explicitly incorporates an adversary as an active player of the game. In this paper we examine one instance of such a model.

3   Voting Protocols

Numerous voting protocols have been proposed in the past. We introduce here two protocols that we will subsequently use to illustrate how voting protocols are analyzed from the information security and economic perspectives.

Voting protocols often involve players (or agents) acting in roles, which are called *principals*. These include a *voting server/election authority*, with a database that processes all the cast votes, stores them, and tallies them. Often, the election authority, who conducts the elections, and the voting server are considered to be one principal. The eligible *voters* are the principals who are legally entitled to vote. When voting electronically, they cast their vote using a *computing platform*. Usually, one considers a *public bulletin board* where votes are published in an authentic way and cannot be altered afterwards. Finally, *auditors* are the principals who check the published information for consistency. Auditors may be voters, party members, candidates, or independent parties.

3.1   Simple Voting Protocol

A simple voting protocol is shown in Fig. 1. This protocol is overly simple; it merely serves to illustrate Eve's role in the following sections. The three involved principals, from left to right, denote a voter, a voting server, and a database where votes are collected. Here we explicitly separate the server from the database to model a traditional three-tier architecture with a presentation tier (browser on the client), a server tier, and a storage tier. In the protocol, a voter sends his vote to the server, which stores the vote in the database. After all votes have been collected, the votes in the database are tallied and the result is published on the server. A voter can read the published result from the server.

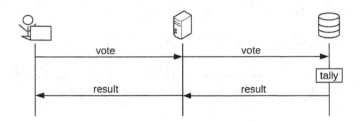

Fig. 1. A simple voting protocol.

3.2   Random Sample Elections

A more complex protocol, but with stronger security guarantees, is random sample elections as introduced by Chaum [9]. The main novelty is that only a random sample of the electorate votes. The motivation is economic: this procedure should be less costly than voting by the entire electorate, and voters may be better informed when they vote less frequently.

In more detail, random sample elections partition the electorate into three sets. The first set consists of the randomly selected (real) voters, whose votes will be counted. The second set consists of *decoy voters* who can ask for, and receive, fake ballots, which they can sell to adversaries. The third set contains those members of the electorate who are not selected and do not ask for fake ballots. Votes cast with fake ballots will have no effect on the tally. Nevertheless, after a decoy voter has ordered a ballot, he behaves exactly as a normal voter when casting his vote. As we explain below, decoy votes are intended to prevent coercion. Additionally, there are auditors, who may be voters or other individuals.

Figure 2 illustrates some of the actions that can take place in random sample elections. As a preliminary step, decoy voters can actively order ballots; in contrast, selected real voters receive ballots without prior actions. This optional step for decoy voters is illustrated by the dashed arrow. Afterwards, the protocol for real voters and decoy voters is identical. First, each voter is provided a pair of

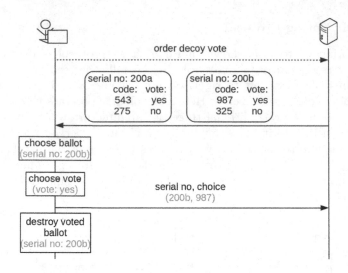

Fig. 2. The voting protocol for random sample elections, illustrated on an example. The dashed arrow indicates the message only sent by decoy voters.

ballots by mail. Each ballot has a serial number, 200*a* and 200*b* in the example, and two answers, yes/no, each with a unique code. A voter can choose either ballot for voting. Second, to cast his vote, the voter enters online the serial number of the chosen ballot and the code of his choice. Figure 2 depicts an example of this in gray. Namely, the voter decides to vote with the ballot with the serial number 200*b* and the vote *yes*. Therefore, he looks up the code corresponding to *yes* on this ballot, which is 987, and he casts his vote by entering the serial number and this code online. Finally, the voter destroys the ballot with the serial number 200*b* so that no one can learn to which vote this code corresponds. He may write down the code 987 to help him remember later what he has sent.

During the voting procedure, the election authority posts information on the bulletin board to enable auditors to verify that the voting procedure was correctly followed. We explain next, on an example, the election authority's internal representation of this information.

Consider a random sample election with two voters, a real voter V_r and a decoy voter V_d. We assume that there are the two pairs of ballots given in Fig. 3. The first pair (the two ballots on the left) is from Fig. 2 and we assume that it was sent to the real voter V_r. The second pair (the two ballots on the right) is sent to the decoy voter V_d. Furthermore, we assume that, as in Fig. 2, V_r selects ballot 200*b* and votes *yes* and that V_d selects ballot 023*a* and votes *yes*.

Figure 4 illustrates the table that is known only to the election authority after the votes are cast. The first column denotes the serial numbers and the codes as appearing on the ballots. The second column indicates which ballots have not been used for casting votes and lists the serial number and codes of these ballots again. Recall that each voter receives two ballots, but only uses one for voting.

serial no: 200a	serial no: (200b)	serial no: (023a)	serial no: 023b
code: vote:	code: vote:	code: vote:	code: vote:
543 yes	(987) yes	(642) yes	555 yes
275 no	325 no	735 no	524 no

Fig. 3. Two pairs of ballots, where the left pair is from a real voter and the right pair is from a decoy voter. Choices are circled in gray.

code	print	vote	voted	decoy
200a, 543	200a, 543	yes	-	-
200a, 275	200a, 275	no	-	-
200b, 987	-	yes	x	-
200b, 325	-	no	-	-
023a, 642	-	yes	x	decoy
023a, 735	-	no	-	decoy
023b, 555	023b, 555	yes	-	decoy
023b, 524	023b, 524	no	-	decoy

Fig. 4. Internal representation of the information stored by the election authority in random sample elections (simplified).

In the example, the ballots 200a and 023b have not been used for casting votes. The third column indicates the vote that corresponds to the respective code in this column. For example, the first row indicates that on the ballot with serial number 200a, the code 543 represents the vote *yes*. The fourth column marks which votes have been chosen. For example, the third row indicates that on ballot 200b, the code 987, which encodes the choice *yes*, has been voted. Finally, the last column indicates whether the respective ballot was sent to a decoy voter, which is the case here for the ballots 023a and 023b.

We will explain in the next section how protocols for posting parts of this information enable verifiability.

4   Information Security Analysis

We first present the information security approach to analyzing security protocols. We start with the simple protocol from Sect. 3 and use it to highlight the importance of adversary models and also the relationship of these models to trust assumptions. Afterwards, we turn to random sample elections.

4.1   Adversary

Trust and compromised principals. In information security, one reasons about the adversary Eve, as formalized by an adversary model, or by trust assumptions. These notions are dual: if we trust a principal, for example a system component, to act in a certain way (e.g., to follow a specification), this is equivalent to assuming that Eve cannot compromise the component and thereby alter its behavior. For example, if we consider a trusted client and server in our simple voting protocol (Fig. 1), we can send messages to the server over the Transport Layer Security protocol TLS (which establishes a secure channel) and hence an adversary who can only observe the network cannot eavesdrop or tamper with transmitted messages, such as votes or election results. However, if we consider a compromised client platform, the adversary can both learn and alter the votes sent. Similarly, if we do not trust the server, i.e., if it can be compromised, then it does not help to use a secure channel to send votes over the network. Eve can still learn and alter the votes because she can learn all the server's secrets.

The following example illustrates that considering different trust assumptions for different usage scenarios is commonplace.

Example 1. The Swiss regulations for electronic voting [22,23] dictate that if at least 30% of the electorate vote electronically, it is assumed that the platform is untrusted but the server is trusted. However, if at least 50% of the electorate vote electronically, it must be assumed that both the platform and the server are untrusted. Equivalently, in the first case, it is assumed that Eve can corrupt just the platform, whereas in the second case, she can corrupt the server as well. Hence two different adversary models are used for the two scenarios.   ∎

Channel assumptions. Continuing with our simple voting protocol, suppose the connection from the voter to the server is not secured by TLS but instead that the unencrypted votes are sent over the insecure network. The voting protocol then does not achieve vote secrecy, even with respect to a weak adversary such as a passive, eavesdropping adversary. It is thus crucial that we state for all principals whether they can be compromised and, moreover, for all communication channels, what Eve's capabilities are.

For online voting, many formalisms assume a Dolev-Yao adversary who can control the network. Assume now that in the simple protocol, votes are not cast online but that the postal service is used instead. Some voting schemes effectively introduce the postal service as an auxiliary (out-of-band) communication channel, which is assumed to be trustworthy, i.e., a secure channel. However, as the following example suggests, one must carefully examine whether such assumptions are justified and what the effects are when these assumptions fail.

Example 2. A reported case of voter fraud took place in the canton of Valais, Switzerland, in March 2017 [21,26]. Normally, ballots are sent to voters by the postal service, after which they are filled out and signed by the voters. The ballots are subsequently cast using the postal service or are hand-delivered to a polling station. In the reported case, some empty ballots were never received by the intended voters. The election protocol used allows voters to order new ballots in such situations. However, when casting their newly ordered ballots, the affected voters noticed that someone else had already voted in their name. The most likely explanation is that the ballots were stolen from their mail boxes and cast by an adversary. Hence, the postal channel did not provide a secure channel from the election authority to the voters, as an adversary had access to the ballots.   ■

Summarizing, the adversary model must precisely define for each principal involved and each channel used how Eve can interact with and possibly compromise them. Otherwise security cannot be meaningfully established. See [4] for an account of how to formalize such models in general. [2,3,5] explain how to formalize channel models and adversaries with a wide range of capabilities.

4.2   Security Properties

There are many security properties relevant for voting protocols. We concentrate on coercion resistance, integrity, and verifiability, and consider them in the context of random sample elections. We also present some additional properties specific to random sample elections.

Coercion resistance. In voting, Eve may try to coerce voters or pay them to vote as she wishes. Sometimes a distinction is made as to whether the voter is willing to collaborate with Eve, for example, for money. In such a context, a protocol where a voter cannot possibly prove that he voted as Eve demanded is more secure with respect to coercion than a protocol where the voter can prove how he voted if he chooses to collaborate with Eve.

In random sample elections, Chaum [9] suggests that coercion resistance can be achieved by employing decoy votes. These votes are indistinguishable from real votes, but they do not contribute to the tally. Since they can be sold, Eve may be less interested in buying votes because she cannot distinguish a real vote from a decoy vote. In terms of the adversary model, the security properties, and the protocol, this can be understood as follows: if decoy votes are effective, Eve will not buy votes and therefore we can exclude the action of vote buying from the adversary model. Of course, if we model an adversary that does not engage in vote buying, coercion resistance holds, independent of the protocol.

Whether or not Chaum's proposal is an adequate countermeasure to vote buying boils down to an economics question. Eve's problem, according to [19], is that she must offer a sufficiently high price for votes in order to attract real votes in addition to the decoy votes that will always be offered to her. Whether Eve engages in vote-buying in such a situation depends on two factors. First, as the share of decoy votes increases, Eve can buy fewer real votes with a given budget. However, an adversary with an extremely large budget might not be deterred by decoy votes. Second, Eve must know the distribution of the real voters' willingness to sell their votes. Otherwise, she risks buying mainly decoy votes if the price is low or, alternatively, vote-buying may be extremely expensive.

Current analysis of decoy votes [19] suggests that an appropriate design of decoy votes is a viable tool to achieve coercion resistance, however, never in an absolute sense. In Sect. 5.3, we will discuss new ways to buy votes when there are decoy votes, which cast doubt on whether decoy votes achieve their intended purpose. Furthermore, we demonstrate that they allow an adversary to distinguish real from decoy voters.

Finally, as a side remark, note that decoy votes may pose a challenge to the credibility of the entire voting process since the electorate is encouraged to interact with the adversary.

Integrity and verifiability. Integrity is the property that data cannot be changed in unauthorized ways, for example, the votes cannot be manipulated. Verifiability is the property that participants or outsiders can establish the integrity of the election results. Equivalently, it is verifiable that no one, including the election authority or even errors in the voting software, can alter the result without this being detected. Verifiability properties are often classified as either *individual verifiability* or *universal verifiability*. Individual verifiability states that each voter can verify that his vote was recorded as cast. Universal verifiability states that auditors, which can be anyone, can verify that the recorded votes were counted correctly by the server. To establish such a property, the election authority often publishes different stages of its computations. For example, it publishes the recorded votes in encrypted form and then publishes the decrypted votes as the final tally. Additionally, the authority proves that the tally corresponds to the encrypted votes.

Verification can be performed in different ways. Take, for example, the problem of showing that the decrypted votes correspond to the encrypted ones. A possible strategy is to verify this by a *cut and choose* argument. In cut and choose, the authority constructs several tables of intermediate results and cryptographically commit to them. Once committed, they cannot change the tables' entries. A random event then decides which columns of each table must be revealed. The revealed columns allow anyone to verify that the tables are consistent, without revealing anything secret. Note that at the time it commits to the tables, the election authority does not know which columns will later be revealed. Therefore, if the consistency checks are verified in many iterations of this procedure, all the computations must have been done correctly with high probability.

Example 3, at the end of this section, illustrates cut and choose on the example of random sample elections. Chaum does not explicitly formalize the considered adversary model in random sample elections. However, the presented mechanism establishes the verifiability of the voting tally even if the election authority is compromised.

If we assume that an adversary cannot compromise the election authority, we are usually not concerned with verifiability properties. If the election authority behaves according to the protocol, the result will not be manipulated. However, if we assume that the election authority can be compromised, then verifiability is important. Also, as the adversary can manipulate each part of the computation, we must ensure that we check all relevant parts, from ballot printing all the way to the fact that the ballots are recorded as cast and counted as recorded.

code	print	vote	voted	decoy
200a, 543	200a, 543	yes	-	-
200a, 275	200a, 275	no	-	-
200b, 987	-	yes	x	-
200b, 325	-	no	-	-
023a, 642	-	yes	x	decoy
023a, 735	-	no	-	decoy
023b, 555	023b, 555	yes	-	decoy
023b, 524	023b, 524	no	-	decoy

(a) Full (internal) representation.

code	print	vote	voted	decoy
023b, 524	023b, 524	no	-	decoy
023a, 735	-	no	-	decoy
200b, 987	-	yes	x	-
023a, 642	-	yes	x	decoy
200b, 325	-	no	-	-
023b, 555	023b, 555	yes	-	decoy
200a, 275	200a, 275	no	-	-
200a, 543	200a, 543	yes	-	-

(b) Check individual verifiability.

code	print	vote	voted	decoy
200b, 325	-	no	-	-
200a, 275	200a, 275	no	-	-
023a, 735	-	no	-	decoy
023a, 642	-	yes	x	decoy
023b, 524	023b, 524	no	-	decoy
200a, 543	200a, 543	yes	-	-
200b, 987	-	yes	x	-
023b, 555	023b, 555	yes	-	decoy

(c) Check print auditing.

code	print	vote	voted	decoy
023b, 555	023b, 555	yes	-	decoy
023a, 735	-	no	-	decoy
200b, 987	-	yes	x	-
200b, 325	-	no	-	-
023b, 524	023b, 524	no	-	decoy
023a, 642	-	yes	x	decoy
200a, 543	200a, 543	yes	-	-
200a, 275	200a, 275	no	-	-

(d) Check final tally.

Fig. 5. Simplified version of cut and choose for random sample elections.

Other Properties. Two other security properties specific to random sample elections are the *integrity* and the *verifiability* of the random selection. This means that the sampled voters are drawn *uniformly at random* from the set of possible voters, that the election authority cannot manipulate the sample group, and that everyone can verify this while still ensuring the anonymity of the real voters. Similarly to establishing the verifiability of the tally, the election authority publishes information on the bulletin board that allows such verification. In particular, the election authority commits to certain values before an unpredictable public random event produces the randomness for the random sampling.

Another important property for random sample elections is the *anonymity of the sample group*. This states that no one can learn who the real voters are. Random sample elections aim to achieve this with decoy voters that can interact with the election authority in exactly the same way as real voters. Hence they are indistinguishable from the perspective of an observing adversary. Interestingly, if the adversary can also interact with real and decoy voters, she can use this to her advantage as we explain in the following section.

Example 3. We present a simplified version of cut and choose for random sample elections, continuing the example from Sect. 3.2. For readability, in Fig. 5a we present again the table that is only known to the election authority. We gray out this table's content to denote that the gray values are not visible on the bulletin board, but only known internally.

Of course, at the beginning of the election, some of these entries are not yet known. In a first phase, which takes place before the ballots are sent to the voters, the election authority fills in the first, third and fifth columns of the table in Fig. 5a, while the second and fourth columns remain empty. The election authority then produces multiple copies of this table, $3k$ copies in this example, and randomly permutes their rows, resulting, for example, in the tables shown in Figs. 5b–d. Then, it encrypts each column of each table with a different secret key and publishes all the resulting encrypted tables on the bulletin board. At this stage, the bulletin board contains $3k$ tables where columns one, three, and five are filled in but the content is not yet readable by the auditors. The columns are encrypted in such a way that they hide the contents of the columns but they can later only be decrypted to the original plain text. With this mechanism, the election authority *commits* to the content without revealing it at this point.

Afterwards, the real voters are chosen, the ballots are sent to the real and decoy voters, and the voters cast their votes. Then, the second and fourth columns are filled into all $3k$ copies of the table, after the votes have been recorded. The resulting columns are again encrypted and published, such that the bulletin board now contains $3k$ full, but hidden tables; this concludes the "cut"-phase.

Next, in the "choose"-phase, the $3k$ tables are divided into three disjoint batches, each containing k tables, based on an unpredictable, random event. The membership of a table to a batch decides which of the table's columns must be revealed on the bulletin board for auditors to inspect. Each table in Figs. 5b–d represents one batch. The white columns depict which columns are revealed for all tables in this batch for the verifiability checks. The gray columns are never revealed. It is important that the event that determines which tables go into which batch is unpredictable so that the election authority cannot prepare the tables in such a way that all the checks go through even when the tables are inconsistent. Furthermore, it is crucial that the columns of all tables have already been committed to, since this allows an auditor to discover if the election authority has manipulated the tables after-the-fact. The following verifiability checks are used by this procedure.

In the first batch, depicted by the table in Fig. 5b, the serial numbers and codes, their repetition in unused ballots, and the voted marks (white columns) are revealed on the bulletin board. This enables every voter to verify that his vote has been recorded as cast. For example, the voter V_r can verify that the ballot 200b was used to cast a vote (because the field in "print" is empty) and that the code 987 was marked as voted. However, no one else learns that the code 987 corresponds to the *yes* vote.

The published columns in Fig. 5c enable voters to verify *print auditing*, that is that the ballots were printed correctly by the election authority. Each voter can check that the code-vote association of his unused ballot is correctly depicted by the table. For example, the voter V_r can check that for the ballot 200a, the code 275 corresponds to *no* and 543 to *yes*, corresponding to the copy of the ballot he still has in his possession. This ensures that the election authority cannot forge votes by printing ballots incorrectly. In particular, because the authority cannot predict which ballot will be chosen by the voter, it cannot know which ballot must be revealed for the consistency check.

In the final batch, as depicted in Fig. 5d, the last three columns of the tables are revealed. This enables all participants to verify the tally. In the example, everyone can see that there are two votes for *yes* and one of them has been sent by a decoy voter and will thus not be counted in the tally.[1] Note that because all tables have different row permutations, this procedure also ensures vote privacy. No auditor of the bulletin board can conclude, for example, that the voter with ballots 200*a* and 200*b* voted *yes* with code 987.   ■

Note that although Chaum does not provide formal models, the protocol we have sketched (and his extensions) are sufficiently detailed that they can be appropriately formalized and verified from the information security perspective.

5   Economic Perspective

In this section, we outline the economic analysis of random sample elections with decoy votes, explore the required security properties, and show that more sophisticated adversaries may violate some of the security properties of random sample elections with decoy votes.

5.1   Economic Analysis

We illustrate the analysis of random sample elections. In the simplest setting with *private values* and *costly voting*, we consider a model that has the following features:

1. There are two alternatives (S and P), representing candidates or issues.
2. The electorate is a given finite set N, which is randomly split into three subsets N_1, N_2 and N_3. Members of N_1 have the right to vote (henceforth called "sample group"), members of N_2 obtain decoy ballots (henceforth "decoy group"), and members of N_3 do not participate in the process. For any given set S, we use $|S|$ to denote its cardinality.
3. Voters $i \in N$ are of two types $t_i = S$ and $t_i = P$, that is, they either prefer S or P.
4. A share λ_S prefers S and a share λ_P prefers P, with $\lambda_S + \lambda_P = 1$.
5. Any voter i's utility is:

	t_i chosen	t_i not chosen
i votes	$1 - c$	$-c$
i does not vote	1	0

---

[1] The actual table in random sample elections is more involved and also includes information allowing one to ascertain that the right voters have been provided with ballots. We refer to [9] for further details, which are not relevant for this paper.

In this table, we have normalized the utility gain to 1 when the preferred alternative is chosen by the sample group. Voting is costly, as citizens need time to make up their minds and to vote. These costs are captured by the parameter c, $0 < c < 1$, which is assumed to be the same for all voters for illustrative purposes.

6. Real and decoy voters decide whether to abstain or to vote for one of the two alternatives. The votes of decoy voters are disregarded.

Finding the equilibria of the above game is the core of the economic analysis. For examples related to this game, see [16]. An immediate observation is that no voter will cast a vote against his preferred alternative. Building on equilibria outcomes, we can then make welfare comparisons relative to the standard voting system where all N citizens vote simultaneously, which serves as a benchmark.

The equilibria can be used to assess whether the voting outcome will achieve a low quality or high quality of collective decisions and whether or not the election generates high costs for the citizens.

In the random sample elections game introduced before, we can immediately observe that the highest decision quality is achieved if and only if

$$\mathcal{S} \text{ is chosen} \Leftrightarrow \lambda_{\mathcal{S}} \geq \frac{1}{2}.$$

Regarding the costs, the best possible situation occurs when nobody votes. In this case, however, no democratic decision-making is possible. Accordingly, there is a trade-off between quality and costs.[2] Typically, this is resolved by a welfare function that incorporates these two objectives or, alternatively, by achieving a certain quality at minimal cost. In most of the well-established costly voting models, the voting outcome does not achieve particularly high quality and the margin between the votes cast for $\mathcal{S}$ and $\mathcal{P}$ is much smaller than the margin between the support for the two alternatives in the entire population. Intuitively, this can be explained as follows: If a voter is in favor of the same decision as most voters are, he will more likely not vote. He can save the cost of voting because it is probable that his favored choice wins anyways. The small difference between votes cast for $\mathcal{S}$ and $\mathcal{P}$ opens up great opportunities for Eve. By manipulating a small number of votes, Eve can arrange that her preferred alternative wins, even if the support for the other alternative is much larger in the entire population.

5.2   Implicit Security Properties

In the following, we review some standard assumptions that are typically taken for granted in the voting model in Sect. 5.1. We show that with the insights provided by information security analysis, these assumptions can be made explicit and can be proven to hold.

---

[2] In general, this does not hold for all citizens. A fraction of voters derives positive value from engaging in deliberation and voting.

Economic models usually assume that the adversary does not interfere with the voting process. However, if one takes Eve seriously, it is easy to imagine different ways that she can affect the outcome of a collective decision directly. First, a small fraction of votes may be manipulated after they have been submitted by the voters, but before they have been made public. The severity of this problem increases the more a voting system tends to compress the vote margin, say by providing members of the majority with lower incentives to turn out than members of the minority. When margins are small, manipulating a few votes may suffice to change the outcome. As we have seen, the property of information security that denotes that no one can alter the votes after they have been cast is *integrity*. Additionally, one can require that everyone must be able to verify that this property holds. This is captured by the properties *individual* and *universal verifiability*.

Second, Eve may want to influence the selection of the voters in the sample group. To ascertain that a protocol is not vulnerable to such attacks, the sample group must be chosen *randomly*, and the *integrity* of the assignment of voters to the sample group must hold. Again, an additional requirement can be that these properties are *verifiable*.

Third, Eve may want to buy certain votes directly from the citizens. For this to be possible, she must have access to the voters' identities, who, in turn, need to prove to Eve that they have voted as agreed. Hence, both the *anonymity* of the sample group and *coercion resistance* are important properties.

Finally, Eve could try and send messages with political content to (targeted) voters to influence their evaluations of alternatives, and ultimately their decisions. This is related to the channel assumptions in the adversary model of information security. If we assume that there are only insecure channels from the election authority to the voter, then Eve could effectively influence voters by forging information as coming from the authority. If, however, the channels from the authority to the voter enable *message authentication*, then Eve cannot convincingly send messages as coming from the authority; this might decrease her chances to influence the voters.

For completeness, we summarize the security requirements needed for the successful implementation of random sample elections. They are: integrity and verifiability of the tally and the selection, random selection of the sample group, anonymity of the sample group, coercion resistance, and message authentication. We have just argued that economic models rely on these properties, which must be established by using the methods of information security. Conversely, as discussed in Sect. 4.2, information security sometimes assumes certain adversary capabilities that are based on economic reasoning, for example the argument that Eve will not buy votes if decoy votes are deployed because they make vote buying ineffective. Economic approaches can help to devise extremely sophisticated adversaries that exploit humans. We demonstrate that if we model a more sophisticated adversary, even with a very low budget she can break the anonymity of the sample group when decoy votes are used.

5.3   Vote Buying

Decoy ballots have been advocated as a viable tool against vote buying. For instance, [19] analyze decoy ballots from a game-theoretic perspective and conclude that they are reasonably immune to vote-buying attempts by malicious adversaries facing budget constraints. In their analysis, they only consider simple attacks by the adversary: she sets a price at which she is willing to buy votes, both from real voters and decoy voters. With the help of a simple model, we briefly discuss how a more sophisticated adversary Eve can separate decoy votes from real votes in the process of vote-buying.[3]

Consider now that the electorate N is composed of risk-neutral citizens, which base their decision solely on expected gains. We also assume that $|N|$ is sufficiently large so that we can work with the law of large numbers, and we denote by p, for $0 < p < 1$, the percentage of citizens who have real votes. These voters are chosen randomly. The rest of the electorate obtains decoy votes.[4] We stress that the parameter p can be chosen by the election designer. Whether one's ballot is real or decoy is private information, and hence, there is no possibility for an outside agent (including Eve) to distinguish between the two types of ballots. For a voter i, let V_i be the utility he obtains from voting. If a voter i has a decoy ballot, his utility is $V_i = 0$. If a voter i has a real ballot, his utility is $V_i = V > 0$. The exact value of V is determined in equilibrium. We assume that the adversary's goal is to buy half of the real votes, which amount to a share $p/2$ of the population.

We consider two possible procedures employed by Eve. First, suppose that she offers each citizen a certain amount x in exchange for his vote. Clearly, if $x < V$, she will only obtain decoy ballots. Hence assume that $x = V$, so that all citizens who are offered the deal accept. In order for Eve to obtain half of the real votes, on average she then needs to offer x to a half of the population since decoy ballots and real ballots are indistinguishable. This means that Eve expects per-capita costs denoted by B where

$$B = \frac{V}{2}.$$

Second, suppose that Eve chooses an entirely different approach and uses so-called "Devil's Raffles", i.e. offering lotteries $L_k = (p_k, q_k), (k = 1, 2, ...)$ of the following kind: with probability p_k, the voter will receive a sure payoff q_k in exchange for his vote, and with probability $1 - p_k$ no transaction will occur and the voter (real or decoy) will keep his ballot. Consider now two lotteries L_1 and L_2 with

$$p_2 := \tfrac{1}{2}$$
$$q_1 := V - \varepsilon$$
$$q_2 := V + \varepsilon$$

---

[3] The simple model we consider is different from, yet similar in spirit to, the one considered by [19].

[4] Thus we assume that $|N_3| = 0$. This is without loss of generality. Moreover, a full-fledged analysis reveals in our setting that all members of N_2 will apply for decoy votes.

for some small value $\varepsilon > 0$. Moreover, let

$$p_1 := \frac{\varepsilon + p_2 q_2}{q_1} = \frac{\varepsilon + \frac{1}{2}(V + \varepsilon)}{V - \varepsilon}. \tag{1}$$

Hence,

$$p_1 \cdot q_1 = \varepsilon + p_2 \cdot q_2 > p_2 \cdot q_2 = \frac{1}{2} \cdot (V + \varepsilon). \tag{2}$$

Thus, the expected payoff from choosing lottery L_1 is higher than that from choosing L_2.

Let us next examine the utilities of citizen i. On the one hand, if he accepts the lottery L_k, for $k \in \{1, 2\}$, he expects

$$\mathbb{E}[i \text{ sells his vote for } L_k] = p_k \cdot q_k + (1 - p_k) \cdot V_i. \tag{3}$$

If, on the contrary, citizen i does not sell his vote, he expects

$$\mathbb{E}[i \text{ does not sell his vote}] = V_i, \tag{4}$$

which is zero for decoy voters and V for real voters.

Since $V_i = 0$ for decoy voters, they will buy lottery L_1 since $p_1 q_1 > p_2 q_2$. For real voters $V_i = V$ and choosing lottery L_2 therefore yields the expected payoff

$$\frac{1}{2}(V + \varepsilon) + \frac{1}{2}V = V + \frac{1}{2}\varepsilon, \tag{5}$$

while selecting L_1 yields

$$p_1(V - \varepsilon) + (1 - p_1)V = V - p_1\varepsilon. \tag{6}$$

Hence real voters will buy lottery L_2.

Eve will offer these lotteries to a share s of the population. In order to obtain, on average, half of the real votes again, s must satisfy

$$s \cdot (p \cdot p_2 + (1 - p) \cdot 0) = p/2 \Leftrightarrow s = \frac{1}{2p_2} = 1.$$

This calculation reflects that $p \cdot p_2$ is the probability that a real voter gives Eve his vote (in lottery two), whereas $(1 - p) \cdot 0$ is the probability that Eve receives a real vote from a decoy voter. The result makes sense: Real voters have a chance of $\frac{1}{2}$ to be able to sell their votes. Hence, the entire electorate must be invited to apply for the lotteries.

We next calculate Eve's expected aggregate costs. For this purpose, we make ε arbitrarily small and neglect it in the calculation. Then the expected budget amounts to

$$B = p \cdot p_2 \cdot q_2 + (1 - p) \cdot p_1 \cdot q_1 \approx p_2 \cdot q_2 = \frac{1}{2} \cdot q_2 = \frac{V}{2}.$$

We obtain two conclusions from an economics perspective. First, attacks with Devil's Raffles are useful to identify who has a decoy ballot and who does not have one because real and decoy voters choose the lottery L_2 and L_1 to sell their votes, respectively. Moreover, Eve can elicit p if it is not known to her with a small budget by selecting small values of p_1 and p_2. Second, regarding the budget needed to obtain half of the real votes: there is no improvement compared to the first procedure where a price is fixed at which a fraction of votes is bought. However, there are more sophisticated forms of Devil's Raffles that also lower the budget [13].

From the security perspective, we learn that a sophisticated adversary can buy votes, even in the presence of decoy ballots. Given this, a protocol using decoy votes is unlikely to provide coercion resistance unless other more effective mechanisms are in place. Repairing this problem would require a protocol redesign. Moreover, the economic analysis demonstrates that decoy votes violate the anonymity of the sample group. Thus even if coercion resistance can be established using decoy ballots, this mechanism should not be used when the anonymity of the sample group is important.

6   Outlook

Through examples, we have shown how the adversary Eve provides an effective interface between security and economics. In particular, information security focuses on what Eve can technically do in a system that incorporates security mechanisms with the aim of achieving security properties. In contrast, economic models investigate what Eve is rationally motivated to do in a self-designed game with the system's participants. We have illustrated how these two viewpoints can complement each other. Economic models implicitly assume security properties that can be made explicit and be proven by using the techniques of information security. Similarly, informal economic arguments motivating the adversary models used in information security must be analyzed with great care. The example of the decoy votes, which are supposed to avoid coercion, shows that sophisticated adversaries can design out-of-the box games that endanger other security properties, such as the anonymity of the sample group.

An important future research direction is certainly to investigate the wide spectrum of adversary models used in election research, their economic justifications, their effects on critical security properties, and as a consequence how voting protocols must be strengthened (or weakened). In addition there are serious concerns that go beyond the actual voting and tallying protocol. Free and fair elections [12] impose requirements before and after the election: including basic freedoms like those of free speech, free press, free movement and assembly, as well as more specialized rights like access to polls and protection from intimidation. Recent elections in America and France have shown that organizations and other countries can attempt to influence public opinion by propaganda or "fake news".

Such election hacking is a major challenge for democracy and an important research direction for both information security and economic research. We conclude with an illustration based on our example from Sect. 5.1. Suppose that Eve manages to send a message about the relative merits of the two alternatives S and P that is perceived to be from a trusted authority and affects through biased information ("fake news") individual evaluations of the alternatives. Assume in our random sample elections game that Eve can manipulate in this way a small fraction of the sample group's members. Two possibilities can occur. First, and less plausibly, assume that it is common knowledge among all voters that Eve has manipulated a fraction of voters who then vote as desired by Eve and that Eve's preferred alternative is also commonly known. Then, the other voters could adjust their decision whether to abstain or not and could—and would—neutralize this manipulation. Second, and more plausibly, assume that Eve's manipulation is hidden. Since vote margins are typically small in costly voting setups, such a hidden manipulation—even of a small fraction of voters—would affect the outcome significantly. This type of manipulation makes voting outcomes extremely vulnerable and developing adequate security countermeasures is a considerable challenge.

References

1. Anderson, R.: Why information security is hard - an economic perspective. In: Proceedings of the 17th Annual Computer Security Applications Conference (ACSAC 2001), pp. 358–365 (2001). http://dl.acm.org/citation.cfm?id=872016.872155
2. Basin, D., Cremers, C.: Modeling and analyzing security in the presence of compromising adversaries. In: Gritzalis, D., Preneel, B., Theoharidou, M. (eds.) ESORICS 2010. LNCS, vol. 6345, pp. 340–356. Springer, Heidelberg (2010). doi:10.1007/978-3-642-15497-3_21
3. Basin, D., Cremers, C.: Know your enemy: compromising adversaries in protocol analysis. ACM Trans. Inf. Syst. Secur. **17**(2), 7:1–7:31 (2014). http://doi.acm.org/10.1145/2658996
4. Basin, D., Cremers, C., Meadows, C.: Model checking security protocols. In: Clarke, E., Henzinger, T., Veith, H. (eds.) Handbook of Model Checking. Chap. 24. Springer (to appear, 2017). ISBN: 9783319105741
5. Basin, D., Radomirovic, S., Schläpfer, M.: A complete characterization of secure human-server communication. In: 2015 IEEE 28th Computer Security Foundations Symposium, pp. 199–213. IEEE Computer Society (2015)
6. Beilharz, H.J., Gersbach, H.: Voting oneself into a crisis. Macroecon. Dyn. **20**(4), 954–984 (2016)
7. Blanchet, B.: An efficient cryptographic protocol verifier based on prolog rules. In: Proceedings of the 14th IEEE Workshop on Computer Security Foundations (CSFW 2001), pp. 82–96 (2001). http://dl.acm.org/citation.cfm?id=872752.873511
8. Caballero, J., Grier, C., Kreibich, C., Paxson, V.: Measuring pay-per-install: the commoditization of malware distribution. In: Proceedings of the 20th USENIX Conference on Security (SEC 2011), p. 13. USENIX Association, Berkeley (2011). http://dl.acm.org/citation.cfm?id=2028067.2028080
9. Chaum, D.: Random-sample voting. http://rsvoting.org/whitepaper/white_paper.pdf. Accessed 7 Jul 2017
10. Dolev, D., Yao, A.: On the security of public key protocols. IEEE Trans. Inf. Theory **29**(2), 198–208 (1983)

11. van Eeten, M.J., Bauer, J.M.: Economics of Malware: Security Decisions, Incentives and Externalities. OECD Science, Technology and Industry Working Papers 2008(1) (2008)
12. Elklit, J., Svensson, P.: What makes elections free and fair? J. Democracy **8**(3), 32–46 (1997)
13. Gersbach, H., Mamageishvili, A., Tejada, O.: Sophisticated Attacks on Decoy Votes. Mimeo (2017)
14. Gersbach, H., Mühe, F.: Vote-buying and growth. Macroecon. Dyn. **15**(5), 656–680 (2011)
15. Gordon, L.A., Loeb, M.P.: The economics of information security investment. ACM Trans. Inf. Syst. Secur. (TISSEC) **5**(4), 438–457 (2002)
16. Krasa, S., Polborn, M.K.: Is mandatory voting better than voluntary voting? Games Econ. Behav. **66**(1), 275–291 (2009)
17. Meier, S., Schmidt, B., Cremers, C., Basin, D.: The TAMARIN prover for the symbolic analysis of security protocols. In: Sharygina, N., Veith, H. (eds.) CAV 2013. LNCS, vol. 8044, pp. 696–701. Springer, Heidelberg (2013). doi:10.1007/978-3-642-39799-8_48
18. Oppliger, R., Schwenk, J., Helbach, J.: Protecting code voting against vote selling. In: Sicherheit 2008: Sicherheit, Schutz und Zuverlässigkeit. Konferenzband der 4. Jahrestagung des Fachbereichs Sicherheit der Gesellschaft für Informatik e.V. (GI), 2.-4. April 2008 im Saarbrücker Schloss. LNI, vol. 128, pp. 193–204. GI (2008)
19. Parkes, D.C., Tylkin, P., Xia, L.: Thwarting vote buying through decoy ballots. In: Proceedings of the 16th Conference on Autonomous Agents and Multiagent Systems, pp. 1679–1681. International Foundation for Autonomous Agents and Multiagent Systems (2017)
20. Schmidt, B., Meier, S., Cremers, C., Basin, D.: Automated analysis of Diffie-Hellman protocols and advanced security properties. In: Proceedings of the 2012 IEEE 25th Computer Security Foundations Symposium (CSF 2012), pp. 78–94 (2012). http://dx.doi.org/10.1109/CSF.2012.25
21. Schweizer Radio und Fernsehen (SRF): Spurensuche nach dem Wahlbetrug im Wallis. https://www.srf.ch/news/schweiz/spurensuche-nach-dem-wahlbetrug-im-wallis. Accessed 22 June 2017
22. Schweizerische Bundeskanzlei: Anhang zur Verordnung der Bundeskanzlei über die elektronische Stimmabgabe, Inkrafttreten: 15 January 2014. https://www.bk.admin.ch/themen/pore/evoting/07979/index.html?lang=de. Accessed 16 June 2017
23. Schweizerische Bundeskanzlei: Verordnung der Bundeskanzlei über die elektronische Stimmabgabe, Inkrafttreten: 15 January 2014. https://www.admin.ch/opc/de/classified-compilation/20132343/index.html#app1. Accessed 16 June 2017
24. Shieh, E., An, B., Yang, R., Tambe, M., Baldwin, C., DiRenzo, J., Maule, B., Meyer, G.: Protect: a deployed game theoretic system to protect the ports of the United States. In: Proceedings of the 11th International Conference on Autonomous Agents and Multiagent Systems, vol. 1, pp. 13–20. International Foundation for Autonomous Agents and Multiagent Systems (2012)
25. Stone-Gross, B., Holz, T., Stringhini, G., Vigna, G.: The underground economy of spam: a botmaster's perspective of coordinating large-scale spam campaigns. LEET **11**, 4 (2011)
26. Tages Anzeiger: Wahlbetrug im Oberwallis–30-jähriger Schweizer verhaftet. http://www.tagesanzeiger.ch/schweiz/standard/Wahlbetrug-im-Oberwallis-30jaehriger-Schweizer-verhaftet/story/14197130. Accessed 22 June 2017
27. Tambe, M.: Security and Game Theory: Algorithms, Deployed Systems, Lessons Learned. Cambridge University Press, Cambridge (2011)

Cryptographic Security Analysis of E-voting Systems: Achievements, Misconceptions, and Limitations

Ralf Küsters[1]([⊠]) and Johannes Müller[2]

[1] University of Stuttgart, Stuttgart, Germany
ralf.kuesters@sec.uni-stuttgart.de
[2] University of Trier, Trier, Germany
muellerjoh@uni-trier.de

Abstract. Rigorous cryptographic security analysis plays an important role in the design of modern e-voting systems by now. There has been huge progress in this field in the last decade or so in terms of formalizing security requirements and formally analyzing e-voting systems. This paper summarizes some of the achievements and lessons learned, which, among others, challenge common believes about the role of and the relationships between central security requirements.

1 Introduction

Privacy, verifiability, accountability, and coercion-resistance are fundamental security requirements for modern e-voting systems. *Privacy* ensures that the way a particular voter voted is not revealed to anybody. Intuitively, *verifiability* guarantees that it is possible to verify that the published election result is correct, even if voting machines/authorities are (partially) untrusted. In the literature, one often finds that verifiability is divided into *individual* and *universal verifiability*. *Accountability* is a stronger form of verifiability: accountability does not only require that it is detected if the published result is incorrect, but that misbehaving parties can be singled out and thus held accountable. This notion so far has gained much less attention than verifiability, although rather than aiming for mere verifiability, modern e-voting system should really strive for accountability in order to be useful in practice, as later explained and further emphasized in this paper. *Coercion-resistance* protects voters against vote buying and coercion. A weaker form of coercion-resistance is called *receipt-freeness*.

In order to find out whether a given voting system achieves its desired security properties, informally analyzing its security is not sufficient since critical aspects can easily be overlooked. Therefore, it is necessary to formally analyze the security of voting systems based on reasonable and formal security definitions.

There have been major achievements in the field of rigorous cryptographic analysis of e-voting systems in the last decade or so. Formal definitions for the

© Springer International Publishing AG 2017
R. Krimmer et al. (Eds.): E-Vote-ID 2017, LNCS 10615, pp. 21–41, 2017.
DOI: 10.1007/978-3-319-68687-5_2

central security requirements have been proposed and intensively been studied (see, e.g., [5,12,31,32,35]). Some of these definitions are formulated in general and widely applicable frameworks so that they can be applied to virtually any e-voting protocols. These frameworks and definitions have been applied to perform rigorous security analysis of various existing e-voting systems (see, e.g., [2,10,13,14,29,31,32,34,35,37,38]), often with surprising results, and newly proposed systems more and more come with security proofs right away (see, e.g., [7,25–28]).

The rigorous approach also has helped to reveal some confusions and common misconceptions concerning security requirements and their relationships, and by this aided the deeper understanding of such requirements, providing a solid formal basis for the design and analysis of e-voting systems.

In this paper, some of these confusions and misconceptions will be highlighted and explained. In particular, based on various works from the literature, we point out the following:

- The still popular notions of individual and universal verifiability together are neither sufficient nor necessary to achieve end-to-end (E2E) verifiability, as explained in Sect. 2.
- E2E verifiability alone is typically insufficient for practical purposes. E-voting systems should really be designed with accountability in mind, a notion presented in Sect. 3.
- While it is commonly believed that coercion-resistance implies privacy, surprisingly, this is not true in general. Moreover, improving the level of privacy can lead to a lower level of coercion resistance (see Sect. 4).

Throughout the paper, we also emphasize the importance of widely applicable security definitions. The definitions which we recall in this paper are all based on a common general framework where systems and protocols are formulated as sets of interactive probabilistic polynomial time Turing machines (see Sect. 2.1). By this, virtually any e-voting system can be modeled in such a framework. All definitions presented here are cryptographic game-based definitions. The definitions also allow one to measure the level of security an e-voting system provides. This is crucial as security typically is not perfect, since, for example, only a fraction of voters perform certain checks.

Before we conclude in Sect. 6, we briefly discuss limitations of the cryptographic analysis of e-voting systems in Sect. 5, such as usability aspects, legal requirements, implementation and deployment issues.

2   Verifiability

E-voting systems are complex hardware/software systems. In such systems, as in all complex systems, it is almost impossible to avoid programming errors. Even worse, components of e-voting systems, such as voters' devices, voting machines, and voting servers, might have deliberately been tampered with. In fact, it has been demonstrated that numerous e-voting systems suffer from flaws that make it possible for more or less sophisticated attackers to change the election result (see, e.g., [19,49,51,52]). Such manipulations are often hard or virtually impossible to detect. In some occasions, announced results were incorrect and/or elections had to be rerun (see, e.g., [23]).

Therefore, besides vote privacy, modern e-voting systems strive for what is called *verifiability*, more precisely end-to-end (E2E) verifiability. Roughly speaking, E2E verifiability means that voters and possibly external auditors should be able to check whether the published election result is correct, i.e., corresponds to the votes cast by the voters, even if voting devices and servers have programming errors or are outright malicious.

In the remainder of this section, we first recapitulate the notion of E2E verifiability and its formal definition. We then discuss other notions of verifiability, in particular the prominent notions of individual and universal verifiability. Following [28,35,37], we show that, unlike commonly believed, these two notions fail to provide a solid basis for verifiability. In particular, they are neither necessary nor sufficient to achieve E2E verifiability.

2.1   E2E Verifiability

About 30 years ago, Benaloh already provided a first definition of E2E verifiability [4]. As discussed in [12], while Benaloh's definition is fairly simple and captures the essence of verifiability, it requires unrealistically strong properties so that it would reject even reasonable e-voting systems.

In [32], Küsters, Truderung, and Vogt introduced a generic framework (the *KTV framework*) for verifiability and, more precisely, the even stronger notion of accountability (see Sect. 3). They also instantiated the framework to define E2E verifiability; also called *global verifiability* in [32], in contrast to individual and universal verifiability (see Sect. 2.2). This framework and definition since then have been used to analyze several e-voting protocols and mix nets [28,29,32,35, 37,38], such as Helios, ThreeBallot, VAV, Wombat Voting, sElect, Chaumian RPC mix nets, and re-encryption RPC mix nets. It can also be applied to other domains, such as auctions and contract signing [32].

Cortier et al. [12] demonstrated that it is possible to cast all formal verifiability definitions from the literature into the generic KTV framework (see also below).

E2E Verifiability in Short. In short, Küsters et al. capture E2E verifiability in the KTV framework as follows: The probability that a run is accepted (by a judge or other observers), but the published result of the election does not correspond to the actual votes cast by the voters is small (bounded by some parameter δ). More specifically, the result should contain all votes of the honest voters, except for at most k honest votes (for some parameter $k \geq 0$), and it should contain at most one vote for every dishonest voter.

In what follows, we first briefly recall the generic KTV framework and then its instantiation which captures E2E verifiability (see [32] for details or the presentation of this framework in [12]). In [32], formalizations both in a symbolic as well as a computational model were presented. Here, as throughout the paper, we concentrate on the computational model.

Protocol Model of the KTV Framework. A protocol is simply modeled as a set of probabilistic polynomial-time interactive Turing machines (ITMs) where the ITMs are connected via named tapes. We also refer to such a set as a *process*. By this, arbitrary protocols can be modeled.

More specifically, a *protocol P* is defined by a set of agents/parties Σ and an ITM π_a for each agent a in Σ. The set Σ may contain voters, voting devices, bulletin board(s), various tellers, auditors, etc. Note that one can easily model voters and voting devices as separate entities (ITMs) in this framework. The program π_a is called the *honest program* of a. By π_P we denote the process consisting of all of these (connected) ITMs. This process is always run with an adversary A which may run an arbitrary (probabilistic polynomial-time) program π_A and which is connected to all other parties. The adversary can model the network and/or dishonest parties. Also, A may statically or dynamically corrupt parties (by sending a corrupt messages to these parties); parties who should not be corruptable would simply ignore corruption messages by the adversary. A *run of P* with adversary π_A is a run of the process $\pi_P \| \pi_A$ (the union of the ITMs in π_P and the ITM π_A).

A Generic Verifiability Definition in the KTV Framework. The KTV framework provides a general definition of verifiability, which in particular can be instantiated to model E2E verifiability (see below). The definition assumes a judge J whose role is to accept or reject a protocol run by outputting accept or reject (on some tape). To make a decision, the judge runs a so-called *judging procedure*, which performs certain checks (depending on the protocol specification), such as verification of zero-knowledge proofs (if any) and taking voter complaints into account. Typically, the judging procedure can be carried out by any party, including external observers and even voters themselves, as the information to be checked is public. Hence, the judge might just be a "virtual" entity.

The generic KTV verifiability definition is centered around a *goal* γ of the protocol. Formally, γ is a set of protocol runs.[1] The goal γ specifies those runs which are correct or desired in some protocol-specific sense. In the context of e-voting and for E2E verifiability, the goal would contain those runs where the announced election result corresponds to the actual choices of the voters.

Now, the idea behind the definition of verifiability in the KTV framework is very simple. Only those runs r should be accepted by the judge in which the goal γ is met, i.e., $r \in \gamma$. In the context of e-voting, if in a run the published result does not correspond to the actual choices of the voters, then the judge should reject the run. More precisely, the definition requires that for all adversaries the probability (over the set of all protocol runs) that a run is accepted by the judge but the goal is not met is bounded by some constant δ (plus a negligible function). Although $\delta = 0$ is desirable, this would be too strong for almost all e-voting protocols. For example, typically not all voters check whether their

---

[1] Note that a single run is determined by the random coins used by the parties involved in the run.

ballots appear on the bulletin board. This give the adversary the opportunity to manipulate or drop some votes without being detected. Therefore, $\delta = 0$ cannot be achieved in general. The parameter δ is called the *verifiability tolerance* of the protocol.

By $\Pr(\pi^{(\ell)} \mapsto \neg\gamma, (\mathsf{J}: \mathsf{accept}))$ we denote the probability that the process π, with security parameter 1^ℓ, produces a run which is not in γ but nevertheless accepted by J.

Definition 1 (Verifiability). *Let P be a protocol with the set of agents Σ. Let $\delta \in [0, 1]$ be the tolerance, $\mathsf{J} \in \Sigma$ be the judge, and γ be a goal. Then, we say that the protocol P is (γ, δ)-verifiable by the judge J if for all adversaries π_A and $\pi = (\pi_P \| \pi_\mathsf{A})$, the probability*

$$\Pr(\pi^{(\ell)} \mapsto \neg\gamma, (\mathsf{J}: \mathsf{accept}))$$

is δ-bounded[2] as a function of ℓ.

We note that the original definition in [32] also captures soundness/fairness: if the protocol runs with a benign adversary, which, in particular, would not corrupt parties, then the judge accepts all runs. This kinds of fairness/soundness can be considered to be a sanity check of the protocol, including the judging procedure, and is typically easy to check.

We note that Definition 1 does not (need to) assume any specific protocol structure, and hence, is widely applicable. It also takes into account real-world uncertainties. As mentioned before and shown in [12], all definitions of verifiability from the literature can be captured by appropriate choices of the goal γ. The specific protocol structures often assumed in such definitions can also easily be captured.

E2E Verifiability in the KTV Framework. In [32], Küsters et al. proposed an instantiation of the generic verifiability definition to capture E2E verifiability. To this end, they introduce a family of goals $\{\gamma_k\}_{k \geq 0}$:[3] the goal γ_k contains exactly those runs of the voting protocol in which (*i*) all but up to k votes of the honest voters are counted correctly, and (*ii*) every dishonest voter votes at most once (see the technical report [33] of [32] or [12] for the formal definition). For example, consider a run of an e-voting protocol with three honest voters and two dishonest voters. Assume that there are two candidates/choices A and B, and that the tallying function returns the number of votes for each candidate. Now, if all honest voters vote for, say, A and the final result is $(A, B) = (2, 2)$, then γ_k is achieved for all $k \geq 1$ but γ_0 is not achieved: one vote of an honest voter is missing (dropped or flipped to a vote for B), and there is at most one vote for every dishonest voter; γ_0 is not satisfied because it requires that all votes of honest voters are counted, which is not the case here.

With this definition of goals, Definition 1 captures E2E verifiability: the probability that the judge accepts a run where more than k votes of honest voters

---

[2] Bounded by δ, plus some negligible function in the security parameter ℓ.

[3] In [12] (Subsect. 10.2), these goals have been refined.

were manipulated or dishonest voters could cast too many votes, is bounded by δ. In security statements about concrete e-voting protocols, δ will typically depend on various parameters, such as k and the probability that voters performs certain checks. While $k = 0$ is desirable, this is in most cases impossible to achieve because, for example, voters might not always perform the required checks, and hence, there is a chance that manipulation of votes goes undetected.

Importantly, this definition of E2E verifiability allows one to *measure* the level of E2E verifiability an e-voting protocol provides.

2.2 Individual and Universal Verifiability

Sako and Kilian [45] introduced the notions of *individual* and *universal verifiability*. These requirements (and subsequent notions, such as *cast-as-intended*, etc.) have become very popular and are still used to design and analyze e-voting systems. According to Sako and Kilian, an e-voting system achieves individual verifiability if "a sender can verify whether or not his message has reached its destination, but cannot determine if this is true for the other voters". Universal verifiability guarantees that it is possible to publicly verify that the tallying of the ballots is correct. That means that the final election result exactly reflects the content of those ballots that have been accepted to be tallied.

The notions of individual and universal verifiability have later been formalized by Chevallier-Mames et al. [8] (only universal verifiability), Cortier et al. [10], and Smyth et al. [48]. As mention in [32] and demonstrated in [12], these notions can also be captured in the KTV framework.

A Common Misconception. Unfortunately, it is often believed that individual together with universal verifiability implies E2E verifiability, which is the security property that e-voting systems should achieve. However, in [32,37], and [28], Küsters et al. have demonstrated that individual and universal verifiability are *neither sufficient nor necessary* for E2E verifiability.

In short, there are e-voting systems, such as ThreeBallot and VAV [42] as well as variants of Helios, that arguably provide individual and universal verifiability but whose verifiability is nevertheless broken, i.e., they do not provide E2E verifiability. Conversely, there are e-voting systems, such as sElect [28], which provide E2E verifiability without having to rely on universal verifiability.

In what follows, we explain these results in more detail.

2.3 Not Sufficient

We recall several attacks that break the E2E verifiability of e-voting systems, even though these systems provide individual and universal verifiability. The first class of attacks uses that (dishonest) voters possibly with the help of malicious authorities might cast malformed ballots. In the second class of attacks (so-called *clash attacks*), the same receipt is shown to different voters who voted for the same candidate, allowing malicious voting devices and authorities to drop or manipulate ballots.

An Illustrative Example: A Modification of Helios. Helios [1] is one of the most prominent remote e-voting systems which, on a high level, works as follows. Trustees share a secret key sk which belongs to a public/private ElGamal key pair (pk, sk). Voters encrypt the candidate of their choice under the public key pk and submit the resulting ciphertext to the bulletin board. Then all ciphertexts are publicly multiplied so that, by the homomorphic property of the ElGamal public-key encryption scheme, the resulting ciphertext encrypts the number of votes for each candidate. Finally, the trustees perform distributed and verifiable decryption of this ciphertext and publish the resulting plaintext as the outcome of the election.

In order to guarantee the integrity of the final result, several zero-knowledge proofs (ZKP) are used. Among others, a voter has to prove that her ciphertext encrypts a valid choice, and, for privacy reasons, that she knows which choice it encrypts.

It has been formally proven that under certain assumptions Helios is E2E verifiable (see, [11,37]). Furthermore, assuming that the voting devices are honest, Helios provides individual verifiability because each voter can check whether her ballot appears on the bulletin board. Universal verifiability follows from the fact that the multiplication of the ciphertexts on the bulletin board is public and that the tellers perform verifiable decryption. Thus, Helios provides E2E verifiability as well as individual and universal verifiability.

To see that individual and universal verifiability together do not imply E2E verifiability consider a modification of Helios in which voters do not have to prove that their votes are correct, i.e., dishonest voters may cast malformed ballots without being detected. Then a (single!) dishonest voter could completely spoil the election result by encrypting an invalid choice. Such a malformed ballot might contain negative votes for certain candidates, and hence, effectively subtracting votes from candidates, or the malformed ballot might contain many more votes for a candidate then allowed. So, such a system certainly does not provide E2E verifiability. At the same time, such a system can still be considered to provide individual and universal verifiability. Voters can still check that their ballots appear on the bulletin board (individual verifiability), and ballots on the bulletin board can still be tallied in a universally verifiable way. But dishonest voters might have spoiled the election result completely and this is not detected.[4]

This simple example demonstrates that, even if an e-voting system achieves individual and universal verifiability, its overall verifiability can nevertheless completely and trivially be broken.

Another Example: ThreeBallot. The attack illustrated above conceptually also applies to the ThreeBallot voting system [42] (also to VAV), but the details of the attack differ. We start by briefly describing how ThreeBallot works.

In ThreeBallot, a voter is given a multi-ballot consisting of three simple ballots. On every simple ballot, the candidates, say A and B, are printed in the same fixed order, say A is listed first and B is listed second. In the secrecy

---

[4] Note that the arguments hold true even when assuming that only eligible voters (honest or dishonest) may vote.

of a voting booth, the voter is supposed to fill out all three simple ballots in the following way: she marks the candidate of her choice on exactly *two* simple ballots and every other candidate on exactly *one* simple ballot. Assume, for example, that a voter votes for candidate A. Then

$$\begin{pmatrix} x \\ o \end{pmatrix}, \begin{pmatrix} x \\ o \end{pmatrix}, \begin{pmatrix} o \\ x \end{pmatrix} \text{ or } \begin{pmatrix} x \\ x \end{pmatrix}, \begin{pmatrix} o \\ o \end{pmatrix}, \begin{pmatrix} x \\ o \end{pmatrix}$$

would be valid multi-ballots to vote for A. After this, the voter feeds all three simple ballots to a voting machine (a scanner) and indicates the simple ballot she wants to get as a receipt. The machine checks the well-formedness of the multi-ballot, prints secretly (pairwise independent) random numbers on each simple ballot, and provides the voter with a copy of the chosen simple ballot, with the random number printed on it. Note that the voter does not get to see the random numbers of the remaining two simple ballots. The scanner keeps all simple ballots (now separated) in a ballot box.

In the tallying phase, the voting machine posts on the bulletin board (electronic copies of) all the cast simple ballots in random order. From the ballots shown on the bulletin board, the result can easily be computed: The number of votes for the ith candidate is the number of simple ballots with the ith position marked minus the total number of votes (since every voter marks every candidate at least ones).

ThreeBallot offers (some level of) individual verifiability because each voter may check whether the simple ballot she has taken as a receipt appears on the bulletin board. Thus, it should be risky for any party to remove or alter simple ballots. Additionally, ThreeBallot offers universal verifiability because the tallying is completely public. However, as Küsters et al. [35] have pointed out, ThreeBallot does not offer E2E verifiability. One variant of the attack presented in [35] assumes that the scanner is dishonest. To illustrate the attack, assume that an honest voter votes for, say, candidate A by submitting a multi-ballot of one of the forms shown above. Now, a dishonest voter which collaborates with the dishonest scanner could create a malformed ballot of the form

$$\begin{pmatrix} o \\ x \end{pmatrix}, \begin{pmatrix} o \\ x \end{pmatrix}, \begin{pmatrix} o \\ x \end{pmatrix},$$

which, together with the ballot of the honest voter (no matter which one of the two kinds shown above), yields two (valid!) votes for candidate B and no vote for candidate A. Clearly, E2E verifiability is broken: a vote for A and one invalid ballot result in two valid votes for B. But no honest voter would complain because none of their single/multi-ballots were manipulated. So, this attack neither invalidates individual verifiability nor universal verifiability, showing again that these notions together do not imply E2E verifiability, and are really insufficient.

Clash Attacks. The idea of individual and universal verifiability not only fails due to undetected malformed ballots. Another problem are *clash attacks* [37], which might break E2E verifiability, while individual and universal verifiability together again do not detect such attacks. As demonstrated in [37], several e-voting system are vulnerable to clash attacks, including several variants of Helios.

To illustrate the attack, consider the Helios voting system, where the voting devices might be dishonest and where the ballots of the voters are published on the bulletin board without voter names or pseudonyms attached to them. Now, if two voters vote for the same candidate, the voting devices might use the same randomness to create the ballots, and hence, the two ballots are identical. However, instead of putting both ballots on the bulletin board, authorities might add only one of them to the bulletin board and the other ballot might be replaced by one for another candidate. The two voters can check individually that "their" ballot appears on the bulletin board (individual verifiability); they do not realize that they are looking at the same ballot, i.e., they do not realize the "clash". Universal verifiability is obviously guaranteed as well. Still, the system does not provide E2E verifiability: a vote of an honest voter was replaced in an undetectable way by another vote.

Adding More Subproperties? Now that we have seen that individual and universal verifiability do not imply the desired security property E2E verifiability, it might be tempting to search for more subproperties that would then, eventually, yield a sufficiently strong verifiability notion.

In [12], it has been demonstrated that all verifiability notions proposed in the literature so far that are split up into additional subproperties, such as individual and universal verifiability, do not provide E2E verifiability, even if more subproperties are added. In [10], for example, a subproperty was introduced that rules out clash attacks but the resulting verifiability notion is still too weak (see [12], Appendix B, for details).

When existing systems are analyzed w.r.t. verifiability or new systems are proposed, one should always check for E2E verifiability as introduced above, as E2E verifiability is the kind of verifiability modern e-voting systems ultimately should aim for. While subproperties, such as individual and universal verifiability, can guide the design of e-voting systems, unless formally proven that their combination in fact implies E2E verifiability, such properties alone might miss important aspects and can therefore not replace E2E verifiability.

2.4   Not Necessary

The examples and attacks above illustrate that the notions of individual and universal verifiability are not sufficient to provide E2E verifiability. Following [28], we now demonstrate that they are not necessary to achieve E2E verifiability either. More specifically, in [28] the remote e-voting system sElect was proposed, and it was shown that it provides E2E verifiability (under reasonable assumptions). But sElect is not universally verifiable.

sElect. sElect [28] is a conceptually simple remote voting system which is based on a Chaumian mix net.

A *Chaumian mix net* consists of mix servers $M_1, \ldots, M_n$ where each one of them holds a public/secret key pair (pk_i, sk_i) of a (CCA2-)secure public-key encryption scheme. The input to the mix net is a set of ciphertexts $c_1, \ldots, c_l$ where each ciphertext c_i is a nested encryption of a plaintext m_i under the public keys of the mix servers in reverse order, i.e.,

$$c_i = \mathsf{Enc}\left(\ldots \mathsf{Enc}\left(m_i, pk_n \right) \ldots, pk_1 \right).$$

When the mix net is executed, the first mix server decrypts the outer encryption layer with its secret key sk_1, shuffles the result,[5] and forwards it to the second mix server, which decrypts the next encryption layer with sk_2, shuffles the resulting ciphertexts, and so on. Finally, the output of the mix net is a random permutation π of the input plaintexts $m_1, \ldots, m_l$. As long as one of the mix servers is honest, the permutation π remains secret. That is, it is not possible to connect the input ciphertexts to their corresponding plaintexts.

Note that there are no ZKPs for correct shuffling or correct decryption, which means that Chaumian mix nets are not universally verifiable.

Now, roughly speaking, sElect works as follows. A voter uses her voting device (a browser) to select the candidate of her choice m_i. Then, the voting device creates a random nonce n_i (which can be done jointly with the voter to decrease trust in the voting device). Afterwards, the device encrypts (m_i, n_i) under the public keys of the mix servers as explained above. For verification purposes, the voter memorizes or writes down the nonce n_i. In addition, the voting device stores this information and the random coins that were used for encryption. In the tallying phase, all input ciphertexts are processed by the mix net as explained above, and the final result is, as well as all intermediate ciphertexts, published on the bulletin board. Each voter is finally invited to use her voting device in order to check whether her candidate m_i appears next to her personal nonce n_i. In addition, the voting device performs a *fully automated verification procedure*. In particular, if the voter's vote and nonce do not appear together in the final result, the voting device can provably single out the mix servers that misbehaved because it has stored all information needed to follow the trace of the voter's ballot through the mix net (and because the mix servers signed certain information).

E2E Verifiability Without Universal Verifiability. It has been formally proven [28] that sElect provides a reasonable level of E2E verifiability (and even accountability) because it is extremely risky for an adversary to manipulate or drop even only a few votes. At the same time, sElect does not rely on universal verifiability. The Chaumian mix net is not verifiable by itself: it takes the voters to perform a simple check. Therefore, the example of sElect shows that universal verifiability is not necessary for E2E verifiability.

---

[5] In order to protect against replay attacks [13], duplicates are removed, keeping one copy only (see [28] for details.).

3   Accountability

In e-voting systems, and for many other cryptographic tasks and protocols (e.g., secure multi-party computation, identity-based encryption, and auctions), it is extremely important that (semi-)trusted parties can be held accountable in case they misbehave. This fundamental security property is called *accountability*,[6] and it is a stronger form of verifiability: it not only allows one to verify whether a desired property is guaranteed, for example that the election outcome is correct, but it also ensures that misbehaving parties can be identified if this is not the case.

Accountability is important for several practical reasons. First of all, accountability strengthens the incentive of all parties to follow their roles because they can be singled out in case they misbehave and then might have to face, for example, severe financial or legal penalties, or might lose their reputation. Furthermore, accountability can resolve disputes that occur when it is only known that some party misbehaved but not which one. This can, for instance, help to increase the robustness of cryptographic protocols because misbehaving parties, such as a dishonest trustee in an e-voting protocol, can be excluded and the protocol can be re-run without the parties that misbehaved.

Unfortunately, despite its importance, accountability is often not taken into account (at least not explicitly), neither to design e-voting protocols nor to analyze their security (see, e.g., [1,7,9,11,15,25–27,43,44]).

In [32], Küsters et al. provided a general formal definition of accountability and emphasized its importance. This formal definition has since been used to analyze different e-voting protocols (Helios, sElect, Bingo Voting), mix nets (re-encryption and Chaumian mix nets with random partial checking), auction schemes (PRST [41]), and contract signing protocols (ASW [3]). These analyses brought forward several accountability issues, e.g., for different versions of Helios [37]. In what follows, we give a brief summary of the accountability definition, for details see the original paper [32].

A Formal Accountability Definition. The accountability definition by Küsters et al. [32] is based on the same generic and expressive protocol model as the verifiability definition (see Sect. 2), and can therefore be applied to all classes of voting protocols and also to other domains.

In contrast to the verifiability definition, the judge now not only accepts or rejects a run, but may output detailed verdicts. A *verdict* is a positive Boolean formula ψ built from propositions of the form $\mathsf{dis}(\mathsf{a})$, for an agent a, where $\mathsf{dis}(\mathsf{a})$ means that (the judge thinks that) agent a misbehaved, i.e., did not follow the prescribed protocol. For example, in a voting protocol with voters $V_1, \ldots, V_n$, a bulletin board B, and trustees $T_1, \ldots, T_m$, if the judge J states, say, $\mathsf{dis}(B) \wedge \mathsf{dis}(T_1) \wedge \ldots \wedge \mathsf{dis}(T_m)$, then this expresses that the judge beliefs that the bulletin board and all trustees misbehaved; the judge would state $\mathsf{dis}(V_i) \vee \mathsf{dis}(B) \vee$

---

[6] In the context of secure MPC, accountability is sometimes called *identifiable abort* [22].

$(\mathsf{dis}(\mathsf{T}_1) \wedge \ldots \wedge \mathsf{dis}(\mathsf{T}_m))$ if she is not sure whether voter V_i. the bulletin board, or all trustees misbehaved.

Who should be blamed in which situation is expressed by a set Ψ of what are called *accountability constraints*. These constrains are of the form

$$C = \alpha \Rightarrow \psi_1 | \cdots | \psi_k,$$

where α is a property of the voting system, similar to the goal γ in Sect. 2.1 (a set of runs of the system, where one run is determined by the random coins used by the parties), and $\psi_1, \ldots, \psi_k$ are verdicts. Intuitively, the set α contains runs in which some desired goal γ of the protocol is not met (due to the misbehavior of some protocol participant). The formulas $\psi_1, \ldots, \psi_k$ are the possible minimal verdicts that are supposed to be stated by J in such a case; J is free to state stronger verdicts (by the fairness condition these verdicts will be true). That is, if a run belongs to α, then C requires that in this run the judge outputs a verdict ψ which logically implies one of ψ_i.

To illustrate the notion of accountability constraints, let us continue the example from above. Let α contain all runs in which the published election result is incorrect, e.g., $\alpha = \alpha_k = \neg\gamma_k$ with the goal γ_k as defined in Sect. 2. Now, consider the following constraints:

$$C_1 = \alpha \Rightarrow \mathsf{dis}(\mathsf{B}) | \mathsf{dis}(\mathsf{T}_1) | \cdots | \mathsf{dis}(\mathsf{T}_m), \tag{1}$$
$$C_2 = \alpha \Rightarrow \mathsf{dis}(\mathsf{V}_1) \vee \cdots \vee \mathsf{dis}(\mathsf{V}_n) \vee \mathsf{dis}(\mathsf{B}) \vee (\mathsf{dis}(\mathsf{T}_1) \wedge \cdots \wedge \mathsf{dis}(\mathsf{T}_m)), \tag{2}$$
$$C_3 = \alpha \Rightarrow \mathsf{dis}(\mathsf{B}) | \mathsf{dis}(\mathsf{T}_1) \wedge \cdots \wedge \mathsf{dis}(\mathsf{T}_m). \tag{3}$$

Constraint C_1 requires that if in a run the published election result is incorrect, then at least one (individual) party among $\mathsf{B}, \mathsf{T}_1, \ldots, \mathsf{T}_m$ can be held accountable by the judge J; note that different parties can be blamed in different runs. Constraint C_2 states that if the published election result is not correct, then the judge J can leave it open whether one of the voters, the bulletin board B, or all trustees misbehaved. Constraint C_3 requires that it is possible to hold B or all trustees accountable.

As pointed out in [32], accountability constraints should provide at least *individual accountability*. That is, the postulated minimal verdicts should at least single out one misbehaving party. In the above example, C_1 and C_3 provide individual accountability, but C_2 does not. In fact, C_2 is very weak, too weak for practical purposes. If a judge states exactly this verdict, there are no real consequences for any party, since no individual party can be held accountable. This is particular problematic if in such a "fuzzy" verdict not only voting authorities are involved but also voters.

A set Φ of constraints for a protocol P is called an *accountability property* of P. Typically, an accountability property Φ covers all relevant cases in which a desired goal γ for P is not met, i.e., whenever γ is not satisfied in a given run r due to some misbehavior of some protocol participant, then there exists a constraint C in Φ which covers r. We write $\Pr\left(\pi^{(\ell)} \to \neg(\mathsf{J}:\Phi)\right)$ to denote the probability that π, with security parameter 1^ℓ, produces a run r such that

J does not satisfies all accountability constrains for this run, i.e., there exists $C = \alpha \Rightarrow \psi_1 | \cdots | \psi_k$ with $r \in \alpha$ but the judge outputs a verdict which does not imply some ψ_i.

Definition 2 (Accountability). *Let P be a protocol with the set of agents Σ. Let $\delta \in [0, 1]$ be the tolerance, $J \in \Sigma$ be the judge, and Φ be an accountability property of P. Then, we say that the protocol P is (Φ, δ)-accountable by the judge J if for all adversaries π_A and $\pi = (\pi_P \| \pi_A)$, the probability*

$$\Pr\left(\pi^{(\ell)} \to \neg(J\colon \Phi)\right)$$

is δ-bounded as a function of ℓ.

Just as for the verifiability definition (Definition 1), the full definition in [32] additionally requires that the judge J is fair, i.e., that she states false verdicts only with negligible probability.

Küsters et al. also showed that verifiability (as defined in Definition 1) can be considered to be a weak form of accountability, and, as mentioned before, verifiability alone is typically too weak for practical purposes.

Instead of explicitly specifying Ψ as necessary in the above definition, there have been attempts to find generic ways to define who actually caused a goal to fail and ideally to blame all of these parties. There has been work pointing into this direction (see, e.g., [16,20,21]). But this problem turns out to be very tricky and has not been solved yet.

4   Coercion-Resistance and Privacy

To achieve verifiability, a voter typically obtains some kind of receipt which, together with additional data published in the election, she can use to check that her vote was counted. This, however, potentially opens up the possibility for vote buying and voter coercion. Besides verifiability, many voting systems therefore also intend to provide so-called *coercion-resistance*.

One would expect that privacy and coercion-resistance are closely related: If the level of privacy is low, i.e., there is a good chance of correctly determining how a voter voted, then this should give the coercer leverage to coerce a voter. Some works in the literature (e.g., [17,39]) indeed suggest a close connection. However, Küsters et al. [35] demonstrated that the relationship between privacy and coercion-resistance is more subtle.

Among others, it turns out that improving the level of privacy of a protocol in a natural way (e.g., by changing the way honest voters fill out ballots) can lead to a *lower* level of coercion-resistance. Clearly, in general, one does not expect privacy to imply coercion-resistance. Still, the effect is quite surprising.

A maybe even more important and unexpected finding that comes out of the case studies in [35] is that the level of privacy of a protocol can be much *lower* than its level of coercion-resistance. The reason behind this phenomenon is basically that it may happen that the counter-strategy a coerced voter may carry out to defend against coercion hides the behavior of the coerced voter, including her vote, better than the honest voting program.

On the positive side, in [35] Küsters et al. proved a theorem which states that under a certain additional assumption a coercion-resistant protocol provides at least the same level of privacy. This is the case when the counter-strategy does not "outperform" the honest voting program in the above sense. The theorem is applicable to a broad class of voting protocols.

In what follows, we explain the subtle relationships between coercion-resistance and privacy in more detail. The findings are based on formal privacy and coercion-resistance definitions proposed in [35] and [31,36], respectively. These definitions build upon the same general protocol model as the one for verifiability, and hence, they are applicable to all classes of voting systems (see, e.g., [28,31,32,34–37]), and they also have been applied to analyze mix nets [29,38]. We only informally introduce the privacy and coercion-resistance definitions in what follows and point to the reader to [31,35,36] for the formal definitions.

Intuitively, the privacy definition in [35] says that no (probabilistic polynomial-time) observer, who may control some parties, such as some authorities or voters, should be able to tell how an honest voter, the voter under observation, voted. More specifically, one considers two systems: in one system the voter under consideration votes for candidate c and in the other system the voter votes for candidate c'; all other honest voters vote according to some probability distribution known by the observer. Now, the probability that the observer correctly says with which system he interacts should be bounded by some constant δ (plus some negligible function in the security parameter). Due to the parameter δ, the definition allows one to *measure* privacy. As discussed in [28], this ability is crucial in the analysis of protocols which provide a reasonable but not perfect level of privacy. In fact, strictly speaking, most remote e-voting protocols do not provide a perfect level of privacy: this is because there is always a certain probability that voters do not check their receipts. Hence, the probability that malicious servers/authorities drop or manipulate votes without being detected is non-negligible. By dropping or manipulating votes, an adversaries obtains some non-negligible advantage in breaking privacy. Therefore, it is essential to be able to precisely tell how much an adversary can actually learn.

For the definition of coercion-resistance (see [31,36]), the voter under observation considered for privacy is now replaced by a *coerced voter* and the observer O is replaced by the *coercer* C. We imagine that the coercer demands full control over the voting interface of the coerced users, i.e., the coercer wants the coerced voter to run a dummy strategy dum which simply forwards all messages between the coerced voter and the coercer C. If the coerced voter in fact runs dum, the coercer can effectively vote on behalf of the coerced voter or decide to abstain from voting. Of course, the coercer is not bound to follow the specified voting procedure. Now, informally speaking, a protocol is called *coercion-resistant* if the coerced voter, instead of running the dummy strategy, can run some *counter-strategy* cs such that (i) by running this counter-strategy, the coerced voter achieves her own goal γ (formally, again a set of runs), e.g., successfully votes for a specific candidate, and (ii) the coercer is not able to distinguish whether the coerced voter followed his instructions (i.e., run dum) or tried to achieve her own goal (by running cs). Similarly to the privacy definition, the probability in (ii) is bounded by some constant δ (plus some negligible function). Again, δ is important in order to be able to measure the level of coercion-resistance a protocol provides: there is always a non-negligible chance for the coercer to know for sure whether the coerced voter followed his instructions or not (e.g., when all voteres voted for the same candidate).

Improving Privacy Can Lower the Level of Coercion-Resistance. To illustrate this phenomenon, we consider the following variant of ThreeBallot (for details of ThreeBallot see Sect. 2). An honest voter is supposed to submit, according to her favorite candidate,

$$\text{either } \begin{pmatrix} x \\ x \end{pmatrix}, \begin{pmatrix} x \\ o \end{pmatrix}, \begin{pmatrix} o \\ o \end{pmatrix} \text{ or } \begin{pmatrix} x \\ x \end{pmatrix}, \begin{pmatrix} o \\ x \end{pmatrix}, \begin{pmatrix} o \\ o \end{pmatrix},$$

and always take the first single ballot $\begin{pmatrix} x \\ x \end{pmatrix}$ as her receipt. The scheme is ideal in terms of privacy because the bulletin board and the receipts do not leak any information apart from the pure election result. However, this scheme does not provide any coercion-resistance. Assume that the coerced voter is instructed to cast

$$\begin{pmatrix} o \\ x \end{pmatrix}, \begin{pmatrix} x \\ x \end{pmatrix}, \begin{pmatrix} o \\ o \end{pmatrix}$$

and take the first single ballot as receipt (which is allowed but never done by honest voters). If the coerced voter actually wants to vote for candidate A, the voter would have to cast

$$\begin{pmatrix} o \\ x \end{pmatrix}, \begin{pmatrix} x \\ o \end{pmatrix}, \begin{pmatrix} x \\ o \end{pmatrix}.$$

But then, as all the honest voters submit

$$\begin{pmatrix} x \\ x \end{pmatrix}, \begin{pmatrix} x \\ o \end{pmatrix}, \begin{pmatrix} o \\ o \end{pmatrix} \text{ or } \begin{pmatrix} x \\ x \end{pmatrix}, \begin{pmatrix} o \\ x \end{pmatrix}, \begin{pmatrix} o \\ o \end{pmatrix},$$

the coercer could easily detect that he was cheated, by counting the number of ballots of type $\begin{pmatrix} o \\ o \end{pmatrix}$ on the bulletin board.

Coercion-Resistance Does Not Imply Privacy. For the original variant of ThreeBallot and the simple variant of VAV, Küsters et al. proved that the level of privacy is much lower than its level of coercion-resistance. The reason behind this phenomenon is basically that the counter-strategy hides the behavior of the coerced voter, including her vote, better than the honest voting program hides the vote. In these voting systems, a receipt an honest voter obtains indeed discloses more information than necessary (for details see [35]).

The following simple, but unlike ThreeBallot and VAV, artificial example, carries this effect to extremes: Consider the ideal voting protocol which collects all votes and publishes the correct result. Now, imagine a voting protocol in which voters use the ideal voting protocol to cast their vote, but where half of the voters publish how they voted (e.g., based on a coin flip). Clearly, the privacy level this protocol provides is very low, namely $\delta \geq \frac{1}{2}$. However, a coerced voter can be more clever and simply lie about how she voted. This protocol indeed provides a high level of coercion-resistance.

As mentioned at the beginning of Sect. 4, in [35] it is shown that if the counter-strategy does not "outperform" the honest voting program (or conversely, the honest voting program does not leak more information than the counter-strategy), then indeed if a voting system provides a certain level of coercion-resistance, then it provides the same level of privacy. Fortunately, in most systems which are supposed to provide coercion-resistance, the counter-strategy indeed does not outperform the honest program.

5   Limitations of Cryptographic Security Analysis

The previous sections were concerned with and highlighted the importance of formally analyzing the security of e-voting systems. However, to obtain a full picture of an e-voting system and to carry out an election, many more aspects have to be taken into account which are beyond formal/cryptographic analysis. Some of these aspects are specific to the field of e-voting, while others apply to virtually all complex systems.

In what follows, we briefly discuss some of these aspects. We start with usability issues and legal requirements, as they are particularly important for e-voting systems.

Usability and Its Relationship to Security. E-voting systems are used by human beings, such as voters, administrators, and auditors. Therefore, the security an e-voting system provides in practice crucially depends on whether, or at least to which degree, the involved human parties follow the protocol.

For example, it is, by now, well-known that many voters are not sensitized enough to verify whether their voting devices created a correct ballot, and even if they are, they often fail to do so because the individual verification procedures, such as Benaloh challenges, are too complex (see, e.g., [24,40]). Similarly to these verification issues, many coercion-resistant e-voting protocols (e.g., Civitas [9]) require that coerced voters successfully deceive their coercer, e.g., by creating faked receipts. It is questionable whether average voters are able to do this.

Therefore, *usability* of e-voting systems is not only important to ensure that all voters can participate, but it also determines whether an e-voting system is secure in the real world: if a security procedure is difficult to use, it worsens the security of the system and may render it insecure. However, it is hard to measure usability; instead, certain usability attributes can be measured and empirically be tested, for example, how often users make the same error.

In order to analyze the impact of a system's usability w.r.t. its security, security notions are necessary which allow one to take usability attributes into account. To some degree, this is incorporated in the security definition presented in the previous sections. For example, Küsters et al. have studied the verifiability levels of Helios, sElect, Bingo Voting, ThreeBallot, and VAV as functions of the probability that a voter (successfully) carries out her verification procedure. For example, for the system sElect [28]. Küsters et al. formally proved that sElect (roughly) provides a verifiability level of $\delta \approx (1-p)^{k+1}$ where p is the probability that an honest voter carries out the verification procedure, i.e., checks whether her vote along with the verification code is in the final result, and where k is the tolerated number of manipulated (honest) votes (see Sect. 2 for details). Hence, the probability that no one complains but more than k votes of honest voters have been manipulated is bounded by $(1 - p)^{k+1}$. Using results from usability studies one can now estimate what realistic values for p are, and hence, better assess the security of a system.

Perceived vs. Provable Security. In addition to the provable security a system provides, the level of security perceived by regular voters might be just as important and even more important for a system to be accepted. Regular voters simply do not understand what a zero-knowledge proof is and for that reason might not trust it. Therefore simplicity and comprehensibility are very crucial, which, for example, was a driving factor for the system sElect [28]. This system features a simple and easy to understand verification procedure, allows for fully automated verification, and uses asymmetric encryption and signatures as the only cryptographic primitives.

Legal Requirements. Since e-voting systems are used in many countries for political elections, they have to provide certain legal requirements which depend on the political system. Unfortunately, it is difficult to formally capture all legal requirements in order to rigorously analyze whether a given e-voting system achieves them. Vice versa, it is also challenging to express formal security definitions in legal terms. There are some approaches that address this problem (see, e.g., [46,47,50]).

Cryptographic Analysis vs. Code-Level Analysis. Cryptographic analysis as considered in this paper, typically does not analyze the actual code of a system but a more abstract (cryptographic) model. Hence, implementation flaws can easily go undetected. While carrying out a full-fledged cryptographic security analysis of an e-voting system is already far from trivial, performing such an analysis on the code-level is even more challenging. A first such analysis for a simple e-voting system implemented in Java has been carried out in [30]. In recent years, there has also been successful code-level analysis of cryptographic protocols, such as TLS (see, e.g., [6,18] for some of the most recent work in this direction).

Implementation and Deployment. It is possible to model strong adversaries and capture potentially flawed program code in a formal model by weak trust assumptions and various kinds of corruptions. However, at least some parties have to be assumed to be honest in essentially all voting systems to achieve a reasonable security level. With the diverse ways systems can be and are attacked within and outside the domain of e-voting, actually guaranteeing the trust assumptions is highly non-trivial. This is even more true in political elections where e-voting systems can be targets of extremely powerful adversaries, such as intelligence agencies and hostile states (see, e.g., [49]).

Even without assuming such powerful adversaries, securely deploying an e-voting system in practice is non-trivial and involves a lot of organizational issues which are not captured nor considered by formal analysis. For example, abstract system descriptions assume that trust is distributed among several trustees and that keys are securely generated and distributed. But it might not always be clear in practice, who the trustees should be. Again, it is therefore important to keep e-voting systems as simple as possible to avoid organizational and technical overheads in order to improve the practical security of systems.

6   Conclusion

The development of secure e-voting systems that are also easy to use, to understand, and to implement is still a big challenge. Rigorous formal analysis is an important piece of the puzzle. This research area has made huge progress in the last decade or so. Many central security requirements have been formulated by now and their relationships have been studied intensively. As explained in this paper, this helped to obtain a better understanding of desired security properties and to overcome some common misconceptions. This alone is already very important to help thinking about the security of e-voting systems and shaping the design of these systems. For newly proposed systems it is more and more common and expected that they come with a cryptographic security analysis. The general formal frameworks and solid formulations of fundamental security requirements are available for such analyses. While rigorous analysis is highly non-trivial and certainly does not and cannot cover all aspects in the design, implementation, and deployment of e-voting systems, it forms an important and indispensable corner stone.

References

1. Adida, B.: Helios: web-based open-audit voting. In: USENIX 2008, pp. 335–348 (2008)
2. Arnaud, M., Cortier, V., Wiedling, C.: Analysis of an electronic boardroom voting system. In: Heather, J., Schneider, S., Teague, V. (eds.) Vote-ID 2013. LNCS, vol. 7985, pp. 109–126. Springer, Heidelberg (2013). doi:10.1007/978-3-642-39185-9_7
3. Asokan, N., Shoup, V., Waidner, M.: Optimistic fair exchange of digital signatures. IEEE J. Sel. Areas Commun. **18**(4), 593–610 (2000)
4. Benaloh, J.D.C.: Verifiable Secret-Ballot Elections. Ph.D. thesis (1987)
5. Bernhard, D., Cortier, V., Galindo, D., Pereira, O., Warinschi, B.: SoK: a comprehensive analysis of game-based ballot privacy definitions. In: S&P 2015, pp. 499–516 (2015)
6. Bhargavan, K., Blanchet, B., Kobeissi, N.: Verified models and reference implementations for the TLS 1.3 standard candidate. In: S&P 2017, pp. 483–502 (2017)
7. Chaidos, P., Cortier, V., Fuchsbauer, G., Galindo, D.: BeleniosRF: a non-interactive receipt-free electronic voting scheme. In: CCS 2016, pp. 1614–1625 (2016)

8. Chevallier-Mames, B., Fouque, P.-A., Pointcheval, D., Stern, J., Traoré, J.: On some incompatible properties of voting schemes. In: Chaum, D., Jakobsson, M., Rivest, R.L., Ryan, P.Y.A., Benaloh, J., Kutylowski, M., Adida, B. (eds.) Towards Trustworthy Elections. LNCS, vol. 6000, pp. 191–199. Springer, Heidelberg (2010). doi:10.1007/978-3-642-12980-3_11
9. Clarkson, M.R., Chong, S., Myers, A.C.: Civitas: toward a secure voting system. In: S&P 2008, pp. 354–368 (2008)
10. Cortier, V., Eigner, F., Kremer, S., Maffei, M., Wiedling, C.: Type-based verification of electronic voting protocols. In: Focardi, R., Myers, A. (eds.) POST 2015. LNCS, vol. 9036, pp. 303–323. Springer, Heidelberg (2015). doi:10.1007/978-3-662-46666-7_16
11. Cortier, V., Galindo, D., Glondu, S., Izabachène, M.: Election verifiability for helios under weaker trust assumptions. In: Kutylowski, M., Vaidya, J. (eds.) ESORICS 2014. LNCS, vol. 8713, pp. 327–344. Springer, Cham (2014). doi:10.1007/978-3-319-11212-1_19
12. Cortier, V., Galindo, D., Küsters, R., Müller, J., Truderung, T.: SoK: verifiability notions for e-voting protocols. In: S&P 2016, pp. 779–798 (2016)
13. Cortier, V., Smyth, B.: Attacking and fixing helios: an analysis of ballot secrecy. In: CSF 2011, pp. 297–311 (2011)
14. Cortier, V., Wiedling, C.: A formal analysis of the Norwegian E-voting protocol. J. Comput. Secur. 25(1), 21–57 (2017)
15. Culnane, C., Ryan, P.Y.A., Schneider, S.A., Teague, V.: vVote: a verifiable voting system. ACM Trans. Inf. Syst. Secur. 18(1), 3:1–3:30 (2015)
16. Datta, A., Garg, D., Kaynar, D.K., Sharma, D., Sinha, A.: Program actions as actual causes: a building block for accountability. In: CSF 2015, pp. 261–275 (2015)
17. Delaune, S., Kremer, S., Ryan, M.: Coercion-resistance and receipt-freeness in electronic voting. In: CSFW-19, pp. 28–42 (2006)
18. Delignat-Lavaud, A., Fournet, C., Kohlweiss, M., Protzenko, J., Rastogi, A., Swamy, N., Béguelin, S.Z., Bhargavan, K., Pan, J., Zinzindohoue, J.K.: Implementing and proving the TLS 1.3 record layer. In: S&P 2017, pp. 463–482 (2017)
19. Epstein, J.: Weakness in depth: a voting machine's demise. IEEE Secur. Priv. 13(3), 55–58 (2015)
20. Feigenbaum, J., Jaggard, A.D., Wright, R.N.: Towards a formal model of accountability. In: NSPW 2011, pp. 45–56 (2011)
21. Gößler, G., Le Métayer, D.: A general framework for blaming in component-based systems. Sci. Comput. Program. 113, 223–235 (2015)
22. Ishai, Y., Ostrovsky, R., Zikas, V.: Secure multi-party computation with identifiable abort. In: Garay, J.A., Gennaro, R. (eds.) CRYPTO 2014. LNCS, vol. 8617, pp. 369–386. Springer, Heidelberg (2014). doi:10.1007/978-3-662-44381-1_21
23. Jones, D., Simons, B.: Broken Ballots: Will Your Vote Count? CSLI Publications (2012)
24. Karayumak, F., Olembo, M.M., Kauer, M., Volkamer, M.: Usability analysis of helios - an open source verifiable remote electronic voting system. In: EVT/WOTE 2011 (2011)
25. Kiayias, A., Zacharias, T., Zhang, B.: DEMOS-2: scalable E2E verifiable elections without random oracles. In: CCS 2015, pp. 352–363 (2015)
26. Kiayias, A., Zacharias, T., Zhang, B.: End-to-end verifiable elections in the standard model. In: Oswald, E., Fischlin, M. (eds.) EUROCRYPT 2015. LNCS, vol. 9057, pp. 468–498. Springer, Heidelberg (2015). doi:10.1007/978-3-662-46803-6_16
27. Kiayias, A., Zacharias, T., Zhang, B.: An efficient E2E verifiable e-voting system without setup assumptions. In: S&P 2017, vol. 15, no. 3, pp. 14–23 (2017)

28. Küsters, R., Müller, J., Scapin, E., Truderung, T.: sElect: a lightweight verifiable remote voting system. In: CSF 2016, pp. 341–354 (2016)
29. Küsters, R., Truderung, T.: Security analysis of re-encryption RPC mix nets. In: Euro S&P 2016, pp. 227–242. IEEE Computer Society (2016)
30. Küsters, R., Truderung, T., Beckert, B., Bruns, D., Kirsten, M., Mohr, M.: A hybrid approach for proving noninterference of java programs. In: CSF 2015, pp. 305–319 (2015)
31. Küsters, R., Truderung, T., Vogt, A.: A game-based definition of coercion-resistance and its applications. In: CSF 2010, pp. 122–136 (2010)
32. Küsters, R., Truderung, T., Vogt, A.: Accountability: definition and relationship to verifiability. In: CCS 2010, pp. 526–535 (2010)
33. Küsters, R., Truderung, T., Vogt, A.: Accountability: definition and relationship to verifiability. Technical report 2010/236, Cryptology ePrint Archive (2010). http://eprint.iacr.org/
34. Küsters, R., Truderung, T., Vogt, A.: Proving coercion-resistance of scantegrity II. In: Soriano, M., Qing, S., López, J. (eds.) ICICS 2010. LNCS, vol. 6476, pp. 281–295. Springer, Heidelberg (2010). doi:10.1007/978-3-642-17650-0_20
35. Küsters, R., Truderung, T., Vogt, A.: Verifiability, privacy, and coercion-resistance: new insights from a case study. In: S&P 2011, pp. 538–553 (2011)
36. Küsters, R., Truderung, T., Vogt, A.: A game-based definition of coercion-resistance and its applications. In: JCS 2012, pp. 709–764 (2012)
37. Küsters, R., Truderung, T., Vogt, A.: Clash attacks on the verifiability of e-voting systems. In: S&P 2012, pp. 395–409 (2012)
38. Küsters, R., Truderung, T., Vogt, A.: Formal analysis of chaumian mix nets with randomized partial checking. In: S&P 2014, pp. 343–358 (2014)
39. Moran, T., Naor, M.: Receipt-free universally-verifiable voting with everlasting privacy. In: Dwork, C. (ed.) CRYPTO 2006. LNCS, vol. 4117, pp. 373–392. Springer, Heidelberg (2006). doi:10.1007/11818175_22
40. Olembo, M.M., Bartsch, S., Volkamer, M.: Mental models of verifiability in voting. In: Vote-ID 2013, pp. 142–155 (2013)
41. Parkes, D., Rabin, M., Shieber, S., Thorpe, C.: Practical secrecy-preserving, verifiably correct and trustworthy auctions. In: ICEC 2006, pp. 70–81 (2006)
42. Rivest, R.L., Smith, W.D.: Three voting protocols: threeballot, VAV and twin. In: EVT 2007 (2007)
43. Ryan, P.Y.A., Rønne, P.B., Iovino, V.: Selene: voting with transparent verifiability and coercion-mitigation. In: Clark, J., Meiklejohn, S., Ryan, P.Y.A., Wallach, D., Brenner, M., Rohloff, K. (eds.) FC 2016. LNCS, vol. 9604, pp. 176–192. Springer, Heidelberg (2016). doi:10.1007/978-3-662-53357-4_12
44. Peter, Y.A., Ryan, D., Heather, J., Schneider, S., Xia, Z.: The prêt à voter verifiable election system, Technical report (2010)
45. Sako, K., Kilian, J.: Receipt-free mix-type voting scheme. In: Guillou, L.C., Quisquater, J.-J. (eds.) EUROCRYPT 1995. LNCS, vol. 921, pp. 393–403. Springer, Heidelberg (1995). doi:10.1007/3-540-49264-X_32
46. Schmidt, A., Heinson, D., Langer, L., Opitz-Talidou, Z., Richter, P., Volkamer, M., Buchmann, J.A.: Developing a legal framework for remote electronic voting. In: VOTE-ID 2009, pp. 92–105 (2009)
47. Schwartz, B., Grice, D.: Establishing a legal framework for e-voting in Canada. Elections Canada (2014)
48. Smyth, B., Frink, S., Clarkson, M.R.: Computational Election Verifiability: Definitions and an Analysis of Helios and JCJ. Number 2015/233 (2015)

49. Springall, D., Finkenauer, T., Durumeric, Z., Kitcat, J., Hursti, H., MacAlpine, M., Halderman, J.A.: Security analysis of the estonian internet voting system, pp. 703–715 (2014)
50. Stein, R., Wenda, G.: The Council of Europe and e-voting: history and impact of REC (2004) 11. In: EVOTE 2014, pp. 1–6 (2014)
51. Wolchok, S., Wustrow, E., Halderman, J.A., Prasad, H.K., Kankipati, A., Sakhamuri, S.K., Yagati, V., Gonggrijp, R.: Security analysis of India's electronic voting machines, pp. 1–14 (2010)
52. Wolchok, S., Wustrow, E., Isabel, D., Halderman, J.A.: Attacking the Washington, D.C. internet voting system. In: Keromytis, A.D. (ed.) FC 2012. LNCS, vol. 7397, pp. 114–128. Springer, Heidelberg (2012). doi:10.1007/978-3-642-32946-3_10

Voting in E-Participation: A Set of Requirements to Support Accountability and Trust by Electoral Committees

Peter Parycek[1], Michael Sachs[1], Shefali Virkar[1(✉)],
and Robert Krimmer[2]

[1] Department for E-Governance in Administration, Danube University Krems,
Krems an der Donau, Austria
{peter.parycek,michael.sachs,
shefali.virkar}@donau-uni.ac.at
[2] Ragnar Nurkse Department for Innovation and Governance,
Tallinn University of Technology, Tallinn, Estonia
robert.krimmer@ttu.ee

Abstract. Voting is an important part of electronic participation whenever it comes to finding a common opinion among the many participants. The impact of the voting result on the outcome of the e-participation process might differ a lot as voting can relate to approving, polling or co-decision making. The greater the impact of the electronic voting on the outcomes of the e-participation process, the more important become the regulations and technologies that stipulate the voting system and its procedures. People need to have trust in the voting system in order to accept the outcomes. Hence, it is important to use thoroughly trustworthy, auditable and secure voting systems in e-participation; especially whenever the voting within the e-participation process is likely to have a significant impact on the outcome. This paper analyses the verdict of the Austrian Constitutional Court in relation to the repeal of the Elections to the Austrian Federation of Students in 2009 where electronic voting was piloted as additional remote channel for casting a ballot. The court states its perspectives on elections and electronic voting which serve as sources for the derivation of legal requirements for electronic voting in this paper, namely requirements for accountability and trust by the electoral committee. Then, possible solutions for the requirements based on scholarly literature are described. The paper does not intend to explicitly provide e-voting solutions for elections, but instead proposes to serve as a basis for discussion of electronic voting in different e-participation scenarios.

Keywords: E-participation · E-voting · Electoral committee · Accountability · Trust

1 Introduction

Electronic participation is characterized by the participation of citizens in political decision-making processes with tools based on modern information and communication technologies (ICTs). Procedures for the participation of citizens in the decision-making

© Springer International Publishing AG 2017
R. Krimmer et al. (Eds.): E-Vote-ID 2017, LNCS 10615, pp. 42–56, 2017.
DOI: 10.1007/978-3-319-68687-5_3

process are possible at all administrative levels, from the municipality to the European Union, but can also be integrated in other contexts such as private organisations. The implementation of electronic participation has the potential to reduce hurdles for participation and to lower the costs of these processes in the long-term [1].

E-participation can be used for various purposes and in different forms, hence, the processes and platforms are often tailor-made for specific contexts. Models that describe e-participation usually divide elements of participation according to the degree of impact each has on the final decision [2]. While low levels of participation, such as accessing information or commenting on ideas, do usually not require strong regulations and high technical security standards, forms of participation with high impact on decision-making outcomes require the implementation of higher standards. As soon as selections and votes are part of the participation process, technical security and detailed regulations are required in order to establish trust in the outcomes of the participatory actions. The greater the impact of the participatory process on the final result, the higher the demands for proper regulations, implementation and secure systems [3].

E-voting in its legally binding context of official elections is the form of e-participation with the most direct impact on the actual decision. Consequently, it is relevant to look closely at e-voting requirements for use in secure voting processes in e-participation.

1.1   Background: The Elections to the Austrian Federation of Students

The elections to the Austrian Federation of Students in 2009 have been the first and only instance of electronic voting in Austria up until now. As the level of participation is traditionally low in the elections to the Austrian Federation of Students [4], e-voting was seen as a means with the potential to increase engagement and to test new technology within a young target group. The implementation of an e-voting pilot as additional remote channel to cast a vote along side the paper ballot in these elections was accompanied by a controversial discussion among students and in the public.

The update of the Regulation of the Elections to the Austrian Federation of Students from 2005[1] came into effect on 3 October 2008 and expired on 13 January 2012. The regulation was challenged by individuals in the Austrian Constitutional Court, which repealed the regulation on e-voting as it was not in alignment with the corresponding Federation of Students law. Consequently, the election was considered invalid. Major issues influencing the verdict of the Constitutional Court pertained to regulations related to the electoral committee and a lack of clear definitions concerning the processes of the verification within the entire voting system. For a comprehensive analysis, see the works of Krimmer, Ehringfeld and Traxl [5, 6].

---

[1] In German: "Hochschülerinnen- und Hochschülerschaftswahlordnung 2005". Available at: https://www.ris.bka.gv.at/Dokument.wxe?Abfrage=Bundesnormen&Dokumentnummer=NOR30006701.

1.2   Relevance for the Electoral Committees and Accountability

The Austrian Constitutional Court dealt extensively with the Austrian Federation of Students elections in 2009, and the relevant judgements can provide guidelines for the implementation of secure e-voting in any context. This paper aims, therefore, to provide a basis for the discussion of possible solutions to legal and technical issues encountered during the adoption of an e-voting system based on the demands made by the Constitutional Court.

In the framework of electronic participation, participatory decision making is usually not legally binding. E-voting regulations for officially binding elections hence address the highest standards of *security*, *audibility* and *reliability*, and are of relevance within the context of co-decision making in e-participation.

One must bear in mind that voting regulations and suffrage differ among countries, and even differ within countries depending on the purpose and context of the voting process. While the requirements formulated in this document may not be directly applicable to different electronic voting contexts they do indeed serve as a base for the creation of tailor-made solutions.

1.3   Structure of the Paper

In order to provide a robust analysis of e-voting as a participatory mechanism, and to present an informed account of the legal concepts and technical solutions underpinning the requirements for secure electronic voting in Austria, this research paper is structured as follows. First, the chapter entitled *Methodology* presents an account of the research design and methodological tools employed by the authors within the context of this research project. The next chapter, *Requirements based on Literature*, examines the selected legal requirements as embedded case studies supported by evidence based in scholarly and practitioner literature. The penultimate chapter, *Discussion*, offers an informed concluding analysis of e-voting and its potential as a tool for greater public engagement; locating the process within the broader conceptual framework of e-participation in Europe. The paper closes with the final chapter, *Acknowledgements*.

2   Methodology

This paper takes into account the legal considerations of the Austrian Constitutional Court ruling regarding the implementation of e-voting in the Elections of the Austrian Federation of Students of 2009 in order to reflect the requirements for secure voting systems that enable the electronic participation of citizens. For this purpose, legal requirements for electronic voting were derived from the verdicts passed by the Austrian Constitutional Court. Possible solutions for these requirements were then extracted in a literature analysis of international scientific works. While the original study takes into consideration all requirements derived from the judgements of the Austrian Constitutional Court, this paper focuses on those that consider the requirements for the electoral committee and those that pertain to system accountability as these can potentially be transferred to other scenarios and contexts of voting as a form of e-participation.

2.1 Deduction of Requirements

Sentences of the Austrian Constitutional Court were analysed for references to e-voting in the Elections of the Austrian Student. Not all judgements with such references included relevant information, for some appeals were rejected as they were not considered lawful or valid. The source of the sentences was the website of the Legal Information System of the Republic of Austria.[2] The following pronouncements of the Constitutional Court were analysed, and they are listed below according to date of sentence and reference number:

- 25 June 2009, V28/09, V29/09 ua
- 10 December 2009, G165/09, V39/09
- 23 February 2010, V89/09
- 9 March 2011, G287/09
- 02 December 2011, WI-1/11, V85/11ua, B1214/10, B1149/10, B898/10
- 5 March 2012, WI-2/11
- 22 August 2014, WI 2/2014

Once all possible legal requirements were extracted from the original texts they were clustered and filtered. These requirements were then further simplified for the purpose of better handling, and redundant requirements were merged with others or deleted. The categories for the clustering were thereafter derived from the content of all requirements and not prior based on literature. In this paper the authors only discuss the requirements that are part of the categories *electoral committee* and *accountability*.

2.2 Literature Research for Solutions

This section consists of a description of the research strategy adopted by the authors whilst conducting a review of existing literature for legal concepts and technological solutions relevant to the research project. To search for literature pertaining to electronic voting in general and to the derived legal requirements in particular, this project made use of one database of peer-reviewed literature (Scopus), one specialist search engine (Google Scholar), and one database of full-text books (Google Books).

The *Scopus Database* was queried specifically for peer-reviewed, scholarly literature. In order to optimally utilize the resource, a systematic conventional query string was constructed to conduct the search within the 'title', 'abstract' and 'keywords' fields of the publications indexed by this database. Searches were also filtered by scholarly discipline in order to narrow down search results and to identify highly relevant material. This research project also made use of the *Google Scholar* search engine to recover full-text sources of material previously discovered using Scopus, to identify clusters of publications authored by the same person, and to obtain new citations

---

[2] https://www.ris.bka.gv.at/defaultEn.aspx.

through a conventional key word search. The *Google Books* database was also queried exhaustively in order to access material from both single-author books and chapters within edited volumes. Here, books identified from earlier literature searches were first looked up, either by publication name or by author/editor name or a combination of the two. A conventional keyword search was also pursued.

3 Requirements Based on Literature

This chapter outlines and analyses the legal requirements for the implementation of secure e-voting in Austria derived from the rulings of the Austrian Constitutional Court. In particular, it discusses in some detail an extensive collection of legal concepts and technical solutions extracted through a systematic literature analysis of international scientific works that are considered relevant to the two sets of legal requirements selected as the embedded case studies for this research paper.

The research findings presented are organised in the following manner: first, the chapter comprises of three sections. The first section presents the derivation of the requirements based on judgements passed in Austria by the Constitutional Court, and introduces the embedded case studies. The second section is then concerned with derived legal requirements for the electoral committee, and the third with derived legal requirements pertaining to electoral accountability. Each stipulated legal requirement is listed individually, and is followed immediately by a discussion that touches upon how existing scholarly literature informs the legal condition conceptually and/or where developments in technology further reflect or advance key fundamental legal concepts.

As this paper does not seek to provide concrete solutions for electronic distance voting, but guidelines for voting at different stages within e-participation processes, literature about remote electronic voting and electronic voting machines was considered for the scholarly discussion below.

3.1 Legal Requirements at a Glance: The Embedded Case Studies

The analysis of the verdicts passed by the Austrian Constitutional Court yielded at total of 28 legal requirements, grouped by these researchers within 5 categories. Of these 5 categories, two – *electoral committee* and *accountability* – were selected as embedded case studies for this research paper.

Out of the 28 requirements identified, 5 relate to the category *electoral committee*. The derived requirements for the category *electoral committee* include that: the electoral committee must be able to carry out all its statutory tasks; the electoral committee must accept/receive the ballot; the electoral committee must examine the electoral authority/eligibility of the elector; the verification of the identity of the person entitled to vote must take place before the transmission of the electoral form; and, a certification of the e-voting system by experts cannot replace the state guarantee of the electoral principles observed by electoral committees.

Another 5 derived requirements may be clustered around the category *accountability*. These include: the electoral committee must be able to determine the election results and their validity; the verification of the validity of the ballot papers must be ensured by the electoral committee; the electoral committee and the judicial authorities of public law must be able to carry out a verification of the electoral principles and results after the election; the essential steps of the electoral process must be reliably verified by the electoral committee (without the assistance of experts) and the judicial authorities of public law; and, the essential steps of the determination of results must be reliably verified by the electoral committee (without the participation of experts).

3.2   Requirements for Trust by Electoral Committees

This section discusses the legal concepts and technical solutions pertaining to the requirements for trust by electoral committees as identified in the scholarly and practitioner literature.

The electoral committee must be able to carry out all its statutory tasks. Today, a large percentage of electoral management bodies (EMBs) use information and communications technologies with the aim of improving administrative procedures associated with the electoral process [7]. Technologies deployed range from the use of basic office automation tools such as word processing and spreadsheets to the application of more sophisticated data processing tools including data base management systems, optical scanning, and geographic information systems [8].

According to Caarls (2010), for an EMB to successfully carry out all its statutory tasks, therefore, it is important that a two-pronged approach be adopted [9]. On the one hand, the tasks and responsibilities of the EMB need to be defined clearly in legislation [10]. The extent to which the EMB is involved with the electoral process has direct bearing on the type and nature of the technological solution it deploys. On the other, it is also vital that personnel within the EMB possess the necessary technical expertise to effectively manage the process of electronic voting [11]. Only when both pre-conditions are fulfilled will the administering electoral body be able to successfully adopt and implement technology solutions to effectively perform and enhance its functions. For technical solutions see also (amongst others) Prosser et al. (2004) [12].

The electoral committee must accept/receive the ballot. Remote electronic voting refers to the election process whereby electors can opt to cast their votes over the Internet, most usually via a Web browser from home, or from possibly any other location where they have Internet access [13]. Whilst many different aspects of this sort of election warrant closer accountability, the focus of this recommendation is on *security*.

Voting in the traditional way, according to Chiang (2009), with physical ballots submitted at a true polling station, is usually done with confidence because the tangible safeguards put in place ensure a tangible return to the electoral management authority [14]. Technology-enabled elections are viewed with suspicion as votes might be intercepted and tampered with at the time of transmission to the electoral authority servers [15].

Just as the revamped election system needs to be seen as both *reliable* and *trustworthy* by electors [16], so must the system be considered impenetrable to external malicious attacks or intent by the administering authority says Pieters (2006). In recognising this, Andreu Riera Jorba and Jordi Castella Roca have developed and patented under United States law a secure electronic voting system that employs interrelated cryptographic processes and protocols to provide reliability to vote casting, ballot recounts, and verification of vote or poll results [17].

The electoral committee must examine the electoral authority/eligibility of the elector. Within the European Union, Ikonomopoulos et al. (2002) have determined that the process of examining the electoral authority/eligibility of the elector is a two-fold procedure. First, the process of determining electors is performed, a step essential for the current voting process, wherein all persons above a certain age have either the right or the obligation to participate in the democratic process [18]. This stage is realised by the state employees working for the electoral authority who determine, according to the national census, each individual's age and legal status. Second, the requirement of providing a means of authentication to each elector then needs to be fulfilled. This is achieved when state employees create a means of identification for every elector, and when these are subsequently received by voters from the state.

Therefore, for an electronic voting system to be at once *secure*, *legitimate* and *complete*, Ikonomopoulos et al. (2002) hold that it is important for the electoral committee be able to determine and establish the electoral authority/eligibility of the elector from a (1) legal, (2) functional, and (3) security systems-requirement perspective. The legal framework for the traditional model of voting advanced above provides us with a basis for the e-voting system requirements specification. In terms of functional requirements, the starting point of any of interaction with the information system is thus the provision of access to system functions that each actor is authorised to perform [18]. Building on this, Ibrahim et al. (2003) have proposed a secure e-voting systems architecture that applies security mechanisms in order to meet the legal security requirements needed for any election process. According to the proposed system, as individuals register themselves with the administrator of e-voting to be counted amongst eligible voters, a validator is made responsible for the verification of elector authority/eligibility and for the production of a ballot ID [19].

The verification of the identity of the person entitled to vote must take place before the transmission of the electoral form. In traditional voting/balloting, the authentication of an elector is generally performed prior to the act of electing, when the elector appears in person to vote at the election centre where they are registered [18]. Ikonomopoulos et al. (2002) outline the process in some detail; wherein the voter arrives at the polling station, presents to the on-duty member of staff his or her identity papers, has them verified by the staffer in question, and is then presented with the current electoral ballot paper. This process is performed to ensure that the elector themselves votes, and consists of an interaction between the elector and the electoral authority as represented by the personnel at the election centre [18].

For Internet voting to be secure, according to Regenscheid et al. (2011), a similar procedural requirement has often to be met: that the identity of the eligible elector needs to be verified prior to the electronic transmission of the electoral form. In the United States of America, for instance, state and local jurisdictions are given the option to employ systems to authenticate Uniformed and Overseas Citizen Absentee Voting Act (UOCAVA) voters before serving them electoral forms, when permitted under state law [20]. However, if voter identification data is indeed used to establish trust that a given ballot was completed and returned by an eligible elector, it is carried out on the premise that the electronic authentication of the person entitled to vote was done prior to any transmission of the electronic ballot form [20].

A certification of the e-voting system by experts cannot replace the state guarantee of the electoral principles observed by electoral committees. Richter (2010) states that "...all forms of voting, including Internet voting have been criticized for not fulfilling the Principle of the Public Nature of the Election which was declared as a constitutional principle in the Voting-Machine-Judgement of the German Federal Constitutional Court (BVerfG09) and which requires verifiability of the election for every citizen without technical knowledge" [21].

According to Gritzalis (2002), electronic voting should be considered only as a complementary means to traditional election processes [22]. He argues that while e-voting can be a cost-effective way to conduct the electoral process and a means of attracting specific groups of people to participate, the continued prevalence of (1) the digital divide within adopting societies, (2) an inherent distrust in the e-voting procedure across populations, and (3) inadequate mechanisms to protect information systems against security risks make it only a supplement to, and not a replacement of, existing paper-based voting systems.

Building on this argument, Caarls (2010) attempts to highlight the issues of trust and confidence as necessary pre-conditions for the uptake of e-voting systems [9]. Here, Caarls argues that an e-voting system cannot be successfully adopted unless citizens trust their current (paper-based) political and administrative systems. Further, she maintains, the introduction of an e-voting system must not result in the exclusion of certain groups within a given population. Security is also paramount, with time needing to be set aside for research into the development of robust and secure system before the eventual roll-out of the project. This is also tightly connected with the topic of verifiability, which will be deal with in the next section.

3.3   Requirements for Accountability

This section considers the legal concepts and technical solutions pertinent to the derived legal requirements for accountability as obtained from the scholarly and practitioner literature.

The electoral committee must be able to determine the election results and their validity. As part of the electoral process, the election authority needs to be able to verify the validity of every ballot cast, and that the tallying of the valid ballots has been correct.

In the electronic voting literature, the term *verifiability* is closely related to the accountability requirement of the integrity of the election result [23]. Gritzalis (2002) contends, therefore, that an e-voting system should allow for its verification by both individual voters (individual verifiability), and also by election officials, parties, and individual observers (institutional or universal verifiability) – despite being in conflict with principles of transparency [22]. Systems providing both types of verification are known as *end-to-end* (E2E) *verifiablility* [24]. However, the ability of currently existing electronic voting systems to enable the election authority to verify the integrity of the election result has been criticised as being flawed by recent scholarship [25].

This is because, as maintained by Gharadaghy and Volkamer (2010), universal verifiability is usually more complex to achieve than individual verifiability for, in order to attain this condition, the election authority needs to ensure that all encrypted votes cast and stored on the database are decrypted appropriately and properly tallied whilst preserving ballot secrecy [24]. Gharadaghy and Volkamer go on to propose two main cryptographic techniques to meet and overcome this challenge: either (1) the application of homomorphic encryption schemes, such as the *Helios 2.0* protocol [26], that allow the encrypted sum of all encrypted votes to be computed without compromising the secrecy of the ballot; or (2) the use of *MIX networks* to anonymize encrypted votes prior to their decryption and eventual tallying [24]. Further, for a discussion of organisational issues see also Krimmer (2016) [27].

The verification of the validity of the ballot papers must be ensured by the electoral committee. It is the task of the electoral committee to ensure the validity of the each of the ballot papers counted towards the final election result.

The need for reliability of the e-voting process, according to Gritzalis (2002), is derived from the democratic need to ensure that the outcome of the election correctly reflects the voters will [22]. In other words, a reliable system should ensure that the outcome of the voting process accurately corresponds to the votes cast. It should be impossible from a systems architecture point of view to exclude from the tally a valid vote and to include an invalid one [28].

Khaki (2014) proposes both basic and advanced security protocols that may be applied by an electoral management body to successfully verify the validity of the submitted ballot papers [29]. Basic security measures advanced by this author include either the use of Message Authentication Code (MAC) keys shared between the voter and the server, or server digital signatures that constitute keys stored on the server. In both cases, the server is able to generate for verification purposes the MAC or digital signature of any vote.

Further, according to Khaki, vote integrity and authenticity can be assured through the use of advanced security measures in the form of voter digital signatures [28], wherein votes are digitally signed by the voter after they have been encrypted in such a manner that the recipient server can validate and verify the signature as authentic but cannot manipulate it. For an early technical proposal see [30].

The electoral committee and the judicial authorities of public law must be able to carry out a verification of the electoral principles and results after the election. In the post-election period, Caarls (2010) recommends that an audit trail be established for all aspects of the systems used in the elections so that "…all changes and decisions can be explained and defended" [9]. Following from this, therefore, audits may be carried out by all the parties involved in the electoral process and can serve many purposes. To paraphrase Norden et al. (2007), such an audit can fulfil the following goals: (1) create public confidence in the election results, (2) deter election fraud, (3) detect and provide information about large-scale systemic errors, (4) provide feedback towards the improvement of voting technology and election administration, (5) set benchmarks and provide additional incentives for election staff to achieve higher standards of accuracy, and (6) confirm, to a high degree of confidence, that a complete manual recount would not affect the election outcome [31].

There exist in the practitioner literature three noteworthy e-voting protocols that overtly permit the electoral management body to carry out such a post-election verification of electoral principles and results [32–34].

A. Punchscan: Fisher et al. (2006) in their seminal paper put forward Punchscan, a hybrid paper/electronic voting system based on a concept delineated by David Chaum in December 2005 [32]. In improving upon the earlier idea, the Punchscan system advanced by Fisher et al. employs a two-layer ballot and receipt system in combination with a sophisticated cryptographic vote-tabulation mechanism called a "Punchboard" that can be used to facilitate the running of an electronic election. During the post-election phase, once the results of the ballot are posted online, auditors may conduct a post-election audit by choosing an area of the Punchboard's decrypt table [32]. Any significant corruption of the Punchboard as a consequence of election malpractice is almost certainly detectable.

B. Helios: Adida (2008) discusses the advantages of Helios, a web-based open-audit voting system [33]. Designed to be deliberately simpler than most complete cryptographic voting protocols, Helios focuses on the central precept of "public auditability" – any group can outsource its election to Helios, and the integrity of that election can be verified even if Helios itself is corrupted. To achieve this, the Helios protocol provides users with the option of two verification programmes written in Python: one for verifying a single encrypted vote produced by the ballot preparation system with the "audit" option selected, and another for verifying the shuffling, decryption, and tallying of an entire election [33].

C. Scantegrity: Chaum et al. (2008) propose Scantegrity, a security enhancement for optical scan voting systems [34]. The Scantegrity voting system combines E2E cryptographic ideas with a widely used vote-counting system to provide the end-user with the strong security guarantees of an E2E set-up whilst not interfering with existing procedural requirements such as a paper audit trail or a manual recount. Scantegrity is furthermore universally verifiable, whereby, using special software of their choice, anyone can verify online that the tally was computed correctly from official data [35]. This makes it particularly useful for those electoral management bodies wishing to carry out a post-electoral audit.

The essential steps of the electoral process must be reliably verified by the electoral committee (without the assistance of experts) and the judicial authorities of public law. From general perspective, in cases where an e-voting system has been deployed, Caarls (2010) advocates that every part of the process be audited post-election; including, the electoral voter register and its compilation, together with the processes of voting, counting, archiving, and the destruction of votes [9]. One part of the audit process could be to verify that the systems used for the election were in fact based on source code certified for use prior to the election. Other parts of the audit process might include the review of other documentation, including the functional and technical system design [9].

In more particular terms of system functionality, and to paraphrase Prandini and Ramilli (2012), e-voting systems are generally evaluated in terms of their security, auditability, usability, efficiency, cost, accessibility, and reliability [36]. The principle of *auditability*, most especially, refers to the necessary pre-condition of there being reliable and demonstrably authentic election records [37] against which due process can be accounted for. Software independence is one form of system auditability, enabling the detection and possible correction of election outcome errors caused by malicious software or software bugs [38]. The concept has been defined by Rivest (2008) as follows: "A voting system is software independent if an (undetected) change or error in its software cannot cause an undetectable change or error in an election outcome" [39].

In other words, the principle of software independence addresses directly the difficulty of assuring oneself that cast ballots will be recorded accurately in adherence to prevailing election principles and standards by complex and often difficult-to-test software in the case of an all-electronic voting system [39]. For users of software-independent voting systems, therefore, verification of the correctness of the election result is possible without there being any lingering concern that the election result was affected or even determined by a software bug or malicious piece of code [38].

The essential steps of the determination of results must be reliably verified by the electoral committee (without the participation of experts). Similar to the legal principle of the "public nature of elections" in Germany [40], which prescribes that all the essential steps of an election are subject to the possibility of open accountability by general public, it is argued here that (when applied to the use of electronic voting machines in Austria) both legal and technical provision needs be made for the electoral management body to be able to verify independently and reliably the essential steps of voting and the ascertainment of the result post-election without its personnel possessing any prior specialist knowledge.

Considered in terms of e-voting in general, the holding makes the security objective of *election* or *end-to-end verifiability* mandatory [41]. This is because, in contrast to conventional paper-based elections, electronics-based ballots are still much less transparent [42]. It may not be possible to observe all the electronic operations performed on data, programming errors are usually difficult to detect, and attacks on a system by malicious code might go unnoticed [26].

Remote electronic voting systems have to, therefore, also be considered from the perspective of their *usability* [43]. The term 'usability', according to Winkler et al. (2009), is often used to describe the perceived ease of use and usefulness of an information technology system [43]. Several studies point out the importance of undertaking a usability evaluation when validating a new e-voting system [44]. Within the context of the discussion, it may be inferred that a verifiable system should be user-friendly to ensure that its users are able to carry out verification processes with relative ease and speed and independent of external specialists.

4   Discussion

It has been a declared target by the Europe Ministers responsible for e-government to empower citizens through information and communication technologies [45]. Citizens shall receive better and more transparent access to information that shall serve as the basis for stronger involvement in the policy process. Hence, information and communication technologies shall enhance citizen participation. New political movements and ideas all across Europe support the surge of an increasingly connected society towards having a stronger say in political processes. Traditional parties seek to open up to outside opinions, at least during election campaigns. These changes in the political landscape must be supported with the necessary tools.

Citizens' participation in general is a complex field with numerous different approaches being adopted to achieve similar aims. It has become evident that there is no single possible solution to resolve the various obstacles in the path of optimal citizen participation, but it has also become obvious that digital technologies, the internet and its networking connectivity can support the management of citizen participation at most stages of engagement.

This research paper focuses on the voting process as an integral part of electronic participation. Votes are used to assess the opinions of participants on comments or proposals which might not necessarily need highly regulated and secure technological systems. Voting can also be used to make the final decision in an e-participation process that might have direct impact on actual implementations in reality or legal regulations. In the latter example, observing regulations and ensuring system security are essential for successful and satisfactory participation.

This paper describes the legal requirements for e-voting as stipulated by the Austrian Constitutional Court in the context of the Austrian Federation of Students Election of 2009. While the derived requirements are only valid for this specific context, they can be a good indication for the way forward in other scenarios.

Large-scale e-participation will involve electronic voting at some point in the process, and this must be manged and implemented in an appropriate manner. Public authorities need to be ready to answer citizens' questions, and to have in place a strategy to help citizens understand the system and its underlying technology. Trust-building is a vital component of the engineering of participatory processes.

The introduction of e-participation should be considered as means of promoting social inclusion, and care must be taken to ensure that its proliferation does not result in the privileging of certain groups within society (those who can afford regular Internet access, for instance) over others. In theory, the use of technology in citizens' engagement widens access to the democratic process by reaching out to and inviting a greater number of people to participate. However, in practice existing digital and social divides circumscribe who actually participates and, if not deployed sensibly, technology could actually worsen prevailing democratic deficits.

Acknowledgements. The work of Robert Krimmer was supported in parts by the Estonian Research Council project PUT1361 and the Tallinn Univerity of Technology project B42.

References

1. Viborg Andersen, K., Zinner Henriksen, H., Secher, C., Medaglia, R.: Costs of e-participation: the management challenges. Transforming Gov. People Process Policy **1**(1), 29–43 (2007)
2. Arnstein, S.R.: A ladder of citizen participation. J. Am. Inst. Planners **35**(4), 216–224 (1969)
3. Schossböck, J., Rinnerbauer, B., Sachs, M., Wenda, G., Parycek, P.: Identification in e-participation: a multi-dimensional model. Int. J. Electron. Gov. **8**(4), 335–355 (2016)
4. Krimmer, R.: e-Voting.at: Elektronische Demokratie am Beispiel der österreichischen Hochschülerschaftswahlen. Working Papers on Information Processing and Information Management 05/2002 of the Vienna University of Economics and Business (2002)
5. Krimmer, R., Ehringfeld, A., Traxl, M.: The use of e-voting in the federation of students elections 2009. In: Krimmer, R., Grimm, R. (eds.) Proceedings of the 4th International Conference on Electronic Voting 2010, pp. 33–44, Bonn (2010)
6. Krimmer, R., Ehringfeld, A., Traxl, M.: Evaluierungsbericht. E-Voting bei den Hochschülerinnen- und Hochschülerschaftswahlen 2009. BMWF, Vienna (2010)
7. Lopez-Pintor, R.: Electoral Management Bodies as Institutions of Governance. Bureau for Development Policy, United Nations Development Programme (2000)
8. ACE Electoral Knowledge Network. Elections and Technology. http://aceproject.org/ace-en/topics/et/onePage. Accessed 21 Apr 2017
9. Caarls, S.: E-voting Handbook: Key Steps in the Implementation of E-enabled Elections. Council of Europe Publishing, Strasbourg (2010)
10. Mozaffar, S., Schedler, A.: The comparative study of electoral governance – introduction. Int. Polit. Sci. Rev. **23**(1), 5–27 (2002)
11. Gillard, S.: Soft-skills and technical expertise of effective project managers. Issues Inf. Sci. Inf. Technol. **6**, 723–729 (2009)
12. Prosser, A., Kofler, R., Krimmer, R., Unger, M.K.: Implementation of quorum-based decisions in an election committee. In: Traunmüller, R. (ed.) EGOV 2004. LNCS, vol. 3183, pp. 122–127. Springer, Heidelberg (2004). doi:10.1007/978-3-540-30078-6_21
13. Rubin, A.D.: Security considerations for remote electronic voting. Commun. ACM **45**(12), 39–44 (2002)
14. Chiang, L.: Trust and security in the e-voting system. Electron. Gov. Int. J. **6**(4), 343–360 (2009)
15. Bishop, M., Wagner, D.: Risks of e-voting. Commun. ACM **50**(11), 120 (2007)
16. Pieters, W.: Acceptance of voting technology: between confidence and trust. In: Stølen, K., Winsborough, W.H., Martinelli, F., Massacci, F. (eds.) iTrust 2006. LNCS, vol. 3986, pp. 283–297. Springer, Heidelberg (2006). doi:10.1007/11755593_21
17. Jorba, A.R., Roca, J.C.: Secure remote electronic voting system and cryptographic protocols and computer programs employed. U.S. Patent No. 7,260,552, 21 August 2007
18. Ikonomopoulos, S., Lambrinoudakis, C., Gritzalis, D., Kokolakis, S., Vassiliou, K.: Functional requirements for a secure electronic voting system. In: Ghonaimy, M.A., El-Hadidi, M.T., Aslan, H.K. (eds.) Security in the Information Society. IAICT, vol. 86, pp. 507–519. Springer, Boston, MA (2002). doi:10.1007/978-0-387-35586-3_40
19. Ibrahim, S., Kamat, M., Salleh, M., Aziz, S.R.A.: Secure E-voting with blind signature. In: Proceedings of 4th National Conference on Telecommunication Technology. NCTT 2003, pp. 193–197. IEEE Publications (2003)
20. Regenscheid, A., Beier, G.: Security Best Practices for the Electronic Transmission of Election Materials for UOCAVA Voters, NISTIR 7711, National Institute of Standards and Technology (NIST) – U.S. Department of Commerce, Gaithersburg, M.D. (2011)

21. Richter, P.: The virtual polling station: transferring the sociocultural effect of poll site elections to remote internet voting. In: Krimmer R., Grimm R. (eds.) Proceedings of the 4th International Conference on Electronic Voting 2010, pp. 79–86. Bonn (2010)
22. Gritzalis, D.A.: Principles and requirements for a secure e-voting system. Comput. Secur. **21**(6), 539–556 (2002)
23. Küsters, R., Truderung, T., Vogt, A.: Accountability: definition and relationship to verifiability. In: Proceedings of the 17th ACM Conference on Computer and Communications Security (CCS 2010), pp. 526–535. ACM, Chicago (2010)
24. Gharadaghy, R., Volkamer, M.: Verifiability in electronic voting - explanations for non security experts. In: Krimmer R., Grimm R. (eds.) Proceedings of the 4th International Conference on Electronic Voting 2010, pp. 151–162. Bonn (2010)
25. Karayumak, F., Olembo, M.M., Kauer, M., Volkamer, M.: Usability analysis of helios-an open source verifiable remote electronic voting system. EVT/WOTE **11**, 5 (2011)
26. Kremer, S., Ryan, M., Smyth, B.: Election verifiability in electronic voting protocols. In: Gritzalis, D.A., Preneel, B., Theoharidou, M. (eds.) Computer Security – ESORICS 2010. LNCS, vol. 6345, pp. 389–404. Springer, Berlin/Heidelberg (2010). doi:10.1007/978-3-642-15497-3_24
27. Krimmer, R.: Verifiability: a new concept challenging or contributing to existing election paradigms? In: Proceedings of the 13th EMB Conference, pp. 102–107, Bucharest (2016)
28. Mitrou, L., Gritzalis, D., Katsikas, S.: Revisiting legal and regulatory requirements for secure e-voting. In: Ghonaimy, M.A., El-Hadidi, M.T., Aslan, H.K. (eds.) Security in the Information Society. IAICT, vol. 86, pp. 469–480. Springer, Boston, MA (2002). doi:10.1007/978-0-387-35586-3_37
29. Khaki, F.: Implementing End-to-End Verifiable Online Voting for Secure, Transparent and Tamper-Proof Elections. IDC Whitepaper 33 W (2014)
30. Prosser, A., Krimmer, R., Kofler, R., Unger, M.K.: The role of the election commission in electronic voting. In: Proceedings of the 38th Annual Hawaii International Conference on System Sciences. HICSS 2005, pp. 119–119. IEEE (2005)
31. Norden, L., Burstein, A., Hall, J.L., Chen, M.: Post-Election Audits: Restoring Trust in Elections, Report by Brennan Center for Justice at The New York University School of Law and The Samuelson Law, Technology and Public Policy Clinic at the University of California, Berkeley School of Law (Boalt Hall) (2007)
32. Fisher, K., Carback, R., Sherman, A.T.: Punchscan: introduction and system definition of a high-integrity election system. In: Preproceedings of the 2006 IAVoSS Workshop on Trustworthy Elections, Robinson College (Cambridge, United Kingdom), International Association for Voting System Sciences (2006). [full citation unavailable]
33. Adida, B.H.: Web-based open-audit voting. In: van Oorschot, P.C. (ed.) Proceedings of the 17th Conference on Security Symposium, pp. 335–348. USENIX Association, Berkley (2008)
34. Chaum, D., Essex, A., Carback, R., Sherman, A., Clark, J., Popoveniuc, S., Vora, P.: Scantegrity: end-to-end voter-verifiable optical scan voting. IEEE Secur. Priv. **6**(3), 40–46 (2008)
35. Sherman, A.T., Carback, R., Chaum, D., Clark, J., Essex, A., Herrnson, P.S., Mayberry, T., Popovenuic, S., Rivest, R.L., Shen, E., Sinha, B., Vora, P.: Scantegrity mock election at Takoma Park. In: Krimmer R., Grimm R. (eds.) Proceedings of the 4th International Conference on Electronic Voting 2010, pp. 35–51. Kollen Druck+Verlag GmbH, Bonn (2010)
36. Prandini, M., Ramilli, M.: A model for e-voting systems evaluation based on international standards: definition and experimental validation. Serv. J. **8**(3), 42–72 (2012)

37. Internet Policy Institute: Report of the National Workshop on Internet Voting: Issues and Research Agenda, An Internet Policy Institute Publication (2001)
38. Rivest, R.L., Virza, M.: Software independence revisited. In: Hao, F., Ryan, P.Y.A. (eds.) Real-World Electronic Voting: Design, Analysis and Deployment. CRC Press, Boca Raton (2017). [full citation unavailable]
39. Rivest, R.L.: On the notion of 'software independence' in voting systems. Philos. Trans. Math. Phys. Eng. Sci. **366**(1881), 3759–3767 (2008)
40. German Federal Constitutional Court (Bundesverfassungsgericht): Use of voting computers in 2005 Bundestag election unconstitutional. Press Release No. 19/2009 of 03 March 2009. https://www.bundesverfassungsgericht.de/SharedDocs/Pressemitteilungen/EN/2009/bvg09-019.html. Accessed 27 Apr 2017
41. Schmidt, A., Heinson, D., Langer, L., Opitz-Talidou, Z., Richter, P., Volkamer, M., Buchmann, J.: Developing a legal framework for remote electronic voting. In: Ryan, P.Y.A., Schoenmakers, B. (eds.) Vote-ID 2009. LNCS, vol. 5767, pp. 92–105. Springer, Heidelberg (2009). doi:10.1007/978-3-642-04135-8_6
42. Enguehard, C.: Transparency in electronic voting: the great challenge. In: IPSA International Political Science Association RC 10 on Electronic Democracy. Conference on "E-democracy - State of the art and future agenda", Jan 2008, Stellenbosch, South Africa, édition électronique (2008)
43. Winckler, M., Bernhaupt, R., Palanque, P., Lundin, D., Leach, K., Ryan, P., Alberdi, E., Strigini, L.: Assessing the usability of open verifiable e-voting systems: a trial with the system Prêt à Voter. In: Proceedings of ICE-GOV (2009)
44. Herrnson, P.S., Niemi, R. G., Hanmer, M.J., Bederson, B.B., Conrad, F.G., Traugott, M.: The importance of usability testing of voting systems. In: Electronic Voting Technology Workshop, Vancouver B.C., Canada, 1 August 2006 (2006)
45. Ministerial Declaration on eGovernment. https://ec.europa.eu/digital-agenda/sites/digital-agenda/files/ministerial-declaration-on-egovernment-malmo.pdf. Accessed 7 May 2017

The Weakness of Cumulative Voting

Josh Benaloh[(✉)]

Microsoft Research, Redmond, WA, USA
benaloh@microsoft.com

Abstract. Cumulative Voting is an electoral system in which each voter is allowed to cast multiple votes — some or all of which may be duplicate votes for a single candidate. It is sometimes used to elect members to a legislative body such as a parliament or city council, and its purpose is to achieve a more proportional representation than that which results from many other voting systems. Cumulative voting is most commonly used in municipal elections in the United States and Europe, but it has also been used for larger elections and is often used by corporations to elect their directors.

In this work, it will be argued that in all practical scenarios, voters who are given the option to split their votes between multiple candidates should refuse to do so and should concentrate all of their votes on a single candidate. Thus, by giving voters multiple votes which the voter may optionally split, many jurisdictions are adding unnecessary complication, confusing voters and increasing the rate of voter errors, and encouraging voters to act against their own interests.

1 Introduction

Cumulative voting is a process wherein a multi-seat body is elected by pooling all of the candidates into a single race and allotting each voter multiple votes (often one per seat to be filled). Candidates are ordered by the number of votes they receive, and the body is filled by taking as many candidates from the top of the ordering as there are seats to be filled [GM05, BDB03]. Cumulative voting is frequently used as an alternative to a partitioned system in which a territory is divided into districts which each elect a single representative [Chr10].

The usual rationale for cumulative voting is to achieve more proportionate representation. For instance, if 60% of a partitioned electorate supports a particular party and the support is distributed homogenously, then one may expect that every district will elect a member of this party and the elected representation will be completely composed of members of this party. In contrast, with cumulative voting it is expected that only 60% of the seats to go to a party that is supported by 60% of the electorate. A minority party with under 10% support that would likely obtain no representation in a partitioned system could obtain proportionate representation with cumulative voting.

Cumulative voting has been adopted in many U.S. jurisdictions including Port Chester, New York [Rae10]; Worcester County, Maryland [Lew94];

© Springer International Publishing AG 2017
R. Krimmer et al. (Eds.): E-Vote-ID 2017, LNCS 10615, pp. 57–65, 2017.
DOI: 10.1007/978-3-319-68687-5_4

Boerne, Texas [Mac10]; and Peoria, Illinois [Sha09]. It was used for more than a century to elect the lower house of the Illinois state legislature [NYT86b, GP01], and is frequently used in Texas school board elections [Nic02]. In most cases, the adoption of cumulative voting is the result of a legal challenge to a district system which was deemed to produce a result that lacked adequate minority representation [PD95]. Cumulative voting is also commonly used in corporate shareholder elections to enable minority shareholders to achieve representation on boards of directors. U.S. Corporations using cumulative voting include Sears-Roebuck [Fly91], Avon [NYT90], Walgreen's [Wal09], Hewlett-Packard [HP009], and Craigslist [DiC10]. Cumulative voting is now required of all Taiwanese corporations [TT009], and a North Dakota constitutional requirement for its use in corporations was recently removed [Mac06].

There has been much research in the social choice literature on the merrits of various voting systems — including cumulative voting (see, for instance, [Tab01]). Chamberlin and Courant [ChCo83] and Monroe [Mon95] offer detailed mechanisms and analyses of rule for achieving proportional representation. This paper does not attempt find the best systems of achieving proportional representation nor does is attempt to compare and contrast cumulative voting versus the more common system of dividing a region into districts and using a simple plurality system to elect a single representative from each district. Instead, it will be argued that within any scenario in which a cumulative voting system might provide value, it is almost always against voters' interests to split their votes. Hence, cumulative voting is, in all practical cases, inferior to the much simpler "at large" system of a *single non-transferable vote* wherein each voter is given only a single vote and the leading overall vote-recipients are elected. Thus, as a practical matter, cumulative voting should *never* be used!

2   When Should Voters Split Their Votes?

A natural question when voters have an option, but no requirement, to split their votes among multiple candidates is when, if ever, should they do so?

The most likely scenario where vote splitting is in a voter's interest is when this voter controls a large fraction of the electorate. This can arise in corporate shareholder settings where a large shareholder may have enough voting power to elect multiple directors. For example, a shareholder with a 40% interest in a corporation that uses cumulative voting to elect a five-member board of directors may want to split these shares and vote 20% for each of two candidates to ensure their election. Similar scenarios may arise when a political party or coalition strategizes over how to best use its support.

Vote splitting can also be in the interest of an individual voter with a relatively small number of votes who has *extremely* precise information about the rest of the electorate. For instance, if 100 voters are each given six votes to cast for a six-member council and a voter knows or has good reason to believe that all of the other 99 voters will cast votes giving 79 votes to each of candidates A_1, A_2, and A_3, 60 votes to each of candidates B_1, B_2, and B_3, and 59 votes to each of candidates C_1, C_2, and C_3, and if this voter prefers candidates C_1, C_2, and C_3 to candidates B_1, B_2, and B_3, then the voter's best strategy is clearly to cast two votes for each of candidates C_1, C_2, and C_3.

In another instance, if an individual voter knows or has good reason to believe that no other voters will split their votes, then it may be in this last voter's interest to split the final vote and thereby have a greater potential to break multiple ties.

Cumulative voting scenarios seem to fall into one of two classes — both of which are better addressed by other voting systems.

The first class is when a large fraction of the total votes is controlled by an entity such as large corporate shareholder or a political party. In these cases, there is already sufficient granularity to allow virtually any desired vote splitting. A shareholder with a 40% stake in a corporation can vote half of these shares for each of two candidates just as easily in the single non-transferable voting case of one vote per share as in the cumulative voting case which allots five votes per share.[1] There are some cases when additional vote granularity may make it slightly easier for a political party to manage its constituents, but these advantages are small and better addressed by alternative voting systems.

In the second class, each individual voter represents only a small fraction of the electorate. It will be shown that, in realistic scenarios, such voters' typical interests are better served by not splitting their votes at all.

3   Voter Utility

A principal tool used in this paper is a voter utility function which assigns a (monetary) value to a vote for each candidate. This function may be implicit and its computation need not be specified. It is only necessary as a pedagogical tool that such a function exist – implicitly or explicitly – for each voter.

The utility function described here is not necessarily the value a voter assigns to election of each candidate nor does it necessarily match the probabilities that a vote for each given candidate would alter the outcome of the election. Instead, the value of a vote for a selected candidate may be regarded as the sum, over all candidates, of the product formed as probability that the vote will elect the selected candidate and displace the other candidate multiplied by the value (positive, negative, or zero) of effecting this change in the electoral outcome.

To be formal, a voter's *view* of an election is a collection of probabilities $\{p_{i,j}\}$ where each $p_{i,j}$ is the voter's (implicit) assessment of the probability that a vote for the candidate denoted by C_i will cause C_i to be elected and candidate C_j to be displaced. The view of a voter is, at least in part, informed by any partial information that the voter may have of the probability distributions of votes cast by other voters.

---

[1] In a *very* small election, a single voter may represent a substantial fraction of an electorate and may benefit from the added granularity of cumulative voting. Such scenarios, e.g. three voters electing a multi-seat board, are not considered to be "realistic" for the purposes of this work.

For any pair of candidates C_i and C_j, the *displacement value* $M_{i,j}$ to a voter is the value to that voter of C_i being elected over C_j.

The voter's *utility function* which describes, for each candidate C_i, the value to that voter of a vote for C_i, can now be defined as

$$U(i) = \sum_j p_{i,j} M_{i,j}.$$

For example, a voter may prefer candidate C_1 over candidate C_2 by a large margin and candidate C_2 over candidate C_3 by a much smaller margin. In this scenario, it might be the case that the voter assigns the highest utility to a vote for C_1 and the lowest to a vote for C_3, but if the voter also perceives candidate C_1 as unlikely to win (or, perhaps, very likely to win) and expects a close election between candidates C_2 and C_3 with only one of the two likely to obtain a seat, then the voter may assign the highest utility to a vote for candidate C_2 instead, since the expected return of this vote may be of higher value than that of a vote for candidate C_1.

A vote for candidate C_i is *optimal* for a voter with utility function U if $U(i) = \max_j U(j)$.

Note again that there is no expectation that voters explicitly compute their utility functions. Instead, the assumption is merely that a function ascribing a value to each possible vote exists implicitly for each voter. Rational voters who each have a single vote to cast should always cast an optimal vote, but it is not assumed that voters act rationally.

Note that describing the utility per vote in this way carries some implicit assumptions. If, for instance, the most important outcome for a voter is that no candidate receives zero votes (perhaps the voter is a judge in a school science fair), then it may well be in the voter's interest to spread votes among as many candidates as possible. Such a goal not captured by the utility function described herein and will not be considered further in this work.

4   A Continuity Assumption

Whether or not utilities are explicitly calculated, it seems very unlikely that the change or addition of a single vote amongst anything beyond a miniscule set of voters would have a significant effect on a rational voter's utility function. Specifically, if a rational voter is presented with two scenarios for the expected distribution of votes which are identical except that a single known vote is added in the second scenario, then the utility functions in these two scenarios are unlikely to differ substantially.

The assumption is characterized as follows.

We say that utility function $U(i) = \sum_j p_{i,j} M_{i,j}$ is *ε-near* utility function $U'(i) = \sum_j p'_{i,j} M'_{i,j}$ if $\max_j |p_{i,j} M_{i,j} - p'_{i,j} M'_{i,j}| \leq \varepsilon$.

Let U be a voter's utility function in a particular election including any partial information about other votes that a voter may have, and let U_j be the utility function for the same election with the additional knowledge that a single vote has been added to the tally of candidate C_j.

We say that u is ε-smooth if for all candidates C_j, U is ε-near U_j.

Lemma 1. *If a voter has two votes to cast and the voter's utility function is ε-smooth, then repeating an optimal vote produces a utility which is within ε of the maximum possible return for all possible vote pairs.*

Commentary. While it seems extremely unlikely that in any practical election, the addition of a single vote would change a voter's utility function enough to change a voter's optimal vote; even if such a scenario were to occur, the benefit of casting a second vote differently from an optimal first vote would be miniscule.

In contrast, in most practical situations casting a second vote which is different from an optimal first vote could result in a return which is substantially less than optimal.

An immediate consequence of this analysis is that a rational voter whose votes constitute only a small fraction of the electorate should almost always cast a second vote (and any subsequent votes) in exactly the same way as the first. **A rational voter should almost never divide votes amongst multiple candidates.**

As noted above, this utility assumption may not be valid for a rational voter who has exceptionally precise information about the ballots of other voters. Additionally, even if a voter has such unrealistically precise information, this information must indicate multiple near-perfect ties between candidates who are each at the threshold of election. In no practical situation with more than a very few voters will such precision be realistic, and the basic claim will hold in all non-trivial practical situations. Hence, in any realistic scenario, it is against a voters interest to split votes; and even in such extraordinarily unusual scenarios where it may be in a voter's interest to split votes, the benefit that a voter could expect from splitting votes would be miniscule.

Since each rational voter should cast all allotted votes for a single candidate, voters could instead each be given a single (non-transferable) vote. This leads to the following principal result.

Lemma 2 (Main Result). *The cumulative voting system of allotting multiple votes to each voter **and** allowing a voter to cast multiple votes for a single candidate complicates implementation, increases voter confusion and errors[2], and encourages voters to act against their own interests by dividing their votes amongst multiple candidates!*

Perhaps the confusion about the value of vote splitting comes from the following scenario. A voter might prefer both candidates C_1 and C_2 to candidate C_3 and believe that all three have a realistic possibility of being elected to the final seat. The voter might decide to cast votes for both candidates C_1 and C_2

---

[2] Some voters may not understand that they are allowed to cast multiple votes or that multiple votes can be cast for the same candidate [BE98, O'M09, Bow03, Wil04].

in order to improve both of their chances of defeating candidate C_3. This may even be a rational strategy in a case where the voter has extraordinarily precise information about the remainder of the electorate.[3] However, the utility argument shows that in any realistic scenario, this voter is virtually certain to be best served by deciding which of candidates C_1 and C_2 to support and casting all votes in favor of this candidate — thereby maximizing the selected candidate's probability of being elected.

5   Related Voting Systems

The cumulative voting system discussed above allocates one vote to each voter for each seat to be filled. One related system is *limited voting* in which each voter receives multiple votes but fewer votes than there are seats to be filled.[4] Another variant is *equal and even cumulative voting* in which the votes of a voter who casts fewer votes than allocated are "stretched" to reach the allocated number (for example, a voter who is allocated four votes and casts only three is recorded as having cast one and a third votes for each of the three selected candidates).

The arguments above regarding standard cumulative voting apply equally well to both limited voting and equal and even cumulative voting. As in standard cumulative voting, it is against the interest of individual voters with a small fraction of the total vote to divide their votes amongst multiple candidates.

6   Single Non-transferable Votes

A *single non-transferable* voting system gives just one vote to each voter – regardless of the number of candidates to be elected. As with cumulative voting, the candidates who receive the most votes are elected. Single non-transferable voting can be thought of as one extreme case of limited voting (with the other extreme being standard cumulative voting). The above analysis indicates that a single non-transferable voting system is essentially always preferable to standard cumulative voting and related systems where voters are each allocated multiple votes.

Jurisdictions and corporations which use cumulative voting should give serious consideration to replacing their electoral systems with single non-transferable voting *or another alternative*. The results herein should not be construed as an endorsement of single non-transferable voting but rather as a relative assessment that single non-transferable voting is superior to cumulative voting and related systems.

---

[3] One such example would be an instance where a voter knows precisely how all other voters *except one* will vote and that this unknown voter will bring either candidate C_1 or C_2 — but not both — within close range of defeating candidate C_3.

[4] Note that limited voting actually comes in two flavors depending on whether or not voters are allowed to cast multiple votes for a single candidate. Its use here applies the case when a candidate *can* receive multiple votes from a single voter.

A common criticism of single non-transferable voting is that a popular candidate can receive far more votes than necessary to be elected, and this can result in disproportionate representation. For example, if 80% of the electorate favors and votes for a particular candidate in an election for a six-member council, this candidate will be elected, but this large majority constituency will be represented by only one of the six council members. (Note that cumulative voting can lead to similarly disproportionate representation.)

The potential for "over-voting" for a candidate leads to substantial strategizing and coalition building among political parties and groups [GM05, NYT86a]. Parties may encourage their constituents to spread their votes amongst multiple candidates in order to attempt to maximize the number of seats that they will win. This strategizing occurs with both single non-transferable voting and cumulative voting.

7 Alternative Electoral Systems

Because of the potential for disproportionate representation and the instability of the strategizing that can result, other voting systems may be considered preferable to single non-transferable voting.

In an environment where there are strict party loyalties and a candidate's party affiliation is considered more important than the candidate's other qualities, a *party list* system may be desirable. In such a system, parties submit ordered lists of candidates, and voters cast votes for a party rather than an individual. Parties are then assigned seats in proportion to the number of votes they receive, and each party's seats are assigned to candidates in accordance with their pre-submitted lists.

When party loyalty is not strict, a preferential voting system such as *single transferable vote (or STV)* may be used. With STV, voters are asked to rank candidates preferentially. Candidates who receive a necessary quota of first-choice votes are elected, and excess votes are given to the next candidate on each voter's list – diluted according to the excess. For example, if a candidate receives twice the number of first-choice votes necessary to be elected, that candidate is elected and all ballots on which that candidate is listed first are transferred to their second choice candidate with half of their original value (now worth one half vote each). This process is iterated until all seats are filled. As with other preferential voting systems, some process must also be provided for eliminating candidates that have not received sufficient support to continue.

A third option is to allow elected candidates to carry their level of support into the body to which they have been elected. For example, if candidate C_1 receives 40% support, candidates C_2 and C_3 each receive 20% support, candidate C_4 receives 10% support, and the remaining 10% of support is distributed amongst other candidates, then candidates C_1, C_2, C_3, and C_4 could be deemed elected with candidate C_1 carrying four legislative votes, candidates C_2 and C_3 each carrying two legislative votes, and candidate C_4 carrying a single legislative vote.

Each of these systems has merits and weaknesses. There is substantial literature on other voting systems, and Chamberlin and Courant [ChCo83] and Monroe [Mon95] offer valuable rules against which proportional voting systems can be measured. The decision of whether to use one of these systems, single non-transferable votes, or some other alternative is dependent upon numerous factors including political realities, the desired electoral effects, and traditional voting patterns. It is clear, however, that cumulative voting and related systems should almost never be considered among the alternatives.

8   Conclusions and Further Work

There is no clear best choice for how to elect a multi-seat body that proportionately represents the voting electorate. One increasingly popular approach is cumulative voting, but it has been argued here that cumulative voting is inferior in virtually all respects to the option of a single non-transferable voting system.

While single non-transferable voting has some significant weaknesses when compared to other alternatives, it dominates cumulative voting in every practical respect. There are simply no realistic scenarios in which the option of cumulative voting can be justified. Additional comparative analysis of single non-transferable voting and other alternatives intended to achieve proportional voting will help communities select the voting systems best suited to their needs.

Acknowledgements. The author gratefully acknowledges illuminating and helpful conversations with Seny Kamra, Ron Rivest, Dan Shumow, and Vanessa Teague as well as helpful comments from anonymous reviewers regarding this work.

References

[BDB03] Bowler, S., Donovan, T., Brockington, D.: Local Experiments with Alternative Elections. Ohio State University Press, Electoral Reform and Minority Representation (2003)

[BE98] Brischetto, R.R., Engstrom, R.L.: Is cumulative voting too complex? Evidence from exit polls. Stetson Law Rev. **27**(25), 816–817 (1998)

[Bow03] Bowen, G.: Yorktown voting system will be decided in court. Victoria Advocate (2003)

[ChCo83] Chamberlin, J.R., Courant, P.N.: Representative deliberations and representative descisions: proporational representation and the borda rule. Am. Polit. Sci. Rev. **77**(3), 718–733 (1983)

[Chr10] Börgers, C.: Mathematics of Social Choice. Society for Industrial and Applied Mathematics (2010)

[DiC10] DiColo, J.A.: EBay-craigslist fight digs into sharing of confidential data. Wall Street Journal (2010). New York

[Fly91] Flynn, J.: Bolting the boardroom door at sears. Business Week (1991)

[GM05] Gallagher, M., Mitchell, P.: The Politics of Electoral Systems. Oxford University Press, Oxford (2005)

[GP01] Goze, K., Patchen, K.L.R.: Panel backs return to cumulative voting. Highland Park News (2001)

[HP009] Hewlett-Packard Company Corporate Governance Guideline, November 2009

[Lew94] Lewis, N.A.: Maryland County embroiled in voting rights suit. The New York Times (1994)

[Mac06] MacIver, D.: ND Chamber of Commerce promotes 'Vote Yes on Measure 2'. Mouse River Journal (2006). Towner, ND

[Mac10] MacCormack, Z.: Boerne election change may face new challenge. San Antonio Express-News (2010)

[Mon95] Burt, L.: Monroe fully proportional representation. Am. Polit. Sci. Rev. **89**(4), 925–940 (1995)

[Nic02] Nichols, J.: A voting reform that works is transforming Texas. The Nation (2002)

[NYT86a] Cumulative voting. The New York Times (1886)

[NYT86b] Effect of cumulative voting. The New York Times (1886)

[NYT90] Avon proxy fight sought. The New York Times (1990)

[O'M09] O'Malley, K.: United States of America v. Euclid City School Board. United States District Court - Northern District of Ohio - Eastern Division – Case 08-CV-2832, p. 20 (2009)

[PD95] Pides, R.H., Donoghue, K.A.: Cumulative Voting in the United States, pp. 272–276. University of Chicago Legal Forum (1995)

[Rae10] Rae, L.: New voting system taking shape in Port Chester. Journal News (White Plains, New York) (2010)

[Sha09] Sharp, J.: Cumulative voting gets little attention. Peoria Journal Star (2009)

[Tab01] Tabarrok, A.: President Perot or fundamentals of voting theory illustrated with the 1992 election. Publ. Choice **106**, 275–297 (2001)

[TT009] Corporate governance in the spotlight. Taipei Times (2009)

[Wal09] Walgreen's 2009 Proxy Statement (2009)

[Wil04] Wilson, J.: Professor's analysis: cumulative voting OK. Amarillo Global News (2004)

No More Excuses: Automated Synthesis of Practical and Verifiable Vote-Counting Programs for Complex Voting Schemes

Lyria Bennett Moses[1], Rajeev Goré[2], Ron Levy[3], Dirk Pattinson[2(✉)],
and Mukesh Tiwari[2]

[1] Faculty of Law, UNSW, Sydney, Australia
[2] Research School of Computer Science, ANU, Canberra, Australia
dirk.pattinson@anu.edu.au
[3] College of Law, ANU, Canberra, Australia

Abstract. We argue that electronic vote-counting software can engender broad-based public trust in elections to public office only if they are formally verified against their legal definition and only if they can produce an easily verifiable certificate for the correctness of the count. We then show that both are achievable for the Schulze method of vote-counting, even when the election involves millions of ballots. We argue that our methodology is applicable to any vote-counting scheme that is rigorously specified. Consequently, the current practice of using unverified and unverifiable vote counting software for elections to public office is untenable. In particular, proprietary closed source vote-counting software is simply inexcusable.

1 Introduction

The integrity of electronic elections depends on many factors and spans the entire process from vote-casting to vote-counting, and the determination of winners. The notion of *universal verifiability* of vote counting (any voter can check that the announced result is correct on the basis of the published ballots [15]) has long been recognised as being central, both for guaranteeing correctness, and building trust, in electronic elections. For vote-counting (on which we focus in this paper), verifiability means that every stakeholder, or indeed any member of the general public, has the means to check that the computation of election winners is correct.

In practice, however, the computer software used to determine winners from the set of ballots cast, offers no such assurance. This applies for example to the software used in the Australian state of New South Wales (where the vote-counting software is closed-source and proprietary) and to the eVACS system used in the Australian Capital territory (where the vote-counting software has been open-sourced), see e.g. [2,9,10].

In this paper, we argue that both *verification* of the computer software that counts votes, and *verifiability* of individual counts are critical for building trust in

© Springer International Publishing AG 2017
R. Krimmer et al. (Eds.): E-Vote-ID 2017, LNCS 10615, pp. 66–83, 2017.
DOI: 10.1007/978-3-319-68687-5_5

an election process where ballots are being counted by computer. We moreover demonstrate by means of a case study that both are achievable for elections of realistic sizes. Given the mission-critical importance of correctness of vote-counting, both for the legal integrity of the process and for building public trust, together with the fact that both can be achieved technologically, we argue that it is imperative to replace the currently used, black-box software for vote-counting with a counterpart that is both verified, and produces verifiable certificates that guarantee correctness.

The leading analogy that informs our notion of verifiability of ballot counting is that of counting by hand. We argue that the result of a count is correct, if we have evidence that every action performed by a counting official is consistent with the (legal) description of the voting protocol. In a setting where votes are counted by hand, this is precisely the duty (and purpose) of election scrutineers. In the absence of scrutineers, and as a thought experiment that is evidently impractical, one can envisage one, or several, cameras that record the entire vote-counting process to a level of detail that allows us to ascertain the validity of every step that has been undertaken to determine the election result.

Correctness can then be verified independently by an analysis of the recording, and potential errors can be identified by exhibiting precisely that part of the recording where an incorrect action has been taken. The notion of certificate for the correctness of an electronic count implements this metaphor: instead of producing a recording of a hand-count, we record every individual step that has been undertaken by the software to determine the outcome electronically. We understand this data as a *certificate* that can then subsequently be either machine-checked in its entirety, or spot-checked for validity by humans.

This de-couples the process of *counting* the votes by computer from the process of *verifying* that ballots have been correctly tallied. We argue this notion of externally certifying electronic vote counting, together with transparency of the entire process, is imperative to building public trust in the integrity of electronic vote counting.

Our goal is therefore to closely integrate three pieces of data: the set of ballots cast, the winner(s) of the election, and the certificate data that links both. This leads to the following key requirements:

1. the ability to verify that a certificate is correctly constructed
2. the ability to verify that the certificate is indeed based on the ballots cast
3. the ability to verify that a correctly constructed certificate indeed provides evidence for the claimed set of winners.

As long as all three requirements are met, we accept *any* valid certificate as evidence of the correctness of the count, irrespective of the means by which it was constructed. In particular, this completely eliminates the need for trust in computer hardware or individuals operating the computing machinery.

We demonstrate, by means of a case study, that all three requirements can be met simultaneously, and that the software that produces these results scales to the size of real-world elections.

For the case study, we choose the Schulze method [26]. Despite the fact that the Schulze Method is not used for elections to public office, it provides an interesting case study for our purposes, as there is a non-trivial gap to bridge between certificates and the winning conditions of the vote counting scheme (item 3 above). We close this gap by giving formal proofs that connect certificates with the actual winning conditions.

One important aspect of our work is that it adds value to the integrity of the electoral process along several dimensions. First, the formal specification enforces a rigid analysis of the voting protocol that eliminates all disambiguities inherent in a textual specification of the protocol. While an independent re-implementation of the protcol (assuming that all votes are published) may give assurance of the officially announced result, the question of correctness remains open if both programs diverge. Checking the validity of a certificate, on the other hand, allows us to precisely pinpoint any discrepancies. Finally, it is much simpler to implement a program that *validates* a certificate compared to a fully-blown re-implementation of the entire voting protocol which increases the number of potential (electronic) scrutineers.

Related Work. This paper discusses the notions of verification, and verifiability, from the perspective of law and trust, and we use the Schulze method as an example to show that both can be achieved in realistic settings. We do not describe the formalisation in detail which is the subject of the companion paper [24]. Apart from the analysis of verifiably correct vote-counting from the perspective of law and trust, the main technical differences between this paper and its companion is scalability: we refine both proofs and code given in [24] to effortlessly scale to millions of ballots.

Formal specification and verification of vote-counting schemes have been discussed in [3,8] but none of these methods produce verifiable results, and as such rely on trust in the tool chain that has been used in their production. The idea of evidence for the correctness of a count has been put forward in [23] as a technical possibility. This paper complements the picture by (a) establishing verification and verifiability also as legal desiderata, and (b) showing, by means of a case study, that both can be achieved for real-world size elections.

2 Verification and Verifiability

Verification is the process of proving that a computer program implements a specification. Here, we focus on *formal* verification [12], where the specification consists of formulae in a formal logic, and the correctness proof of a program consists of applying logical deduction rules. This takes place inside a (formal) theorem prover that then validates the correctness of each and every proof step. One crucial aspect of this is that every correctness proof itself is machine-checked which gives the highest possible level of correctness, as the proof-checking functionality of a theorem prover is a comparatively small and heavily scrutinised part of the entire system.

As a consequence, once we are satisfied with the fact that the *specification* of the program indeed expresses the intended notion of correctness, we have *very* high assurance that the results of the computation are indeed correct.

In order to ascertain that the results of a verified program are indeed correct, one therefore needs to

1. read, understand and validate the formal specification: is it error free, and does it indeed reflect the intended functionality?
2. scrutinize the formal correctness proof: has the verification been carried out with due diligence, is the proof complete or does it rely on other assumptions?
3. ensure that the computing equipment on which the (verified) program is executed has not been tampered with or is otherwise compromised, and finally
4. ascertain that it was indeed the verified program that was executed in order to obtain the claimed results.

The trust in correctness of any result rests on all items above. The last two items are more problematic as they require trust in the integrity of equipment, and individuals, both of which can be hard to ascertain once the computation has completed. The first two trust requirements can be met by publishing both the specification and the correctness proof so that the specification can be analysed, and the proof can be replayed. Both need a considerable amount of expertise but can be carried out by (ideally more than one group of) domain experts. Trust in the correctness of the result can still be achieved if a large enough number of domain experts manage to replicate the computation, using equipment they know is not compromised, and running the program they know has been verified. As such, trust in *verified* computation mainly rests on a relatively small number of domain experts.

The argument for correctness via *verification* is that we have guarantees that *all* executions of a program are correct, and we therefore argue that this in particular applies to any one given instance.

Verifiability, on the other hand, refers to the ability to independently ascertain that a *particular* execution of a program did deliver a correct result. This is usually achieved by augmenting the computation so that it additionally produces a certificate that can be independently checked, and attests to the correctness of the computation, see e.g. [1]. Attesting to the correctness of the computation therefore requires to

1. ensure that the certificate is valid (usually by means of machine-checking it)
2. ensure that the certificate is indeed associated to the computation being scrutinized, i.e. it matches both input and output of the computation
3. establish that a valid certificate indeed guarantees the correctness of the computation.

Here, the first two items are mechanical and can be accomplished by relatively simple and short, independently developed computer programs for which little expert knowledge, other than basic programming skills, are necessary. The difficulty lies in establishing the third requirement: to verify that a correct certificate indeed implies the correctness of the result.

To maximise trust, reliability and auditability of electronic vote counting, we argue that both approaches need to be combined. To ensure (universal) verifiability, we advocate that vote-counting programs do not only compute a final result, but additionally produce an independently verifiable certificate that attests to the correctness of the computation, *together* with a formal verification that valid certificates indeed imply the correct determination of winners. In other words, we solve the problem outlined under (3) above by giving a *formal*, machine-checkable proof of the fact that validity of certificates indeed implies correct determination of winners. In contrast to scrutiny sheet published by electoral authorities, a certificate of this type contains all the data needed to reconstruct the count.

Given a certificate-producing vote-counting program, external parties or stakeholders can then satisfy themselves to the correctness of the count by checking the certificate (and whether the certificate matches the election data), and validate, by means of machine-checking the formal proof given for item (3) that validity of certificates indeed entails the correctness of the count. In particular, once it has been established (and vetted by a large enough number of domain experts) that valid certificates do indeed imply correctness, this step does not have to be repeated for each individual election. For every particular election, trust in the correctness of the count can be established solely by machine-checking the generated certificates. As argued above, this task can be accomplished by a large class of individuals with basic programming skills.

In fact, we go one step further: we demonstrate that fully verified programs can be employed to count real-size elections that involve millions of ballots and produce both independently verifiable and provably correct certificates. While the use of verified programs is not essential for building trust in the correctness of the count (as long as certificates are validated), it gives us formal assurance that the certificates produced will *always* be valid.

3   Legal Aspects of Verification and Verifiability

Any system for counting votes in democratic elections needs to satisfy at least three conditions: (1) each person's vote must be counted accurately, according to a mandated procedure, (2) the system and process should be subjectively trusted by the electorate, (3) there should be an objective basis for such trust, or in other words the system must be trustworthy. While subjective trust cannot be guaranteed through greater transparency [21], transparency about both the voting system and the actual counting of the vote in a particular election are important in reducing errors and ensuring an accurate count, promoting public trust and providing the evidential basis for demonstrated trustworthiness. In particular, it is a lack of transparency that has been the primary source of criticism of existing systems, both in the literature [7,9] and among civil society organisations [27] (for example, blackboxvoting.org and trustvote.org). International commitment to transparency is also demonstrated through initiatives such as the Open Government Partnership. Another important concept referred to both in the literature and by civil society organisations is public accountability, which requires both giving an "account" or explanation to the public and when called on (for example, in court) as well as being held publicly responsible for failures. Transparency is thus a crucial component of accountability, although the latter will involve other features (such as enforcement mechanisms) that are beyond the scope of this paper.

There are two contexts in which transparency is important in the running of elections. First, there should be transparency in Hood's sense [14] as to the process used in elections generally. This is generally done through legislation with detailed provisions specifying such matters as the voting method to be used as well as the requirements for a vote to count as valid. In a semi-automated process, this requires a combination of legislation (instructions to humans) and computer code (instructions to machines). The second kind of transparency, corresponding to Meijer's use of the term [20], is required in relation to the performance of these procedures in a specific election. In a manual process, procedural transparency is generally only to intermediaries, the scrutineers, who are able to observe the handling and tallying of ballot papers in order to monitor officials in the performance of their tasks. While the use of a limited number of intermediaries is not ideal, measures such as allowing scrutineers to be selected by candidates (e.g. Commonwealth Electoral Act 1918 (Australia) s 264) promote public confidence that the procedure as a whole is unbiased. However imperfect, procedural transparency reduces the risk of error and fraud in execution of the mandated procedure and enhances trust.

Electronic vote counting ought to achieve at least a similar level of transparency along both dimensions as manual systems in order to promote equivalent levels of trust. Ideally, it would go further given physical limitations (such as the number of scrutineers able to fit in a room) apply to a smaller part of the process. The use of a verified, and fully verifiable system is transparent in both senses, with members of the public able to monitor both the rules that are followed and the workings and performance of the system in a particular instance.

First, the vote counting procedure needs to be transparent. For electronic vote counting, the procedure is specified in both legislation (which authorises the electronic vote counting procedure) and in the software employed. The use of open source code ensures that the public has the same level of access to instructions given to the computer as it has to legislative commands given to election officials. The use of open source code is crucial as is demonstrated through a comparison of different jurisdictions of Australia. In Australia, for example, the Federal Senate and NSW state election vote counting are based on proprietary black box systems while the Australian Capital Territory uses open source eVACS software [2,9,10]. This has significant impact on the ability of researchers to detect errors both in advance of elections and in time to correct results [9]. Private verification systems have been less successful, in both Australia and the US, in providing equivalent protection against error to open source software [7,9]. Further, private verification provides a lower level of public transparency than the use of manual systems which rely on public legislation (instructions to humans) as the primary source of vote counting procedures [7]. It should also be noted that there are few public advantages in secrecy since security is usually enhanced by adopting an open approach (unless high quality open source vote counting software were unavailable), and private profit advantages are outweighed by the importance of trust in democratic elections.

Second, verifiability provides a method of ascertaining the correctness of results of a specific election. External parties are able to check a certificate to confirm that the counting process has operated according to the rules of the voting procedure. Under a manual process, tallying and counting can only be confirmed by a small number of scrutineers directly observing human officials. The certification process allows greater transparency not limited to the number of people able to fit within a physical space, although we recognise that physical scrutiny is still required for earlier elements of the voting and vote counting process (up to verification of optical scanning of ballots). Certification reduces the risk of error and fraud that would compromise accuracy and provides an evidence-base for trustworthiness. It is also likely to increase subjective public trust, although this will require engagement with the public as to the nature of verification involved. While it is likely that in practice checking will be limited to a small group with the technical expertise, infrastructure and political interest to pursue it, knowledge as to the openness of the model is likely to increase public trust. Currently in Australia, neither open source nor proprietary vote counting systems provide an equivalent level of procedural transparency for monitoring the count in a particular election (for example, compare Commonwealth Electoral Act 1918 (Australia) s 273A).

Ultimately, legislation, computer code (where relevant) and electoral procedures need to combine to safeguard an accurate count in which the public has justified confidence. The verification and verifiability measures suggested here go further to ensure this than current methods used in Australia and, as far as we are aware, public office elections around the world.

In the remainder of the paper, we describe a particular voting method (the Schulze method) to demonstrate that we can achieve both verification and verifiability for real-world size elections.

4   The Schulze Method

The Schulze Method [26] is a preferential voting scheme that elects a single winner. While not used for elections to public office, it provides us with an example that show-cases all aspects of verifiability discussed in Sect. 2, as the correspondence between valid certificates and election winners is not trivial, i.e. a valid certificate cannot immediately be matched to the winning condition. We bridge this gap by a formal proof that we outline in Sect. 5.

In Schulze counting, each ballot expresses a preference ordering over the set of candidates where all candidates need to be ranked, but candidates may be given equal preference. The requirement of ranking all candidates can be relaxed by assuming that non-ranked candidates tie for last position.

From a social choice perspective, the Schulze voting scheme has been shown to satisfy a large number of desirable properties, such as monotonicity, independence of clones, and reversal symmetry, established in the original paper [26].

From a game theoretic perspective, it has also been experimentally established that the Schulze Method is better than other, more established voting schemes such as plurality and instant-runoff voting and Borda count [25]. Despite the fact that the Schulze method isn't used in elections for public office, there is rapid uptake in a large number of organisations, including e.g. various national branches of the Pirate Party and numerous open software initiatives.

Academically, the Schulze method has been investigated further, and it has been established that Schulze voting is resistant to bribery and control [22] in the sense that both problems are computationally infeasible, but have been found to be fixed-parameter tractable with respect to the number of candidates [13].

The Schulze Method is guaranteed to always elect a Condorcet winner, that is, a candidate that a majority prefers to every other candidate in a pairwise comparison.

The distinguishing feature of Schulze counting is the resolving of cycles in collective preferences. These situations appear to arise in real elections [16] and it has been demonstrated that different choices of resolving cycles indeed lead to different outcomes. Consider for example the following scenario taken from [6] where we have three candidates A, B, and C and the following distribution of votes:

$$4 : A > B > C \qquad 3 : B > C > A \qquad 2 : B > A > C \qquad 4 : C > A > B$$

where the number before the colon indicates the multiplicity of the vote, and $>$ indicates the order of preference so that e.g. $3 : B > C > A$ denotes three votes where B is preferred over C who is in turn preferred over A. In this example, a majority of candidates prefer A over B as eight ballots prefer A over B compared to five ballots preferring B over A. Similarly, a majority of candidates prefer B over C, and a majority prefer C over A, leading to a cyclic collective preference relation.

The main idea of the method is to resolve cycles by considering *transitive preferences* or a generalised notion of margin. That is, if $m(c, d)$ is the margin between candidates c and d (the difference between the number of votes that rank c higher than d and the number of votes that rank d higher than c), Schulze voting considers *paths* of the form

$$c_1 \xrightarrow{m(c_1,c_2)} c_2 \xrightarrow{m(c_2,c_3)} c_3 \quad \cdots \quad c_{n-1} \xrightarrow{m(c_{n-1},c_n)} c_n$$

i.e. sequences of candidates annotated with the margin between successive candidates. A path like the above induces the path-based margin $\min\{m(c_i, c_{i+1} \mid 1 \leq i < n\}$ between c_1 and c_n given as the minimum of the margins between successive candidates, and the *generalised margin* between two candidates c and d is the largest path-based margin considering all possible paths between c and d.

This allows us to replace the *margin* used to determine Condorcet winners by the *generalised margin* introduced above. The key result of Schulze's paper [26] (Sect. 4.1) is that the induced ordering is now indeed transitive.

A *Schulze Winner* can then be taken to be a candidate that is not defeated by any other candidate in a pairwise comparision, using generalised margins. In symbols, candidate c is a winner if $g(c, d) \geq g(d, c)$ for all other candidates d, where $g(\cdot, \cdot)$ denotes generalised margins.

In the above example, we have the following margins (on the left) and generalised margins (on the right):

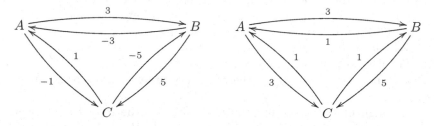

Note that the margins on the left are necessarily symmetric in the sense that $m(x, y) = -m(y, x)$ as margins are computed as the difference between the number of ballots that rank x higher than y and the number of ballots that rank y higher than x. This property is no longer present for generalised margins, and A is the (only) winner as A wins every pairwise comparison based on generalised margins. In summary, vote counting according to the Schulze method can be described as follows:

1. compute the *margin function* $m(c, d)$ as the number of ballots that strictly prefer c over d, minus the number of ballots that strictly prefer d over c
2. compute the *generalised margin function* $g(c, d)$ as the maximal path-based margin between c and d
3. Compute winning candidate, i.e. candidates for which $g(c, d) \geq g(c, d)$, for all other candidates d, and apply tie-breaking if more than one winning candidate has been elected.

It has been shown in Schulze's original paper that at least one winner in this sense always exists, and that this winner is unique in most cases, i.e. Schulze counting satisfies the resolvability criterion.

5   Provably Correct and Verifiable Schulze Counting

Our implementation of the Schulze method consists of three parts:

Formal Specification. First, we provide a formal specification of the winning condition for elections counted according to Schulze. This takes the form of a logical formula that directly reflects the voting scheme.

Certificate. Second, we establish what counts as a *certificate* for the winning condition to hold, and give a formal proof that existence of a certificate for winning is equivalent to winning in the sense of the initial specification. The main difference between both notions of winning is that the former is a mere logical assertion, whereas the latter is formulated in terms of verifiable data.

Proofs. Third, we provide a full proof of the fact that the existence of a certificate is logically equivalent to the specification being met. Moreover, we give a full proof of the fact that winners can always be computed correctly, and certificates can be produced, for any set of ballots.

We exemplify the relationship of these components with a simple example. Consider the notion of being a list of integers sorted in ascending order. The *formal specification* of this operation consists of two sentences:

- the elements of the resulting list should be in ascending order
- the elements of the resulting list should be a permutation of the elements of the input list.

In this case, we don't need to certify that a list is sorted: this can be checked easily (in linear time). Ascertaining that the result list is a permutation of the input list is (slightly) less trivial. Here, a *certificate* can be a recipe that permutes the input list to the resulting list: to verify that the resulting list is indeed a permutation, the only thing the verifier needs to do is to alter the input list according to the given recipe, and then checking whether the two lists are equal.

In this case, the computation produces *two* pieces of data: we not only get to see the sorted list, but also a permutation that witnesses that the resulting list is a permutation of the input list. A *proof* then amounts to establishing that given

- the input list, and the (sorted) resulting list, and
- a recipe that permutes the input list to its sorted version

we can conclude that the sorting operation indeed meets the formal specification.

The main (and important) difference between the specification and the certificate is that the former is merely a proposition, i.e. a statement that can either be true or false. The certificate, on the other hand, gives us concrete means to *verify* or ascertain the truth of the specification. The proofs provide the glue between both: if a certificate-producing computation delivers a result together with a certificate, we in fact know that the specification holds. On the other hand, we need to establish that every correct computation can in fact be accompanied by a valid certificate.

For vote counting, our development takes place inside the Coq theorem prover [5] that is based on the Calculus of Inductive Constructions. Technically, Coq distinguishes logical formulae or propositions (that are of type Prop) from data (that is of type Set or Type). The former are correctness assertions and are erased when programs are generated from proofs, whereas the latter are computed values that are preserved: our certificates therefore need to be Types. To give a simple example, a function that sorts a list will take a list (say, of integers) and produce a sorted list, where the fact that the list is sorted is expressed as a proposition, so that sorted lists are pairs where the second component is a proof that the first component is ordered, and is deleted by extraction. To make sorting of lists *verifiable*, we would need to *additionally* output a certificate, i.e. data from which we can infer that the result list is really a permutation of the input list.

The logical specification of the winning condition is based on an integer-valued *margin function* and a *path* between candidates:

```
Variable marg : cand -> cand -> Z.

Inductive Path (k: Z) : cand -> cand -> Prop :=
| unit c d : marg c d >= k -> Path k c d
| cons c d e : marg c d >= k -> Path k d e -> Path k c e.
```

Paths are additionally parameterised by integers that give a lower bound on the path-based margin (the *strength* of the path in the terminology of [26]). We interpret an assertion Path k c d as the existence of a path between c and d that induces a path-based margin of at least k. Such a path can be constructed if the margin between c and d is $\geq k$ (the unit constructor). Alternatively, a path between c and e of strength $\geq$ k can be obtained if there is there is candidate d for which the margin between c and d is $\geq$ k and d and e are already connected by a path of strength $\geq$ k (via the cons constructor). This gives the following formula that expresses that a candidate c wins a Schulze vote:

```
Definition wins_prop (c: cand) :=
 forall d : cand, exists k : Z,
  Path k c d /\ (forall l, Path l d c -> l <= k).
```

Simply put, it says that for each candidate d, there exists an integer k and a path from c to d of strength k, and any other path going the reverse direction induces at most the same path-based margin. In terms of the generalized margin function, candidate c wins, if for every candidate d, the generalized margin between c and d is greater than or equal to the generalised margin between d and c. We reflect the fact that the above is a logical proposition in the name of the formula. The certificate for winning then needs to consist of data that evidences precisely this.

One crucial component of a certificate that evidences that a particular candidate c is a Schulze-winner therefore consists of displaying a sufficiently strong path between c and any other candidate. We achieve this by pairing the propositional notion of path with a type-level notion PathT that can be displayed as part of a certificate for winning, and will not be erased by extraction.

```
Inductive PathT (k: Z) : cand -> cand -> Type :=
| unitT c d : marg c d >= k -> PathT k c d
| consT c d e : marg c d >= k -> PathT k d e -> PathT k c e.
```

The second part of the winning condition, i.e. the non-existence of a stronger path going the other way, is more difficult to evidence. Rather than listing all possible paths going the other way, we use *co-closed sets* of pairs of candidates which leads to smaller certificates. Given an integer k, a set $S \subseteq$ cand $\times$ cand of candidate pairs is *k*-coclosed if none of its elements (c, d) can be connected by a path of strength k or greater. This means that

- for any element (c, d) $\in S$, the margin between c and d is $< k$, and
- if (c, d) is in the co-closed set and m is a candidate (a "midpoint"), then either the margin between c and m is $< k$, or m and d cannot be connected by a path of strength $\geq k$.

The second condition says that c and d cannot be connected by a path of the form c, m, ..., d whose overall strength is $\geq k$.

We represent co-closed sets by boolean functions of type cand -> cand -> bool and obtain the following formal definitions:

```
Definition coclosed (k : Z) (f : (cand * cand) -> bool) :=
  forall x, f x = true -> W k f x = true.
```

where W: (cand -> cand -> bool) -> (cand -> cand -> bool) is an operator on sets of pairs of candidates that is given by

```
Definition W (k: Z) (p: cand * cand -> bool) (x: cand * cand) :=
  andb (marg_lt k x)
  (forallb (fun m => orb (marg_lt k (fst x, m)) (p (m, snd x)))
           cand_all).
```

and marg_lt is a boolean function that decides whether the margin between two candidates is less than a given integer, and cand_all is a list containing all candidates that stand for election.

The *certificate* for a candidate c to be winning can then be represented by a table where for every other (competing) candidate d, we have

- an integer k and a path from c to d of strength k, and
- a k+1-coclosed set that evidences that no path of strength $> k$ exists between d and c.

This leads to the following definition and equivalence proof where f plays the role of coclosed set:

```
Definition wins_type c := forall d : cand,
  existsT (k : Z), ((PathT k c d) *
    (existsT (f : (cand * cand) -> bool),
      f (d, c) = true /\ coclosed (k + 1) f))%type.

Lemma wins_type_prop : forall c, wins_type c -> wins_prop c.
Lemma wins_prop_type : forall c, wins_prop c -> wins_type c.
```

and `existsT` is a type-level existential quantifier (technically, a Σ-type).

Going back to the trichotomy of specification, certificate and proof outlined at the beginning of the section, the first lemma (`wins_type_prop`) says that the existence of a certificate indeed implies the validity of the specification. The second lemma (`wins_prop_type`) tells us that the notion of the certificate is so that any correct computation can indeed be certified. That is, the notion of certificate is general enough to certify *all* correct computations.

It is precisely the formal proof of equivalence of both notions of winning that formally justifies our notion of certificate, as it ensures that a valid certificate *indeed* witnesses the winning condition. This implements the third requirement discussed on page 2.

The considerations so far rely on a previously computed margin function. To obtain a formal specification and ensuing notion of certificates, all we need to do is to provide a way of constructing the margin function step-by-step. We do this by exhibiting two stages of the count:

1. in the first state, we process all ballots and iteratively update the margin function until all ballots have been processed. This gives us the margin function on which subsequent computations are based.
2. in the second step, we compute winners, and evidence for winning, on the basis of the margin function we have constructed in the first step.

The complete specification then takes the form of an inductive type that *only* allows us to construct valid stages of the count. In more detail, we have four constructors:

- `ax` where we construe all ballots as uncounted, and start with the zero margin
- `cvalid` where we update the margin function based on a formal ballot
- `cinvalid` where we discard an informal ballot and do not change the margin
- `fin`, where we assume that all ballots have been processed, and we finalise the count by providing winners, and evidence for winning.

As a consequence, *every* element of this type represents a valid state of the computation, and a count in state `fin` describes the result of the process.

```
Inductive Count (bs : list ballot) : State -> Type :=
  | ax us m : us = bs -> (forall c d, m c d = 0) ->
    Count bs (partial (us, []) m)          (* zero margin      *)
  | cvalid u us m nm inbs : Count bs (partial (u :: us, inbs) m) ->
    (forall c, (u c > 0)%nat) ->           (* u is valid       *)
    (forall c d : cand,
      ((u c < u d) -> nm c d = m c d + 1) (* c preferred to d *) /\
      ((u c = u d) -> nm c d = m c d)      (* c, d rank equal  *) /\
      ((u c > u d) -> nm c d = m c d - 1))(* d preferred to c *) ->
    Count bs (partial (us, inbs) nm)
  | cinvalid u us m inbs : Count bs (partial (u :: us, inbs) m)  ->
    (exists c, (u c = 0)%nat)              (* u is invalid     *) ->
    Count bs (partial (us, u :: inbs) m)
  | fin m inbs w (d: (forall c, (wins_type m c)+(loses_type m c))):
```

```
Count bs (partial ([], inbs) m)        (* no ballots left *) ->
(forall c, w c = true <-> (exists x, d c = inl x)) ->
(forall c, w c = false <-> (exists x, d c = inr x)) ->
Count bs (winners w).
```

The formulation above relies on the following assumptions. First, ballots are represented as functions from candidates into natural numbers that represent the ranking. We assume that preferences start with 1 and interpret 0 as the failure to denote a preference for a given candidate which renders the vote invalid. A State is either a partial count that consists of a list of unprocessed ballots, a list of informal ballots, and a partially constructed margin function, or of a boolean function that determines the election winners. We have elided the definition of *losing* that is dual to that of winning.

The task of computing the winners of a Schulze election given a list bs of ballots is then reduced to exhibiting a boolean function w: cand -> bool that determines the winners, and an element of the type Count bs (winners w). While the first part (the boolean function) is the result of the computation, the second part (the element of the Count-type) consists of the verifiable certificate for the correctness of the count.

We exemplify the nature of certificates by returning to the example presented in Sect. 4. We construe e.g. the ballot $A > B > C$ as the function $A \mapsto 1$, $B \mapsto 2$ and $C \mapsto 3$. Running a Schulze-election then corresponds to executing the function that computes winners, which produces the following certificate (we have added some pretty-printing):

```
V: [A1 B2 C3,..], I:   [], M: [AB:0 AC:0 BC:0]
------------------------------------------------
V: [A1 B2 C3,..], I:   [], M: [AB:1 AC:1 BC:1]
------------------------------------------------

               . . .
------------------------------------------------
V: [A2 B3 C1], I:   [], M: [AB:2 AC:0 BC:6]
------------------------------------------------
V: [], I: [], M: [AB:3 AC:-1 BC:5]
----------------------------------------

winning: A
   for B: path A --> B of strenght 3, 4-coclosed set:
     [(A,A),(B,A),(B,B),(C,A),(C,B),(C,C)]
   for C: path A --> B --> C of strenght 3, 4-coclosed set:
     [(A,A),(B,A),(B,B),(C,A),(C,B),(C,C)]
losing: B
   exists A: path A --> B of strength 3, 3-coclosed set:
     [(A,A),(B,A),(B,B),(C,A),(C,B),(C,C)]
losing: C
   exists A: path A --> B --> C of strength 3, 3-coclosed set:
     [(A,A),(B,A),(B,B),(C,A),(C,B),(C,C)]
```

The initial stages are the construction of the margin function, where the first component are the ballots to be processed. Here, a ballot of the form A2, B3, C1 represents a first preference for C, a second preference for A and a third preference for B. The partial margin function is displayed in the rightmost column, and lists pairwise margins, for example AB:1 encodes $m(A, B) = 1$. Note that the margin function is symmetric, i.e. $m(x, y) = -m(y, x)$ so that the above is a complete representation. We do not have any invalid votes so that the I-component always remains empty. The ellipsis (. . .) indicates the omission of some steps of constructing the margin which we have elided to save space. Once the margin is fully constructed, we present evidence, in this case, for A winning the election (and everybody else losing). As described above, this evidence consists of a path, and a coclosed set, for each candidate distinct from A. The subsequent entries (that we haven't discussed in this paper) show that every candidate except A is not winning. A losing candidate (in this example, e.g. B) is a candidate for which there exists a competitor (here: A) so that the generalised margin of A over B is strictly larger than the generalised margin of B over A. This is evidenced similarly to winning candidates, by giving a path and a co-closed set.

6   Experimental Results

We report on the results of implementing the Schulze method in the Coq theorem prover [5] that automatically extracts into the OCaml programming language [18]. Coq comes with an extraction mechanism [19] that allows us to extract both functions and proofs into executable code via the Haskell, Ocaml and Scheme programming languages. As Coq is written in OCaml itself, the OCaml extraction mechanism is the best developed, and OCaml produces faster executables than the other two languages. As Coq is based on constructive logic, we can turn both functions written in Coq, as well as proofs into executable code. Given that the correctness of the count is witnessed by an inductive data type, counting itself amounts to populating this type, and we use a mix of proofs (showing that a count exists amounts to a function that produces a count) and verified functional programs (that compute data directly), using the latter for performance-critical tasks.

The most performance critical aspect of our code is the margin function. Recall that the margin function is of type cand -> cand -> Z and that it depends on the *entire* set of ballots. Internally, it is represented by a closure [17] so that margins are re-computed with every call. The single largest efficiency improvement in our code was achieved by memorization, i.e. representing the margin function (in Coq) via list lookup. With this (and several smaller) optimisation, we can count millions of votes using verified code. Below, we include our timing graphs, based on randomly generated ballots while keeping number of candidates constant i.e. 4.

On the left, we report timings (in seconds) for the computation of winners, whereas on the right, we include the time to additionally compute a universally verifiable certificate that attests to the correctness of the count. This is consistent

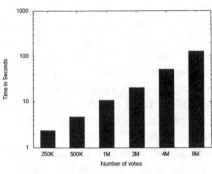

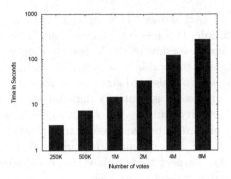

(a) Computation of Winners

(b) Computation of Winners and Certificate

Fig. 1. Experimental results

with known computational complexity of Schulze counting i.e. linear in number of ballots and cubic in candidates. The experiments were carried out on a system equipped with Intel core i7 processor and 16 GB of RAM. We notice that the computation of the certificate adds comparatively little in computational cost (Fig. 1).

At this moment, our implementation requires that we store *all* ballots in main memory as we need to parse the entire list of ballots before making it available to our verified implementation so that the total number of ballots we can count is limited by main memory in practise. We can count real-world size elections (8 million ballot papers) on a standard, commodity desktop computer with 16 GB of main memory.

7   Discussion and Further Work

This paper argues that there is no excuse to use vote counting software in elections to public office (or otherwise) that is neither *verified* (i.e. the correctness of the software has been established using formal methods) nor *verifiable* (i.e. stakeholders can independently ascertain the correctness of individual executions of the software). We have argued that both verification and verifiability are desiderata from the perspective of law and trust. Finally, our experimental results show that both verification and verifiability can be achieved in realistic settings.

Our case study (Schulze voting) was chosen as it showcases how we can bridge a non-trivial gap between certificates and the winning conditions of the voting scheme under consideration. Despite the fact that the Schulze method is not used for elections to public office, we are convinced that the same programme can (and should!) be carried out for other preferential voting schemes.

As the precise notion of certificate depends on the exact description of the voting protocol, it is clear that this paper merely provides a case study. For other voting systems, in particular the notion of certificate needs to be adapted to in fact witness the correctness of the determination of winners. As a toy example, this has been carried out for first-past-the-post (plurality) voting and a simple version of single transferable vote [23]. The more realistic scenario of single transferable vote with fractional transfer values is being considered in [11] where real-word size case studies are being reported. Given that the nature of certificates is crucially dependent on the voting protocol under scrutiny, the complexity and size of certificates necessarily differs from case to case. While our general experience seems to indicate that computing certificates incurs little overhead, this remains to be investigated more formally.

One aspect that we have not considered here is encryption of ballots to safeguard voter privacy which can be incorporated using protocols such as shuffle-sum [4] and homomorphic encryption [28]. The key idea here is to formalise a given voting scheme based on encrypted ballots, and then to establish a homomorphic property: the decryption of the result obtained from encrypted ballots is the same as the result obtained from the decrypted ballots. We leave this to further work.

References

1. Arkoudas, K., Bringsjord, S.: Computers, justification, and mathematical knowledge. Minds Mach. **17**(2), 185–202 (2007)
2. Australian Electoral Commission. Letter to Mr Michael Cordover, LSS4883 Outcome of Internal Review of the Decision to Refuse your FOI Request no. LS4849 (2013). http://www.aec.gov.au/information-access/foi/2014/files/ls4912-1.pdf. Accessed 14 May 2017
3. Beckert, B., Goré, R., Schürmann, C., Bormer, T., Wang, J.: Verifying voting schemes. J. Inf. Sec. Appl. **19**(2), 115–129 (2014)
4. Benaloh, J., Moran, T., Naish, L., Ramchen, K., Teague, V.: Shuffle-sum: coercion-resistant verifiable tallying for STV voting. IEEE Trans. Inf. Forensics Secur. **4**(4), 685–698 (2009)
5. Bertot, Y., Castéran, P., Huet, G., Paulin-Mohring, C.: Interactive Theorem Proving and Program Development: Coq'Art: The Calculus of Inductive Constructions. Texts in Theoretical Computer Science. An EATCS Series. Springer, Heidelberg (2004). doi:10.1007/978-3-662-07964-5
6. Brandt, F., Conitzer, V., Endriss, U., Lang, J., Procaccia, A.D.: Introduction to computational social choice. In: Brandt, F., Conitzer, V., Endriss, U., Lang, J., Procaccia, A.D. (eds.) Handbook of Computational Social Choice. Cambridge University Press, Cambridge (2016)
7. Carrier, M.A.: Vote counting, technology, and unintended consequences. St Johns Law Rev. **79**, 645–685 (2012)
8. Cochran, D., Kiniry, J.: Votail: a formally specified and verified ballot counting system for Irish PR-STV elections. In: Pre-proceedings of the 1st International Conference on Formal Verification of Object-Oriented Software (FoVeOOS) (2010)
9. Conway, A., Blom, M., Naish, L., Teague, V.: An analysis of new south wales electronic vote counting. In: Proceedings of ACSW 2017, pp. 24:1–24:5 (2017)
10. Elections ACT. Electronic voting and counting (2016). http://www.elections.act.gov.au/elections_and_voting/electronic_voting_and_counting. Accessed 14 May 2017

11. Ghale, M.K., Goré, R., Pattinson, D.: A formally verified single transferable vote scheme with fractional values. In: Krimmer, R., Volkamer, M., Binder, N.B., Kersting, N., Schürmann, C. (eds.) E-Vote-ID 2017. LNCS, vol. 10615, pp. 163–182. Springer, Cham (2017)
12. Hales, T.: Formal proof. Not. AMS **55**, 1370–1380 (2008)
13. Hemaspaandra, L.A., Lavaee, R., Menton, C.: Schulze and ranked-pairs voting are fixed-parameter tractable to bribe, manipulate, and control. Ann. Math. Artif. Intell. **77**(3–4), 191–223 (2016)
14. Hood, C.: Transparency. In: Clarke, P.B., Foweraker, J. (eds.) Encyclopedia of Democratic Thought, pp. 700–704. Routledge, London (2001)
15. Kremer, S., Ryan, M., Smyth, B.: Election verifiability in electronic voting protocols. In: Gritzalis, D., Preneel, B., Theoharidou, M. (eds.) ESORICS 2010. LNCS, vol. 6345, pp. 389–404. Springer, Heidelberg (2010). doi:10.1007/978-3-642-15497-3_24
16. Kurrild-Klitgaard, P.: An empirical example of the condorcet paradox of voting in a large electorate. Publ. Choice **107**(1/2), 135–145 (2001)
17. Landin, P.J.: The mechanical evaluation of expressions. Comput. J. **6**(4), 308 (1964)
18. Leroy, X., Doligez, D., Frisch, A., Garrigue, J., Rémy, D., Vouillon, J.: The OCaml system release 4.04 documentation and user's manual. Technical report, Institut National de Recherche en Informatique et en Automatique (INRIA) (2016)
19. Letouzey, P.: Extraction in Coq: an overview. In: Beckmann, A., Dimitracopoulos, C., Löwe, B. (eds.) CiE 2008. LNCS, vol. 5028, pp. 359–369. Springer, Heidelberg (2008). doi:10.1007/978-3-540-69407-6_39
20. Meijer, A.: Transparency. In: Bovens, M., Goodin, R.E., Schillemans, T. (eds.) The Oxford Handbook of Public Accountability, pp. 507–524. Oxford University Press, Oxford (2014)
21. O'Neill, O.: A Question of Trust. Cambridge University Press, Cambridge (2002)
22. Parkes, D., Xia, L.: A complexity-of-strategic-behavior comparison between Schulze's rule and ranked pairs. In: Hoffmann, J., Selman, B. (eds.) Proceedings of AAAI 26, pp. 1429–1435. AAAI Press (2012)
23. Pattinson, D., Schürmann, C.: Vote counting as mathematical proof. In: Pfahringer, B., Renz, J. (eds.) AI 2015. LNCS, vol. 9457, pp. 464–475. Springer, Cham (2015). doi:10.1007/978-3-319-26350-2_41
24. Pattinson, D., Tiwari, M.: Schulze voting as evidence carrying computation. In: Ayala-Rincón, M., Muñoz, C.A. (eds.) ITP 2017. LNCS, vol. 10499. Springer, Cham (2017). doi:10.1007/978-3-319-66107-0_26
25. Rivest, R.L., Shen, E.: An optimal single-winner preferential voting system based on game theory. In: Conitzer, V., Rothe, J. (eds.) Proceedings of COMSOC 2010. Duesseldorf University Press (2010)
26. Schulze, M.: A new monotonic, clone-independent, reversal symmetric, and Condorcet-consistent single-winner election method. Soc. Choice Welfare **36**(2), 267–303 (2011)
27. Vogl, F.: Waging War on Corruption: Inside the Movement Fighting the Abuse of Power. Rowman & Littlefield, Lanham (2012)
28. Yi, X., Paulet, R., Bertino, E.: Homomorphic Encryption and Applications. SpringerBriefs in Computer Science. Springer, Heidelberg (2014). doi:10.1007/978-3-319-12229-8

Public Evidence from Secret Ballots

Matthew Bernhard[2(✉)], Josh Benaloh[1], J. Alex Halderman[2],
Ronald L. Rivest[8], Peter Y.A. Ryan[3], Philip B. Stark[4], Vanessa Teague[6],
Poorvi L. Vora[7], and Dan S. Wallach[5]

[1] Microsoft Research, Redmond, USA
[2] University of Michigan, Ann Arbor, USA
matber@umich.edu
[3] University of Luxembourg, Luxembourg City, Luxembourg
[4] University of California at Berkeley, Berkeley, USA
[5] Rice University, Houston, USA
[6] University of Melbourne, Melbourne, Australia
[7] The George Washington University, Washington, USA
[8] Massachusetts Institute of Technology, Cambridge, USA

Abstract. Elections seem simple—*aren't they just about counting?* But
they have a unique, challenging combination of security and privacy
requirements. The stakes are high; the context is adversarial; the electorate needs to be convinced that the results are correct; and the secrecy
of the ballot must be ensured. They also have practical constraints: time
is of the essence, and voting systems need to be affordable and main-
tainable, as well as usable by voters, election officials, and pollworkers.
It is thus not surprising that voting is a rich research area spanning
theory, applied cryptography, practical systems analysis, usable security,
and statistics. Election integrity involves two key concepts: *convincing
evidence that outcomes are correct* and *privacy*, which amounts to *convincing assurance that there is no evidence* about how any given person
voted. These are obviously in tension. We examine how current systems
walk this tightrope.

1 Introduction: What Is the Evidence?

It is not enough for an election to produce the correct outcome. The electorate
must also be convinced that the announced result reflects the will of the people.
For a rational person to be convinced, evidence is required.

Modern technology—computer and communications systems—is fragile and
vulnerable to programming errors and undetectable manipulation. No current
system that relies on electronic technology alone to capture and tally votes can
provide convincing evidence that election results are accurate without endanger-
ing or sacrificing the anonymity of votes.[1]

A more in-depth version of this paper can be found at https://arxiv.org/abs/1707.
08619.

[1] Moreover, the systems that come closest are not readily usable by a typical voter.

© Springer International Publishing AG 2017
R. Krimmer et al. (Eds.): E-Vote-ID 2017, LNCS 10615, pp. 84–109, 2017.
DOI: 10.1007/978-3-319-68687-5_6

Paper ballots, on the other hand, have some very helpful security properties: they are readable (and countable, and re-countable) by humans; they are relatively durable; and they are tamper-evident. Votes cast on paper can be counted using electronic technology; then the accuracy of the count can be checked manually to ensure that the technology functioned adequately. Statistical methods allow the accuracy of the count to be assessed by examining only a fraction of the ballots manually, often a very small fraction. If there is also convincing evidence that the collection of ballots has been conserved (no ballots added, lost, or modified) then this combination—voter-verifiable paper ballots, a mechanized count, and a manual check of the accuracy of that count—can provide convincing evidence that announced electoral outcomes are correct.

Conversely, absent convincing evidence that the paper trail has been conserved, a manual double-check of electronic results against the paper trail will not be convincing. If the paper trail has been conserved adequately, then a full manual tally of the ballots can correct the electronic count if the electronic count is incorrect.

These considerations have led many election integrity advocates to push for a voter-verifiable paper audit trail (VVPAT[2]) in the absence of paper ballots.

In the 2016 U.S. presidential election, about three quarters of Americans voted using systems that generated voter-verifiable paper records. The aftermath of the election proved that even if 100% of voters had used such systems, it would not have sufficed to provide convincing evidence that the reported results are accurate.

- No state has laws or regulations to ensure that the paper trail is conserved adequately, and that evidence to that effect is provided.
- No state had laws or regulations that ensured adequate manual scrutiny of the paper to determine that the electronically-generated results were correct.
- Many states that have a paper trail also have laws that make it hard for anyone to check the results using the paper trail—even candidates with war chests for litigation. Not only can other candidates fight attempts to check the results, the states themselves can fight such attempts. This treats the paper as a nuisance, rather than a safeguard.

The bottom line is that the paper trail is not worth the paper it's printed on. Clearly this must change.

Other approaches like *software independence* and *end-to-end verifiability* offer tools to improve electronic voting systems, but these methods have not been broadly applied.

---

[2] The VVPAT consists of a cash-register style printout of each vote that the voter can check but cannot touch. Voter-marked paper ballots or ballots marked using a ballot-marking device are preferable to VVPAT because voters may not check the VVPAT record.

1.1   Why so Hard?

Several factors make it difficult to generate convincing evidence that reported results are correct. The first is the trust model.

No one is trusted. In any significant election, voters, election officials, and equipment used to vote cannot necessarily be trusted by anyone with a stake in the outcome. Voters, operators, system designers, and external parties are all potential adversaries.

The need for evidence. Because officials and equipment may not be trustworthy, elections should be *evidence-based*. Any observer should be able to verify the reported results based on trustworthy evidence from the voting system. Many in-person voting systems fail to provide sufficient evidence; and as we shall see Internet systems scarcely provide any at all.

The secret ballot. Perhaps the most distinctive element of elections is the *secret ballot*, a critical safeguard that defends against vote selling and voter coercion. In practical terms, voters should not be able to prove how they voted to anyone, *even if they wish to do so*. This restricts the types of evidence that can be produced by the voting system. For example, the voting system may not provide votes encrypted by the voter as evidence, because the voters may choose to reveal their selections and the randomness used during encryption in response to bribery or coercion.

The challenge of voting is thus to use fragile technology to produce trustworthy, convincing *evidence* of the correctness of the outcome while protecting voter *privacy* in a world *where no person or machine may be trusted*. The resulting voting system and its security features must also be *usable* by regular voters.

The aim of this paper is to explain the important requirements of secure elections and the solutions already available from e-voting research, then to identify the most important directions for research, which we present as **Open Problems** throughout.

Prior to delving into our discussion, we need to make a distinction in terminology. *Pollsite* voting systems are those in which voters record and cast ballots at predetermined locations, often in public areas with strict monitoring. *Remote* voting refers to a system where voters fill out ballots anywhere, and then send them to a central location to cast them, either physically mailing them in the case of vote-by-mail, or sending them over the Internet in the case of Internet voting.

Section 2 defines the requirements related to notions of election evidence, Sect. 3 on privacy and voter authentication, and Sect. 4 on more general usability, availability and local regulatory requirements. Section 5 describes the cryptographic, statistical, and engineering tools that have been developed for designing voting systems with verifiably correct election outcomes. Section 6 concludes with the promise and problems associated with Internet voting.

2   Secure Voting Requirements: Trust, Verifiability, and Evidence

For an election to be accepted as legitimate, the outcome should be convincing to all—and in particular to the losers—leaving no valid grounds to challenge the outcome. Whether elections are conducted by counting paper ballots by hand or using computer technology, the possibility of error or fraud necessitates assurances of the accuracy of the outcome.

It is clear that a naive introduction of computers into voting introduces the possibility of wholesale and largely undetectable fraud. If we can't detect it, how can we prevent it?

2.1   Risk Limiting Audits

Statistical post-election audits provide assurance that a reported outcome is correct, by examining some or all of an *audit trail* consisting of durable, tamper-evident, voter-verifiable records. Typically the audit trail consists of paper ballots.

The *outcome* of an election is the set of winners. An outcome is incorrect if it differs from the set of winners output by a perfectly accurate manual tabulation of the audit trail.

Definition 1. *An audit of an election contest is a* **risk-limiting audit (RLA)** *with risk limit α if it has the following two properties:*

1. *If the reported contest outcome under audit is incorrect, the probability that the audit enables outcome correction is at least $1 - \alpha$.*
2. *The audit will not indicate a need to alter a reported outcome that is correct.*

Together, these two properties imply that post-RLA, either the reported set of winners is the set that a perfectly accurate hand count of the audit trail would show, or an event which altered the election's outcome has occurred and was not detected by the audit (this event has probability no larger than bound α). RLAs amount to a limited form of probabilistic error correction: by relying on the audit trail, they have a known minimum probability of correcting the reported outcome if it is incorrect. They are not designed to detect (or correct) an incorrectly-reported tally, only an incorrectly-reported outcome.

The following procedure is a trivial RLA: with probability $1 - \alpha$, perform a full manual tally of the audit trail. Amend the outcome to match the set of winners the full hand count shows if that set is different.

The art in constructing RLAs consists of maintaining the risk limit while performing *less work* than a full hand count when the outcome is correct. Typically, this involves framing the audit as a sequential test of the statistical hypothesis that the outcome is incorrect. To reject that hypothesis is to conclude that the outcome is correct. RLAs have been developed for majority contests, plurality contests, and vote-for-k contests and complex social choice functions including D'Hondt—see below. RLAs have also been devised to check more than one election contest simultaneously [84].

2.2   Software Independence

Rivest and Wack introduced a definition targeted specifically at detecting misbehavior in computer-based elections:

Definition 2. *[68] A voting system is* **software independent** *if an undetected change or error in its software cannot cause an undetectable change or error in an election outcome.*

Software independence clearly expresses that it should not be necessary to trust software to determine election outcomes, but it does not say what procedures or types of evidence should be trusted instead. A system that is not software independent *cannot* produce a convincing evidence trail, but neither can a paper-based system that does not ensure that the paper trail is complete and intact, a cryptographic voting system that relies on an invalid cryptographic assumption, or a system that relies on audit procedures but lacks a means of assuring that those procedures are properly followed. We could likewise demand independence of many other kinds of trust assumptions: hardware, paper chain-of-custody, cryptographic setup, computational hardness, procedures, good randomness generation *etc.*

Rivest and Wack also define a stronger form of the property that includes error recovery:

Definition 3. *[68] A voting system is* **strongly software independent** *if it is software independent and a detected change or error in an election outcome (due to the software) can be corrected without rerunning the election.*

A strongly software-independent system can recover from software errors or bugs, but that recovery in turn is generally based on some other trail of evidence.

Software independence can be viewed as a form of tamper-evident system: a material software problem leaves a trace. Strongly software independent systems are resilient: not only do material software problems leave a trace, the overall election system can recover from those problems.

One mechanism to provide software independence is to record votes on a paper record that provides physical evidence of voter's intent, can be inspected by the voter prior to casting the vote, and—if preserved intact—can later be manually audited to verify the election outcome. Risk-limiting audits (see Sect. 5.2) can then achieve a prespecified level of assurance that results are correct; machine assisted risk-limiting audits [20], can help minimize the amount of labor required.

> **Open problems:**
> – How can systems handle errors in the event that elections don't verify? Can they recover?

2.3   End-to-end Verifiability

The concern regarding fraud and desire for transparency has motivated the security and crypto communities to develop another approach to voting system assurance: *end-to-end verifiability* (E2E-V). An election that is end-to-end verifiable achieves software independence together with the analagous notion of hardware independence, as well as independence from actions of election personnel and vendors. Rather than attempting to verify thousands of lines of code or closely monitor all of the many processes in an election, E2E-V focuses on providing a means to detect errors or fraud in the process of voting and counting. The idea behind E2E-V is to enable voters themselves to monitor the integrity of the election. This is challenging because total transparency is not possible without undermining the secret ballot, hence the mechanisms to generate such evidence have to be carefully designed.

Definition 4. *(adapted from [14]).*
  A voting system is **end-to-end verifiable** *if it has the following three kinds of verifiability:*

– **Cast as intended:** *Voters can independently verify that their selections are correctly recorded.*
– **Collected as cast:** *Voters can independently verify that the representation of their vote is correctly collected in the tally.*
– **Tallied as collected:** *Anyone can verify that every well-formed, collected vote is correctly included in the tally.*

If verification relies on trusting entities, software, or hardware, the voter and/or auditor should be able to choose them freely. Trusted procedures, if there are any, must be open to meaningful observation by every voter.

Note that the above definition allows each voter to check that her vote is correctly collected, thus ensuring that attempts to change or delete cast votes are detected. In addition, it should also be possible to check the list of voters who cast ballots, to ensure that votes are not added to the collection (*i.e.,* to prevent ballot-box stuffing). This is called *eligibility verifiability* [53,81].

2.4   Collection Accountability

In an E2E-V election protocol, voters can check whether their votes have been properly counted, but if they discover a problem, there may not be adequate evidence to correct it. An election system that is *collection-accountable* provides voters with evidence of any failure to collect their votes.

Definition 5. *An election system is* **collection accountable** *if any voter who detects that her vote has not been collected has, as part of the vote-casting protocol, convincing evidence that can be presented to an independent party to demonstrate that the vote has not been collected.*

Another form of evidence involves providing each voter with a code representing her votes, such that knowledge of a correct code is evidence of casting a particular vote [27]. Yet another mechanism is a suitable paper receipt. Forensic analysis may provide evidence that this receipt was not forged by a voter [7,11].

Open problems:
- Can independently verifiable evidence be provided by the voting system for incorrect ballot casting?

2.5 Dispute Resolution

While accountability helps secure the election process, it is not very useful if there is no way to handle disputes. If a voter claims, on the basis of accountability checks provided by a system, that something has gone wrong, there needs to be a mechanism to address this. This is known as *dispute resolution*:

Definition 6. *[46] A voting system is said to have* **dispute resolution** *if, when there is a dispute between two participants regarding honest participation, a third party can correctly resolve the dispute.*

An alternative to dispute resolution is dispute freeness:

Definition 7. *[50] A* **dispute free** *voting system has built-in prevention mechanisms that eliminate disputes between the active participants; any third party can check whether an active participant has cheated.*

Open problems:
- Can dispute resolution for all classes of possible errors exist in a given system?
- Are there other reasonable definitions and mechanisms for dispute resolution?
- Can a system offer complete dispute resolution capabilities in which every dispute can be adjudicated using evidence produced by the election system?

2.6 From Verifiable to Verified

Constructing a voting system that creates sufficient evidence to reveal problems is not enough on its own. That evidence must actually be used—and used appropriately—to ensure the accuracy of election outcomes.

An election result may not be verified, even if it is generated by an end-to-end verifiable voting system. For verification of the result, we need several further conditions to be satisfied:

- Enough voters and observers must be sufficiently diligent in performing the appropriate checks.

- Random audits (including those initiated by voters) must be sufficiently extensive and unpredictable that attempts at election manipulation have a high chance of being detected.
- If checks fail, this must be reported to the authorities who, in turn, must take appropriate action.

These issues involve complex human factors, including voters' incentives to participate in verification. Little work has been done on this aspect of the problem.

An E2E-V system might give an individual voter assurance that her vote has not been tampered with *if* that voter performs certain checks. However, sufficiently many voters must do this in order to provide evidence that the election outcome as a whole is correct. Combining risk-limiting audits with E2E-V systems can provide a valuable layer of protection in the case that an insufficient number of voters participate in verification.

Finally, another critical verification problem that has received little attention to date is how to make schemes that are recoverable in the face of errors. We do not want to have to abort and rerun an election every time a check a fails. Certain levels of detected errors can be shown to be highly unlikely to affect the outcome, and hence can be tolerated. Other types and patterns of error can be handled and corrected for, either post hoc or dynamically.

Both Küsters *et al.* [55] and Kiayias *et al.* [52] model voter-initiated auditing [10] and its implications for detection of an incorrect election result. Both definitions turn uncertainty about voter initiated auditing into a bound on the probability of detecting deviations of the announced election result from the truth.

Open problems:
- Can systems be designed so that the extent and diligence of checks performed can be measured?
- Can verification checks be abstracted from the voter, either by embedding them in other election processes or automating them?

---

3   Secure Voting Requirements: Voter Authentication, Privacy, Receipt-Freeness and Coercion-Resistance

This section focuses on secure voting system requirements related to authenticating the voter and ensuring that the evidence provided for verifiability cannot be used to coerce or bribe the voter to vote in a certain manner.

3.1   Voter Authentication

A significant challenge for election systems is the credentialing of voters to ensure that all eligible voters, and no one else, can cast votes. This presents numerous questions: what kinds of credentials should be used? How should they be issued? Can they be revoked or de-activated? Are credentials good for a single election or for an extended period? How difficult are they to share, transfer, steal, or forge? Can the ability to create genuine-looking forgeries help prevent coercion? These questions must be answered carefully, and until they are satisfied for remote voting, pollsite voting is the only robust way to address these questions—and even then, in-person credentialing is subject to forgery, distribution, and revocation concerns (for instance, the Dominican Republic recently held a pollsite election where voters openly sold their credentials [35]). In the U.S., there is concern that requiring in-person credentialing, in the form of voter ID, disenfranchises legitimate voters.

> **Open problems:**
> – Is there a sufficiently secure way to distribute credentials for Internet voting?
> – Is a traditional PKI sufficient to ensure eligibility for remote voting?
> – How does use of a PKI change coercion assumptions?

3.2   Privacy, Receipt Freeness, and Coercion Resistance

In most security applications, privacy and confidentiality are synonymous. In elections, however, privacy has numerous components that go well beyond typical confidentiality. Individual privacy can be compromised by "normal" election processes such as a unanimous result. Voters may be coerced if they can produce a proof of how they voted, even if they have to work to do so.

Privacy for votes is a means to an end: if voters don't express their true preferences then the election may not produce the right outcome. This section gives an overview of increasingly strong definitions of what it means for voters to be free of coercion.

Basic Confidentiality. We will take *ballot privacy* to mean that the election does not leak any information about how any voter voted beyond what can be deduced from the announced results. Confidentiality is not the only privacy requirement in elections, but even simple confidentiality poses significant challenges. It is remarkable how many deployed e-voting systems have been shown to lack even the most basic confidentiality properties (e.g., [21,24,34,42,59]).

Perhaps more discouraging to basic privacy is the fact that remote voting systems (both paper and electronic) inherently allow voters to eschew confidentiality. Because remote systems enable voters to fill out their ballots outside a controlled environment, anyone can watch over the voter's shoulder while she fills out her ballot.

In an election—unlike, say, in a financial transaction—even the candidate receiving an encrypted vote should not be able to decrypt it. Instead, an encrypted (or otherwise shrouded) vote must remain confidential to keep votes from being directly visible to election authorities.

Some systems, such as code voting [26] and the Norwegian and Swiss Internet voting schemes, defend privacy against an attacker who controls the computer used for voting; however, this relies on assumptions about the privacy and integrity of the code sheet. Some schemes, such as JCJ/Civitas [45], obscure who has voted while providing a proof that only eligible votes were included in the tally.

Several works [33, 55], following Benaloh [16] formalize the notion of privacy as preventing an attacker from noticing when two parties swap their votes.

> **Open problems:**
> - Can we develop more effective, verifiable assurance that vote privacy is preserved?
> - Can we build privacy for remote voting through computer-based systems?

Everlasting Privacy. Moran and Naor expressed concern over what might happen to encrypted votes that can still be linked to their voter's name some decades into the future, and hence decrypted by superior technology. They define a requirement to prevent this:

Definition 8. *[60] A voting scheme has* **everlasting privacy** *if its privacy does not depend on assumptions of cryptographic hardness.*

Their solution uses perfectly hiding commitments to the votes, which are aggregated homomorphically. Instead of privacy depending upon a cryptographic hardness assumption, it is the integrity of an election that depends upon a hardness assumption; and only a real-time compromise of the assumption can have an impact.

Systemic Privacy Loss. We generally accept that without further information, a voter is more likely to have voted for a candidate who has received more votes, but additional data is commonly released which can further erode voter privacy. Even if we exclude privacy compromises, there are other privacy risks which must be managed. If voters achieve privacy by encrypting their selections, the holders of decryption keys can view their votes. If voters make their selections on devices out of their immediate control (*e.g.* official election equipment), then it is difficult to assure them that these devices are not retaining information that could later compromise their privacy. If voters make their selections on their own devices, then there is an even greater risk that these devices could be infected with malware that records (and perhaps even alters) their selections (see, for instance, the Estonian system [82]).

> **Open problems:**
> - Are there ways to quantify systemic privacy loss?
> - How can elections minimize privacy loss?
> - How can elections provide verifiable integrity while minimizing privacy loss?

Receipt-Freeness. The problem of preventing coercion and vote-selling was considered solved with the introduction of the *Australian* ballot. The process of voting privately within a public environment where privacy can be monitored and enforced prevents improper influence. Recent systems have complicated this notion, however. If a voting protocol provides a receipt but is not carefully designed, the receipt can be a channel for information to the coercive adversary.

Benaloh and Tuinstra [15] pointed out that passive privacy is insufficient for resisting coercion in elections:

Definition 9. *A voting system is* **receipt free** *if a voter is unable to prove how she voted even if she actively colludes with a coercer and deviates from the protocol in order to try to produce a proof.*

Traditional elections may fail receipt-freeness too. In general, if a vote consists of a long list of choices, the number of possible votes may be much larger than the number of likely voters. This is sometimes called (a failure of) the *short ballot assumption* [71]. Prior to each election, coercers assign a particular voting pattern to each voter. When the individual votes are made public, any voter who did not cast their pattern can then be found out. This is sometimes called the *Italian attack*, after a once prevalent practice in Sicily. It can be easily mitigated when a vote can be broken up, but is difficult to mitigate in systems like IRV in which the vote is complex but must be kept together. Mitigations are discussed in Sects. 5.2 and 5.3.

Incoercibility has been defined and examined in the universally composable framework in the context of general multiparty computation [22,90]. These definitions examine whether the protocol introduces additional opportunities for coercion that are not present when the computation is performed by a trusted party. With some exceptions (such as [5]), they usually focus on a passive notion of receipt-freeness, which is not strong enough for voting.

Coercion Resistance. Schemes can be receipt-free, but not entirely resistant to coercion. Schemes like Prêt à Voter [74] that rely on randomization for receipt-freeness can be susceptible to *forced randomization*, where a coercer forces a voter to always choose the first choice on the ballot. Due to randomized candidate order, the resulting vote will be randomly distributed. If a specific group of voters are coerced in this way, it can have a disproportionate impact on the election outcome.

If voting rolls are public and voting is not mandatory, this has an effect equivalent to *forced abstention*, wherein a coercer prevents the voter from voting. Schemes that rely on credentialing are also susceptible to coercion by *forced surrender of credentials*.

One way to fully resist forced abstention is to obscure who voted. However, this is difficult to reconcile with the opportunity to verify that only eligible voters have voted (eligibility verifiability), though some schemes achieve both [41].

Moran and Naor [60] provide a strong definition of receipt freeness in which a voter may deviate actively from the protocol in order to convince a coercer that she obeyed. Their model accommodates forced randomization. A scheme is resistant to coercion if the voter can always pretend to have obeyed while actually voting as she likes.

Definition 10. *A voting scheme S is* **coercion resistant** *if the following holds:*
There exists a strategy for a coerced voter V such that, for any strategy adopted by the Coercer C, V is able to cast her intended vote in a manner that is indistinguishable to C from her having followed C's instructions.

Coercion resistance is defined in [45] to include receipt freeness and defence against forced-randomization, forced abstention and the forced surrender of credentials. More general definitions include [56], which incorporates all these attacks along with Moran and Naor's notion of a coercion resistance strategy.

Note that if the coercer can monitor the voter throughout the vote casting period, then resistance is futile. For in-person voting, we assume that the voter is isolated from any coercer while she is in the booth (although this is questionable in the era of mobile phones). For remote voting, we need to assume that voters will have some time when they can interact with the voting system (or the credential-granting system) unobserved.

More Coercion Considerations. Some authors have tried to provide some protection against coercion without achieving full coercion resistance. *Caveat coercitor* [39] proposes the notion of *coercion evidence* and allows voters to cast multiple votes using the same credential.

Open problems:
– Can we design usable, verifiable, coercion-resistant voting for a remote setting?

---

4   Other Secure Voting Requirements

In this section we briefly review more general secure voting system requirements such as usability, availability and those resulting from local election regulations.

4.1   Availability

Denial-of-Service (DoS) is an ever-present threat to elections which can be mitigated but never fully eliminated. A simple service outage can disenfranchise voters, and the threat of attack from foreign state-level adversaries is a pressing concern. Indeed, one of the countries that regularly uses Internet voting, Estonia, has been subject to malicious outages [89].

A variant of DoS specific to the context of elections is *selective DoS*, which presents a fundamentally different threat than general DoS. Voting populations are rarely homogeneous, and disruption of service, for instance, in urban (or rural) areas can skew results and potentially change election outcomes. If DoS

96   M. Bernhard et al.

cannot be entirely eliminated, can service standards be prescribed so that if an outcome falls below the standards it is vacated? Should these standards be dependent on the reported margin of victory? What, if any, recovery methods are possible? Because elections are more vulnerable to minor perturbations than most other settings, selective DoS is a concern which cannot be ignored.

4.2 Usability

A voting system must be *usable* by voters, poll-workers, election officials, observers, and so on. Voters who may not be computer literate—and sometimes not literate at all—should be able to vote with very low error rates. Although some error is regarded as inevitable, it is also critical that the interface not drive errors in a particular direction. For instance, a list of candidates that crosses a page boundary could cause the candidates on the second page to be missed. Whatever security mechanisms we add to the voting process should operate without degrading usability, otherwise the resulting system will likely be unacceptable. A full treatment of usability in voting is beyond the scope of this paper. However, we note that E2E-V systems (and I-voting systems, even when not E2E-V) add additional processes for voters and poll workers to follow. If verification processes can't be used properly by real voters, the outcome will not be properly verified. One great advantage of statistical audits is to shift complexity from voters to auditors.

Open problems:
 – How can usability be integrated into the design process of a voting system?
 – How can we ensure full E2E-V, coercion resistance, etc., in a usable fashion?

4.3 Local Regulatory Requirements

A variety of other mechanical requirements are often imposed by legal requirements that vary among jurisdictions. For example:

 – Allowing voters to "write-in" vote for a candidate not listed on the ballot.
 – Mandating the use of paper ballots (in some states without unique identifying marks or serial numbers; in other states *requiring* such marks)
 – Mandating the use of certain social choice functions (see section on Complex Election Methods below).
 – Supporting absentee voting.
 – Requiring or forbidding that "ballot rotation" be used (listing the candidates in different orders in different jurisdictions).
 – Requiring that voting equipment be certified under government guidelines.

Newer electronic and I-voting systems raise important policy challenges for real-world adoption. For example, in STAR-Vote [7], there will be multiple copies of every vote record: mostly electronic records, but also paper records. There may be instances where one is damaged or destroyed and the other is all that remains. When laws speak to retention of "the ballot", that term is no longer well-defined. Such requirements may need to be adapted to newer voting systems.

Complex Election Methods. Many countries allow voters to *select, score, or rank* candidates or parties. Votes can then be tallied in a variety of complex ways [19,76]. None of the requirements for privacy, coercion-resistance, or the provision of verifiable evidence change. However, many tools that achieve these properties for traditional "first-past-the-post" elections need to be redesigned.

An election method might be complex at the voting or the tallying end. For example, party-list methods such as D'Hondt and Sainte-Laguë have simple voting, in which voters select their candidate or party, but complex proportional seat allocation. Borda, Range Voting, and Approval Voting allow votes to be quite expressive but are simple to tally by addition. Condorcet's method and related functions [80,88] can be arbitrarily complex, as they can combine with any social choice function. Instant Runoff Voting (IRV) and the Single Transferable Vote (STV) are both expressive and complicated to tally. This makes for several challenges.

Open problems:

- Which methods for cast-as-intended verification (e.g. code voting [26]) work for complex voting schemes?
- How do Risk-limiting audits apply to complex schemes? (See Sect. 5.2)
- How can complex ballots mitigate failures of the *short ballot assumption* [71]?
- Can we achieve everlasting privacy for complex elections?

---

5   How Can We Secure Voting?

The goal of this section is to provide a state-of-the-art picture of current solutions to voting problems and ongoing voting research, to motivate further work on open problems, and to define clear directions both in research and election policy.

5.1   The Role of Paper and Ceremonies

Following security problems with direct-recording electronic voting systems (DREs) noted in [21,34,59,92] and others, many parts of the U.S. returned to the use of paper ballots (as have many places around the world). If secure custody of the paper ballots is assumed, paper provides durable *evidence* required to determine the correctness of the election outcome. For this reason, when humans vote from untrusted computers, cryptographic voting system specifications often use paper for security, included in the notions of dispute-freeness, dispute resolution, collection accountability and accountability [54] (all as defined in Sect. 2).

Note that the standard approach to dispute resolution, based on non-repudiation, cannot be applied to the voting problem in the standard fashion, because the human voter does not have the ability to check digital signatures or digitally sign the vote (or other messages that may be part of the protocol) unassisted.

Dispute-freeness or accountability are often achieved in a polling place through the use of cast paper ballots, and the evidence of their chain of custody (e.g., wet-ink signatures). Paper provides an interface for data entry for the voter—not simply to enter the vote, but also to enter other messages that the protocol might require—and data on unforgeable paper serves many of the purposes of digitally signed data. Thus, for example, when a voter marks a *Prêt à Voter* [74] or *Scantegrity* [27] ballot, she is providing an instruction that the voting system cannot pretend was something else. The resulting vote encryption has been physically committed to by the voting system—by the mere act of printing the ballot—before the voter "casts" her vote.

Physical ceremony, such as can be witnessed while the election is ongoing, also supports verifiable cryptographic election protocols (see Sect. 5.3). Such ceremonies include the verification of voter credentials, any generation of randomness if required for the choice between cast and audit, any vote-encryption-verification performed by election officials, etc.

The key aspect of these ceremonies is the chance for observers to see that they are properly conducted.

Open problems:
– Can we achieve dispute-resolution or -freeness without the use of paper and physical ceremony?

5.2 Statistics and Auditing

Two types of Risk Limiting Audits have been devised: *ballot polling* and *comparison* [12,57,83]. Both types continue to examine random samples of ballots until either there is strong statistical evidence that the outcome is correct, or until there has been a complete manual tally. "Strong statistical evidence" means that the p-value of the hypothesis that the outcome is incorrect is at most α, within tolerable risk.

Both methods rely on the existence of a *ballot manifest* that describes how the audit trail is stored. Selecting the random sample can include a public ceremony in which observers contribute by rolling dice to seed a PRNG [31].

Ballot-polling audits examine random samples of individual ballots. They demand almost nothing of the voting technology other than the reported outcome. When the reported outcome is correct, the expected number of ballots a ballot-polling audit inspects is approximately quadratic in the reciprocal of the (true) margin of victory, resulting in large expected sample sizes for small margins.

Comparison audits compare reported results for randomly selected subsets of ballots to manual tallies of those ballots. Comparison audits require the voting system to commit to tallies of subsets of ballots ("clusters") corresponding to identifiable physical subsets of the audit trail. Comparison audits have two parts: confirm that the outcome computed from the commitment matches the reported outcome, and check the accuracy of randomly selected clusters by manually inspecting the corresponding subsets of the audit trail. When the reported cluster tallies are correct, the number of clusters a comparison audit inspects is approximately linear in the reciprocal of the reported margin. The efficiency of comparison audits also depends approximately linearly on the size of the clusters. Efficiency is highest for clusters consisting of individual ballots: individual cast vote records. To audit at the level of individual ballots requires the voting system to commit to the interpretation of each ballot in a way that is linked to the corresponding element of the audit trail.

In addition to RLAs, auditing methods have been proposed with Bayesian citeRivestShenspsbayes or heuristic [69] justifications.

All post-election audits implicitly assume that the audit trail is adequately complete and accurate, and that a full manual count would reflect the correct contest outcome. *Compliance audits* are designed to determine whether there is convincing evidence that the audit trail was curated well, by checking ballot accounting, registration records, pollbooks, election procedures, physical security of the audit trail, chain of custody logs, and so on. *Evidence-based elections* [86] combine compliance audits and risk-limiting audits to determine whether the audit trail is adequately accurate, and if so, whether the reported outcome is correct. If there is not convincing evidence that the audit trail is adequately accurate and complete, there cannot be convincing evidence that the outcome is correct.

Audits in Complex Elections. Generally, in traditional and complex elections, whenever an election margin is known and the infrastructure for a comparison audit is available, it is possible to conduct a rigorous risk-limiting comparison audit. This motivates many works on practical margin computation for IRV [18, 25, 58, 79].

However, such an audit for a complex election may not be efficient, which motivates the extension of Stark's *sharper discrepancy measure* to D'Hondt and related schemes [85]. For Schulze and some related schemes, neither efficient margin computation nor any other form of RLA is known (see [43]); a Bayesian audit [28, 70] may nonetheless be used when one is able to specify suitable priors.

Open problems:
- Can comparison audits for complex ballots be performed without exposing voters to "Italian" attacks?
- Can risk-limiting or other sound statistical audits be developed for systems too complex to compute margins efficiently?
- Can the notion of RLAs be extended to situations where physical evidence is not available (i.e. Internet voting)?

5.3 Cryptographic Tools and Designs

Major Approaches to Voting Cryptography. Typically E2E-V involves providing each voter with a *protected receipt*—an encrypted or encoded version of their vote—at the time the vote is cast. The voter can later use her receipt to check whether her vote is included correctly in the tabulation process. Furthermore, given the set of encrypted votes (as well as other relevant information, like the public keys), the tabulation is *universally verifiable*: anyone can check whether it is correct. To achieve this, most E2E-V systems rely on a public bulletin board, where the set of encrypted ballots is published in an append-only fashion.

The votes can then be turned into a tally in one of two main ways. *Homomorphic encryption* schemes [16,30] allow the tally to be produced on encrypted votes. *Verifiable shuffling* transforms a list of encrypted votes into a shuffled list that can be decrypted without the input votes being linked to the (decrypted) output. There are efficient ways to prove that the input list exactly matches the output [6,40,63,77,87].

Techniques for Cast-as-Intended Verification. How can a voter verify that her cast vote is the one she wanted? *Code Voting*, first introduced by Chaum [26], gives each voter a sheet of codes for each candidate. Assuming the code sheet is valid, the voter can cast a vote on an untrusted machine by entering the code corresponding to her chosen candidate and waiting to receive the correct confirmation code. Modern interpretations of code voting include [44,73,93].

The alternative is to ask the machine to encrypt a vote directly, but verify that it does so correctly. Benaloh [9] developed a simple protocol to enable vote encryption on an untrusted voting machine. A voter uses a voting machine to encrypt any number of votes, and casts only one of these encrypted votes. All the other votes may be "audited" by the voter. If the encryption is audited, the voting system provides a proof that it encrypted the vote correctly, and the proof is public. The corresponding ballot cannot be cast as the correspondence between the encryption and the ballot is now public, and the vote is no longer secret. Voters take home receipts corresponding to the encryptions of their cast ballots as well as any ballots that are to be audited. They may check the presence of these on a bulletin board, and the correctness proofs of the audited encryptions using software obtained from any of several sources. However, even the most diligent voters need only check that their receipts match the public record and that any ballots selected for audit display correct candidate selections. The correctness proofs are part of the public record that can be verified by any individual or observer that is verifying correct tallying.

A Rigorous Understanding of E2E-V Protocols. In addition to the work of Adida on assisted-human interactive proofs (AHIPs, see [1]), there has been some work on a rigorous understanding of one or more properties of single protocols, including the work of Moran and Naor [61,62] and Küsters et al. [54].

There have also been formalizations of voting protocols with human participants, such as by Moran and Naor [61] (for a polling protocol using tamper-evident seals on envelopes) and Kiayias et al. [51]. However, there is no one model that is sufficient for the rigorous understanding of the prominent protocols used/proposed for use in real elections. The absence of proofs has led to the overlooking of vulnerabilities in the protocols in the past, see [38,47–49].

Many systems use a combination of paper, cryptography, and auditing to achieve E2E-V in the polling place, including Markpledge [3,64], Moran and Naor's scheme [60], Prêt à Voter [74], Scantegrity II [23], Wombat [8,72], STAR-Vote [7] and Demos [52]. Their properties are summarised in Table 1.

The cryptographic literature has numerous constructions of end-to-end verifiable election schemes (e.g., [7,23,36,44,64,65,71,72,74,78]). There are also various detailed descriptions of what it means to verify the correctness of the output of E2E-V systems (e.g., [15,52,60]). Others have attempted to define alternative forms of the E2E-V properties [32,54,66]. There are also less technical explanations of E2E-V intended for voters and election officials [14,91].

Open problems:
- Can we develop a rigorous model for human participants and the use of paper and ceremonies in cryptographic voting protocols?
- Can we examine rigorously the combination of statistical and cryptographic methods for election verification?

Techniques for Coercion Resistance. Some simple approaches to coercion resistance have been suggested in the literature. These include allowing multiple votes with only the last counting and allowing in-person voting to override remotely cast votes (both used in Estonian, Norwegian, and Utah elections [17,37,82]). It is not clear that this mitigates coercion at all. Alarm codes can also be provided to voters: seemingly real but actually fake election credentials, along with the ability for voters to create their own fake credentials. Any such approach can be considered a partial solution at best, particularly given the usability challenges.

One voting system, *Civitas* [29], based on a protocol by Juels, Catalano and Jakobsson [45], allows voters to vote with fake credentials to lead the coercive adversary into believing the desired vote was cast. Note that the protocol must enable universal verification of the tally from a list of votes cast with both genuine and fake credentials, proving to the verifier that only the ones with genuine credentials were tallied, without identifying which ones they were.

Open problems:
- Can we develop cryptographic techniques that provide fully coercion resistant remote voting?

Cryptographic Solutions in Complex Elections. Cast-as-intended verification based on creating and then challenging a vote works regardless of the scheme (*e.g.* Benaloh challenges). Cut-and-choose based schemes such as Prêt à Voter and Scantegrity II need to be modified to work.

Both uses of end-to-end verifiable voting schemes in government elections, the Takoma Park run of Scantegrity II and the Victorian run of Prêt à Voter, used IRV (and one used STV). Verifiable IRV/STV counting that doesn't expose individual votes to the Italian attack has been considered [13], but may not be efficient enough for use in large elections in practice, and was not employed in either practical implementation.

Open problems:
- Is usable cast-as-intended verification for complex voting methods possible?

Table 1 summarizes how various election systems built out of these tools satisfy the definitions given in Sects. 2, 3, and 4.

6   A Look Ahead

Voting has always used available technology, whether pebbles dropped in an urn or marked paper put in a ballot box; it now uses computers, networks, and cryptography. The core requirement, to provide public evidence of the right result from secret ballots, hasn't changed in 2500 years.

Computers can improve convenience and accessibility over plain paper and manual counting. In the polling place there are good solutions, including Risk Limiting Audits and end-to-end verifiable systems. These must be more widely deployed and their options for verifying the election result must actually be used.

Many of the open problems described in this paper—usable and accessible voting systems, dispute resolution, incoercibility—come together in the challenge of a remote voting system that is verifiable and usable without supervision. The open problem of a system specification that (a) does not use any paper at all and (b) is based on a simple procedure for voters and poll workers will motivate researchers for a long time. Perhaps a better goal is a hybrid system combining paper evidence with some auditing or cryptographic verification.

Research in voting brings together knowledge in many fields—cryptography, systems security, statistics, usability and accessibility, software verification, elections, law and policy to name a few—to address a critical real-world problem.

The peaceful transfer of power depends on confidence in the electoral process. That confidence should not automatically be given to any outcome that seems plausible—it must be earned by producing evidence that the election result is what the people chose. Insisting on evidence reduces the opportunities for fraud, hence bringing greater security to citizens the world over.

Table 1. Applying our threat model to fielded and proposed voting schemes
–Note that certain features like credentialing and availability are excluded, as these factors impact all systems in roughly equivalent ways.

	fielded	coercion resistance	everlasting privacy	software independence	take-home evidence	ballot cast assurance	collection accountable	verifiably cast-as-intended	verifiably collected-as-cast	verifiable counted-as-collected	paper/electronic/hybrid	write-ins supported	preferential ballots supported
Poll-site techniques in widespread use													
Hand-counted in-person paper	●	●	●	●	○	○	○	●	○	●[7]	p	●	●
Optical-scan in-person paper	●	●	●	●	○	○	○	●	○	●[7]	h	●	●
DRE (with paper audit trail)	●	●	○	●	○	○	○	◐[7]	●	●[7]	h	●	●
Paperless DRE	●	●	○	○	○	○	○	○	○	○	e	●	●
Poll-site systems from research													
Prêt-à-voter [74]	●[1]	●	○	●	●	●	◐[12]	●	●	●	h	○	●
Scantegrity [27]	●[1]	●	○	●	●	●	◐[12]	●	●	●	h	◐	○
STAR-Vote [7]	◐[2]	●	◐[6]	●	●	●	◐[13]	◐[14]	●	●	h	○	○
Wombat [72]	◐[3]	●	◐[6]	●	●	●	◐[13]	◐[14]	●	●	h	○	○
VeriScan [11]	○	●	◐[6]	●	●	●	◐[13]	◐[14]	●	●	h	○	○
Scratch and Vote [4]	○	●	○	●	●	●	◐[12]	●	●	●	h	◐	◐
MarkPledge [64]	○	●	◐[6]	●	●	●	●	●	●	●	e	○	○
ThreeBallot [67]	○	●	●	●	●	●	◐[12]	●	●	◐	h	○	○
Remote voting systems and techniques													
Helios [2]	◐[3]	○[5]	◐[6]	●	●	●[8]	◐	○	◐[7]	●	e	○	○
Remotegrity [93]	◐[1]	○	◐[6]	●	●	○	●	●	●	●	h	○	○
Civitas [29]	◐[3]	●	◐[6]	○	●[8]	○	●	●	●	●	e	◐	●
Selene [75]	○	●	◐[6]	●	○	○	●	●	●	●[7]	e	○	●
Norway [37]	●	○[5]	○	○	○	○	◐[11]	○	○	◐[7]	e	●	●
Estonia [82]	●	○[5]	○	○	◐[9]	○	○	○	○	○	e	○	○
iVote [42]	●[4]	○[5]	○	○	○	○	○	◐[10]	◐[10]	○	e	●	●
Paper ballots returned by postal mail	●	○	●	●	○	○	○	○	○	●[7]	p	●	●

● = provides property   ○ = does not provide property   ◐ = provides property with provisions

1 Used in small trial elections
2 Pending deployment
3 Used in private sector elections
4 Absentee voting only
5 Allows multiple voting
6 Possible with PPAT
7 With sufficient auditing
8 Receipts sent by email
9 Temporary email receipt
10 Queryable (phone system)
11 Queryable (code sheets)
12 Enhanced with pre- and post-election auditing
13 Enhanced with auditing during elections
14 To the extent the paper resists forgery

Acknowledgments. This work was supported in part by the U.S. National Science Foundation awards CNS-1345254, CNS-1409505, CNS-1518888, CNS-1409401, CNS-1314492, and CNS-1421373, the Center for Science of Information STC (CSoI), an NSF Science and Technology Center, under grant agreement CCF-0939370, the Maryland Procurement Office under contract H98230-14-C-0127, and FNR Luxembourg under the PETRVS Mobility grant.

References

1. Adida, B.: Advances in Cryptographic Voting Systems. Ph.D. thesis, MIT, July 2006
2. Adida, B.: Helios: web-based open-audit voting. In: 17th USENIX Security Symposium, August 2008. vote.heliosvoting.org
3. Adida, B., Neff, C.A.: Efficient receipt-free ballot casting resistant to covert channels. IACR Cryptology ePrint Archive, 2008 (2008)
4. Adida, B., Rivest, R.L., Scratch, V.: Self-contained paper-based cryptographic voting. In: ACM Workshop on Privacy in the Electronic Society (2006)
5. Alwen, J., Ostrovsky, R., Zhou, H.-S., Zikas, V.: Incoercible multi-party computation and universally composable receipt-free voting. In: Gennaro, R., Robshaw, M. (eds.) CRYPTO 2015. LNCS, vol. 9216, pp. 763–780. Springer, Heidelberg (2015). doi:10.1007/978-3-662-48000-7_37
6. Bayer, S., Groth, J.: Efficient zero-knowledge argument for correctness of a shuffle. In: Pointcheval, D., Johansson, T. (eds.) EUROCRYPT 2012. LNCS, vol. 7237, pp. 263–280. Springer, Heidelberg (2012). doi:10.1007/978-3-642-29011-4_17
7. Bell, S., Benaloh, J., Byrne, M.D., DeBeauvoir, D., Eakin, B., Fisher, G., Kortum, P., McBurnett, N., Montoya, J., Parker, M., Pereira, O., Stark, P.B., Wallach, D.S., Winn, M.: STAR-vote: a secure, transparent, auditable, and reliable voting system. USENIX J. Election Technol. Syst. **1**(1), 8 (2013)
8. Ben-Nun, J., Fahri, N., Llewellyn, M., Riva, B., Rosen, A., Ta-Shma, A., Wikström, D.: A new implementation of a dual (paper and cryptographic) voting system. In: 5th International Conference on Electronic Voting (2012)
9. Benaloh, J.: Simple verifiable elections. In: USENIX/ACCURATE Electronic Voting Technology Workshop, August 2006
10. Benaloh J.: Ballot casting assurance via voter-initiated poll station auditing. In: USENIX/ACCURATE Electronic Voting Technology Workshop, August 2007
11. Benaloh, J.: Administrative and public verifiability: can we have both? In: USENIX/ACCURATE Electronic Voting Technology Workshop, August 2008
12. Benaloh, J., Jones, D., Lazarus, E., Lindeman, M., Stark, P.B.: Soba: Secrecy-preserving observable ballot-level audit. In: Proceedings of the USENIX Accurate Electronic Voting Technology Workshop (2011)
13. Benaloh, J., Moran, T., Naish, L., Ramchen, K., Teague, V.: Shuffle-sum: coercion-resistant verifiable tallying for STV voting. IEEE Trans. Inf. Forensics Secur. **4**(4), 685–698 (2009)
14. Benaloh, J., Rivest, R., Ryan, P.Y., Stark, P., Teague, V., Vora, P.: End-to-end verifiability. arXiv:1504.03778 (2015)
15. Benaloh, J., Tuinstra D.: Receipt-free secret-ballot elections. In: 26th ACM Symposium on Theory of Computing (1994)
16. Benaloh J.D.C.: Verifiable Secret-ballot Elections. Ph.D. thesis, Yale (1987). AAI8809191

17. Bernhard, M.: What happened in the Utah GOP caucus. https://mbernhard.com/Utahvoting.pdf
18. Blom, M., Stuckey, P.J., Teague, V.J., Tidhar, R.: Efficient computation of exact IRV margins. arXiv:1508.04885 (2015)
19. Brams, S.: Mathematics and Democracy. Princeton University Press, Princeton (2008)
20. Calandrino, J.A., Halderman, J.A., Felten, E.W.: Machine-assisted election auditing. In: USENIX/ACCURATE Electronic Voting Technology Workshop, August 2007
21. California Secretary of State's Office: Top-to-bottom review of electronic voting systems (2007). http://wwws.os.ca.gov/elections/voting-systems/oversight/top-bottom-review/
22. Canetti, R., Gennaro, R.: Incoercible multiparty computation. In: 37th IEEE Symposium on Foundations of Computer Science (1996)
23. Carback, R., Chaum, D., Clark, J., Conway, J., Essex, A., Herrnson, P.S., Mayberry, T., Popoveniuc, S., Rivest, R.L., Shen, E., Sherman, A.T., Vora, P.L.: Scantegrity II municipal election at Takoma Park: the first E2E binding governmental election with ballot privacy. In: 18th USENIX Security Symposium, August 2010
24. Carter Center: Expert study mission report–Internet voting pilot: Norway's 2013 parliamentary elections, March 2014. http://www.regjeringen.no/upload/KRD/Kampanjer/valgportal/valgobservatorer/2013/Rapport_Cartersenteret2013.pdf
25. Cary, D.: Estimating the margin of victory for instant-runoff voting. In: USENIX/ACCURATE Electronic Voting Technology Workshop/Workshop on Trustworthy Elections, August 2011
26. Chaum, D.: SureVote: technical overview. In: IAVoSS Workshop on Trustworthy Elections (2001)
27. Chaum, D., Carback, R., Clark, J., Essex, A., Popoveniuc, S., Rivest, R.L., Ryan, P.Y.A., Shen, E., Sherman, A.T., Scantegrity, I.I.: End-to-end verifiability for optical scan election systems using invisible ink confirmation codes. In: USENIX/ACCURATE Electronic Voting Workshop, August 2008
28. Chilingirian, B., Perumal, Z., Rivest, R.L., Bowland, G., Conway, A., Stark, P.B., Blom, M., Culnane, C., Teague, V.: Auditing australian senate ballots. arXiv preprint arXiv:1610.00127 (2016)
29. Clarkson, M., Chong, S., Myers, A.C.: Civitas: a secure remote voting system. Technical report, Cornell University Computing and Information Science Technology Report, May 2007. http://www.truststc.org/pubs/545.html
30. (Cohen), J.B., Fischer, M.J.: A robust and verifiable cryptographically secure election scheme. In: 26th Annual Symposium on Foundations of Computer Science (1985)
31. Cordero, A., Wagner, D., Dill, D.: The role of dice in election audits - extended abstract. In: IAVoSS Workshop On Trustworthy Elections (2006)
32. Cortier, V., Galindo, D., Küsters, R., Müller, J., Truderung, T.: Verifiability Notions for E-Voting Protocols. Technical report, Technical Report 2016/287, Cryptology ePrint Archive (2016). http://eprint.iacr.org/2016/287
33. Delaune, S., Kremer, S., Ryan, M.: Verifying privacy-type properties of electronic voting protocols: a taster. In: Chaum, D., Jakobsson, M., Rivest, R.L., Ryan, P.Y.A., Benaloh, J., Kutylowski, M., Adida, B. (eds.) Towards Trustworthy Elections. LNCS, vol. 6000, pp. 289–309. Springer, Heidelberg (2010). doi:10.1007/978-3-642-12980-3_18

34. Feldman, A.J., Halderman, J.A., Felten, E.W.: Security analysis of the Diebold AccuVote-TS voting machine. In: USENIX/ACCURATE Electronic Voting Technology Workshop, August 2007
35. Fieser, E.: People Openly Sell Votes for $20 in the Dominican Republic, May 2016. http://www.bloomberg.com/news/articles/2016-05-16/people-openly-sell-their-votes-for-20-in-the-dominican-republic
36. Fisher, K., Carback, R., Sherman, A.T.: Punchscan: introduction and system definition of a high-integrity election system. In: IAVoSS Workshop on Trustworthy Elections (2006)
37. Gjøsteen, K.: The norwegian internet voting protocol. In: Kiayias, A., Lipmaa, H. (eds.) Vote-ID 2011. LNCS, vol. 7187, pp. 1–18. Springer, Heidelberg (2012). doi:10.1007/978-3-642-32747-6_1
38. Gogolewski, M., Klonowski, M., Kubiak, P., Kutyłowski, M., Lauks, A., Zagórski, F.: Kleptographic attacks on e-voting schemes. In: Müller, G. (ed.) ETRICS 2006. LNCS, vol. 3995, pp. 494–508. Springer, Heidelberg (2006). doi:10.1007/11766155_35
39. Grewal, G.S., Ryan, M.D., Bursuc, S., Ryan, P.Y.: Caveat coercitor: Coercion-evidence in electronic voting. In: 34th IEEE Symposium on Security and Privacy (2013)
40. Groth, J.: A verifiable secret shuffle of homomorphic encryptions. J. Cryptol. **23**(4), 546–579 (2010)
41. Haenni, R., Spycher, O.: Secure Internet Voting on Limited Devices with Anonymized DSA Public Keys, August 2011
42. Halderman, J.A., Teague, V.: The new south wales ivote system: security failures and verification flaws in a live online election. In: Haenni, R., Koenig, R.E., Wikström, D. (eds.) VOTELID 2015. LNCS, vol. 9269, pp. 35–53. Springer, Cham (2015). doi:10.1007/978-3-319-22270-7_3
43. Hemaspaandra, L.A., Lavaee, R., Menton, C.: Schulze and ranked-pairs voting are fixed-parameter tractable to bribe, manipulate, and control. In: International Conference on Autonomous Agents and Multiagent Systems (2013)
44. Joaquim, R., Ribeiro, C., Ferreira, P.: VeryVote: a voter verifiable code voting system. In: Ryan, P.Y.A., Schoenmakers, B. (eds.) Vote-ID 2009. LNCS, vol. 5767, pp. 106–121. Springer, Heidelberg (2009). doi:10.1007/978-3-642-04135-8_7
45. Juels, A., Catalano, D., Jakobsson, M.: Coercion-resistant electronic elections. In: ACM Workshop on Privacy in the Electronic Society, November 2005
46. Kaczmarek, T., Wittrock, J., Carback, R., Florescu, A., Rubio, J., Runyan, N., Vora, P.L., Zagórski, F.: Dispute resolution in accessible voting systems: the design and use of audiotegrity. In: Heather, J., Schneider, S., Teague, V. (eds.) Vote-ID 2013. LNCS, vol. 7985, pp. 127–141. Springer, Heidelberg (2013). doi:10.1007/978-3-642-39185-9_8
47. Karlof, C., Sastry, N., Wagner, D.: Cryptographic voting protocols: a systems perspective. In: 14th USENIX Security Symposium, August 2005
48. Kelsey, J., Regenscheid, A., Moran, T., Chaum, D.: Attacking Paper-Based E2E Voting Systems. In: Chaum, D., Jakobsson, M., Rivest, R.L., Ryan, P.Y.A., Benaloh, J., Kutylowski, M., Adida, B. (eds.) Towards Trustworthy Elections. LNCS, vol. 6000, pp. 370–387. Springer, Heidelberg (2010). doi:10.1007/978-3-642-12980-3_23
49. Khazaei, S., Wikström, D.: Randomized partial checking revisited. In: Dawson, E. (ed.) CT-RSA 2013. LNCS, vol. 7779, pp. 115–128. Springer, Heidelberg (2013). doi:10.1007/978-3-642-36095-4_8

50. Kiayias, A., Yung, M.: Self-tallying elections and perfect ballot secrecy. In: Naccache, D., Paillier, P. (eds.) PKC 2002. LNCS, vol. 2274, pp. 141–158. Springer, Heidelberg (2002). doi:10.1007/3-540-45664-3_10
51. Kiayias, A., Zacharias, T., Zhang, B.: Ceremonies for end-to-end verifiable elections. IACR Cryptology ePrint Archive, 2015 (2015)
52. Kiayias, A., Zacharias, T., Zhang, B.: End-to-end verifiable elections in the standard model. In: Oswald, E., Fischlin, M. (eds.) EUROCRYPT 2015. LNCS, vol. 9057, pp. 468–498. Springer, Heidelberg (2015). doi:10.1007/978-3-662-46803-6_16
53. Kremer, S., Ryan, M., Smyth, B.: Election verifiability in electronic voting protocols. In: Gritzalis, D., Preneel, B., Theoharidou, M. (eds.) ESORICS 2010. LNCS, vol. 6345, pp. 389–404. Springer, Heidelberg (2010). doi:10.1007/978-3-642-15497-3_24
54. Küsters, R., Truderung, T., Vogt, A.: Accountability: definition and relationship to verifiability. In: 17th ACM Conference on Computer and Communications Security (2010)
55. Küsters, R., Truderung, T., Vogt, A.: Verifiability, privacy, and coercion-resistance: New insights from a case study. In: 32nd IEEE Symposium on Security and Privacy (2011)
56. Küsters, R., Truderung, T., Vogt, A.: A game-based definition of coercion resistance and its applications. J. Comput. Secur. 20(6), 709–764 (2012)
57. Lindeman, M., Stark, P.B., Yates, V.S.: BRAVO: ballot-polling risk-limiting audits to verify outcomes. In: USENIX Electronic Voting Technology Workshop/Workshop on Trustworthy Elections, August 2012
58. Magrino, T.R., Rivest, R.L., Shen, E., Wagner, D.: Computing the margin of victory in IRV elections. In: USENIX Electronic Voting Technology Workshop/Workshop on Trustworthy Elections, August 2011
59. McDaniel, P., et al.: EVEREST: evaluation and validation of election-related equipment, standards and testing, December 2007. http://www.patrickmcdaniel.org/pubs/everest.pdf
60. Moran, T., Naor, M.: Receipt-free universally-verifiable voting with everlasting privacy. In: Dwork, C. (ed.) CRYPTO 2006. LNCS, vol. 4117, pp. 373–392. Springer, Heidelberg (2006). doi:10.1007/11818175_22
61. Moran, T., Naor, M.: Basing cryptographic protocols on tamper-evident seals. Theor. Comput. Sci. 411, 1283–1310 (2010)
62. Moran, T., Naor, M.: Split-ballot voting: everlasting privacy with distributed trust. ACM Trans. Inf. Syst. Secur. 13(2), 16 (2010)
63. Neff, C.A.: A verifiable secret shuffle and its application to e-voting. In: ACM Conference on Computer and Communications Security. ACM (2001)
64. Neff C.A.: Practical high certainty intent verification for encrypted votes (2004). http://www.votehere.net/vhti/documentation
65. Popoveniuc, S., Hosp, B.: An Introduction to Punchscan. In: IAVoSS Workshop on Trustworthy Elections, August 2006
66. Popoveniuc, S., Kelsey, J., Regenscheid, A., Vora, P.L.: Performance requirements for end-to-end verifiable elections. In: USENIX Electronic Voting Technology Workshop/Workshop on Trustworthy Elections, August 2010
67. Rivest, R.L.: The Three Ballot voting system (2006). https://people.csail.mit.edu/rivest/Rivest-TheThreeBallotVotingSystem.pdf
68. Rivest, R.L.: On the notion of "software independence" in voting systems. Philos. Trans. R. Soc. A Math. Phys. Eng. Sci. 366, 3759–3767 (2008)
69. Rivest, R.L.: DiffSum: a simple post-election risk-limiting audit. CoRR abs/1509.00127 (2015)

70. Rivest, R.L., Shen, E.: A Bayesian method for auditing elections. In: USENIX Electronic Voting Technology Workshop/Workshop on Trustworthy Elections, August 2012
71. Rivest, R.L., Smith, W.D.: Three voting protocols: ThreeBallot, VAV, and Twin. In: USENIX/ACCURATE Electronic Voting Technology Workshop, August 2007
72. Rosen, A., Ta-shma, A., Riva, B., Ben-Nun, J.Y.: Wombat voting system. http://www.wombat-voting.com
73. Ryan, P.Y.A.: Prêt à voter with confirmation codes. In: 2011 Electronic Voting Technology Workshop/Workshop on Trustworthy Elections, August 2011
74. Ryan, P.Y.A., Bismark, D., Heather, J., Schneider, S., Xia, Z.: Prêt à voter: a voter-verifiable voting system. IEEE Trans. Inf. Forensics Secur. 4(4), 662 673 (2009)
75. Ryan, P.Y.A., Roenne, P.B., Iovino V.: Selene: Voting with Transparent Verifiability and Coercion-Mitigation. Cryptology ePrint Archive, Report 2015/1105 (2015). http://eprint.iacr.org/
76. Saari, D.G.: Geometry of voting (2012)
77. Sako, K., Kilian, J.: Receipt-free mix-type voting scheme. In: Guillou, L.C., Quisquater, J.-J. (eds.) EUROCRYPT 1995. LNCS, vol. 921, pp. 393–403. Springer, Heidelberg (1995). doi:10.1007/3-540-49264-X_32
78. Sandler, D.R., Derr, K., Wallach, D.S.: VoteBox: a tamper-evident, verifiable electronic voting system. In: 17th USENIX Security Symposium, July 2008
79. Sarwate, A.D., Checkoway, S., Shacham, H.: Risk-limiting audits and the margin of victory in nonplurality elections. Stat. Polit. Policy 4(1), 29–64 (2013)
80. Schulze, M.: A new monotonic, clone-independent, reversal symmetric, and condorcet-consistent single-winner election method. Soc. Choice Welfare 36(2), 267–303 (2011)
81. Smyth, B., Ryan, M., Kremer, S., Kourjieh, M.: Towards automatic analysis of election verifiability properties. In: Armando, A., Lowe, G. (eds.) ARSPA-WITS 2010. LNCS, vol. 6186, pp. 146–163. Springer, Heidelberg (2010). doi:10.1007/978-3-642-16074-5_11
82. Springall, D., Finkenauer, T., Durumeric, Z., Kitcat, J., Hursti, H., MacAlpine, M., Halderman, J.A.: Security analysis of the Estonian Internet voting system. In: 21st ACM Conference on Computer and Communications Security (2014)
83. Stark, P.: Conservative statistical post-election audits. Ann. Appl. Stat. (2008)
84. Stark, P.B.: Super-simple simultaneous single-ballot risk-limiting audits. In: Proceedings of the 2010 International Conference on Electronic Voting Technology/Workshop on Trustworthy Elections, August 2010
85. Stark, P.B., Teague, V.: Verifiable European elections: risk-limiting audits for d'hondt and its relatives. USENIX J. Election Technol. Syst. 1(3), 18–39 (2014)
86. Stark, P.B., Wagner, D.A.: Evidence-based elections. IEEE Secur. Priv. Mag. 10(05), 33–41 (2012)
87. Terelius, B., Wikström, D.: Proofs of restricted shuffles. In: Bernstein, D.J., Lange, T. (eds.) AFRICACRYPT 2010. LNCS, vol. 6055, pp. 100–113. Springer, Heidelberg (2010). doi:10.1007/978-3-642-12678-9_7
88. Tideman, T.N.: Independence of clones as a criterion for voting rules. Soc. Choice Welfare 4(3), 185–206 (1987)
89. Trayno, I.: Russia accused of unleashing cyberwar to disable Estonia, May 2007. http://www.theguardian.com/world/2007/may/17/topstories3.russia
90. Unruh, D., Müller-Quade, J.: Universally composable incoercibility. In: Rabin, T. (ed.) CRYPTO 2010. LNCS, vol. 6223, pp. 411–428. Springer, Heidelberg (2010). doi:10.1007/978-3-642-14623-7_22

91. U.S. Vote Foundation and Galois: The future of voting: End-to-end verifiable Internet voting specification and feasibility assessment study (2015). https://www.usvotefoundation.org/sites/default/files/E2EVIV_full_report.pdf
92. Wallach, D.: Security and Reliability of Webb County's ES&S Voting System and the March 06 Primary Election. Expert Report in Flores v, Lopez (2006)
93. Zagórski, F., Carback, R.T., Chaum, D., Clark, J., Essex, A., Vora, P.L.: Remotegrity: design and use of an end-to-end verifiable remote voting system. In: Jacobson, M., Locasto, M., Mohassel, P., Safavi-Naini, R. (eds.) ACNS 2013. LNCS, vol. 7954, pp. 441–457. Springer, Heidelberg (2013). doi:10.1007/978-3-642-38980-1_28

Towards a Mechanized Proof of Selene Receipt-Freeness and Vote-Privacy

Alessandro Bruni, Eva Drewsen, and Carsten Schürmann(✉)

IT University of Copenhagen, Copenhagen, Denmark
{albr,carsten}@itu.dk, edrewsen@gmail.com

Abstract. Selene is a novel voting protocol that supports individual verifiability, Vote-Privacy and Receipt-Freeness. The scheme provides tracker numbers that allow voters to retrieve their votes from a public bulletin board and a commitment scheme that allows them to hide their vote from a potential coercer. So far, however, Selene was never studied formally. The Selene protocol was neither completely formalized, nor were the correctness proofs for Vote-Privacy and Receipt-Freeness.

In this paper, we give a formal model for a simplified version of Selene in the symbolic model, along with a machine-checked proof of Vote-Privacy and Receipt-Freeness. All proofs are checked with the Tamarin theorem prover.

1 Introduction

The original motivation of the Selene voting protocol [17] was to design a voting protocol that is verifiable, usable, and guarantees Vote-Privacy (VP) and Receipt-Freeness (RF). Selene's hallmark characteristics is that it does not require voters to check their votes on a bulletin board using long hashes of encrypted ballots, but instead works with readable and memorisable tracker numbers.

Selene is a voting protocol that could, at least in theory, be used in binding elections. One way to increase the confidence in its correctness is to use formal methods. The more complex a protocol the more likely are design mistakes, and the earlier such mistakes can be found and fixed, the better it is for all stakeholders involved. Selene uses an ElGamal crypto system, two independent phases of mixing, Pedersen style trap-door commitments and zero-knowledge proofs of knowledge.

In this paper we apply Tamarin to mechanize the proofs of correctness for VP and RF for Selene. First, we model Selene in the Tamarin language. The first model corresponds to the original Selene protocol described in Sect. 2. Using

This work was funded in part through the Danish Council for Strategic Research, Programme Comission on Strategic Growth Technologies under grant 10-092309. This publication was also made possible by NPRP grant NPRP 7-988-1-178 from the Qatar National Research Fund (a member of Qatar Foundation). The statements made herein are solely the responsibility of the authors.

R. Krimmer et al. (Eds.): E-Vote-ID 2017, LNCS 10615, pp. 110–126, 2017.
DOI: 10.1007/978-3-319-68687-5_7

Tamarin, we prove VP and RF, but only under the assumptions that coercer and voters do not collude. Tamarin constructs a counter example otherwise. We then strengthen the model according to a fix that was already described in the original Selene paper and then show VP and RF. Tamarin can no longer find a counter example.

For the purpose of mechanization, we also develop a precise message sequence chart for full Selene, which we then simplify further to become suitably representable in Tamarin. Tamarin is described in Sect. 3. While working with Tamarin, we also discovered a few completeness issues with the implementation of Tamarin that are currently being worked on by the Tamarin team.

Contributions. We describe a formalisation of Selene. A description of the full formalization can be found in [9]. We propose a simplified model of Selene, where explicit mixing is replaced by random multi-set reductions. We formalise our simplified model of Selene in Tamarin, and express the properties of VP and RF in our model. We describe the counter example and the modified model for which show VP and RF. All Tamarin proof scripts can be found at https://github.com/EvaSleva/selene-proofs.

Related work. The extended version of the original Selene paper [17] includes in the appendix a partial argument of correctness of the main construction, however it does not provide a formal proof of the scheme. Other voting protocols have undergone formal analysis, such as the FOO [11], Okamoto [15] and Lee et al. [13], which have been analysed in [7]. An analysis of Helios [2] is presented in [5] and of the Norwegian e-voting protocol [12] in [6]. The arguments are partly formalized, for example in the applied π-calculus [1] and the theorem prover ProVerif [4]. Recently the Dreier et al. [8] extended the equational reasoning of multiset rewrite rules in Tamarin, which have been pivotal for our development, and applied this technique to the analyses of the FOO and Okamoto protocols.

Organization. This paper is organized as follows. In Sect. 2 we describe the full Selene voting protocol as described in [17] as message sequence charts. In Sect. 3 we give a brief introduction into the Tamarin tool and explain syntactic categories and the Tamarin rewrite engine. In Sect. 4, we describe then the two Tamarin models, and present the result of mechanizing the proofs of VP and RF. Finally, we conclude and assess results in Sect. 7.

2   The Selene Voting Protocol

The purpose of Selene is to construct a receipt-free scheme ensuring individual verifiability, i.e. voters can check that their vote is tallied in the final result. Selene achieves this by giving each user a *tracker number* that will point to their vote on a public bulletin board, containing all cast votes. The scheme maintains *vote-privacy*, since none of the involved parties—besides the voters themselves—learns who cast each vote; *individual verifiability*, since the protocol gives a proof to the voters that their vote has been tallied; and *receipt-freeness*, since voters have no way of proving how they voted to a potential coercer, because they can fake the proof that should convince the coercer how they voted.

The involved parties in the protocol are the *Voters* (V_i); an *Election Authority* (EA) responsible for checking their identities and issuing the tracking numbers; a *Web Bulletin Board* (WBB) that publishes the intermediate stages of the voting process, as well as the anonymized, decrypted votes; a *Mixnet* (M) performing distributed re-encryption of the tracking numbers and the votes; and a number of *Tellers* (T), performing distributed threshold decryption of the votes.

Tracker numbers must remain unlinkable to the voter from the perspective of the various parties involved; at the same time, one must be assured that each voter is given a distinct tracker number. This problem is solved by the distributed Mixnet carrying along proofs of re-encryption. The Tellers produce a Pedersen-style commitment for each voter to their tracker number, also in a distributed fashion; they also decrypt the votes and tracker numbers, which are finally posted publicly on the Bulletin Board. To ensure that the computations are performed correctly, non-interactive zero knowledge proofs are carried throughout the protocol.

2.1 Re-Encryption Mixnets and Pedersen-Style Commitments

At the heart of the Selene protocol are two useful properties of the ElGamal cryptosystem, which we now briefly review: it can perform randomized re-encryptions and can act as a commitment scheme.

The ElGamal encryption scheme operates under a cyclic group $\mathbb{G}$ of order q and generator g. For any given private key $sk \in \mathbb{Z}_q$; the corresponding public key is $pk = g^{sk}$; the encryption of a message $m \in \mathbb{G}$ intended for the owner of sk is the ElGamal tuple $(\alpha, \beta) = (g^r, m \cdot pk^r)$ given a uniformly random choice of $r \in \mathbb{Z}_q$; finally, decryption is performed by computing $m = \frac{\beta}{\alpha^{sk}}$.

Re-encryption. Given an encryption pair $(\alpha, \beta) = (g^r, m \cdot pk^r)$ with $m \in \mathbb{G}$ and uniformly random $r \in \mathbb{Z}_q$, one can compute a randomized re-encryption of m without knowing the secret key sk. Computing the pair $(\alpha \cdot g^{r'}, \beta \cdot pk^{r'})$ with uniformly random $r' \in \mathbb{Z}_q$, is equal to $(g^{(r+r')}, m \cdot pk^{(r+r')})$ and hence decrypts to the same value of m while being indistinguishable from the former encryption without having the secret key sk. Shuffling mixnets chain this sort of encryption on a set of encrypted values, such that if at least one link in the mixnet is kept secret, the final cipher texts will be unlinkable to the original input, albeit encrypting the same values.

Pedersen-style commitments. ElGamal cryptosystems also allow to commit to a message without revealing it right away. Given a message $m \in \mathbb{M}$, with $\mathbb{M} \subseteq \mathbb{G}$ and small $|\mathbb{M}|$ (e.g. the number of random tracker numbers chosen for the election), one computes the commitment of m as $\beta = g^m \cdot pk^r$ for some randomly uniform $r \in \mathbb{Z}_q$. To reveal the message m, simply output $\alpha = g^r$ and compute $\gamma = \frac{\beta}{\alpha^{sk}} = g^m$, then check against all $m' \in \mathbb{M}$ to find the matching $g^{m'} = \gamma$.

The Pedersen-style commitment scheme constitutes the core of the individual verifiability and receipt-freeness in Selene. First, the voters can be convinced that the protocol behaved correctly by committing in advance to the tracking number that will be linked to their vote, which they can publicly check. It is in fact believed to be hard to compute a reveal message α' that decrypts to a different m' knowing only m, pk and r, as it reduces to solving the discrete logarithm problem. Most importantly, the voters (knowing sk and α) can construct the fake α' by computing $\alpha' = g^{\frac{m-m'}{sk}} \cdot \alpha$. This makes it practically impossible for anyone but the voter to construct a fake receipt, thus the voters can trust that the protocol behaved correctly, whereas a potential coercer cannot trust any receipt from the voter. For a more detailed explanation of Pedersen-style commitment schemes we refer to the original paper [16].

2.2 Protocol Steps

We will now explain the main steps of Selene. Before voting begins, each voter V_i must be given a tuple on the WBB containing their public key, the encrypted tracker number and the trap door commitment to the tracker number: $(pk_i, \{g^{n_i}\}_{pk_T}, \beta)$. This process is as follows:

Set up. All voters are assumed to have their public/secret key pairs: $(pk_i = g^{sk_i}, sk_i)$. The election authority publicly creates unique tracker numbers n_i for each voter, computes g^{n_i} and the ElGamal encryption under the teller's public key: $\{g^{n_i}\}_{pk_T}$. These terms are posted on the WBB:

$$(n_i, g^{n_i}, \{g^{n_i}\}_{pk_T})$$

These are put through a sequence of verifiable re-encryption mixes and the shuffled numbers are assigned to the voters and posted on the WBB:

$$(pk_i, \{g^{n_{\pi(i)}}\}_{pk_T})$$

Since the numbers have gone through multiple mixes, no single teller knows this assignment. The shuffling is verifiable however, so it preserves the original tracker numbers.

Creation of trap-door commitments. The trapdoor commitments are created in a distributed fashion among the tellers. For each voter i, each teller j creates a fresh random $r_{i,j}$, computes $\{g^{r_{i,j}}\}_{pk_T}$ and $\{pk_i^{r_{i,j}}\}_{pk_T}$. For each voter, the product of the second elements are formed:

$$\{pk_i^{r_i}\}_{pk_T} = \prod_{j=1}^{t} \{pk_i^{r_{i,j}}\}_{pk_T}$$

where by exploiting the multiplicative homomorphic property of ElGamal:

$$r^i := \sum_{j=1}^{t} r^{i,j}$$

Then the product of $\{pk_i^{r_i}\}_{pk_T}$ and $\{g^{n_{\pi(i)}}\}_{pk_T}$ is formed to obtain the encrypted trapdoor commitment: $\{pk_i^{r_i} \cdot g^{n_{\pi(i)}}\}_{pk_T}$. The commitments are decrypted and posted on the WBB along with the voter's identity and the encrypted tracker number:

$$(pk_i, \{g^{n_{\pi(i)}}\}_{pk_T}, (pk_i^{r_i} \cdot g^{n_{\pi(i)}}), \qquad)$$

All these steps with proofs and audits are also posted. The last entry is left blank for the vote. The tellers keep their $g^{r_{i,j}}$ terms secret for now.

Voting. Each voter encrypts and signs their vote $Sign_{V_i}(\{Vote_i\}_{pk_T})$ and sends it along with a proof of knowledge of the plaintext. The signature and proof are needed to ensure "ballot independence" [19] and to prevent an attacker copying the vote as their own. The server checks for duplication, checks proofs and pairs off the vote with the key corresponding to the private key which it was signed. The entry on the WBB now looks like this:

$$(pk_i, \{g^{n_{\pi(i)}}\}_{pk_T}, (pk_i^{r_i} \cdot g^{n_{\pi(i)}}), Sign_{V_i}(\{Vote_i\}_{pk_T}))$$

Decryption and tabulation. For each row on the WBB, the second and fourth terms (which are the tracker and vote) are taken out and put through verifiable, parallel, re-encryption mixes, and threshold decrypted. We then have a list of pairs: $(g^{n_{\pi(i)}}, Vote_i)$ from which the tracker can be derived:

$$(n_{\pi(i)}, Vote_i)$$

Revealing the trackers. After the trackers and votes have been available for a suitable amount of time, the voter receives the $g^{r_{i,j}}$ terms from all the tellers through a private channel and combines them to form g^{r_i}, which is the α term of the ElGamal encryption under the voters' PKs. The $g^{n_{\pi(i)}} \cdot pk_i^{r_i}$ posted earlier is the β component, and the voter can now form the ElGamal cryptogram: $(g^{r_i}, g^{n_{\pi(i)}} \cdot pk_i^{r_i})$, which they can decrypt with their secret key to reveal $g^{n_{\pi(i)}}$ and hence $n_{\pi(i)}$.

In case of coercion, it is easy for the voter to compute an alternative $(g^{r_i'})$, which will open the encryption to any tracker number they would like. However, this is hard to do without the secret key, so it would not be feasible for an attacker to reveal the wrong tracker to the voter. Due to space limitations, we refer to [9] for the full formalization of Selene.

3   Tamarin

Tamarin is a specialised theorem prover for security protocols based on labelled multiset rewriting. It can prove both trace properties and equivalence properties on labelled transition systems. Tamarin supports convergent equational theories and the AC theories for Diffie-Hellman and multisets [8, 18]. In Tamarin models, multiset rewriting rules encode both the protocol specification and the Dolev-Yao attacker. Because of its multiset semantics, the tool supports precise analysis of protocols with state and unbounded numer of sessions, however at the cost of non-termination, since the problem is undecidable in general.

Definition 1 (Rules, facts, terms, equational theories and semantics).
A term is either a variable x or a function $f(t_1,\ldots,t_n)$ of fixed arity n, with $t_1,\ldots,t_n$ terms. Equality of terms $=_E$ is defined as the smallest reflexive, symmetric and transitive closure of a user-defined equational theory E. Variables are annotated with a sort system, with a top generic sort msg and two incompatible sub-sorts: ˜ for nonces and \$ for public messages. Facts are of the form $\mathsf{F}(t_1,\ldots,t_n)$, with fixed arity n and $t_1,\ldots,t_n$ terms. There are six reserved fact symbols: Fr for fresh nonces; In and Out for protocol input and output; KU, KD and K for attacker knowledge. All other facts are user-defined. Persistent facts are prefixed with the ! (bang) modality, and can be consumed arbitrarily often.

A labelled multiset rewrite rule is a rule of the form $l\!-\!\lfloor a\rfloor\!\mapsto\! r$, where the multisets of facts l, a and r represent the rule premise, label and conclusion. We omit the brackets when $a = \emptyset$. A state S is a multiset of facts. We define the semantics of a rule $l\!-\!\lfloor a\rfloor\!\mapsto\! r$ as the relation $S \xrightarrow{\ \sigma(a)\ } S'$ with substitution σ where $\sigma(l) \subseteq_E S$ and $S' = S \setminus_E \sigma(l) \uplus \sigma(r)$.

Functions and equations model cryptography symbolically: for example asymmetric encryption and decryption with the equation $adec(aenc(m, pk(sk)), sk) =_E m$, saying that the encryption of m using $pk(sk)$ only succeeds with the corresponding secret key sk. In Sect. 4.2 we present a more advanced equational theory that covers the commitment and re-encryption schemes used in Selene.

Observational Equivalences. Tamarin supports both trace-based properties and observational equivalence in the models. Trace-based peoperties suffice to model secrecy and authentication. However in this work we focus on observational equivalences, i.e. show that an adversary cannot distinguish between two systems, specified by the left and the right projections of special terms $diff(t_1, t_2)$ occurring in the model. To define observational equivalence we split the rules into *system rules (Sys)*, *environment rules (Env)* and *interface rules (IF)*. In the following, $\mathcal{F}^{\#}$ and $\mathcal{G}^{\#}$ are finite multisets of facts and ground facts, while ρ is the set of all rule recipes. For a detailed definition of these concepts see [3].

Definition 2 (Observational Equivalence). *Two sets of multiset rewrite rules S_A and S_B are observational equivalent with respect to an environment Env, written $S_A \approx_{Env} S_B$, if, given the labelled transition system defined by the rules $S_A \cup IF \cup Env$ and $S_B \cup IF \cup Env$, there is a relation $\mathcal{R}$ containing the initial states, such that for all states $(S_A, S_B) \in \mathcal{R}$ we have:*

- *If $S_A \xrightarrow[a]{r} S'_A$ and r is the recipe of a rule in $Env \cup IF$, then there exists action $a' \in \mathcal{F}^{\#}$, and $S'_B \in \mathcal{G}^{\#}$, such that $S_B \xrightarrow[a']{r} S'_B$, and $(S'_A, S'_B) \in \mathcal{R}$.*
- *If $S_A \xrightarrow[a]{r} S'_A$ and r is the recipe of a rule in S_A, then there exist recipes $r_1,\ldots,r_n \in \rho$ of rules in S_B, actions $a_1,\ldots,a_n \in \mathcal{F}^{\#}$, $n \geq 0$, and $S'_B \in \mathcal{G}^{\#}$, such that $S_B \xrightarrow[a_1]{r_1} \ldots \xrightarrow[a_n]{r_n} S'_B$, and $(S'_A, S'_B) \in \mathcal{R}$.*
- *We have the same in the other direction.*

Tamarin does not directly prove observational equivalences: it rather proves a stronger notion of equivalence, called *mirroring of dependency graphs*. A *dependency graph* is defined as a graph where the nodes are ground rule instances, and there is a directed arc from a rule r_1 to r_2 iff r_1 produces a fact that is consumed by r_2. Furthermore, it is required that all input facts have incoming edges, that non-persistent facts are consumed at most once, and that exactly one rule has no outgoing edges (the goal rule). *Mirroring* is defined as an isomorphism between two graphs modulo the equational theory. Let $mirrors(dg)$ denote the mirrors of a dependency graph dg.

To prove mirroring, Tamarin constructs all possible instantiations of dependency graphs for the left- and right-hand side systems, and shows that for each dependency graph on one side, there exists one on the other that mirrors it. If such construction is possible, then we say that the two systems are *dependency graph equivalent*. We will not dive into the details however, but rather present the essential result of the proof technique that this paper uses.

Theorem 1 (Dependency graph equivalence implies observational equivalence). *Let S be a bi-system. If $L(S) \sim_{DG,Env} R(S)$ then $L(S) \approx_{Env} R(S)$*

Our proofs of vote-privacy and receipt-freeness in Selene rely on constructing two systems using *diff*-terms and then checking whether *mirroring* holds. For a full explanation of Tamarin and the techniques we just briefly covered, we refer to the official documentation [20] and research papers [3,8,14,18].

4   Selene Tamarin Model

Assumptions. To make the protocol amenable to formal verification we have made the following assumptions in the model: firstly, we assume that all the participants in the protocol behave honestly, except the attacker and the voter being coerced. Selene claims to be secure even under partially compromised Tellers and Mixnets, by using threshold and distributed encryption schemes. The original Selene paper does not commit to specific schemes in this regard, and these are complex verification problems out of reach for current symbolic theorem provers like Tamarin. Instead of explicitly modeling them, we only model their defining features and assume a proper implementation. Furthermore, our voting system is restricted to two voters and two candidates. For modeling vote-privacy and receipt-freeness properties in voting systems two voters are enough [7], hence this restriction does not pose further limitations in the analysis.

Simplifications to the Protocol. Given said assumptions we have made the following simplifications to our model. Since the protocol is honest, we do not need to model zero knowledge proofs, e.g. reencryption proofs in Selene: by the model each entity executes the protocol, hence no proof of computation is needed. Only one teller is modelled, as multiple tellers in Selene are used to perform cryptographic operations (e.g. reencryption of the tracker numbers) without having access to the decrypted data so that one dishonest teller cannot link a decrypted tracker number to the voter. Since we assume that the tellers are honest, we do not need more than one. Similarly we do not model the mixnet explicitly, and we take advantage of the non-determinism of Tamarin rules, and of the associative-commutative multiset operators, to ensure that the link is lost between the identities of the voters and their tracker numbers, at least from the perspective of the attacker. In our model, every occurrence of mixing is replaced with a synchronisation point and a multiset operation. Finally, whenever an authentic and confidential channel is required in the protocol, we model that with a linear fact that is not accessible to the attacker, whereas if the channel is only authentic, but public, the attacker receives the value separately.

4.1   The Protocol

We model our protocol after the scheme presented in Fig. 1. As discussed earlier, the Mixnet does not appear in our simplified scheme, whose behaviour we model with the non-deterministic semantic of rewrite rules. We assume that each voter V_i has a public key pk_i, and the teller public key is pk_T. Initially the EA generates a unique tracker number for each voter V_i, and publishes them through the WBB. With respect to the full version, we omit the zero-knowledge proofs, the re-encryption mixing and the distributed decryption, as we assume to trust the Tellers, Mixnet and the Election Authority.

The teller then creates a commitment to the tracker number for each voter with their public key, and posts them on the WBB. Voters can now cast their vote by sending to their teller the encrypted and signed choice. After voting has ended, the encrypted votes are posted on the WBB along with the voter identity and commitment. Again the model omits the second pass of re-encryption randomisation by the mixnet, and posts directly the decrypted vote and tracker number on the WBB.

After a suitable period, the randomness of the commitments is sent to the voters. The voters can then combine this with their commitment to find their tracker number, and check the corresponding vote on the WBB.

4.2   Modelling Approach

Channels. Selene assumes the existence of secure and authentic communication channels. We model these by the use of linear facts that ensure a correspondence between inputs and outputs, and add a corresponding Out fact when the communication is also public, e.g.:

$$\mathsf{Fr}(\tilde{x}) \rightarrow \mathsf{SendValue}(\tilde{x}), \mathsf{Out}(\tilde{x}) \qquad \text{(AuthCh)}$$

We use this approach as an alternative to explicitly modelling encryption in public channels: this has the advantage of greatly reducing the search space.

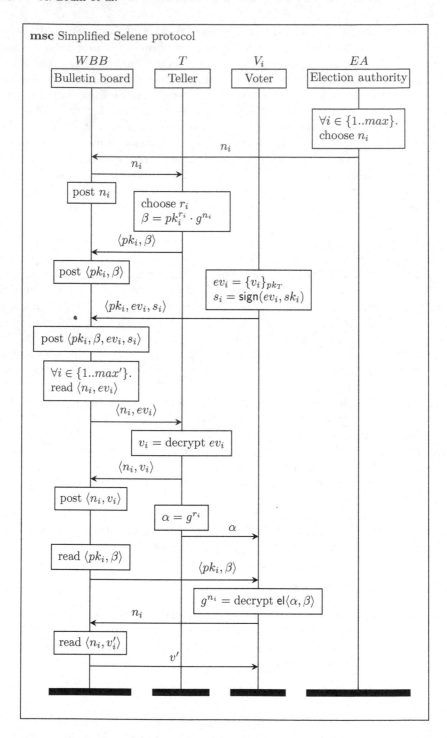

Fig. 1. Simplified Selene protocol

Equations. Trap-door commitments are the central cryptographic primitive of the Selene protocol. We model them with the functions $commit/3$, $open/3$ and $fake/4$. The term $commit(m, r, pk)$ models a commitment to value m using the randomness r and the public key $pk = pk(sk)$. To open the commitment one applies $open(commit(m, r, pk(sk)), r, sk)$. Those in possession of the secret key sk can construct a receipt $fake(m, r, sk, m_2)$ for another message m_2, and it should hold that $open(commit(m, r, pk(sk)), fake(m, r, sk, m_2), sk) = m_2$. Thus we have:

$$open(commit(n_1, r, pk(sk)), r, sk) \to n_1$$
$$commit(n_2, fake(n_1, r, sk, n_2), pk(sk)) \to commit(n_1, r, pk(sk))$$

These equations do not produce a confluent rewriting system, and it is therefore not convergent, and this can cause Tamarin to produce false results. We use the Maude Church-Rosser checker to produce their Knuth-Bendix completion and get:

$$open(commit(n_1, r, pk(sk)), fake(n_1, r, sk, n_2), sk) \to n_2$$

However adding this equation still does not make it confluent, since the checker keeps finding new and larger critical pairs whenever the resulting equation is added. In order to fix this we add the equation:

$$fake(n_2, fake(n_1, r, sk, n_2), sk, n_3) \to fake(n_1, r, sk, n_3)$$

Using the Maude Church-Rosser checker this is now confirmed to yield a confluent rewriting system [10].

Shuffling. When the full Selene protocol of Sect. 2 requires shuffling the votes through a re-encryption mixnet, we use multisets to model the reordering, for example:

$$\mathsf{SendTracker}(n_1), \mathsf{SendTracker}(n_2) \to$$
$$\mathsf{!PublishTrackers}(n_1 + n_2), \mathsf{Out}(n_1 + n_2) \quad \text{(Shuffle)}$$
$$\mathsf{!PublishTrackers}(n_1' + n_2') \to \quad \text{(Receive)}$$

In Tamarin, the AC symbol $+$ denotes multiset union. It is therefore possible to match the two rules (Shuffle) and (Receive) both with the substitution $\{n_1/n_1', n_2/n_2'\}$ and $\{n_1/n_2', n_2/n_1'\}$, making irrelevant the order of inputs and outputs. Furthermore, this rule acts as a synchronization point.

4.3   Basic Model

In this section, we describe the common rules between the models used for the vote-privacy and receipt-freeness proofs of Sects. 5 and 6. Our models have a fixed set of agents, that is two voters V_1 and V_2 and a teller T. Rule (Setup) generates the keys for both agents, and outputs the corresponding public keys. The state of each agent is initialised with a predicate $\mathsf{St}_{\mathsf{X0}}$ where X denotes the agent type and the arguments denote their knowledge, including—for the voters—their choice of candidates specified using *diff* terms. Two teller instances are created to interact with each of the voters. The fact EA starts the generation of the random tracker numbers by the Election Authority, as described by the next rule.

$$
\begin{aligned}
&\mathsf{Fr}(^\sim\!sk_{V_1}), \mathsf{Fr}(^\sim\!sk_{V_2}), \mathsf{Fr}(^\sim\!sk_T)\!-\!\!\lceil\mathsf{OnlyOnce}\rceil\!\mapsto \\
&\qquad \mathsf{Out}(pk(^\sim\!sk_{V_1})), \mathsf{Out}(pk(^\sim\!sk_{V_2})), \mathsf{Out}(pk(^\sim\!sk_T)), \\
&\qquad \mathsf{St}_{\mathsf{V0}}(\mathrm{V}_1, \mathit{diff}(\mathrm{A},\mathrm{B}), {}^\sim\!sk_{V_1}, pk(^\sim\!sk_{V_1})), \\
&\qquad \mathsf{St}_{\mathsf{V0}}(\mathrm{V}_2, \mathit{diff}(\mathrm{B},\mathrm{A}), {}^\sim\!sk_{V_2}, pk(^\sim\!sk_{V_2})), \\
&\qquad \mathsf{St}_{\mathsf{T0}}(\mathrm{T}, {}^\sim\!skT, pk(^\sim\!sk_{V_1})), \\
&\qquad \mathsf{St}_{\mathsf{T0}}(\mathrm{T}, {}^\sim\!skT, pk(^\sim\!sk_{V_2})), \\
&\qquad \mathsf{EA}(pk(^\sim\!sk_{V_1}), pk(^\sim\!sk_{V_2}))
\end{aligned}
\qquad\text{(Setup)}
$$

In rule (EA) the Election Authority generates the tracker numbers n_i and outputs them publicly. The trackers are shuffled using the $+$ operator, and the pk_Vs are used to ensure that both voters don't get assigned the same tracker.

$$
\begin{aligned}
&\mathsf{EA}(pk_{V_1}, pk_{V_2}), \mathsf{Fr}(^\sim\!n_1), \mathsf{Fr}(^\sim\!n_2) \rightarrow \\
&\qquad !\mathsf{ShuffleTrackers}(\langle^\sim\!n_1, pk_{V_1}\rangle + \langle^\sim\!n_2, pk_{V_2}\rangle), \\
&\qquad \mathsf{Out}(^\sim\!n_1, {}^\sim\!n_2)
\end{aligned}
\qquad\text{(EA)}
$$

Rule (T1) represents the teller receiving one shuffled tracker n_i from the multiset produced by EA. The teller assigns n_i to a voter V_i by creating a commitment to its value with the voter's public key and a newly generated random value α, then stored in the state fact. The commitment is published on the WBB using both $\mathsf{PostCommitment}$ and an Out fact:

$$
\begin{aligned}
&\mathsf{let}\ \beta_i = commit(n_i, \alpha_i, pk_{V_i})\ \mathsf{in} \\
&!\mathsf{ShuffleTrackers}(\langle n_i, pk_{V_i}\rangle + y), \mathsf{Fr}(\alpha_i), \mathsf{St}_{\mathsf{T0}}(T, {}^\sim\!sk_T, pk_{V_i}) \rightarrow \\
&\qquad \mathsf{Out}(\langle pk_{V_i}, \beta_i\rangle), !\mathsf{PostCommitment}(pk_{V_i}, \beta_i), \\
&\qquad \mathsf{St}_{\mathsf{T1}}(T, {}^\sim\!sk_T, pk_{V_i}, \alpha_i, n_i, \beta_i)
\end{aligned}
\qquad\text{(T1)}
$$

Rule (V1) enacts the voting stage. To simplify the model and since we assume a trusted teller, voting is represented by a predicate $\mathsf{SendVote}$ that includes the choice and the teller's public key:

$$
\mathsf{St}_{\mathsf{V0}}(V_i, v_i, {}^\sim\!sk_{V_i}, pk_{V_i}) \rightarrow \mathsf{SendVote}(v_i, pk_{V_i}), \mathsf{St}_{\mathsf{V1}}(V_i, v_i, {}^\sim\!sk_{V_i}, pk_{V_i}) \qquad\text{(V1)}
$$

Rules (T2) and (T2-Sync) represent the teller receiving the two votes cast, revealing to each voter the randomness to recover their tracker numbers, synchronising and outputting both pairs of vote and tracker number publicly.

$$\text{SendVote}(v_i, pk_{V_i}), \text{St}_{T1}(T, {}^{\sim}sk_T, pk_{V_i}, \alpha_i, n_i, \beta_i) \rightarrow$$
$$\text{SendSecretToVoter}(\alpha_i), \text{PassVote}(v_i, n_i) \qquad \text{(T2)}$$
$$\text{PassVote}(v_1, n_1), \text{PassVote}(v_2, n_2) \rightarrow$$
$$!\text{PublishVote}(\langle n_1, v_1 \rangle + \langle n_2, v_2 \rangle), \text{Out}(\langle n_1, v_1 \rangle + \langle n_2, v_2 \rangle) \qquad \text{(T2-Sync)}$$

Finally, rule (V2) models the checking phase, where the voter retrieves their commitment and their secret randomness to compute their tracker number. The rule also checks that the vote is posted correctly on the bulletin board by requiring the presence of the corresponding tuple in *PublishVote*.

$$\text{let } n_i = open(\beta_i, \alpha_i, {}^{\sim}sk_{V_i}) \text{ in}$$
$$\text{SendSecretToVoter}(\alpha_i), !\text{PostCommitment}(pk_{V_i}, \beta_i),$$
$$!\text{PublishVote}(\langle n_i, v_i \rangle + y), \text{St}_{V1}(V_i, v_i, {}^{\sim}sk_{V_i}, pk_{V_i}) \rightarrow \qquad \text{(V2)}$$

5 Vote-Privacy

Vote-privacy is the basic requirement to any electronic voting system, where running the protocol should not reveal the intention of each voter. Obviously one cannot simply model vote-privacy as an observational equivalence property where one voter votes in two possible ways and the rest remains unchanged, since the result would show up in the final tally. Instead, Delaune et al. [7] define vote-privacy as an equivalence between two systems where two voters V_1 and V_2 swap their choices of candidates A and B. The public outcome of the election remains unchanged, hence an attacker must observe the difference between the two systems from other information that is exchanged throughout the election.

The model introduced in Sect. 4.3 is sufficient to prove vote-privacy of Selene: it produces two systems where the two candidates V_1 and V_2 swap their votes A and B, using the *diff* terms. Tamarin can prove mirroring automatically, hence by Theorem 1 we conclude that they are observationally equivalent.

6 Receipt-Freeness

Receipt-freeness is a stronger property than vote-privacy. To be receipt-free, a protocol must not reveal the choice of a voter even when the voter reveals all their private information to an attacker [7].

Selene claims to be receipt-free as long as the underlying vote-casting scheme is receipt-free. The extra information the voter has in Selene is a commitment to the tracking number linked to their vote, and a receipt that opens the commitment. However each voter can fake their own receipt hence the attacker cannot infer from the voter's private information whether the receipt is fake or real [17].

6.1 Modelling

Like in vote-privacy, the model shows two systems in which two voters swap votes. However, V_1 always outputs a receipt for A regardless of how they voted.

The coercer should not be able to determine that V_1 is producing fake receipts. We modify the model of Sect. 4.3 by splitting the rule (V2) into the rules (V2-1) and (V2-2). Rule (V2-2) is identical to (V2) for voter V_2 and only checks that their vote appears on the WBB, while (V2-1) outputs the secret information of V_1 (the coerced voter), including their secret key, the desired tracker number, and either a fake or a real receipt:

$$\text{let } n_1 = open(\beta, \alpha, \tilde{} sk_V) \text{ in}$$
$$\mathsf{SendSecretToVoter}(\alpha), !\mathsf{PostCommitment}(pk_V, \beta),$$
$$!\mathsf{PublishVote}(\langle n_1, v \rangle + \langle n_2, \mathit{diff}(B, A) \rangle),$$
$$\mathsf{St}_{V1}(V_1, v, \tilde{} sk_V, pk_V) \rightarrow$$
$$\qquad \mathsf{Out}(\tilde{} sk_V), \mathsf{Out}(\beta),$$
$$\qquad \mathsf{Out}(\mathit{diff}(n_1, n_2)),$$
$$\qquad \mathsf{Out}(\mathit{diff}(\mathit{fake}(n_1, \alpha, \tilde{} sk_V, n_1), \mathit{fake}(n_1, \alpha, \tilde{} sk_V, n_2))),$$
$$\qquad \mathsf{Out}(\mathit{diff}(v, A)) \qquad\qquad\qquad\qquad\qquad\qquad \text{(V2-1)}$$

Here, V_1 checks for their vote, as well V_2's vote, and saves this tracker number as n_2. In the first system V_1 actually voted for A as the coercer wanted, and outputs the real receipts. In the second system V_1 voted for B, but outputs fake receipts, as if they voted for A. In the rule's conclusion V_1 outputs all the available values, which are: the private key $\tilde{} sk_V$, the commitment β, the tracker number n_1, or n_2, the secret randomness, and finally either the actual vote or the fake vote.

The randomness is a *fake* function that either opens the commitment to the voter's real tracker number n_1, or to the other tracker number n_2. As a modeling expedient we use the term $\mathit{fake}(n_1, \alpha, \tilde{} sk_V, n_1)$ to denote the real receipt for V_1, instead of simply α. This is required because Tamarin converts the directed equational theories into rewrite rules, and hence the rules produced for the *fake* constructors would not apply to the basic αs. Using the model just presented Tamarin automatically proves receipt-freeness for the protocol.

Attack. The scheme poses a problem if the voter accidentally picks the coercer's own tracker number, or a tracker number of another voter under coercion. This does not reveal the voter's actual vote, but the coercer will know the voter is lying. This is a known flaw in the protocol and is also explained in the paper presenting Selene. We can reproduce this attack in our model by changing the rule (V2-2) to also output V_2's tracker number:

$$\text{let } n_1 = open(\beta, \alpha, \tilde{} sk_V) \text{ in}$$
$$\mathsf{SendSecretToVoter}(\alpha), !\mathsf{PostCommitment}(pk_V, \beta),$$
$$!\mathsf{PublishVote}(\langle n_1, v \rangle + y), \mathsf{St}_{V1}(V_2, v, \tilde{} sk_V, pk_V) \rightarrow \mathsf{Out}(n_1) \qquad \text{(V2-2)}$$

In fact, if the adversary knows both tracker numbers, then they can compare the trackers and see that they match when V_1 chooses to fake their receipt, while they differ when V_1 behaves honestly, violating the observational equivalence.

Fix. The authors of Selene [17] proposed a construction that removes the possibility of voters picking the coercer's tracker number. Each voter v gets $|C|$ additional tracker numbers that point to fake votes cast for each candidate of the possible choices C. The bulletin board contains $|C| \cdot v + v$ tracker-vote pairs, and computing the final tally amounts to removing $|C| \cdot v$ votes to each candidate. If a voter is being coerced and wants to reveal a fake receipt, they only need to pick one of their fake trackers that points to the desired candidate.

We model this fix in a simplified version of our original model, where we remove the non-determinism in the shuffling that contributes to space explosion. Tamarin could not terminate within 16 h on the full version using a server with 16 Intel Xeon cores and 120 GB of RAM. The partial model has no EA and does not output the trackers or the pairs on a public WBB. It works as follows: the teller generates three tracker numbers for each voter, but only creates a commitment to the first one, which will act as the voter's real tracker number.

$$\text{let } \beta = commit(n_0, \alpha_i, pk_{V_i}) \text{ in}$$
$$\mathsf{Fr}(n_0), \mathsf{Fr}(n_1), \mathsf{Fr}(n_2), \mathsf{Fr}(\alpha_i),$$
$$\mathsf{St_{T0}}(T, \tilde{}\,sk_T, pk_{V_i}, v_i') \rightarrow$$
$$\mathsf{Out}(\langle pk_{V_i}, \beta_i \rangle), !\mathsf{PostCommitment}(pk_{V_i}, \beta_i),$$
$$\mathsf{St_{T1}}(T, \tilde{}\,sk_T, pk_{V_i}, v_i', \alpha_i, n_0, n_1, n_2) \qquad \text{(T1')}$$

After receiving the vote, the teller assigns each tracker to a vote. The real vote is therefore assigned to the voter's real tracker number and to one other tracker number. All $|C| + 1$ trackers are published along with their corresponding vote. For each voter $|C|$ trackers are published along with the voter's identity, so the voter can use these in case of coercion. The extra tracker, that also points to the voter's actual cast vote, is removed from set, and therefore not published with the voter's identity.

$$\mathsf{SendVote}(v_i, pk_{V_i}), \mathsf{St_{T1}}(T, \tilde{}\,sk_T, pk_{V_i}, v_i', \alpha_i, n_0, n_1, n_2) \rightarrow$$
$$\mathsf{SendSecretToVoter}(\alpha_i),$$
$$!\mathsf{PublishTracker}(pk_{V_i}, n_0), !\mathsf{PublishTracker}(pk_{V_i}, n_2),$$
$$!\mathsf{PublishVote}(n_0, v_i), !\mathsf{PublishVote}(n_1, v_i), !\mathsf{PublishVote}(n_2, v_i') \qquad \text{(T2')}$$

The difference in the checking phase is that V_1 needs to check the WBB for their personal tracker number corresponding to the coercer's desired candidate. Both votes can then be checked using the voter's two tracker numbers. The process is unchanged for voter V_2.

let $n_0 = open(\beta, \alpha, \tilde{sk}_V)$ in

SendSecretToVoter(α), !PostCommitment(pk_V, β),

!PublishTracker(pk_V, n_F), !PublishVote(n_0, v), !PublishVote($n_F, diff$(B, A)),

$St_{V1}(V_1, v, \tilde{sk}_V, pk_V) \rightarrow$

    Out($\tilde{sk}_V$), Out(β),

    Out($diff(n_0, n_F)$),

    Out($diff(fake(n_0, \alpha, \tilde{sk}_V, n_0), fake(n_0, \alpha, \tilde{sk}_V, n_F))$),

    Out($diff(v, A)$)   (V2-1')

As with the previous RF model, we can prove that the two systems produced by this model satisfy mirroring, therefore issuing a fake certificate for each candidate allows us to prove receipt-freeness even when the attacker knows the other voter's vote. This alternative protocol ensures a stronger type of receipt-freeness in which other voters' receipts can also be revealed.

7 Conclusions

In this work we built mechanised proofs receipt-freeness and vote-privacy for Selene, which claims to also offer individual and universal verifiability. Selene uses re-encryption mixnets and Pedersen-style commitment schemes, which lead to complex equational theories that were out of reach for many cryptographic theorem provers, including ProVerif [4]. We overcame the limitation on mixing by using the AC multiset operator of Tamarin, and built a confluent equational theory for the commitment scheme used in Selene.

Our models show that the Selene scheme preserves vote-privacy and that it is receipt-free as long as the fake receipts do not match the choice of another colluding voter. We also model the proposed fix, whereby each voter receives a fake tracker numbers for each candidate. These proofs confirm the claims of the original paper [17], albeit under the stricter condition that the Tellers, Mixnet and Election Authority are honest and not compromised. These restrictions were necessary since distributed re-encryptions and decryptions produce state explosions that makes it infeasible to find a proof, even when running on a virtual server with 16 Intel Xeon cores and 120 GB of RAM.

We believe that this study contributes to a better understanding of Selene, and to discover necessary conditions for its security, such as the synchronisation points required after the setup and the voting phases. As future work, it will be interesting to explore how to relax the assumption that all principals behave honestly and introduce zero-knowledge proofs to ensure their correct behaviour. Also, this study has not considered universal verifiability: while the protocol maintains individual verifiability—and that can be checked as a correspondence property in our current model—checking universal verifiability requires combining Selene with other receipt-free, universally verifiable schemes.

References

1. Abadi, M., Fournet, C.: Mobile values, new names, and secure communication. In: ACM SIGPLAN Notices, vol. 36, pp. 104–115. ACM (2001)
2. Adida, B.: Helios: Web-based open-audit voting. In: USENIX Security Symposium, vol. 17, pp. 335–348 (2008)
3. Basin, D., Dreier, J., Sasse, R.: Automated symbolic proofs of observational equivalence. In: Proceedings of the 22nd ACM SIGSAC Conference on Computer and Communications Security, pp. 1144–1155. ACM (2015)
4. Blanchet, B., Abadi, M., Fournet, C.: Automated verification of selected equivalences for security protocols. J. Logic Algebraic Program. **75**(1), 3–51 (2008)
5. Cortier, V., Smyth, B.: Attacking and fixing helios: an analysis of ballot secrecy. J. Comput. Secur. **21**(1), 89–148 (2013)
6. Cortier, V., Wiedling, C.: A formal analysis of the norwegian e-voting protocol. J. Comput. Secur. **25**(1), 21–57 (2017)
7. Delaune, S., Kremer, S., Ryan, M.: Verifying privacy-type properties of electronic voting protocols. J. Comput. Secur. **17**(4), 435–487 (2009)
8. Dreier, J., Duménil, C., Kremer, S., Sasse, R.: Beyond subterm-convergent equational theories in automated verification of stateful protocols. In: 6th International Conference on Principles of Security and Trust (POST) (2017)
9. Drewsen, E.: Formal analysis of the selene voting protocol. Master's thesis, IT University of Copenhagen, June 2017
10. Durán, F., Meseguer, J.: On the church-rosser and coherence properties of conditional order-sorted rewrite theories. J. Logic Algebraic Program. **81**(7–8), 816–850 (2012)
11. Fujioka, A., Okamoto, T., Ohta, K.: A practical secret voting scheme for large scale elections. In: Seberry, J., Zheng, Y. (eds.) AUSCRYPT 1992. LNCS, vol. 718, pp. 244–251. Springer, Heidelberg (1993). doi:10.1007/3-540-57220-1_66
12. Gjøsteen, K.: The norwegian internet voting protocol. In: Kiayias, A., Lipmaa, H. (eds.) Vote-ID 2011. LNCS, vol. 7187, pp. 1–18. Springer, Heidelberg (2012). doi:10.1007/978-3-642-32747-6_1
13. Lee, B., Boyd, C., Dawson, E., Kim, K., Yang, J., Yoo, S.: Providing receipt-freeness in mixnet-based voting protocols. In: Lim, J.-I., Lee, D.-H. (eds.) ICISC 2003. LNCS, vol. 2971, pp. 245–258. Springer, Heidelberg (2004). doi:10.1007/978-3-540-24691-6_19
14. Meier, S.: Advancing automated security protocol verification. Ph.D. thesis, ETH Zürich (2013)
15. Okamoto, T.: Receipt-free electronic voting schemes for large scale elections. In: Christianson, B., Crispo, B., Lomas, M., Roe, M. (eds.) Security Protocols 1997. LNCS, vol. 1361, pp. 25–35. Springer, Heidelberg (1998). doi:10.1007/BFb0028157
16. Pedersen, T.P.: Non-interactive and information-theoretic secure verifiable secret sharing. In: Feigenbaum, J. (ed.) CRYPTO 1991. LNCS, vol. 576, pp. 129–140. Springer, Heidelberg (1992). doi:10.1007/3-540-46766-1_9
17. Ryan, P.Y.A., Rønne, P.B., Iovino, V.: Selene: voting with transparent verifiability and coercion-mitigation. In: Clark, J., Meiklejohn, S., Ryan, P.Y.A., Wallach, D., Brenner, M., Rohloff, K. (eds.) FC 2016. LNCS, vol. 9604, pp. 176–192. Springer, Heidelberg (2016). doi:10.1007/978-3-662-53357-4_12

18. Schmidt, B.: Formal analysis of key exchange protocols and physical protocols. Ph.D. thesis, Citeseer (2012)
19. Smyth, B., Bernhard, D.: Ballot secrecy and ballot independence: definitions and relations. Technical report, Cryptology ePrint Archive, Report 2013/235 (version 20141010: 082554) (2014)
20. The Tamarin Team. Tamarin-Prover Manual, April 2017

Trust Implications of DDoS Protection in Online Elections

Chris Culnane[1], Mark Eldridge[2], Aleksander Essex[3](✉), and Vanessa Teague[4]

[1] Department of Computer and Information Systems,
University of Melbourne, Melbourne, Australia
christopher.culnane@unimelb.edu.au
[2] School of Computer Science, University of Adelaide, Adelaide, Australia
mark.eldridge@student.adelaide.edu.au
[3] Department of Electrical and Computer Engineering,
University of Western Ontario, London, Canada
aessex@uwo.ca
[4] Department of Computing and Information Systems,
University of Melbourne, Melbourne, Australia
vjteague@unimelb.edu.au

Abstract. Online elections make a natural target for distributed denial of service attacks. Election agencies wary of disruptions to voting may procure DDoS protection services from a cloud provider. However, current DDoS detection and mitigation methods come at the cost of significantly increased trust in the cloud provider. In this paper we examine the security implications of denial-of-service prevention in the context of the 2017 state election in Western Australia, revealing a complex interaction between actors and infrastructure extending far beyond its borders.

Based on the publicly observable properties of this deployment, we outline several attack scenarios including one that could allow a nation state to acquire the credentials necessary to man-in-the-middle a foreign election in the context of an unrelated *domestic* law enforcement or national security operation, and we argue that a fundamental tension currently exists between trust and availability in online elections.

1   Introduction

Democratically elected governments may still aspire to the old principle of being *of the people, by the people, and for the people*. But when it comes to contemporary deployments of internet voting, the technology underpinning *how* governments are elected is a different story, and we are beginning to observe local elections carrying an increasingly multi-national footprint.

In this paper we present an analysis of the 2017 state election of Western Australia (WA) as one such case study. We found a complex interaction between jurisdictions extending far beyond WA's borders. The election software was created by a Spanish based company. The election servers were hosted in the neighbouring state of New South Wales. Voters connected to the election website via a

© Springer International Publishing AG 2017
R. Krimmer et al. (Eds.): E-Vote-ID 2017, LNCS 10615, pp. 127–145, 2017.
DOI: 10.1007/978-3-319-68687-5_8

U.S. based cloud provider. They were presented with a TLS certificate that was shared with dozens of unrelated websites in countries such as the Philippines, Lithuania, and Argentina, and that was served out of data centers in countries such as Japan, Poland, and China.

In particular this work focuses on the implications of cloud-based distributed denial of service (DDoS) protection in an election setting, revealing the existence of a tension between availability and authentication.

1.1 Background

The acceptance of an election result should not come down to trust, but it often does. Some systems, such as fully scrutinised manual counting, Risk Limiting Audits [13] and end-to-end verifiable cryptographic systems [3,5,7,11,12,16], allow voters and observers to derive evidence of an accurate election result, or to detect an inaccurate result.

Australia's iVote Internet voting system, implemented by third-party vendor Scytl, does not provide a genuine protocol for verifying the accuracy of the election outcome, relying instead on a collection of trusted and semi-trusted authorities and auditors [10]. At the time of writing, it is the largest continuing Internet voting system in the world by number of votes cast.[1] The Western Australian run was, however, very small: about 2000 votes were received, out of an electorate of 1.6 million. Election day was March 11th 2017, but iVote was available during the early voting period starting on 20th February.

For recent elections conducted in the Australian states of Western Australia and New South Wales, the iVote system was used in conjunction with Imperva Incapsula, a global content delivery network which provides mitigation of Distributed Denial of Service (DDoS) attacks.

DDoS attacks involve using a large number of connections to flood a target website, overloading systems and preventing legitimate users from logging in. It was a DDoS attack which was blamed for the failure of the Australian Government online eCensus system in August 2016 [4,14]. To mitigate these attacks, Incapsula's systems act as a TLS proxy, intercepting secure connections between the voter and the iVote servers and filtering malicious traffic.

Following our analysis of the unintended consequences of TLS proxying in the Western Australian Election, a subsequent by-election in New South Wales used Incapsula only for registrations and demonstration of iVote, not for the actual voting process itself. However, valid TLS certificates for the Western Australian and New South Wales election systems continue to be served by Incapsula servers all over the world. This illustrates the difficulty of reversing a decision to outsource trust.

Contributions. Our contributions are threefold. Firstly, we provide an analysis of the front-end iVote protocol, including the associated credential exchange and key derivation.

---

[1] The largest as a fraction of the electorate is Estonia's.

Secondly, we analyse the implications of running an internet voting system through a cloud based DDoS protection service acting as a non-transparent TLS proxy. We provide the results of a global scan to assess the scale with which Western Australian election related TLS certificates had been globally deployed. We identify and discuss the misconfigurations we discovered in the case of the Western Australian state election 2017, and analyse the feasibility of a malicious TLS proxy performing a brute force attack on voter credentials.

Finally, we examine the injection of JavaScript performed by the DDoS protection service, and provide a proof of concept of how this could be utilised by a malicious entity to compromise voter credentials and modify ballots. We disclosed our findings to the Western Australian Electoral Commission, both before and during the election. They addressed the server misconfiguration, but continued to use the cloud based DDoS protection service for the duration of the election.

Paper Organization. The rest of the paper is organized as follows. Section 2 describes the iVote protocol, and how a voter's cryptographic credentials can be recovered by a man-in-the-middle observing messages exchanged between the client and iVote server. Section 3 describes technical findings of the cloud-based DDoS protection service, focusing on their certificate management practices. Based on these findings Sect. 4 proposes two attack scenarios that could allow the cloud provider (or a coercive entity) to man-in-the-middle an election. Section 5 presents additional findings and Sect. 6 concludes.

2   The iVote Protocol

In this section we describe the iVote protocol. In particular we observed that partial votes are sent—and stored on the server—encrypted by a symmetric key which is only protected by a key derived from the voter's ID and PIN. As we shall discuss, this leads to the potential to recover votes via a brute force attack of the `iVoteID` or `PIN`. When combined with the wider issue of using the same TLS Proxy for registration as voting, the brute force attack becomes viable.

2.1   Key Findings

In iVote the secret keys used to construct an encrypted and digitally signed ballot are cryptographically derived from two values: a voter's ID and PIN. Knowledge of these two values is sufficient information to allow an attacker to impersonate a voter and cast a valid ballot on their behalf. iVote seemingly acknowledges the sensitivity of these values.

The key finding of this section is that the iterative hashing scheme used by iVote to protect the ID/PIN pair can be brute forced in practice by a man-in-the-middle observing messages exchanged between a voter's client and the iVote server. While transport layer security (TLS) protects these values from the view of most network observers, as we explain in Sect. 3, the non end-to-end nature of TLS in DDoS prevention exposes these values to the cloud provider.

2.2 Methodology

Publicly available technical documentation of the iVote system as deployed in WA is limited. Significant information about the system and its configuration, however, can be observed from its public internet-facing components via a demonstration website set up by the Western Australian Electoral Commission (WAEC) to allow voters to practice voting. To test the implementation we created our own local server based on the publicly available JavaScript. There were, however, two main limitations to this approach: (1) the practice website did not include the registration step, and as such we were unable to observe network messages exchanged during this phase, and (2) the responses by the practice iVote server were mocked, and may not convey the full functionality of the live election website. Following our initial analysis, we contacted the WEAC on Feb 17th, 2017 with a report of our findings, which WAEC acknowledged the same day.

2.3 Voter Experience

An iVote election has three main phases:

1. **Registration.** A voter visits a registration website, enters her name, her registered address and her date of birth. She may possibly be asked for further identifiers such as a passport number. She then chooses and submits a 6-digit PIN, which we will refer to as PIN. An 8-digit iVote ID number, which we will refer to as iVoteID, is sent to her via an independent channel such as by post or SMS.
2. **Voting.** The voter visits the voting website and enters her iVoteID and her PIN. Her vote is encrypted in her browser using JavaScript downloaded over TLS from the voting server. If she wishes, she may pause voting and resume later—to facilitate this, a partially-completed vote is stored (encrypted) on the server while she is voting. When she submits her vote, she receives a 12-digit receipt number.
3. **Verification.** All submitted votes are copied to a third-party verification server. After voting, the voter may call this service, enter her iVoteID, PIN and Receipt number, and then hear her vote read back to her.

2.4 Protocol Overview

A complete overview of the protocol is both beyond the scope of this paper, and beyond what can be observed from the public-facing elements of the system. We do, however, have sufficient information to outline how a brute force attack to recover voter credentials could proceed. A high-level overview of login and ballot casting is depicted in Fig. 1, with additional details as follows.

Login. The voter first enters their `iVoteID` and `PIN` into the login page in the browser. A cryptographic key derivation implementation in client-side JavaScript then uses these values to derive a value, `voterID`, as follows. First a string is created of the form `iVoteID + "," + Base64(SHA256(PIN)) + "," + "voterid"`. This string is used as the password input to the password-based key derivation function `PKCS#5 PBKDF2WithHmacSHA1`. The function uses the generated password along with a salt of 20 null bytes; it performs 8000 iterations and outputs a key of length 16 bytes. The result is hex encoded before being posted to the server as `voterID`.

The purpose for this seems to be to protect the `iVoteID` and `PIN` by not sending them to the server directly. However, as we discuss in Sect. 2.6, this protection is insufficient as it is computationally feasible to recover these values from `voterID` through brute-force search.

Voter Credentials. If the `voterID` submitted to the server corresponds to a registered voter, the server responds with a file `credential.json`. An outline of this file is shown in Listing 1. The demo system uses an internal mocked response for a sample user, however we conjecture the real election server simply stores a database of `voterId`/`credential.json` pairs, and responds with the associated `credential.json` whenever a valid `voterID` is presented.

```
1   {
2       "v": "1",
3       "challenge_object": "Base64 Challenge Object",
4       "vad": {
5           "vk": "{
6               "salt": "Base64Encoded Salt",
7               "secrets": {
8                   "symmetric": "Base64Encoded AES Key"
9               },
10              "store": "Base64Encoded PKCS12 KeyStore"
11          }",
12          "vkp": "Base64Encoded salt and password for KeyStore",
13          "eeca": "Base64Encoded CA Certificate",
14          "svca": "Base64Encoded CA Certificate",
15          "azca": "Base64Encoded CA Certificate",
16          "ab": "Base64Encoded Certificate to Verify XML Signatures",
17      },
18      "cert": "Base64Encoded Client Certificate"
19  }
```

Listing 1: Voter Credential File Skeleton

The `vad` object contains a number of keys and certificates. The `vk` object represents a Scytl KeyStore, which combines a `PKCS#12` keystore with a JSON object of encrypted secrets. The underlying `PKCS#12` keystore is protected by what the code refers to as the *long password*. The first step to deriving the *long password* is to derive an AES key to decrypt the password contained in `vkp`. To do this a string is created similar to the one created during the login phase.

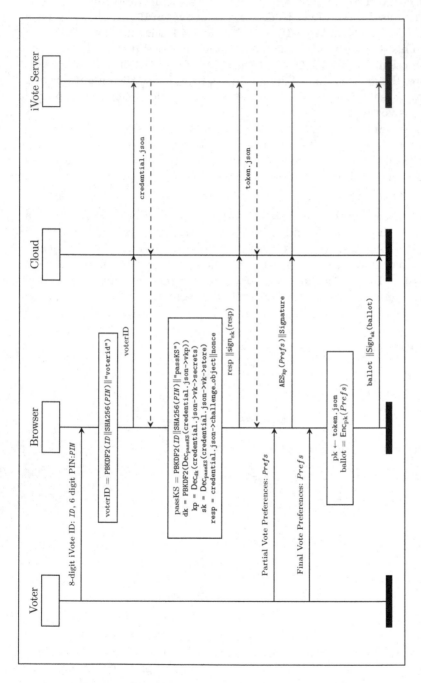

Fig. 1. iVote Protocol. High-level overview of login and ballot casting protocol (*n.b.*, some details omitted for brevity). The TLS connection is not end-to-end between the browser and iVote server, exposing brute-forcible voter credentials to the cloud provider. (This is an instance of a PKCS#5 PBKDF2WithHmacSHA1 function, with a salt consisting of 20 null bytes, performing 8000 iterations, and generating a key of 16 bytes.)

This string has the form: `iVoteID + "," + Base64(SHA256(PIN)) + "," + "passKS"`. The string differs from the one constructed at login time using the suffix "passKS" instead of "voterid".

This password string, along with the salt value in `vkp`, is passed to another instance of `PKCS#5 PBKDF2WithHmacSHA1` that performs 8000 iterations. The result is a 16-byte key, which is then used to initialise an AES cipher, using GCM (Galois/Counter Mode) with no padding. The GCM nonce length is 12 bytes and the tag length is 16 bytes. The nonce is the first 12 bytes of the password value stored in `vkp`. The remaining value of `vkp` is decrypted to form what the code calls the *derived password*.

The *long password* is finally generated by a `PBKDF2WithHmacSHA1` that performs a single iteration on the *derived password* along with the salt value from `vk`, yielding a 16 byte key. This value is used as both a password for the `PKCS#12` key store, and as an AES Key to decrypt the values in the secrets object. The keys in the `secrets` object in `vk` are Base64Encoded ciphertexts. The *long password* is used to initialize an AES Cipher using GCM with no padding. The GCM nonce length is 12 bytes and the tag length is 16 bytes. The nonce is the first 12 bytes of the value in the `secrets` object, with the remainder being the ciphertext that is to be decrypted.

The final outcome of this intricate sequence of client-side key derivations and decryptions is an AES symmetric key `kp` which is used by the browser to encrypt partial votes, which we will continue in further detail in Sect. 2.5.

Token. The `credential.json` file is further processed and the contents extracted, in addition the server's signature on the received challenge is verified. In response to a valid signature, the browser generates a random nonce, concatenates it with the server's challenge, and returns this as a signed message. The purpose of this check appears to be a means of confirming that a client has successfully recovered their private signing key in the keystore.

The response is posted to `vote-encoder/token/{voterKeysId}?v=1` where v is taken from the configuration file, and `voterKeysId` comes from the voter certificate common name, which contains the string "VoterAuth_" followed by the `votersKeysId`. The `voterKeysId` value is important because it is used during all subsequent posts, including voting and partial votes. It is unclear how this value is derived or who generates it, but we suspect it is generated by the registration server during the credential file generation.

Finally, the server responds to the token post with `token.json` that contains the public-key group parameters for encrypting ballot preferences, the Election Markup Language for the various races, and any partial votes that have been recorded. The specifics of the encryption and signature of voter ballot preferences are outside the scope of this paper.

2.5   Partial Votes

When a voter completes a voting screen, either the Legislative Assembly (lower house) or Legislative Council (upper house), a partial vote of all currently entered preferences is created and sent to the server. The submission is sent to `vote-encoder/partial_vote/{voterKeysId}?v=1`, with JSON object shown in Listing 2. The `eo` string is encrypted with the secret key contained in the `secrets` object in `credential.json`, which was extracted as part of the credential file processing, discussed in the previous section. When a partial vote is contained within the Token Response the same AES key contained in the `secrets` object is used to decrypt its contents and restore the screen for the user. The crucial consequence of this is that unlike the final vote which is submitted under the encryption of a randomly generated AES key, which is in turn encrypted with the public key of the election, the partial vote is only protected by the AES key stored in the credential file.

```
1  {
2      "token":"Base64 Copy of Token from Server",
3      "eo":"Base64 Encrypted String",
4      "signature":"Base64 Siganture of Vote",
5      "cert":"Base64 Encoded PEM Certificate of Voter Sign cert"
6  }
```

Listing 2: Partial Vote Skeleton

Given that the credential file itself is only protected by the an encryption key derived from the `iVoteID` and `PIN`, if the `iVoteID` and `PIN` are susceptible to brute force attacks, both the receiving server, and any TLS proxies in between, would have the ability to recover votes. The attack is not mitigated by the fact the final vote could be different, since the partial votes are always submitted as the voter moves between the screens, and as such, the attacker need only look for the last partial vote submission prior to final submission to be sure of the contents of the final vote.

2.6   Brute Forcing Voter Credentials

One important question is how hard it would be for a man-in-the-middle to recover a voter's credentials from observed messages exchanged between the browser and iVote server. Since WA opted to disable re-voting for their election, a near real-time attack capability is needed in order to construct a valid (but malicious) ballot and transparently swap it into the voter's session before they can cast. We now show that this requirement can feasibly be satisfied in practice.

As described in Sect. 2.4 the `voterId` value sent by the browser at login time is derived from the voter's $iVoteID$ and PIN, and knowledge of these values would be sufficient to recover all the voter's other cryptographic values from `credential.json` and `token.json` files.

Recall the `voterID` value is essentially 8000 iterations of SHA1 applied to $iVoteID$, an 8-digit system-assigned value concatenated with PIN, a 6-digit user-chosen value. This implies a brute-force upper bound of

$$8 \cdot 10^3 \cdot 10^8 \cdot 10^6 \approx 2^{60}$$

operations. In other words, the `voterID` value provides 60 bits of security in the best case.

This falls well below the minimum recommended NIST 112-bit security level [15]. As a comparison, at the time of writing the Bitcoin network was able to perform 2^{62} `SHA1` hashes per second.[2]

In practice, however, the voterID space may not be uniformly distributed. Only a few thousand *iVoteIDs* were actually used. Moreover since the registration server is also covered by the DDoS cloud provider, we may assume that a man-in-the-middle would also be able to observe the set of *iVoteIDs* in the context of the registration step and associate an ID with a unique IP address. Under the assumption of a known *iVoteID*, the search space to recover the voter's credential would be

$$8 \cdot 10^3 \cdot 10^6 \approx 2^{33}$$

hashes. This space could be searched nearly instantly using a moderately sized GPU cluster. For example, contemporary bitcoin mining ASICs now achieve hash rates in the tera-hash-per-second (*i.e.*, $>2^{40}$) range. Investment in expensive and difficult to procure custom hardware, however, is not necessary. The rise of inexpensive elastic cloud computing puts this attack within reach of nearly any budget, and recent work has examined offering crypto brute forcing as a service. Heninger *et al.* [18], for example, have deployed hundreds of concurrent instances on Amazon EC2 in pursuit of factoring RSA moduli.

As a more immediate timing comparison demonstrating the real-world feasibility of this attack, we implemented our own program to brute force `voterID`s in a threaded Python program using the Hashlib implementation of PBKDF2 and deployed it on Digital Ocean. Using a single 20-core droplet, our unoptimized (non-GPU) implementation was able to recover a 6-digit PIN in approximately 7 min at a cost of USD \$0.11. With 10 concurrent droplets (Digital Ocean's default account max) the time to recovery is less than 1 min, which we believe would plausibly be less than the time taken by the average vote to read, mark and cast a ballot. Using a GPU-optimized hashing implementation (e.g., Hashcat), however, we expect this time can be reduced to the millisecond range while retaining a comparable cost of pennies per recovered credential.

3   Distributed Denial of Service Protection

Imperva Incapsula is a US-based cloud application delivery company which provides numerous security services to websites including prevention and mitigation of DDoS attacks. In this section we present a technical analysis of relevant aspects of their service as used by the Western Australian Electoral Commission (WAEC) for the 2017 WA State Election.

---

[2] https://blockchain.info/stats.

3.1 Key Findings

Our key finding in regards to the DDoS prevention service deployed in the 2017 WA State Election are threefold:

1. Encryption is not end-to-end between the voter and the iVote server;
2. The cloud provider's practice involves the bundling of dozens of unrelated website domains into a single certificate's subject alternate name (SAN) list; and
3. An internet-wide scan we conducted found valid TLS certificates for the election website being served by servers around the world.

Taken together we argue that this opens the possibility of a foreign nation being able to obtain the private key necessary to man-in-the-middle WA voters through an unrelated domestic law enforcement or national security operation. It also risks compromising the election as a result of error or malfeasance by server administrators all over the world.

Additionally, we discovered that the system initially deployed for the election did not correctly protect against DDoS attacks, despite the presence of Incapsula's DDoS mitigation service. Due to misconfiguration of the iVote server, we were able to determine the true IP address for the WA iVote server via historical domain registrations for the NSW iVote system used in 2015, which was also being used to host the WA iVote system.

Upon discovering this vulnerability we notified the WAEC, who reconfigured the server to stop accepting connections that did not originate from Incapsula's systems.

3.2 Non End-to-End TLS

In a typical TLS handshake the server presents its certificate to the client. Completing a TLS handshake takes time, and saving the session state requires the server allocate memory. This and other strategies allow attackers with access to numerous hosts to overwhelm a server by flooding it with connection requests. When a DDoS mitigation service is involved, the TLS handshake is slightly altered to allow the service to identify and filter malicious requests by forcing incoming connections to be made through its infrastructure before being forwarded on to the destination in a separate connection. The result is that the service provider becomes an intermediary for all traffic to the iVote server.

Incapsula's DDoS mitigation service operates by placing Incapsula servers between the user and the destination website as a non-transparent TLS proxy, intercepting all communications to and from the website in order to filter malicious connections. For example, when connecting to the iVote Core Voting System (CVS) at https://ivote-cvs.elections.wa.gov.au, the voter's connection first travels to a server owned by Incapsula where it is decrypted, scanned, and then forwarded on to the iVote server managed by the WAEC. This interaction is shown in Fig. 2.

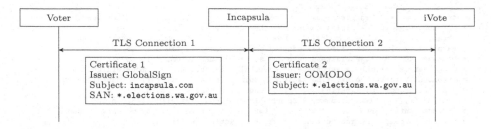

Fig. 2. Non end-to-end TLS. Communication between a voter's browser and the iVote server pass through an Incapsula server and are decrypted, inspected, and re-encrypted under a different key.

Nominally, if the iVote server was correctly covered by DDoS prevention, we should not have been able to observe its certificate, as the server would ignore any connection originating from a non-Incapsula IP address[3]. However, a misconfiguration of the iVote server made it possible to identify its true IP address, allowing us to request its TLS certificate directly. This issue is discussed in more detail in Sect. 5.2.

The interception of connections allows Incapsula to filter out malicious traffic during DDoS attacks, but also allows Incapsula to see all traffic travelling through their systems. This behaviour is by design: modern DDoS mitigation methods rely on scanning the plaintext traffic being transmitted to the server they are protecting [2,20]. Without this ability, they would have a much harder time determining the good connections from the bad ones. What it means, however, is that the voter's interaction with the voting server exists as plaintext at some point after leaving the voter's computer, but before reaching the election servers.

This fact is problematic since TLS authentication remains the only meaningful form of server authentication in iVote, and using a cloud provider for DDoS protection necessarily outsources this trust. Putting valid keys on a variety of third-party servers throughout the world brings all of them into the set of trusted parties, and increases the likelihood of a key leaking. Furthermore, ballot secrecy in iVote depends critically on the assumption that a voter's identity disclosed during registration cannot be linked with a cast ballot making non end-to-end encryption a concern in this matter as well.

3.3 Large-Scale Certificate Sharing

DDoS protection need not require a customer to surrender its private keys to the cloud provider [2,20]. Instead, Incapsula outwardly presents their own certificate in the handshake, which includes the iVote server's domain (ivote-cvs.elections.wa.gov.au) in the Subject Alternate Name (SAN) exten-

---

[3] https://www.incapsula.com/blog/make-website-invisible-direct-to-origin-ddos-atta cks.html.

```
incapsula.com, *.1strongteam.com, *.absolutewatches.com.au, *.advancemotors.com.au,
*.alconchirurgia.pl, *.amplex.com.au, *.bohemiocollection.com.au,
*.cheapcaribbean.com, *.compareit4me.com, *.elections.wa.gov.au, *.everafterhigh.com,
*.farmerslifeonline.com, *.floraandfauna.com.au, *.heypennyfabrics.com.au,
*.homeaway.com.ph, *.jetblackespresso.com.au, *.lifemapco.com, *.lovemyearth.net,
*.maklernetz.at, *.mobile-vertriebe.de, *.mobile.zurich.com.ar, *.monsterhigh.com,
*.mycommunitystarter.co.uk, *.noosacivicshopping.com.au, *.oilsforlifeaustralia.com.au,
*.planetparts.com.au, *.purina.lt, *.redsimaging.com.au, *.rlicorp.com,
*.roundup.fr, *.sassykat.com.au, *.spendwellhealth.com, *.sublimation.com.au,
*.uat.user.zurichpartnerzone.com, *.woodgrove.com.au, *.yamahamotor-webservice.com,
*.zlaponline.com, *.zurich-personal.co.uk, *.zurich.ae, *.zurich.co.jp,
*.zurich.es, *.zurich.jp, *.zurichlife.co.jp, *.zurichseguros.pt, 1strongteam.com,
absolutewatches.com.au, advancemotors.com.au, alconchirurgia.pl, amplex.com.au,
bohemiocollection.com.au, compareit4me.com, farmerslifeonline.com,
floraandfauna.com.au, heypennyfabrics.com.au, homeaway.com.ph, jetblackespresso.com.au,
lifemapco.com, lovemyearth.net, mycommunitystarter.co.uk, noosacivicshopping.com.au,
oilsforlifeaustralia.com.au, planetparts.com.au, purina.lt, redsimaging.com.au,
roundup.fr, sassykat.com.au, spendwellhealth.com, sublimation.com.au, woodgrove.com.au,
zurich.ae, zurich.es, zurich.jp, zurichlife.co.jp
```

Fig. 3. Subject alternate names in the Incapsula certificate. The same digital certificate used to prove the identity of *.elections.wa.gov.au to WA voters is also used to prove the identity of websites listed above. This list was transient and changed several times in the month leading up to election day.

sion of their certificate. Specifically Incapsula includes the wildcard domain *.elections.wa.gov.au in the SAN.

Obtaining this secondary certificate is a financial expense, and Incapsula shares one certificate among numerous websites in order to reduce cost [20]. Specifically it lists itself as the certificate's subject, and packs numerous domains of its customers' into a single certificate's SAN. When a WA voter visits the iVote website https://ivote-cvs.elections.wa.gov.au, their browser is presented with a certificate with dozens of other unrelated domains in the SAN. A list of these domains is given in Fig. 3, and includes websites for widely varying sectors and countries of origin.

Through a combination of collecting our own TLS handshakes with the iVote server as well as Censys [9] data we observed this certificate over a two month period prior to the election and found the SAN list changed several times, presumably as some clients joined and others left. For example, on Feb 1st the SAN included several casinos (pandora-online-casino.com, caribiccasino.com, regalo-casino.com, doublestarcasino.com), but they disappeared shortly after. Importantly, visitors to any of these other websites are, in turn, presented with the *same* certificate.

3.4   International Certificate Footprint

Incapsula's global network consists of 32 data centres (Points of Presence, or PoPs), located across the Americas, Europe, the Middle East, and the Asia Pacific region.[4] Due to the design of Incapsula's network, TLS certificates hosted

---

[4] https://www.incapsula.com/incapsula-global-network-map.html.

in one PoP are propagated worldwide, so that users in any region served by Incapsula can have their connection proxied by the nearest PoP available. As stated by Incapsula:[5] *"When using Incapsula, our servers become the intermediate for all traffic to your website, including SSL traffic. To facilitate this, Incapsula needs a valid SSL certificate for your domain installed on all its servers worldwide."*

We found Incapsula servers serving valid TLS certificates for `*.elections.wa.gov.au` from locations around the world, including Eastern and Western Europe, China, North and South America, and various points in Australia.

These servers were identified through domain name look-ups for ivote-cvs.elections.wa.gov.au originating from within each country, and subsequent TLS connections, using a Virtual Private Network (VPN). Our timing analysis strongly indicates that the TLS certificates were being served directly by these servers, and not proxied from elsewhere.

Internet Scan. We conducted an internet wide scan of the IPv4 space on election day (March 11, 2017), collecting all TLS certificates served over port 443 using `zgrab`.[6] In total we found 153 distinct IPs serving certificates containing `*.elections.wa.gov.au` in the subject alternate name. A traceroute and timing analysis showed that these IPs were consistent with cities in which Incapsula advertises data centers (see Footnote 8). We were able to identify points of presence serving WA's certificate in Australia, Canada, China, France, Germany, Japan, Poland, Singapore, Spain, Switzerland, United Kingdom, and throughout the United States.

4   Man in the Middle Attack Scenarios

In this section we outline two scenarios in which a man-in-the-middle could recover credentials necessary to be able to cast a valid ballot on a voter's behalf.

4.1   Modify the Scripts the DDoS Provider Is Already Injecting

Overview and Significance. In this first scenario, a malicious cloud provider injects Javascript into the voter's client with the aim of capturing their credentials. Since the cloud provider sits between the voter and iVote server, injecting a malicious script is an obvious but risky approach for the cloud provider if both the presence the script and its malicious purpose were detected. The significance of our particular attack scenario, however, makes use of the following observations: (1) the cloud provider is already rewriting server content to injecting their own JavaScript as part of their DDoS profiling functionality, and (2) the script payloads are already being obfuscated.

We created a proof-of-concept vote-stealing script that leaks the voter's ID and PIN in the tracking cookie, and incorporated it into the script already being injected by the cloud provider at no increased file size.

---

[5] https://www.incapsula.com/blog/incapsula-ssl-support-features.html.
[6] https://github.com/zmap/zgrab.

Script Injection for System Profiling. When a voter connects to the iVote WA Core Voting System using the address https://ivote-cvs.elections.wa.gov.au, the connection is proxied through Incapsula's servers using an Incapsula-controlled TLS certificate. The initial response to a voter's connection sets a number of Incapsula cookies.

In addition the response is modified by Incapsula to include JavaScript code at the end of the HTML response. The included code inserts a `<script>` element to cause the browser to load an additional JavaScript file, the contents of which are obfuscated as a string of hex values. The included code is designed to perform fingerprinting of the voter's system. The HTTP responses for the resource files do not contain x-cdn or x-iinfo headers, strongly suggesting they are served by the Incapsula proxy (as would be expected), rather than by the iVote server.

When expanded into a more readable format, the injected JavaScript code is revealed as a tracking function. The code is designed to probe various parts of the voter's computer, including: the web browser they are using; any browser plugins they have installed; the operating system being used; their CPU type; and other information designed to fingerprint individual user connections. Additionally, this cookie calculates a digest of all other cookies set on the page, including those set by the server.

This information is written into a profile cookie that is temporarily stored on the voter's computer. This profile cookie has an extremely short life of just 20 s, after which it will be deleted. Due to this being loaded during the page load the remaining requests within the page will send this cookie to the server before it disappears from the voter machine. As such, unless spotted within the 20 s period, or all requests/responses are being logged by the voter, it will be difficult for a voter to detect that this profiling cookie was ever set or sent to the server. The cookie is named __utmvc, which is similar to a Google Analytics cookie (__utmv), however, it does not appear to be related. The Google __utmv cookie is a persistent cookie used to store custom variables. The reason for the choice of naming is not immediately clear.

Cookies and Voting. While the concept of profiling and tracking cookies may seem invasive, there is nothing overtly malicious about this behaviour. Indeed, the entire web advertising industry is built to perform similar tasks, in order to track individual users across websites and better serve advertisements.

For Incapsula, the tracking cookie most likely forms part of the DDoS mitigation process: Incapsula can determine which requests are likely to be from legitimate users. Combined with the profiling cookie, Incapsula can perform an analysis of the requesting device and alter its behaviour accordingly.

In the context of iVote, however, this behaviour poses a significant risk for voter security. As discussed in the introduction to this article, the iVote system is designed with the assumption that the encryption and authentication covering the communication between voter and server (Transport Layer Security, or TLS) is secure. If a third party has the ability to intercept this communication and inject malicious JavaScript into server responses, it would be possible to hijack the entire voting process.

The JavaScript we have witnessed being injected into server responses is non-malicious, however, there remains the potential for this to not always be the case. For example, a rogue Incapsula employee or a foreign intelligence service with access to Incapsula's systems could alter the injected JavaScript. If this occurred, it would be possible to steal the iVoteID and PIN from the voter, and subsequently modify their ballot, with a very low chance of detection by either the voter or the iVote server itself.

Furthermore, with Incapsula's cookies already being used to identify voters between both the registration server and voting server, it would also be trivial for such an attacker to link voters with their vote, removing the secrecy of their ballot and opening voters to the risk of vote-buying or coercion.

The device fingerprinting behaviour of the injected JavaScript may also allow these attacks to be performed in a selective fashion. Recent research by Cao *et al.* [6] has shown that these fingerprinting methods can be used to identify users with a high degree of confidence, even across different browsers on the same device. This may provide an attacker with the ability to selectively target individual voters or electoral divisions, and to avoid targeting voters who may notice changes to the injected JavaScript (such as security researchers).

Proof of Concept. We developed a short script that would leak the iVoteID and PIN by setting it in the profiling cookie. As such, the information would be leaked without need for any additional requests, making detection extremely difficult. Furthermore, due to the original injected script from Incapsula not being minimised, we were able to construct a malicious injection script that maintained all the functionality of the original, along with our additional malicious code, while still maintaining exactly the same length.

To achieve this we added two onChange listeners to the iVoteID and PIN input boxes. We use these onChange listeners to take a copy of the values entered and set them inside the profiling cookie. The advantage of this is that we are not adding any additional cookies, or requests, in order to leak the information, but instead using an existing side channel.

In order to facilitate this we had to extend the lifetime of the profiling cookie. During testing we extended it to 1 hour, but realistically it only needs to be extended by a few minutes, the only requirement is that the cookie exists at the point the iVoteID and PIN is entered by the voter.

4.2 Foreign Access to TLS Private Keys

In this attack scenario a cloud provider uses the brute force attack described in Sect. 2.6 to recover the iVoteID and PIN from the passively observed voterID value sent by the browser at login time. In comparison to the script injection attack above, this approach is completely passive and has the benefit of being undetectable at the cost of increased computational resources. Any cloud provider, therefore, must be trusted not to pursue such an attack unless the combined ID/PIN space was made cryptographically strong.

A more interesting scenario is one in which the cloud provider (a multi-national company operating in many jurisdictions) must inadvertantly grant a foreign power the ability to man-in-the-middle an election through the course of prosecuting an otherwise lawful national security request.

As discussed in Sect. 3.4, valid TLS certificates for `*.elections.wa.gov.au` are served by Incapsula servers worldwide, with the associated TLS private keys also stored on these servers. The TLS certificates served by Incapsula's servers are multi-use certificates covering a number of domains, as described in Sect. 3.3. This design has significant implications for the security of the TLS private keys associated with these certificates.

For example: a foreign government, as part of a legitimate domestic sur-veillance operation, may request that Incapsula provide access to the TLS private key for the domain `*.example.com` served by a PoP located in the foreign country. If this domain is contained in the same TLS certificate as `*.elections.wa.gov.au`, obtaining this private key would also provide the for-eign government with the ability to perform man-in-the-middle attacks on voters using iVote.

5   Additional Findings

5.1   Verifiability

The iVote system incorporates a telephone verification service [1], which allows a voter to dial a provided number and connect with an interactive voice response (IVR) system.

The telephone verification service requires the voter's `iVoteID`, `PIN`, and the receipt number provided by the iVote server after a vote has been successfully cast. After these three numbers have been provided, the telephone verification service reads back the list of candidates, in preference order, chosen by the voter in their completed ballot.

During the 2015 New South Wales state election, which also used the iVote system, Halderman and Teague identified several potential attacks against this telephone verification system [10]. These attacks could allow an attacker who had manipulated iVote ballots to avoid detection by voters who were attempting to verify that their vote was cast as intended.

One of these attacks is known as a "clash attack," and is designed to trick voters by manipulating the registration and vote confirmation pages to provide the `iVoteID`, `PIN`, and receipt number of a previous like-minded voter with the same candidate preferences. The previous voter's ballot has been allowed to be recorded unmodified, and is then used as verification evidence for multiple voters. The actual votes of these voters can then be manipulated at-will with little chance of detection.

Crucially, the clash attack relies on accurate prediction of how a voter will vote prior to registration, so that they can be provided with the `iVoteID` and

PIN of a like-minded voter who has submitted an unmodified ballot. In addition, the attack relies upon providing voters with a PIN rather than allowing them to choose one. This may raise the suspicions of voters who are aware that the iVote system is supposed to allow them to choose their own PIN.

For the 2017 WA State Election, the clash attack could be significantly improved as a consequence of Incapsula being used to proxy all voter connections to both the registration and voting servers. An attacker with access to Incapsula's systems could directly link each voter's registration details with their completed ballot, provided that the voter registers and votes using the same browser (and potentially across browsers as well [6]).

Due to Incapsula's position as a DDoS mitigation service for a number of other online services, such an attacker would also have the ability to identify voters (and their likely voting preferences) with significantly more accuracy than if they only had access to the iVote system itself. This would allow for more accurate clash attacks to be performed.

5.2 Bypassing DDoS Mitigation

It is assumed that the use of Incapsula's service to proxy iVote connections was an attempt to protect the iVote system from potential Distributed Denial of Service (DDoS) attacks during the 2017 WA state election.

DDoS mitigation services such as Incapsula operate by intercepting connections to a service (in this case, iVote), thereby hiding the true public IP Address of the service. If this protection is applied correctly, any attacker wishing to attack the iVote system will be forced to do so via Incapsula's systems—thereby allowing Incapsula's robust infrastructure to withstand the attack and filter legitimate connections through to the iVote system. For this protection to be effective, the true IP address of the service must be properly hidden from attackers [19].

During the first several days of voting in the 2017 WA State Election, it was possible to identify the public IP address of the server hosting the iVote Core Voting System (CVS) for the WA election (https://ivote-cvs.elections.wa.gov. au), through specific requests to known iVote infrastructure in Sydney, NSW. This infrastructure could be publicly identified through DNS queries and other methods requiring little sophistication on the part of an attacker. With knowledge of this address, it would have been possible for an attacker to perform DDoS attacks against the iVote system directly, rendering Incapsula's protection ineffective.

Recommended practice for the use of DDoS mitigation services such as Incapsula is to prevent the identification of the true IP address of the service being protected, through techniques such as blocking all traffic from sources other than Incapsula itself [8,17]. These protections were not correctly implemented for the WA state election until we noticed the problem, several days after the opening of iVote, and notified the WAEC.

6   Conclusion

We have shown that utilizing cloud based DDoS protection servers can have a significant impact on the trust model of an internet based election. Furthermore, we have analysed the increased risks of tracking and interception associated with such services, and provided a proof of concept demonstrating how malicious JavaScript could be injected into a voting client in order to read or alter completed ballots.

At the time of writing, more than two months after the election, the Western Australian Electoral Commission has published neither the raw voting data for iVote, nor the verification success and failure statistics. Even if the votes were broadly similar to those cast on paper, and the verification failure rate was small, that would not constitute genuine evidence that the votes were accurately recorded. A lack of transparency in the process is simply no longer acceptable. In light of the trusted nature of cloud providers, their single point of failure, and the remote nature of potential attackers, the need for evidence-based election outcomes is greater than ever.

Acknowledgements. The authors thank the Western Australian Election Commission for quick acknowledgement and response to our disclosure. Thanks also to Yuval Yarom and the anonymous reviewers for helpful feedback.

References

1. How to use iVote. https://www.elections.wa.gov.au/ivote/how-use-ivote. Accessed 15 May 2017
2. SSL FAQ. http://support.cloudflare.com/hc/en-us/articles/204144518-SSL-FAQ
3. Adida, B.: Helios: web-based open-audit voting. In: USENIX Security Symposium, pp. 335–348 (2008)
4. Australian Senate: Economics References Committee: 2016 Census: issues of trust. http://www.aph.gov.au/Parliamentary_Business/Committees/Senate/Economics/2016Census/Report
5. Bell, S., Benaloh, J., Byrne, M.D., Debeauvoir, D., Eakin, B., Kortum, P., McBurnett, N., Pereira, O., Stark, P.B., Wallach, D.S., Fisher, G., Montoya, J., Parker, M., Winn, M.: Star-vote: a secure, transparent, auditable, and reliable voting system. In: Electronic Voting Technology Workshop/Workshop on Trustworthy Elections (EVT/WOTE 2013) (2013)
6. Cao, Y., Li, S., Wijmans, E.: (Cross-)browser fingerprinting via OS and hardware level features. In: Proceedings of Network & Distributed System Security Symposium (NDSS) (2017)
7. Chaum, D., Carback, R., Clark, J., Essex, A., Popoveniuc, S., Rivest, R.L., Ryan, P.Y., Shen, E., Sherman, A.T.: Scantegrity II: end-to-end verifiability for optical scan election systems using invisible ink confirmation codes. EVT **8**, 1–13 (2008)
8. Cohen, E.: How to make your website invisible to direct-to-origin DDoS attacks. https://www.incapsula.com/blog/make-website-invisible-direct-to-origin-ddos-attacks.html. Accessed 15 May 2017

9. Durumeric, Z., Adrian, D., Mirian, A., Bailey, M., Halderman, J.A.: A search engine backed by Internet-wide scanning. In: Proceedings of the 22nd ACM Conference on Computer and Communications Security (2015)

10. Halderman, J.A., Teague, V.: The New South Wales iVote system: security failures and verification flaws in a live online election. In: Haenni, R., Koenig, R.E., Wikström, D. (eds.) VOTELID 2015. LNCS, vol. 9269, pp. 35–53. Springer, Cham (2015). doi:10.1007/978-3-319-22270-7_3

11. Jonathan (Yoni) Ben-Nun, Rosen, A., Ta-shma, A., Riva, B.: Wombat voting system (2012). https://wombat.factcenter.org

12. Kiayias, A., Zacharias, T., Zhang, B.: DEMOS-2: scalable E2E verifiable elections without random oracles. In: Proceedings of the 22nd ACM SIGSAC Conference on Computer and Communications Security, pp. 352–363. ACM (2015)

13. Lindeman, M., Stark, P.B.: A gentle introduction to risk-limiting audits. IEEE Secur. Priv. 10(5), 42–49 (2012)

14. MacGibbon, A.: Review of the events surrounding the 2016 eCensus. http://apo.org.au/node/70705

15. National Institute of Standards and Technology (NIST): NIST Special Publication 800-57, Part 1, Revision 4. Recommendation for Key Management. Part 1: General (2016)

16. Ryan, P.Y., Bismark, D., Heather, J., Schneider, S., Xia, Z.: Prêt à voter: a voter-verifiable voting system. IEEE Trans. Inf. Forensics Secur. 4(4), 662–673 (2009)

17. Sullivan, N.: DDoS prevention: protecting the origin. https://blog.cloudflare.com/ddos-prevention-protecting-the-origin/. Accessed 15 May 2017

18. Valenta, L., Cohney, S., Liao, A., Fried, J., Bodduluri, S., Heninger, N.: Factoring as a service. Cryptology ePrint Archive, Report 2015/1000 (2015). http://eprint.iacr.org/2015/1000

19. Vissers, T., Van Goethem, T., Joosen, W., Nikiforakis, N.: Maneuvering around clouds: bypassing cloud-based security providers. In: Proceedings of the 22nd ACM SIGSAC Conference on Computer and Communications Security, pp. 1530–1541. ACM (2015)

20. Zeifman, I.: The Bits and Bytes of Incapsula SSL Support. https://www.incapsula.com/blog/incapsula-ssl-support-features.html. Accessed 15 May 2017

Updated European Standards for E-voting

The Council of Europe Recommendation Rec(2017)5 on Standards for E-voting

Ardita Driza Maurer[✉]

Centre for Democracy Studies Aarau (ZDA),
University of Zurich, Zurich, Switzerland
ardita.drizamaurer@uzh.ch

Abstract. The Council of Europe is the only international organization to have issued recommendations on the regulation of the use of e-voting. The 2004 Recommendation to member States, Rec(2004)11 and the two 2010 Guidelines on certification and on transparency were recently repealed and replaced by Rec (2017)5 on Standards for e-voting and the associated Guidelines on its implementation. We discuss the 2017 Recommendation and the main novelties introduced by it. The Recommendation extends the definition of e-voting to include pure e-counting. It enlists 49 standards which set objectives that e-voting should fulfill to comply with the principles and conditions for democratic elections of the European electoral heritage. Detailed guidelines for the implementation of the objectives are collected in a lower level document, the Guidelines on the implementation of the provisions of Rec(2017)5. The guidelines are expected to be completed through further work. The main differences between the old and the new Council of Europe standards on e-voting are outlined. Correlations are illustrated. The expected use, impact and evolution of the Recommendation and Guidelines are briefly explained.

Keywords: Council of Europe · E-voting · Principles · Standards · Requirements · Recommendation Rec(2017)5 · (old) Recommendation Rec (2004)11

1 Introduction

Since the beginning of the Millennium e-voting has been a recurrent theme at the Council of Europe, both at the national and international levels.[1] Discussions and implementations of e-voting have taken place in several countries. Given the interest of

---

[1] The Council of Europe is an international organization established in 1949 by a number of like-minded European countries, to safeguard and realize the ideals and principles which are their common heritage, as stated in article 1 of the Statute of the Council of Europe (ETS 1). Today it includes 47 member States covering all European Union members as well as Albania, Andorra, Armenia, Azerbaijan, Bosnia and Herzegovina, Georgia, Iceland, Liechtenstein, Republic of Moldova, Monaco, Montenegro, Norway, Russian Federation, San Marino, Serbia, Switzerland, The former Yugoslav Republic of Macedonia, Turkey and Ukraine. Other countries with a "special guest" or "observer" status include Canada, Mexico, U.S., Holy See, Japan, countries in Central Asia etc.

© Springer International Publishing AG 2017
R. Krimmer et al. (Eds.): E-Vote-ID 2017, LNCS 10615, pp. 146–162, 2017.
DOI: 10.1007/978-3-319-68687-5_9

member States, the Council of Europe has elaborated standards offering guidance to countries on how to regulate the use of e-voting. It has also provided a forum for regular discussion between national experts.[2] Standards have both influenced developments in member States and have been influenced by them [1, 2].

A first Recommendation elaborated by national experts was adopted on 30 September 2004 by the Committee of Ministers of the Council of Europe. *Recommendation Rec(2004)11 on legal, operational and technical standards for e-voting* included 112 standards and requirements. Two guidelines were approved at the 2010 biannual review meeting: *Guidelines on transparency of e-enabled elections* (16 provisions) and *Guidelines for developing processes that confirm compliance with prescribed requirements and standards in the region* (*Certification of e-voting systems*) (14 provisions). The guidelines were meant to provide a practical tool to facilitate the implementation of the 2004 Recommendation, in particular its paragraphs 20 to 23 (transparency) and 111, 112 (certification).

After discussions and a report on the need to update Rec(2004)11 and the associated guidelines [1],[3] the Committee of Ministers set up in April 2015 an "Ad hoc committee of legal experts on legal, operational and technical standards for e-voting" (CAHVE) with the mandate to prepare a new Recommendation updating Rec(2004)11 in the light of recent technical and legal developments related to e-enabled elections in the Council of Europe member States [3].[4]

The results of CAHVE's work which took place between 2015 and 2016 are a new *Recommendation Rec(2017)5 on standards for e-voting* (49 provisions), its *Explanatory Memorandum*, as well as the *Guidelines on the implementation of the provisions of Recommendation Rec(2017)5 on standards for e-voting* [4–6].[5] All three documents were approved by CAHVE in November 2016. On 14 June 2017 the Committee of Ministers adopted the new Recommendation Rec(2017)5 and took note of the other documents.[6] At the same time it repealed the 2004 Recommendation and the 2010 guidelines on transparency and on certification.[7]

This article presents the new Rec(2017)5 and the main novelties that it introduces. We start by an overview of literature on the old standards, highlighting the main

---

[2] Biannual meetings to review the implementation of Rec(2004)11 have been organised by the Council of Europe. Meetings documents are available at https://www.coe.int/en/web/electoral-assistance/e-voting .

[3] An informal meeting of experts on the question of the update was held in Vienna in December 2013, https://www.coe.int/en/web/electoral-assistance/informal-meeting-of-experts-e-voting.

[4] The author of this article was appointed lead legal expert. She prepared a roadmap for the update and led the draft update of the Recommendation. Intermediary and final results were approved by CAHVE at its October 2015 and November 2016 meetings. More on http://www.coe.int/en/web/electoral-assistance/e-voting.

[5] The guidelines also include examples of effective implementation of standards in specific contexts, called "good practice. Examples of good practice are included for information purposes.

[6] The mandate of CAHVE foresaw an update of Rec(2004)11. However given its innovative character, it was decided that Rec(2017)5 and the associated Guidelines shall repeal and replace the old documents instead of simply modifying them (see § 27, Explanatory Memorandum).

[7] https://www.coe.int/en/web/electoral-assistance/-/council-of-europe-adopts-new-recommendation-on-standards-for-e-voting.

suggestions for improvement made therein (Sect. 2). Next, we discuss the new Recommendation (Sect. 3). We start by clarifying the terms "principle", "standard" and "requirement" used in the Recommendation and the associated documents. The bulk of this chapter discusses the new standards and highlights the main differences with Rec (2004)11. Most novelties are based on suggestions coming from literature. Finally we comment on the practical use of the standards; their influence on member States' regulations; their future development (Sect. 4) and present some concluding remarks (Sect. 5). Apart from a quick overview of literature on the old recommendation (Sect. 2), the article mainly addresses documents of the Council of Europe, in particular those in relation to the update work of CAHVE.

2 Suggestions from Literature

Writings that focus on the Council of Europe e-voting standards, namely on the old Rec (2004)11 and associated guidelines, can be grouped in four categories.

The first category includes writings that examine the Rec(2004)11 itself and make proposals for improvement. The second category consists of evaluations of specific uses of e-voting in the region. Authors refer to Rec(2004)11 and to the associated guidelines as legal benchmarks and sometime identify weak points in these documents which they criticize and/or suggest improving. In the third category we include writings that focus on specific aspects of e-voting (often technical ones, but also social, etc.). When examining their topic or building new solutions, authors do refer to detailed requirements derived from legal principles. The ways in which such requirements are derived and their content are interesting from the perspective of updating the recommendation and the guidelines. Finally, a fourth category regroups the documents of experts working with the Council of Europe on the elaboration of standards on e-voting, mainly in the CAHVE group which prepared Rec(2017)5.

We do not aim here to list[8] and discuss the writings in each category (for details on this see [1, 7]). Our point is to present an overview of suggestions to improve Rec (2004)11[9] resulting from each category of writings (the four identified categories are as many different perspectives on the standards developed by the Council of Europe). To illustrate our purpose, we will refer to a few writings from each category.

The interest of presenting improvement suggestions from literature is that they were effectively considered by experts during the update and several are reflected in the new Rec(2017)5. Of the 250 provisions (proposed standards) that were considered by CAHVE, 142 came from the old Recommendation and the Guidelines; and around one

---

[8] The Centre for Direct Democracy (ZDA) of the University of Zurich (iVoting project) has established and maintains a bibliography more specifically on internet voting covering all official reports in the field and academic production from a legal or social science perspective. It can be consulted at http://www.preferencematcher.com/edc/?page_id=338 (follow the link to the latest version).

[9] A detailed list of proposals for improvement, including those coming from academic research, was considered by CAHVE experts during the updating work in 2015-2016 (see next paragraph and footnote).

hundred came from literature, namely from technical publications (third category) and OSCE/ODIHR evaluations of e-voting implementations in the region (second category).[10] Not all suggestions from literature are "original" or "unique". There are much repetitions, redundancies, etc. in between them. Consolidation was necessary before their integration in the Rec(2017)5 could be considered and eventually decided by CAHVE.

Writings that examine the merits of the standards of Rec(2004)11 (first category) are not numerous. Rec(2004)11's approach of thinking e-voting "by analogy" with paper-based channels is criticized [7, 8]. One of the reasons is that different voting channels face different types of risk and this should also be reflected in the respective regulations. Another conclusion is that it is important to distinguish between issues of public policy and issues of technical implementation. A certain number of issues, for instance whether to opt for absolute or relative secrecy, are to be decided (and regulated) as a matter of public policy not of voting technology (alone).

Some writings examine Rec(2004)11 standards from the perspective of evaluation/certification against standards [9] and highlight its many flaws related to consistency, completeness and scope, over-/under-specification, redundancy, maintainability, extensibility. A restructuring is proposed with operational and technical requirements grouped under each of the five rights (principles) identified in appendix I of Rec(2004)11. Others propose a restructuring in the form of a merger of the high-level recommendations of Rec(2004)11 with the detailed standards of US Voluntary Voting System Guidelines (VVSG)[11] to obtain a document useful for system certification purposes [10]. This group's main input could be summarized as the need for well-structured standards and the need for coherency and consistency within the Recommendation and between it and the associated documents. As for their other proposal, of having a Recommendation against which to evaluate and certify e-voting systems, we will see below (in 3.1 and 4.1) whether the Recommendation can, alone, become such a legal benchmark, or not.

Some writings evaluate specific implementations of e-voting in the region against the Council of Europe standards (Rec(2004)11 and the associated guidelines)(second category of writings). When doing so, authors identify a number of problems with Rec (2004)11 itself. For instance, several standards included in Rec(2004)11 are too detailed to be applied to all kinds of e-voting (as the Recommendation aims to). The need for trade-offs between standards is ignored by Rec(2004)11. Also, the lack of consideration for national provisions and the perceived pretention of the Recommendation to cover a maximum of situations is criticized. One document in particular crystallizes these empirical findings, the 2012 IFES (Barrat, Goldsmith) evaluation of the Norwegian internet voting system's conformity with international standards [11]. Here, the general conclusion is that when it comes to a specific implementation of

---

[10] This working document has not been published but can be obtained from the Council of Europe. The small group of experts that compiled the list, consolidated it and finally produced the draft of the new Recommendation and Guidelines included A. Driza Maurer (lead), J. Barrat, R. Krimmer, M. Volkamer and S. Neumann.

[11] https://www.eac.gov/voting-equipment/voluntary-voting-system-guidelines/.

e-voting, a better interweaving between international standards and national regulations is necessary. The former are by definition higher level and less detailed than the latter.

The third category of writings includes technical writings which present solutions for e-voting or its evaluation, or which evaluate such solutions. Solutions and evaluations should respect legal principles (such as universal, equal, free and secret elections) which stem from international treaties and national constitutions. However, principles are too abstract for this purpose and need to be spelled out or "translated" into detailed requirements. So, these writings usually start by identifying a number of detailed requirements, for instance security ones, based on which they build their systems/evaluation work. Although they do not necessarily refer to the standards of Rec(2004)11, the methods used to derive detailed technical requirements from general and broad legal principles are of interest also from the perspective of restructuring and updating the Recommendation and the associated guidelines. Instead of many, consider the contribution from Neumann and Volkamer (and references) [12] in which they derive technical requirements from constitutional provisions and propose metrics to estimate the fulfillment of these requirements within concrete voting systems.

Suggestions and conclusions of experts working on the update of the standards (fourth category of documents) will be referred to throughout the following chapters.

All above-mentioned writings have one common feature: they directly or indirectly advocate an update of Rec(2004)11 and provide indications of the direction to be taken. These suggestions were considered and eventually reflected in Rec(2017)5 and the associated guidelines, as we will see below.

3   Council of Europe Rec(2017)5 on Standards for E-Voting

3.1   Principles, Standards, Requirements

The terms "principles", "standards" and "requirements" are all mentioned in Rec(2017)5.What is their meaning and what's the relationship between them?

Rec(2017)5 recommends the governments of members States to respect all the *principles* of democratic elections and referendums in their legislation and practice of e-voting. It also recommends them to be guided in their legislation, policies and practice by the *standards* included in the Appendix I to Rec(2017)5. And it says that the interconnection between the abovementioned standards and those included in the accompanying Guidelines should be taken into account. Finally standard 36, Appendix I, says that member States shall develop technical, evaluation and certification *requirements* and shall ascertain that they fully reflect the relevant legal and democratic principles.

"Principles" refers to high level electoral principles to be found in universal instruments such as art. 21 of the Universal Declaration of Human Rights and art. 25 section b of the International Covenant on Civil and Political Rights (periodic, universal, equal, secret, free elections) as well as in European (regional) instruments such as art.3 of Protocol I to the European Convention on Human Rights which foresees free, periodic and secret elections (universal and equal suffrage are also included according to the European Court of Human Rights[12] (see also §5, Explanatory Memorandum). The preamble of Rec(2017)5 mentions obligations and commitments undertaken by the member states within a number of treaties and conventions[13], however the list is not exhaustive.[14] At the national level, the same principles defined in the same way, or more largely, as well as additional principles are found in the national constitution, and maybe also in the formal law (i.e. law adopted by the highest legislative authority, usually the Parliament and, in certain countries like Switzerland, also subject to a popular vote). An example of an additional principle which only exists at the national level is "the public nature of elections" in Germany [13]. In some federal countries, where the sub-state entity has some degree of autonomy in electoral matters, the same principles or even additional, local ones, are to be found in the respective documents (e.g. in cantonal constitutions in Switzerland or State laws in the U.S.). For a detailed account of regulatory frameworks of e-voting in 13 countries (Germany, Austria, Brazil, India, Estonia, France, Argentina, Finland, Mexico, Switzerland, United States, Australia and Venezuela) see the respective chapters in [14].

The Council of Europe's core mission is to safeguard and realize the principles which are common heritage of its member States (art. 1 of its Statute), including principles for democratic elections. Principles which are common heritage are also referred to as the European constitutional heritage. Part of it is the so-called European electoral heritage. Principles of the European electoral heritage (which stem from various instruments) have been identified and collected in a document adopted in 2002: the Code of Good Practice in Electoral Matters [15] of the European Commission for Democracy through Law (Venice Commission). Although non-binding, the Code is the reference document of the Council of Europe when it comes to higher level principles for democratic elections.

The Code identifies the following elements: universal, equal, free, secret, direct suffrage; frequency of elections, respect for fundamental rights, regulatory levels and stability of electoral law, procedural safeguards (organisation of elections by an impartial body, observation of elections, an effective system of appeal, organisation and

---

[12] See e.g. the ECtHR judgment of 2 March 1987, *Mathieu-Mohin and Clerfayt*, series A 113, § 54.

[13] The International Covenant on Civil and Political Rights (ICCPR) (1966), the United Nations Convention on the Elimination of All Forms of Racial Discrimination (ICERD) (1966), the United Nations Convention on the Elimination of All Forms of Discrimination against Women (CEDAW) (1979), the United Nations Convention on the Rights of Persons with Disabilities (CRPD) (2006), the United Nations Convention against Corruption (UNCAC) (2003), the Convention for the Protection of Human Rights and Fundamental Freedoms (CEDH) (1950), in particular its Protocol No.1 (CEDH-P1) (1952), the European Charter of Local Self-Government (ETS No. 122), the Convention on Cybercrime (ETS No. 185), the Convention for the Protection of Individuals with Regard to Automatic Processing of Personal Data (ETS No. 108), the Additional Protocol to the Convention for the Protection of Individuals with Regard to Automated Processing of Personal Data regarding supervisory authorities and transborder data flows (ETS No.181) and the Convention on the Standards of Democratic Elections, Electoral Rights and Freedoms in the Member States of the Commonwealth of Independent States (CDL-EL(2006)031rev).

[14] One could add the Convention on the Political Rights of Women (CPRW) (1952), the International Convention on the Protection of the Rights of All Migrant Workers and Members of Their Families (ICRMW) (1990), the Convention concerning Indigenous and Tribal Peoples in Independent Countries, ILO C169 (1989), the UN Convention against Corruption (UNCAC) (2003).

operation of polling stations, funding, and security). The Recommendation follows the same structure (see also §§ 13 and 14 Explanatory Memorandum). However, not all principles call for special attention when implementing e-voting. The standards in Rec (2017)5 address only those matters (principles and conditions for implementing them) that require specific measures to be taken when e-voting is introduced (§ 15 Explanatory Memorandum).

"Legal standards" refers to provisions contained in the Appendix I to the Rec(2017) 5 (Appendix II, Glossary of terms, under "standard"). The Recommendation contains legal standards on e-voting which set objectives that e-voting shall fulfill to conform to the principles of democratic elections. The aim is to harmonize the implementation of the principles when e-voting is used in member States. Standards are common to the Council of Europe region. Unless specific mention, standards apply to all forms of e-voting. Standards which are specific only to one or to some forms do mention this (§§ 4, 5, 7, 8, 28 Explanatory Memorandum).

Legal standards are to be distinguished from "technical standards" which refer to a technical norm, usually in the form of a formal document that establishes uniform engineering or technical criteria, methods, processes and practice (Appendix II, Glossary of terms). The Recommendation and the associated Guidelines deal with legal standards.

The specificity of the Guidelines is that they offer instructions on the implementation of the standards. They are less "binding"[15] than the Recommendation and are expected to evolve rapidly over time (§26 Explanatory Memorandum) to reflect changes in law and technology. Also, the present (June 2017) version of the Guidelines needs to be completed through further work to address all forms and all aspects of e-voting covered by the new Recommendation.

"Requirement" is defined in the Recommendation (Appendix II) as a singular, documented need of what a particular product or service should be or perform. Standard 36 (Appendix I) says that it's up to member States to develop technical, evaluation and certification requirements. Member States shall furthermore ascertain that requirements fully reflect relevant legal principles and shall keep the requirements up-to-date.

Requirements for a specific e-voting solution to be used in a given context, must be defined with respect to that specific solution and context. They must be derived from the international, national and, as the case may be, local legal principles applicable. So, by definition, e-voting detailed requirements cannot be decided in an international document like the Recommendation which is supposed to cover many different uses of e-voting in all 47 member States.

The hierarchy between principles (top), standards (middle) and requirements (bottom of the pyramid) reflects the hierarchy of the respective instruments from where they stem: international conventions/treaties, national constitution and formal law (top) –

---

[15] The Recommendation has no binding force *per se*. However it has an important influence and may even acquire binding effect, in certain cases (see Sect. 4.2 below).

international recommendations/soft law[16], national material law (middle) – lower level regulations (bottom). The hierarchy means conformity with the higher level.

3.2 Main Features and Novelties of Rec(2017)5

New definition and broader scope of e-voting. E-voting was until recently defined in two different ways by the two main international organisations active in the electoral field in the region. Rec(2004)11 of the Council of Europe defined e-voting as the *casting* of the vote through electronic means. OSCE/ODIHR, the international organization on observation of elections in the region, understands e-voting as the use of information and communication technologies (ICT) applied to *the casting and counting* of votes [16].

The new Rec(2017)5 defines e-voting as *the use of electronic means to cast and/or count the vote* (Appendix II, Glossary of terms) (see also §8 Explanatory Memorandum) thus including also the electronic scanning and counting of paper ballots. As a result, both organizations now share a common understanding of e-voting which contributes to a better understanding of the standards applicable to it in the region.

Some experts feared that by broadening the scope of e-voting to include pure e-counting of paper ballots, the Recommendation would become less sharp or less relevant. CAHVE was willing to take this risk, given the importance of raising awareness on the regulation of the use of ICT to vote and/or to count votes.

Recommendations. The Committee of Ministers took three decision (points I, II, III at the end of the preamble of Rec(2017)5). It decided (point I) to issue six recommendations (i to vi) to governments of members States that introduce, revise or update as the case may be, domestic legislation and practice in the field of e-voting (I). The Committee recommends (i) to respect all the principles of democratic elections and referendums when introducing e-voting; (ii) to assess and counter risks by appropriate measures; (iii) to be guided in their legislation, policies and practice by the standards included in Appendix I and to consider those included in the Guidelines; (iv) to review their policy and experience of e-voting and to provide the Council of Europe with a basis for holding review meetings at least every two years following its adoption. Governments are further invited (v) to share their experience in this field as well as (vi) to translate and disseminate as widely as possible the new recommendation more

---

[16] Soft-law documents include political commitments, comments to treaty/convention provisions, recommendations, good practices, etc. Examples are the comments to art.25 ICCPR, the Council of Europe recommendations or the Venice Commission's Codes of good practice. The preamble of Rec(2017)5 refers to a number of soft law instruments (the list is not exhaustive): Recommendation No. R (99) 5 of the Committee of Ministers to member States on the protection of privacy on the Internet; Recommendation Rec(2004)15 of the Committee of Ministers to member States on electronic governance; Recommendation CM/Rec(2009)1 of the Committee of Ministers to member States on electronic democracy; the document of the Copenhagen Meeting of the Conference on the Human Dimension of the OSCE; the Code of Good Practice in Electoral Matters, adopted by the Council for democratic elections of the Council of Europe and the European Commission for Democracy through Law and supported by the Parliamentary Assembly, the Congress of Local and Regional Authorities and the Committee of Ministers of the Council of Europe.

specifically among electoral management bodies, citizens, political parties, observers, NGOs, academia, providers of solutions and e-voting controlling bodies.

The other decisions were to regularly update the provisions of the Guidelines that accompany the Recommendation (point II) and to repeal the old Recommendation (2004)11 and the Guidelines thereto (point III).

Novelties. All the following new elements were discussed and decided by CAHVE during the update [17].

Recommendation i maintains that e-voting should respect all the principles of democratic elections and referendums but drops the previous comparison that it should be *"as reliable and secure as"* other (paper based) methods. The interpretation of this comparison proved problematic in the past [7]. Furthermore the benchmark is respect for all principles of democratic elections and referendums. So standards should be derived directly from the applicable principles.

Recommendation ii stresses the need to assess risks, namely those specific to e-voting and to adopt appropriate measures to counter them.

According to recommendation iii, whereas the Recommendation is intended to provide a stable framework, Guidelines are meant to be updated on a regular basis (a novelty decided by the Committee of Ministers in point II). The relationship between standards included in Appendix I and those in the Guidelines which implement them is underlined – which is also new.

Recommendation iv introduces a review policy for the Recommendation which is based on the previous practice of biannual meetings, which however had no clear basis in the Rec(2004)11 given that the (2004) rec. v foresaw (only) one (first) review meeting *within two years after the adoption* of Rec(2004)11.[17] The present Recommendation clarifies that review meetings are to be held *at least every two years following its adoption.* The update of the Guidelines, among others, will be considered and decided by member States at the periodic review meetings (§12 Explanatory Memorandum).

Recommendation vi encourages translation and dissemination policies. Such provision is recently automatically included in all Council of Europe recommendations.

Standards and Guidelines. The old standards included 142 provisions (112 in Rec (2004)11 and 30 in the associated guidelines). The new standards include 143 provisions (49 in Rec(2017)5 and 94 in the associated Guidelines). It is foreseen that the new Guidelines should be completed, i.e. expanded (§12 Explanatory Memorandum). By looking at the figures alone (142 and 143) one could say that, so far, things have not changed very much. This is not so. The structure of the old and new documents, the type and content of standards, the relations between them, all have changed. The new 143 standards are different from the old 142 ones. Several are totally new. The table

---

[17] Rec. v Rec(2004)11 read as follows: «in order to provide the Council of Europe with a basis for possible further action on e-voting within two years after the adoption of this Recommendation, the Committee of Ministers recommends that ….". In French "…afin de fournir au Conseil de l'Europe une base à partir de laquelle il pourra élaborer les actions futures en matière de vote électronique dasn les deux ans après l'adoption de cette recommandation, le Comité des Ministres recommande que…».

appended at the end of this paper illustrates some of the changes, namely "what happened" to the 112 standards of Rec(2004)11.

Novelties. Since the beginning of the updating process it was decided that the new Recommendation should be homogenous, as opposed to the old one which contained a mixture of higher and lower level standards [17]. The new Rec(2017) includes only higher level, stable standards. Guidelines are grouped under the corresponding standard in the Guidelines. Besides their detailed nature, the reason for putting the guidelines in a separate document is that they are supposed to evolve frequently to take stock of legal and technical developments. As an instrument, the Guidelines are more easily and quickly reviewed than the Recommendation, which is a more rigid and stable document.

Now, there is a clear interweaving between higher principles and conditions for implementing them (identified by the Code of good practice and reflected as headings in Appendix I of Rec(2017)5), standards (derived from the principles and included in the Appendix I) and implementation guidelines of the standards (in the Guidelines).

For instance, to ensure compliance with the principle of universal suffrage as defined in the Code (see also §14 Explanatory Memorandum), the following objectives must be met: an e-voting system shall be easy to understand and use by all voters (1); shall be designed, as far as practicable, to enable voters with special needs and the disabled to vote independently (2); in case of remote e-voting, this channel shall be only a complementary and optional one unless and until it is universally accessible (3); and, in case of remote e-voting again, voters' attention shall be drawn as to the validity of their e-vote (4). To streamline the implementation of standard 1 (interface easy to understand and use), the following guidelines are proposed: the presentation of the voting options on the devices used by voters should be optimized for the average voter who does not have specialized computer knowledge (a); voters should be involved in the design of the e-voting system (b); consideration should be given to the compatibility of new products with existing ones (c). And so on with the other principles, standards and guidelines.

Several new standards have been included in the Recommendation. They were previously in the guidelines or suggested by research. Their inclusion translates regional consensus on these new objectives that e-voting must fulfil to conform to the principles. Prominent examples are standards 15, 17 and 18 which introduce individual and universal verifiability; standard 20 on data minimisation; standard 29 which stipulates that the responsibilities of the electoral management body with respect to e-voting should be clarified in the relevant regulation and that this one should foresee that the EMB has the control over e-voting systems; standard 36 which says that member States develop technical, evaluation and certification requirements, that they ascertain that requirements fully reflect relevant legal principles and that they keep requirements up to date; or standard 40 which says that the electoral management body shall be responsible for the respect and enforcement of all requirements even in the presence of failures and attacks.

Many other provisions, initially inherited from the old standards were reviewed, corrected, clarified (see also [18]). Examples include standard 9 which now takes into account the multiple voting possibility (see criticism of the previous standard in [11]) or standard 23 which takes into account the verifiability proofs.

4   Use, Impact and Evolution of Rec(2017)5

4.1   Use of Rec(2017)5

International, national and local regulatory instruments of e-voting. The adoption of the old Rec(2004)11 was preceded by a Venice Commission report on the compatibility of remote voting and electronic voting with the standards of the Council of Europe [19].[18] The report notes that electronic voting is neither generally permitted by human rights nor ruled out a priori. Instead, its acceptability depends on the standards implemented in the procedure. The report concludes that e-voting's compatibility depends primarily on adequate provision, through national legislation and legal practice, of the prescribed conditions, taking particular account of technical and social conditions.

This remains true and illustrates the importance of a good regulatory framework for e-voting. International standards are only one part of it. Additionally, national and, as the case may be, local regulations apply to the of e-voting in a specific case. The challenge is to have a coherent corpus of international-national-local regulations. While Rec(2017)5 contributes to clarifying the international standards, work is still necessary at the national level (in most cases). Yet, as shown by several authors in this conference and elsewhere (examples include [14, 20–22]) the national legislator faces several difficulties and dilemmas when regulating e-voting.

By clarifying the application of European principles of democratic elections to e-voting, Rec(2017)5 clarifies the corpus of international regulations that apply to e-voting. The work of CAHVE to update the European standards to take stock of experiences and developments in the technical and legal fields, followed a clear, previously agreed strategy. It can serve as an example to the national legislator too. The challenges and ambitions are similar. Furthermore the national legislator should (according to rec.iii) build upon the Council of Europe documents and does not need to start to regulate e-voting from scratch.

What about national legal specificities? The Recommendation recognizes that countries may have additional principles. They may make a stricter or broader interpretation of the European principles and standards. There may be exceptions and restrictions or the need to apply one principle in a stricter way and another one in a looser way, etc. At the end, such decisions are to be taken by the national authority. However, some basic conditions should be respected. Such decisions should be taken by the competent authority. They are based on law, are in the general interest, respect proportionality, etc. The overall aim of democratic elections should be respected (see also §18 Explanatory Memorandum).

---

[18] The word "standards" in the title of this Venice Commission report from 2004 corresponds to the concept "principles" as defined in this paper and as referred to in Rec(2017)5. This inconsistency illustrates the fact that e-voting challenges legal regulations among others because it requires a very well structured and coherent body of regulations, including terminology, which of course is far from being the case.

Rec(2017)5 and certification of e-voting solutions. Compliance with the European standards alone does not guarantee the democratic quality of a specific e-election. National (and, as the case may be, local) principles apply to the use of e-voting in a specific context. Detailed requirements should be derived from all applicable principles, including national and local ones. This task, as well as ensuring that such requirements comply with higher principles and are up-to-date, fall on member States (standard 36). It follows that detailed requirements for a specific use of e-voting cannot logically be put in a document like the Recommendation which ambitions to cover all kinds of e-voting in all 47 member States (see also Sect. 3.1 above).

Detailed requirements are necessary in order to evaluate and certify a specific e-voting system to be used in a given election. It follows that such certification cannot be done against the standards included in the Recommendation alone. Whether it is possible and whether it makes sense to have a "partial certification" against the European standards alone is another question which is not discussed in the Recommendation.

4.2   Impact of the Recommendation

As a soft-law instrument (not binding by definition), the Recommendation has however an important influence on member States and may even become binding, in certain circumstances. This is briefly explained below (for more details see [23]).

Influence. As a legal instrument, a recommendation indicates unanimous agreement regarding the measures contained in it. According to articles 15 (§a and b) and 20 of the Council of Europe Statutes, a recommendation requires the unanimous vote of the representatives casting a vote and the presence of a majority of the representatives entitled to sit on the Committee. So Rec(2017)5 contains unanimously accepted interpretations of the principles on democratic elections as applied to e-voting and this in the whole region and for all kinds of e- elections.

According to [19] where the contracting States share a common or homogenous standard on a question related to the ECHR's guarantees, this tends to favour acceptance of this standard at European level as well. Where it is impossible to identify a common point of view among the various member States, national authorities have greater scope for discretion. This gives the standards in the Recommendation a clear advantage. This also explains why they are used as legal benchmark for evaluating e-voting by observers [16].

Furthermore, as foreseen in the Council of Europe Statue, Rec(2017)5 recommends that governments keep under review their policy on e-voting and experience of it (rec. iv). They are encouraged to share their experience in this field (rec. v) and to translate and disseminate it (rec. vi). All this helps increase acceptance of the Recommendation.

Possible binding character. Soft law instruments reflect common agreement on the interpretation of conventional principles. In the Council of Europe region, the European Court of Human Rights (ECtHR), which rules on alleged violations of the rights set out in the ECHR, including of the right to free elections by secret ballot (P1-3), adopts a dynamic interpretation of the rights and freedoms granted by the Convention. With the aim to ensure the effectiveness of rights, the Court considers the Convention as being a living instrument which must be interpreted in the light of present-day conditions.[19] In practice, this means that the Court makes a dynamic interpretation of the Convention: in interpreting the principles in the light of present conditions, the Court seeks guidance (some say legitimacy) in the common trends of legal and social developments in the region. In the electoral field, Venice Commission's Code of Good practice in electoral matters is regularly referred to by the Court. This may be the case, in the future, with Rec(2017)5. When included in a Court judgment (binding on member states) the referenced soft law provision becomes binding.

4.3   Future Work on E-voting at the Council of Europe

The new Recommendation foresees periodical review meetings at least every two years and introduces a review mechanism for the Guidelines. These new elements were strongly supported by national experts at CAHVE.

The Recommendation provides precious guidance to member States. However it only includes a set of minimum standards applicable throughout the region. Countries can and actually do more, going beyond the minimum European standard, namely to reflect their specific traditions and needs. At some point, there may be a broader, regional consensus, on new standards. Such novelty will probably be reflected in (a new version of) the recommendation.

For instance, the old Guidelines on transparency suggested that countries experiment verifiability techniques which allow for more transparency. However the old Recommendation had no provisions on verifiability. A few years later, almost all countries that were using e-voting (both remote internet voting and e-voting on voting machines at polling stations) introduced mandatory regulations requiring certain verifiability tools (individual and/or universal verifiability tools) as a precondition for allowing e-voting.[20] The new Rec(2017)5 now has integrated such consensus and recommends the introduction of verifiability tools to create a chain of trust (provisions §15 - §18) in the text of the recommendation itself.

It is the task of the review meetings to monitor such developments and decide as the case may be to update the Guidelines. A possible decision, at some later point, to update the Recommendation will require the preliminary approval of the Committee of Ministers.

5   Conclusion

This paper explains the new European standards on e-voting, the novelties introduced by Rec(2017)5 compared to the previous Rec(2004)11 and the underlying motivations, inputs and work to update/produce the new standards. It further explains the relations and mutual influences between international and national standards and comments on the future development of the European standards.

---

[19] Constant case law of the ECtHR.

[20] This happened for instance in Norway, Estonia, Switzerland, Belgium.

If there is one general conclusion to be drawn, it is about the importance of maintaining a regular dialogue between international standard setting bodies, national authorities and experts, academia and other e-voting interested stakeholders on the interpretation of standards, their implementation and their possible evolution. This has taken place in the past at the Council of Europe and is foreseen to continue in the future. Thanks to this dialogue the new Rec(2017)5 and the associated Guidelines have integrated lessons learned from past developments and have adopted the necessary structure and mechanisms that allow them to remain up-to-date in the future.

Appendix

See Table 1.

Table 1. Correlation between (old) Rec(2004)11 standards and the Rec(2017)5 and accompanying Guidelines. Decisions with respect to the old standards (under Explanation)

Standards Rec(2004) 11 (App. I, II and III)	Standards Rec (2017)5 (App. I) and Guidelines[a]	Explanation	Standards Rec(2004) 11 (App. I, II and III)	Standards Rec (2017)5 (App. I) and Guidelines	Explanation
1	1	Changed	57	30a	Unchanged
2	Discarded	Out of scope	58	49	Changed
3	2	Unchanged	59	39	Changed
4	3	Unchanged	60	39c	Changed
5	9	Changed	61	1, 2a	Changed
6	9	Changed)	62	1b	Unchanged
7	9	Changed	63	2a	Unchanged
8	6	Changed	64	1c	Changed
9	10	Changed	65	1a	Changed
10	12	Unchanged	66	35	Changed
11	12a	Changed	67	discarded Mentioned in Explanatory Memorandum	Over-specified
12	10b	Unchanged	68	discarded	Over-specified
13	13	Changed	69	31a, 43, 40j	Changed
14	16	Changed	70	40i, 40 k, 40 l-i	Changed
15	10c	Changed	71	40i, 40 k	Changed
16	19	Changed	72	40j	Changed
17	26, 19	Changed	73	42a	Changed
18	26, 19	Changed	74	40 l-ii	Unchanged

(continued)

Table 1. (*continued*)

Standards Rec(2004) 11 (App. I, II and III)	Standards Rec (2017)5 (App. I) and Guidelines[a]	Explanation	Standards Rec(2004) 11 (App. I, II and III)	Standards Rec (2017)5 (App. I) and Guidelines	Explanation
19	18, 19	Changed	75	40 h, 40i, 40 m	Changed
20	32	Changed	76	47, 47a	Changed
21	32	Changed	77	40e	Unchanged
22	32c	Changed	78	21	Changed
23	34	Unchanged	79	40 g	Unchanged
24	33	Unchanged	80	41a	Changed
25	37	Changed	81	21, 21a	Changed
26	15-18	Changed	82	7	Changed
27	Discarded	Unclear	83	33a	Unchanged
28	40	Changed	84	39b	Unchanged
29	40-49	Changed	85	40, 37, 39	Changed
30	40	Changed	86	48	Unchanged
31	42	Unchanged	87	discarded	out of scope
32	41	Changed	88	discarded	out of scope
33	41b, 41c	Unchanged	89	48	Changed
34	40, 44, 45, 46	Changed	90	11, 10a	Changed
35	21, 45	Changed	91	49a	Unchanged
36	32	Changed	92	15	Changed
37	32	Changed	93	23b, 23c	Changed
38	32	Changed	94	7, 8, 9	Changed
39	Discarded	Registering is not considered	95	15	Changed
40	Discarded	Out of scope	96	28 k	Split
41	Discarded	Bad practice	97	48	Changed
42	Discarded	Out of scope	98	30b	Changed
43	Discarded	Out of scope	99	30d	Unchanged
44	9	Changed	100	39	Changed
45	32	Changed	101	39, 39a-c	Changed
46	32	Changed	102	39	Unchanged
47	5	Changed	103	39a	Unchanged
48	5, 10, 11	Changed	104	39	Changed
49	5	Language	105	41e	Changed
50	4, 32	Changed	106	26	Changed
51	23	Changed	107	39	Changed
52	23	Changed	108	15–18	Changed

(*continued*)

Table 1. (*continued*)

Standards Rec(2004) 11 (App. I, II and III)	Standards Rec (2017)5 (App. I) and Guidelines[a]	Explanation	Standards Rec(2004) 11 (App. I, II and III)	Standards Rec (2017)5 (App. I) and Guidelines	Explanation
53	23, 24	Unchanged	109	40, 41	Changed
54	Discarded	Unclear	110	40, 41	Unchanged
55	26b		111	36, 37	Changed
56	30, 34	Changed	112	Discarded	

[a] Standards in Rec(2017)5 are numbered 1, 2, 3, etc. Provisions in the Guidelines should be numbered by letters a, b, c, etc. which follow the number of the respective standard. E.g. guidelines to standard 1 are numbered 1a, 1b, 1c, etc. Due to a formatting error, the numbering in the document Guidelines published on the website of the Council of Europe is different. E.g. guidelines to standard 1 are now numbered 7a, 7b, 7c and so on. However, this should be corrected soon and the numbering adopted here should correspond to the one on the published document, https://search.coe.int/cm/Pages/result_details.aspx?ObjectID=0900001680 726c0b - last consulted 4.08.2017.

References

1. Driza Maurer, A.: Report on the possible update of the Council of Europe Recommendation Rec (2004)11 on legal, operational and technical standards for e-voting (2013). https://rm.coe.int/168059be23
2. Wenda, G., Stein, R.: Ten Years of Rec(2004)11 – The Council of Europe and E-voting. In: Krimmer, R., Volkamer, M. (eds.) Proceedings of Electronic Voting 2014 (EVOTE 2014), TUT Press, Tallinn, pp. 105–110
3. Council of Europe, Terms of Reference of the Ad hoc committee of experts on legal, operational and technical standards for e-voting (2015). https://search.coe.int/cm/Pages/result_details.aspx?ObjectId=09000016805c40c4
4. Council of Europe, Committee of Ministers, Recommendation CM/Rec(2017)5 of the Committee of Ministers to member States on standards for e-voting (Adopted by the Committee of Ministers on 14 June 2017 at the 1289th meeting of the Ministers' Deputies) (2017)
5. Council of Europe, Ad hoc Committee of Experts on Legal, Operational and Technical Standards for e-voting (CAHVE), Explanatory Memorandum to Recommendation CM/Rec (2017)5 of the Committee of Ministers to member States on standards for e-voting (Item considered by the GR-DEM at its meetings on 20 April and 1 June 2017) (2017)
6. Council of Europe, Ad hoc Committee of Experts on Legal, Operational and Technical Standards for e-voting (CAHVE), Guidelines on the implementation of the provisions of Recommendation CM/Rec(2017)5 on standards for e-voting (Item considered by the GR-DEM at its meetings on 20 April and 1 June 2017) (2017)
7. Driza Maurer, A.: Ten Years Council of Europe Rec(2004)11: Lessons learned and Outlook. In: Krimmer, R., Volkamer, M. (eds.) Proceedings of Electronic Voting 2014 (EVOTE2014), TUT Press, Tallinn, pp. 111–120
8. Jones, D.W.: The European 2004 Draft E-Voting Standard: Some critical comments (2004). http://homepage.cs.uiowa.edu/~jones/voting/coe2004.shtml
9. McGaley, M., Gibson, J.P.: A Critical Analysis of the Council of Europe Recommendations on e-voting (2006). https://www.usenix.org/legacy/event/evt06/tech/full_papers/mcgaley/mcgaley.pdf

10. Prandini, M., Ramilli, M.: Taking the best of both worlds: a comparison and integration of the U.S. and EU approaches to e-voting systems evaluation. In: Proceedings of the 44th Hawaii International Conference on System Sciences (HICSS-44). IEEE Computer Society Press (2011)

11. Barrat, J., Goldsmith, B.: Compliance with International Standards, Norwegian e-vote project   (2012).   http://www.regjeringen.no/upload/KRD/Prosjekter/e-valg/evaluering/Topic7_Assessment.pdf

12. Neumann, S., Volkamer, M.: A holistic framework for the evaluation of internet voting systems. In: Zissis, D., Lekkas, D. (eds.) Design, Development and Use of Secure Electronic Voting Systems. IGI Global Book Series (2014)

13. Bundesverfassungsgericht (German Constitutional Court), Decision 2 BvC 3/07, 2 BvC 4/07, 3 March 2009 http://www.bundesverfassungsgericht.de/entscheidungen/cs20090303_2bvc000307.html

14. Driza Maurer, A., Barrat, J. (eds.): E-Voting Case Law – A Comparative Analysis. Routledge, London (2015, 2017)

15. European Commission for Democracy through Law (Venice Commission), Code of Good Practice on Electoral Matters - Guidelines and explanatory report (2002). http://www.venice.coe.int/webforms/documents/default.aspx?pdffile=CDL-AD(2002)023rev-e

16. OSCE/ODIHR, Handbook for the observation of new voting technologies (2013). http://www.osce.org/odihr/elections/104939

17. Driza Maurer, A. (CAHVE(2015)2add), Report on the scope and format of the update of Rec (2004)11 (2015). https://rm.coe.int/168059ace6

18. Driza Maurer, A. Update of the Council of Europe Recommendation on Legal, Operational and Technical Standards for E-Voting – a Legal Perspective. In: Tagungsband IRIS (Internationales Rechtsinformatik Symposion), Universität Salzburg (2016)

19. European Commission for Democracy through Law (Venice Commission)/Grabenwarter, Ch., Report on the compatibility of remote voting and electronic voting with the standards of the Council of Europe (2004). http://www.venice.coe.int/webforms/documents/CDL-AD (2004)012.aspx

20. Hill, R.: E-Voting and the law. issues, solutions, and a challenging question. In: Krimmer, R., et al. (eds.) Proceedings of E-VOTE-ID 2016, pp. 123–138. TUT Press, Tallinn (2016)

21. Loeber, L.: Legislating for e-enabled elections: dilemmas and concerns for the legislator. In: Krimmer, R., et al. (eds.) Proceedings of E-VOTE-ID 2016, pp. 139–160. TUT Press, Tallinn (2016)

22. Barrat, J. (Coord.): El voto electronic y sus dimensiones jurídicas : entre la ingenua complacencia y el rechazo precipitado, Iustel (2016)

23. Driza Maurer, A.: The european standards applicable to innovative services in electoral processes, report for Venice commission. In: International Conference Innovative Services and Effective Electoral Operations, Borjomi, Georgia, 27 February 2017

A Formally Verified Single Transferable Voting Scheme with Fractional Values

Milad K. Ghale, Rajeev Goré, and Dirk Pattinson$^{(\boxtimes)}$

Research School of Computer Science, ANU, Canberra, Australia
dirk.pattinson@anu.edu.au

Abstract. We formalise a variant of the Single Transferable Vote scheme with fractional transfer values in the theorem prover Coq. Our method advocates the idea of vote counting as application of a sequence of rules. The rules are an intermediate step for specifying the protocol for vote-counting in a precise symbolic language. We then formalise these rules in Coq. This reduces the gap between the legislation and formalisation so that, without knowledge of formal methods, one can still validate the process. Moreover our encoding is modular which enables us to capture other Single Transferable Vote schemes without significant changes. Using the built-in extraction mechanism of Coq, a Haskell program is extracted automatically. This program is guaranteed to meet its specification. Each run of the program outputs a certificate which is a precise, independently checkable record of the trace of computation and provides all relevant details of how the final result is obtained. This establishes correctness, reliability, and verifiability of the count.

1 Introduction

Elections are at the heart of democratic systems, where people choose whom they perceive as the fittest candidate according to their preferences. Consequently, providing public trust into correctness of elections, including the count of votes, becomes crucial. Usually this trust is established by allowing observers of each party, or members of the public, to scrutinise the count, thereby ascertaining the authenticity of the final outcome of the election. Moreover, scrutiny sheets are published later to provide detail about the process.

In practice, scrutiny leaves much to be desired. For example, costly mistakes have happened in Australia so that the whole election was cancelled and had to be re-run again [9]. Because of such incidents, and the cost of hand-counted elections, use of computers for vote counting has received more attention. Unfortunately, the source code of the program used to count votes is kept secret in most cases as it is "commercial in confidence" [2]. These programs merely output the final result without giving information as to how and through what exact steps they reached the final result. Since legislation often leaves some corner cases open to interpretation, for instance tie breaking, implementation of the protocol is not straightforward. Due to this inexactness, examining the output of such commercial-in-confidence programs against any other program for

© Springer International Publishing AG 2017
R. Krimmer et al. (Eds.): E-Vote-ID 2017, LNCS 10615, pp. 163–182, 2017.
DOI: 10.1007/978-3-319-68687-5_10

(hopefully) producing the same output becomes extremely difficult. Therefore questions about correctness of the count by these programs are still addressed unsatisfactorily.

Formal verification [6] now is mature enough to solve this problem. In this paper, we understand the process of counting votes in accordance to the protocol as a finite sequence of atomic steps, where uncounted ballots are dealt with and distributed among candidates according to the algorithm laid down by the protocol. Each of these stages can be formally expressed mathematically. For example, every count begins from a set of ballots and continues through some intermediate steps where candidates are elected or excluded until eventually the final stage where winners of the election are declared is reached. We represent every single possible stage of the count (or computation) by formal objects called *judgements*. Judgements are categorised into three kinds: initial, intermediate and final.

Initial judgements are the ones that an election begins with, namely the set of uncounted ballots.

Intermediate judgements consist of recording: the uncounted ballots; the tally of each candidate; elected and excluded candidates; those awaiting their surplus to be transferred; and a backlog of already elected candidates whose surplus still needs to be transferred.

Final judgements are the ones where the election has come to an end by declaring winners.

Therefore at each stage of the count, judgements record all the necessary information that represents a state of the process of tallying the ballots. In every election, the protocol specifies how to move from one point of the count to another, for instance, by electing or eliminating a candidate. Each of these statements telling us what to do in counting are captured by mathematical rules which state when and how precisely one can progress from a given judgement to another judgement (stage of the count). Every rule has side conditions that specify when precisely the rule may be applied. An election count therefore simply becomes a sequence of correctly applied mathematical rules for counting which begin with an initial judgement and end with a final one. For the purpose of this paper, we have translated the *textual* specification of the protocol into a *mathematical,* rule-based formulation. While we have taken care to correctly capture the protocol, this step would need to be validated by legal professionals.

Judgements and rules specified mathematically are formalised in the theorem-prover Coq [1]. We formally prove three main properties of the formalised scheme.

Measure decrease: at each stage of the computation, if there is an applicable rule of counting, applying it decreases a well-defined measure of complexity.

Rule application: whenever we are in a *non-final* stage of the count one can always apply at least one rule. (In fact, *exactly* one rule can be applied.)

Termination: from every non-final judgement, we can always reach a final judgement via rule applications, i.e. a stage where winners are announced.

Coq has a built-in automatic extraction mechanisms [8] that allow us to automatically synthesise functional programs (we choose to extract into Haskell) from Coq code. As we show by experiment, the extracted code is capable of dealing with real-size elections. More importantly, every run of the program produces a *certificate*. This is the trace of the computation performed by the program. It records each single step taken from an initial to a final stage of the count along with the rules applied to move between judgements. The certificate can then be taken and checked for correctness by other programs in which the scrutineers trusts, or simply spot-checked by hand. This allows for a larger group of observers (in particular, more than can fit into the room where hand counting takes place) to ascertain the correctness of the count. Furthermore, we no longer need to be concerned with the integrity of hardware, as the validity of the certificate will guarantee the correctness of the count. Indeed, we no longer need to trust anyone or anything, including the actual program which output the certificate. By itself the certificate implements *universal verifiability* [7] as a qualitative measure of the reliability of elections.

Finally our encoding is *modular*: if the rules are changed, we only need to adapt the (formal) proof of the applicability and the measure decrease theorem. When we prove any assertion about the rules, since the definition of each of them stands alone, we break the assertion into small pieces and prove it for each rule separately, thus minimising number of steps needed to establish the proof obligations. Also, to capture other STV schemes, only part of one single rule might need modification. Combined with the above feature this allows us to prove the same assertions for the new STV encoded fairly smoothly.

Related work. DeYoung and Schürmann [4] pioneered vote counting as computation in a logical system. They use a formal system called Linear Logic [5] as a bridge between the legislation and their formalisation of the voting protocol in the logical framework Celf [11]. The gap between the protocol and linear logic specification is less compared to a direct implementation in a main stream programming language. However, technical understanding of linear logic and its syntax is required to fully follow their formal specification. Furthermore, to the best of our knowledge, their work could not deal with real-size elections. Pattinson and Schürmann [10], and Verity [13] approached the task for dealing with First-Past-The-Post and a simple form of STV in a similar way except that they use type-theory as a bridge between protocol and formalisation, and the theorem-prover Coq to formalise the rules and establish their properties, like existence of winners at each election. Dawson et al. [3] employ the HOL4 theorem prover to formalise Hare-Clark STV. A specification of the scheme is given based on Higher-order Logic. Then an SML program is produced inside HOL4 along with some properties proved about the code which is then manually translated into executable code. There is no proof that the manual transliteration from HOL4 to ML is correct, and no certificate is output after a run of the program. While there is no formal proof of the correctness of the (automated) extraction of code from Coq proofs, our approach, in particular the certificate, increases trust in the final result. Sources of this paper are available at: https:// github.com/MiladKetabGhale/STV-Counting-ProtocolVerification.

2   From Legal Text to Logical Rules

There are many variants of STV schemes used around the world, e.g. in the Netherlands, India, and Australia. They mostly differ in the quota, the mechanism to transfer the surplus, the computation of transfer values, and the method of tie breaking. Our formalisation is based on the ANU-Union STV scheme [12], a basic version of STV that very similar e.g. to the scheme used to elect the Australian Senate. The main features of this scheme are:

Step-by-step surplus transfer. Surplus votes of already elected candidates, who are awaiting for their surplus to be transferred, are dealt with, one at a time, in order of first preferences.

Electing after each transfer. After each transfer of values, candidates that reach the quota are elected immediately.

Fractional transfer. The value of vote transfer is a fractional number determined by a specific formula.

For the description of the protocol, we refer to the votes in excess of the quota that contribute to the election of a candidate as the *surplus votes* (of that candidate). The ANU-Union counting protocol proceeds as follows:

1. decide which ballots are *formal*.
2. determine what the quota exactly is.
3. count the first preference for each *formal* ballot paper and place the vote in the pile of the votes of the preferred candidate.
4. if there are vacancies, any candidate that reaches the quota is declared elected.
5. if all the vacancies have been filled, counting terminates and the result is announced.
6. if the number of vacancies exceeds the number of continuing candidates, all of them are declared elected and the result is announced.
7. if there are still vacancies and all ballots are counted, and there is an elected candidate with surplus, go to step 8 otherwise go to step 9.
8. in case of surplus votes, transfer them to the next continuing preference appearing on each of those votes at a fractional value according to the following formula:

$$\text{new value} = \frac{\text{number of votes of elected candidate} - \text{quota}}{\text{number of votes of elected candidate}} \tag{1}$$

   Subsequent transfer values are computed as the product of the current transfer value with previous transfer value.
9. if there are still vacancies and all ballots are counted, and all surplus votes are transferred, choose the candidate with the least amount of votes and exclude that candidate from the list of continuing candidates. Also transfer all of their votes according to the next preference appearing on each of the votes in his pile. The transfer value of the ballots shall remain unchanged.

10. if there is more than one elected candidate, first transfer the surplus of the candidate who has the largest surplus. If after a transfer of surplus, a continuing candidate exceeds the quota, declare them elected and transfer their surplus, only after all of the earlier elected candidates' surpluses have been dealt with.
11. at transfer stage, candidates who are already elected or eliminated receive no vote.

2.1   Formalisation as Logical Rules

We need to introduce some symbols which formally represent concepts in the protocol. Then by using them, we can mathematically express different parts of the protocol. Below is a list of concepts along with the corresponding symbols used to express them.

C	a set of candidates
$\mathbb{Q}$	the set of rational numbers
$\mathsf{List}(C)$	the set of all possible list of candidates
$\mathsf{List}(C) \times \mathbb{Q}$	the set of all (possible) ballots (with transfer values)
B	shorthand for $\mathsf{List}(C) \times \mathbb{Q}$
A	initial list of all of the candidates
st	initial number of vacancies
bs	initial list of ballots cast to be counted
bl	the list of elected candidates whose surplus is to be transferred
b, d	to represent a ballot
ba, ba'	list of ballots
ba_ϵ	empty list of ballots
c, c'	to represent a candidate
t, nt, t'	tally function, from C into $\mathbb{Q}$
p, np	function for computing pile of a candidate, from C to B
e, ne	for characterizing list of elected candidates so far
$[]$	representing empty list of candidates
$l_1 {+}{+} l_2$	list l_2 is appended to the end of list l_1
h, nh	for representing list of continuing candidates in the election
qu	for the quota of the election as a rational number

Before explaining the role of above symbols in the formalisation, we decompose counting of an election into its integral parts. Every *election count* has components which put together form the whole process:

1. candidates competing in the election
2. ballots consisting of a list of candidates to be ranked and a fractional value of the ballot
3. quota of the election
4. stages of the counting (or computation)
5. a group of candidates called *elected* candidates
6. a group of candidates called *continuing* candidates

7. a group of candidates already elected who have exceeded the quota
8. the tally of votes of each candidate
9. the set of ballots that have been counted for each individual candidate.

Here a ballot $b \in B$ has two parts: one part is a list of candidates and the other is the value that the ballot has. So a ballot b is a pair (l, q), for some $l \in \mathsf{List}$ (C) and a number $q \in \mathbb{Q}$. The character $ba \in B$, is reserved to show the set of ballots which require to be counted in each single state of the count (ba for "ballots requiring attention"). The current tally for each candidate is represented by the function t. Item 9 above is expressed by the function pile p. At each stage of the count for any candidate c, $p(c)$ determines which votes are given to the candidate c. The list $bl \in \mathsf{List}(C)$ which is the backlog, is the list of already elected candidates whose votes are yet to be transferred. The notation e (for "elected") and h (for "hopeful", as c already represents candidates) respectively represent the list of elected and continuing candidates at each stage.

We must formally express stages of the computation that occur during a counting process. For this purpose, we introduce three kinds of *judgements*, which encapsulate the concept of *stages of the computation*. When forming a judgement, there could be *assumptions* that are hypothesised in order to assert that judgement. The symbol $\vdash$ is used to enclose those assumptions in the judgement.

Initial. $bs, st, A \vdash \mathsf{initial}(ba)$ where A is the initial list of all continuing candidates, bs is the initial list of all ballots, and st is the initial number of vacancies.

In an election, assuming we have an initial list of ballots bs, initial number of vacancies st, and a list A of all candidates competing in the election, $\mathsf{initial}(ba)$ is an initial stage of computation, where ba is the list of uncounted formal ballots.

Intermediate. $bs, st, A \vdash \mathsf{state}(ba, t, p, bl, e, h)$ where A, bs and st are as above.

In an election, assuming we have an initial list of ballots bs, initial number of vacancies st, and a list A of all candidates competing in the election, $\mathsf{state}(ba, t, p, bl, e, h)$ is an intermediate stage of the computation, where ba is the list of uncounted ballots at this point, for a candidate c, $t(c)$ is the tally recording the number of votes c has received up to this point, $p(c)$ is the pile of votes counted towards the tall of candidate c, bl is the list of elected candidates whose surpluses have not yet been transferred, e is the list of elected candidates by this point, and h is the list of continuing candidates up to this stage.

Final. $bs, st, A \vdash \mathsf{winners}(w)$ where A, bs and st are as above.

In an election, assuming we have an initial list of ballots bs, initial number of vacancies st, and a list A of all candidates competing in the election, $\mathsf{winners}(w)$ is a final stage of the computation, where w is the final list consisting of all of the declared elected candidates.

Assumptions on the left of the turnstile symbol ($\vdash$) are not shown from now on to improve readability of the formalisation and we shall employ the term *judgement* interchangeably with *stage of computation*. Also we note that our computations make no essential use of the employed concepts such as continuing candidates as lists of candidates instead of a set of candidates, and ballots as lists instead of multi-sets. The rules defined later are ignorant of the order of continuing candidates or the ballots cast. Therefore use of lists is simply a matter of convenience in view of the formalisation in a theorem prover.

Now we are in a position to present formal rules capturing the scheme. For each of the rules, there are *side conditions* stated inside the definitions of the rules. They are propositions which impose constraints on the formalisation of rules so that we can apply the rules only if those conditions are met. These conditions are formal counterpart of the protocol clauses. Satisfying them when applying rules ascertains us that the protocol is (formally) met.

The first rule *start* specifies how the process of computation begins. An initial list of ballots $ba \in$ List (B) is filtered so that *informal* ballots are eliminated. Based on the number of *formal* ballots the quota qu is determined. Here we use the Droop quota, but later we explain that one can simply choose a different formulation of qu suited for their particular STV scheme.

Definition 1 (start). *Let the list of uncounted ballots ba and the judgement initial (ba) be given. Then by the counting rule* start, *we can transit to the judgement* state $(ba', nt, np, [], [], A)$ *where*

$$\frac{\textit{initial } (ba)}{\textit{state } (ba', nt, np, [], [], A)} \; start$$

1. ba' *is the list of formal ballots,* $qu = \frac{length(ba')}{st+1} + 1$ *is the quota (a fractional value in the ANU union voting protocol)*
2. *the list of formal ballots appended to the list of informal ballots is a permutation of the list of total ballots.*
3. *for every candidate c, the tally $nt(c)$ is zero and the pile $np(c)$ is empty, i.e. $\forall c, nt(c) = 0$ and $np(c) = ba_\epsilon$*
4. *no one is elected yet, i.e. $e = []$, and no one has any surplus yet, i.e. $bl = []$*

The second rule *count* states how votes are counted. Assume we are in a stage state (ba, t, p, bl, e, h). The rule *count* determines what the next stage of the computation is. First of all ba should not be empty, as it would not make sense to count because there would be no ballots to deal with. Besides, the rule asserts that the next judgement is of an intermediate kind. Therefore it will look like state$(ba_\epsilon, nt, np, nbl, ne, nh)$. Moreover, it tells us what each of the components are exactly. ba_ϵ is the empty list of ballots. Take a candidate c. If $c \notin h$ then c receives no vote and therefore $np(c) = p(c)$ and also the tally of c will remain the same so that $nt(c) = t(c)$. But if $c \in h$, then we collect all of those votes which prefer the candidate c and collect them into a list l_c and finally append l_c to the rest of the votes which c already has (namely $p(c)$). Subsequently, the tally of c is updated by adding the fractional values of all of the votes which favour c by adding the second component of each ballot in $np(c)$. When moving through the rule *count*, no one is declared elected or excluded from the election, and no change happens to the backlog as well, i.e. $nh = h$, $ne = e$, $nbl = bl$. Therefore only ba, t, and p are updated when we apply *count*. The rule deals with all of the uncounted ballots in ba in on step.

Definition 2 (count). *Suppose for ba $\in List(B)$, $t : C \to \mathbb{Q}$, $p : C \to List(B)$, bl $\in List(C)$, and $e, h \in List(C)$, and state(ba, t, p, bl, e, h) is an intermediate stage of the computation and ba is not empty. Then the* count *inference rule states that we can move to state$(ba_\epsilon, nt, np, bl, e, h)$ as our next stage of the computation with the conditions below met.*

$$\frac{state(ba, t, p, bl, e, h)}{state(ba_\epsilon, nt, np, bl, e, h)} \ count$$

1. *if a candidate c is not continuing, then c's pile and tally remain the same, i.e. $\forall c \notin h$, $np(c) = p(c)$ and $nt(c) = t(c)$*
2. *if a candidate c is continuing, then find all of the ballots which have c as their first continuing preference and put them in the pile of c, i.e. $\forall c \in h$, $np(c) = p(c) ++ l_c$, and $nt(c)$ equals to the sum of values of the ballots in the updated pile*

After counting the first preferences, we are expected to check if any candidates have reached the quota and subsequently declare them elected. The rule *elect* takes in an intermediate judgement and checks who has reached the quota and declares all of them elected in one go. The rule computes the fractional value of the surplus of each of those candidates according to the mentioned formula and puts those elected candidates into the backlog *bl* in order of the amount of votes they have received. Notice that the rule cannot be applied if *ba* is not empty.

Definition 3 (elect). *Assume state $(ba_\epsilon, t, p, bl, e, h)$ is a judgement and ba_ϵ is the empty list of ballots. Then we have the following rule whenever there exists $l \in List (C)$, a list of candidates to be elected, such that each of the conditions below hold:*

$$\frac{state \ (ba_\epsilon, t, p, bl, e, h)}{state \ (ba_\epsilon, t, np, nbl, ne, nh)} \ elect$$

1. *length of the list l is less than or equal to $st - length(e)$ (there are enough vacant seats)*
2. *every candidate in the list l has reached (or exceeded) the quota qu*
3. *the list l is ordered with respect to the number of votes each elected candidate (whose name appears in l) has received.*
4. *the updated list of elected candidates ne, contains every already elected candidates (in e) plus the ones appearing in the list l*
5. *the updated list nh has every continuing candidate whose name is in h, except those whose name also exists in l*
6. *nbl equals to bl appended by the list l, i.e. $nbl = bl ++ l$*
7. *if a candidate c is not in the list l, then pile of c is kept the same, i.e. $\forall c \notin l, np(c) = p(c)$*
8. *if a candidate c is in l, then update their pile by keeping the votes already attributed to them, but changing the value of those votes to a new fractional value according to formula (1).*

Definition 4 (ewin). *Let state* (ba, t, p, bl, e, h) *be a stage of the computation. The inference rule* ewin *asserts that* winners (e) *is the next judgement, provided that* length $(e) = $ st.

$$\frac{state\ (ba, t, p, bl, e, h)}{winners\ (e)}\ ewin$$

Close to the above, is the rule *hwin* which finishes the counting process if the sum of the number of elected and continuing candidates does not exceed st.

Definition 5 (hwin). *If state* (ba, t, p, bl, e, h) *is a judgement and* (length (e) + length $(h) \leq$ st), *then we can transit to the stage* winners $(e\ ++\ h)$.

$$\frac{state\ (ba, t, p, bl, e, h)}{winners\ (e\ ++\ h)}\ hwin$$

The sixth rule *transfer* tells us how and when to transfer votes. In order to apply the rule, the list of uncounted ballots should be empty, the backlog must contain at least one elected candidate and the number of elected candidates must be strictly less than the vacancies. Moreover, no continuing candidate should have reached the quota so it is impossible to elect someone. We then remove the candidate who is at the head position of the backlog and update the list of uncounted ballots, the pile of this particular candidate and the backlog.

Definition 6 (transfer). *Suppose state* $(ba_\epsilon, t, p, bl, e, h)$ *is the current judgement. Then the rule* transfer *allows us to progress the count to state* (nba, t, np, nbl, e, h)

$$\frac{state\ (ba_\epsilon, t, p, bl, e, h)}{state\ (nba, t, np, nbl, e, h)}\ transfer$$

and the side conditions for applying the rule are

1. *there are still seats to fill, i.e.* length $(e) <$ st
2. *no candidate has reached the quota, i.e.* $\forall c', c' \in h \rightarrow (t(c) < qu)$
3. *there exist a list* $l \in List(C)$ *and a candidate* c' *such that*
   3.1 c' *is the first candidate in the backlog and* l *is the tail of* bl, *i.e.* $bl = c' :: l$
   3.2 *remove* c' *from the backlog* bl *and update it, i.e.* $nbl = l$
   3.3 *move the votes in the pile of* c' *to the list of uncounted ballots,* $nba = p(c')$
   3.4 *empty the pile of* c', *i.e.* $np(c') = ba_\epsilon$
   3.5 *do not tamper with pile of candidates other than* c', *i.e.* $\forall c'', c'' \neq c' \rightarrow np(c'') = p(c'')$.

The last rule *elim* deals with excluding the weakest candidate among continuing candidates when there is no ballot to count, no one has been elected, or there are no votes to transfer. We find the candidate with the least amount of votes, put his votes into the list of ballots to be counted and update this particular candidate's pile and remove him from the list of candidates.

Definition 7 (elim). *Suppose state $(ba_\epsilon, t, p, [], e, h)$ is the current stage of computation. If st $<$ (length (e) + length (h)), and no candidate has reached the quota then subject to the side conditions below, the rule* elim *progresses to the judgement state $(nba, t, np, [], e, h)$.*

$$\frac{state\ (ba_\epsilon, t, p, [], e, h)}{state\ (nba, t, np, [], e, h)}\ elim$$

1. *All continuing candidates are below the quota*
2. *there exists a weakest candidate c' such that*

    2.1 *other continuing candidates have strictly more votes than c'*

    2.2 *exclude c' from current continuing list of candidates (namely h) and update it to nh*

    2.3 *remove the ballots in the pile of c' without changing the value of those ballots and put them in the list of uncounted ballots, i.e. $nba = p(c')$ and $np(c') = ba_\epsilon$.*

    2.4 *do not tamper with the pile of other candidates, i.e. $\forall c'', c'' \neq c' \rightarrow np(c'') = p(c'')$*

Remark 1. In the formulation of the rule **elim** above, note that it allows the exclusion of *one* candidate (with the least number of votes). The rule does not specify any tie-breaking. That is, if two (or more) candidates tie for the smallest tally, *one* of them can be eliminated non-deterministically. To conform with the specification, *any* tie-breaking scheme may be used. Put differently: the specification that we give does not mandate any way of tie breaking, as long as a candidate with the least tally is chosen.

3   Formalisation as Inductive Types

Formal rules expressing the protocol were laid down in the previous section. Each of the notions introduced previously have an equivalent in the Coq formalisation. To express some of them, using Coq libraries is enough, such as rational numbers and lists. However, notions such as judgement, ballot and candidate must be defined by the user. Coq provides the user with powerful tools to state their desirable notions and properties by means of *dependent inductive types*.

In a nutshell, a *type* is a collection of values of similar structure, and a dependent inductive type is a type that depends on additional data. In our case, this data is the set of ballots cast, the initial set of candidates, and the number of vacancies. That is, we only get to speak about an election count once these parameters are fixed.

3.1   ANU-Union STV

Judgements are defined as an inductive type in Fig. 1. Recall that there are three kind of judgements. We only describe the Coq formalisation of intermediate judgements in detail. In Fig. 1, the second item asserts that state is a

```
Inductive FT-Judgement :=
  | initial: list ballot -> FT-Judgement
  | state:   list ballot
             * (cand -> Q)
             * (cand -> list ballot)
             * list cand
             * {elected: list cand | length elected <= st}
             * {hopeful: list cand | NoDup hopeful}
             * Q -> FT-Judgement
  | winners: list cand -> FT-Judgement.
```

Fig. 1. Inductive definition of judgements

constructor which takes in seven values each of which has a type on its own. For example the type of the first argument is `list ballot`, and the second one is of type `(cand ->Q)`.

Recall that an intermediate judgement was of the form state (ba, t, p, bl, e, h). The definition above captures such a stage introduced earlier. However, there are two small differences in our encoding and mathematical representation of the last section. Here, we have added one more argument to an intermediate state which is of type Q (for rational numbers) and represents the quota qu. In addition, we require that the list of elected candidates doesn't exceed the number of available seats, and that the list of continuing candidates is duplicate-free. In Coq-notation, this is achieved by adding the respective constraints as in Fig. 1.

Elected candidates. The first one is the formalisation we have chosen for list of elected candidates. What it expresses is that a value of this type is a pair like (a, p_a), such that a is a list of candidates (thus of type `list cand`) and p_a is a *constraint* that the length of this value a (which is a list) does not exceed the number of vacancies, namely st.

Continuing candidates. The second one is the type of continuing candidates. Similarly values of this types are composed of two parts; a list part and proof showing the list component has *no duplicate*.

Owing to the additional constraints on elected and continuing candidates, we must discharge the corresponding proof obligation for every theorem formally established in Coq.

Now we can talk about the encoding of rules. Due to space limitation only one of them is described here. Figure 2 is the encoding for the logical formalisation of the rule *elim* given earlier in Definition 7. Each number in Fig. 2 corresponds to the number given to the clauses in Definition 7. Items † are the premise and conclusion of the elim rule, respectively. Recall that continuing candidates are represented as values which have two parts: a list component and a constraint component about that list. The function `proj1-sig` takes a value e of such type and returns the list part. The property `eqe` encodes the idea that the list part of updated continuing candidates is exactly equal to the list part of the old continuing candidates, except that it does not contain the weakest candidate c.

```
Definition elim (prem: FT-Judgement) (conc: FT-Judgement) : Prop
:= exists nba t p np e h nh,
    †      prem = state ([], t, p, [], e, h, qu)
    †'     ∧ length (proj1-sig e) + length (proj1-sig h) > st
    1      ∧ (forall c, In c (proj1-sig h) -> (t(c) < qu)
    2      ∧ exists c,
      2.1    ((forall d, In d (proj1-sig h) -> (t(c) <= t(d)))
      2.2    ∧ eqe c (proj1-sig nh) (proj1-sig h)
      2.3    ∧ nba = p(c)
      2.3    ∧np(c)=[]
      2.4    ∧ (forall d, d <> c -> np (d) = p (d)))
    †      ∧ conc = state (nba, t, np, [], e, nh, qu).
```

Fig. 2. Coq definition of elim rule

```
Definition eqe {A: Type} (x:A) (l: list A) (nl: list A) : Prop :=
    exists (l1 l2: list A),
    l = l1 ++ l2 /\ nl = l1 ++[x]++ l2 /\ not(In x l1) /\ not(In x l2).
```

Fig. 3. Definition of eqe

We argue that there is no essential gap from the mathematical specification of the protocol defined earlier to the Coq formalisation. Other formal rules are encoded similarly in correspondence to their formal counterpart in the last section. Having defined rules of counting, we can state and prove properties about their behaviour. We establish three main properties about them.

To prove the first result, by defining a well-founded ordering on the set $\mathbb{N}$ and extending it to a lexicographic ordering on the set $\mathbb{N} \times \mathbb{N} \times \mathbb{N} \times \mathbb{N}$, we impose a complexity measure on judgements.

Definition 8 (measure on judgements). *The complexity measure FT_m is defined on* non-final *judgements as*

$$FT_m : \{j : FT\text{-}Judgement \,|\, non\text{-}final\,(j)\} \longrightarrow \mathbb{N} \times \mathbb{N} \times \mathbb{N} \times \mathbb{N}$$

1. $FT_m(\mathit{initial}(ba)) = (1,0,0,0)$, *for any ba*
2. $FT_m(\mathit{state}(ba,t,p,bl,e,h,qu)) = (0, \mathit{length}(h), \mathit{length}(bl), \mathit{length}(ba))$

This imposed complexity measure is well-behaved with respect to the lexicographic ordering imposed.

Theorem 1 (Measure decrease). *Given the definition of FT-Judgements, rules of counting, and the ordering defined on non-final judgements, application of any of the rules to a non-final judgement decreases the complexity measure.*

Proof. Proof of the theorem proceeds by separating in into lemmas each of which shows the same assertion for a single rule. Each of the rules that we apply reduces at least one of the components of the measure. Since every component is finite, we reach to a base eventually.

Theorem 2 (Rule application). *For the FT-Judgements and rules of counting defined, at each non-final stage, at least one rule is applicable.*

Proof. We provide a sketch of the proof. First we check what kind of judgement the current stage of computation is.

1. If it is an initial, we apply the rule *initial-step*.
2. If it is an intermediate stage like $state(ba, t, p, bl, e, h, qu)$, then we first check whether ba is an empty list of ballots. If ba is empty then there are two possibilities at first instance: $(\text{length}(e) + \text{length}(h)) \leq st$, or $(\text{length}(e) + \text{length}(h)) > st$.
2.1 If $(\text{length}(e) + \text{length}(h)) \leq st$ we have two possibilities: $(\text{length}(e) + \text{length}(h)) = st$, or $(\text{length}(e) + \text{length}(h)) < st$. In case of the former, we can apply the rule *ewin*. If the latter occurs then the rule *hwin* is applicable.
2.2 But if $(\text{length}(e) + \text{length}(h)) > st$, we have two possibilities: bl is empty, or bl is not empty. If the former, then *elim* is applicable. Otherwise the rule *transfer* is applied.
2.3 If ba is not empty then *count* applies.

Remark 2. The structure of the proof along with tactics used in the Coq proof of the above theorem provides us with a stronger assertion: at each non-final stage of the computation, *exactly* one rule is applicable. Hence by checking carefully when and how the rules are applied, one can see our encoding matches exactly with expectations of the protocol. For instance, as the protocol specifies, if there are ballots requiring attention, they must be counted first before anything else can happen in the process of the count. It is impossible to apply any rule other than *count* if ba is not empty.

Theorem 3 (Termination). *Beginning from a non-final judgement, we always reach a final judgement.*

Proof. Given a non-final judgement by Theorem 2 we know there is one applicable rule. By Theorem 1 the application of rules is a finite process. Hence we reach to a final stage eventually.

We note that *all* proofs are fully formalised in the Coq code that accompanies the paper.

3.2 Certificate

The extracted Haskell programme, described in the next section, provides a trace of the computation.

Example 1. Suppose in an election, there are three candidates and two vacancies, where the initial set of ballots is $ba = [b_1, b_2, b_3, b_4, b_5]$.

$$b_1 = ([A, C], 1) \quad b_2 = ([A, B, C], 1) \quad b_3 = ([A, C, B], 1)$$
$$b_4 = ([B, A], 1) \quad b_5 = ([C, B, A], 1)$$

We explain how the counting would proceed in the hand-counted case.

start. Ballots which are informal are excluded. Since each ballot is non-empty and does not list a candidate more than once (i.e. represents a preference order) all ballots are formal.

count. First preferences for each candidates are determined and put into their pile. Hence candidate A receives the ballots b_1, b_2, and b_3. Candidate B receives the ballot b_4, and C receives b_5. Tallies are updated so that tally of A becomes 3, and candidate B and C reach 1.

elect. Candidate A exceeds the quota, they are elected and value of surplus votes changes to 0.11 according to the mentioned formula (1). The updated pile of A is $([A, C], 0.11)$, $([A, B, C], 0.11)$, and $([A, C, B], 0.11)$. Nothing changes about C and B at this stage.

transfer. As there are vacancies and no one else has reached or exceeded the quota, surplus of A is dealt with. The list of uncounted ballots is updated to contain the surplus of A.

count. The list of uncounted ballots is dealt with and votes are distributed according to next continuing preference. Therefore, C receives two new votes (each of value 0.11) which are $([C], 0.11)$ and $([C, B], 0.113)$. Candidate B receives one vote, which is $([B, C], 0.11)$.

elim. No continuing candidate has reached the quota, one vacancy is left, and there are no more votes to deal with. So the weakest candidate is found and excluded, which is B.

count. Candidate C receives the vote $([c], 0.11)$ from the excluded candidate B.

hwin. The only continuing candidate, that is C, is elected and as we have filled all the vacancies, a final stage has been obtained.

Figure 4 shows how our formal rules deal with the counting. They proceed according to the protocol specified earlier. The starting point is the initial state initial(ba). Then, sequentially, counting rules are applied until a final stage is obtained. The quota is a fractional value, which is computed by the rule application **start.** Notice that our program computes numbers by using the extracted data type of rational numbers. So the actual arithmetic behind the computation is based on this extracted data type.

In Fig. 4, all rational numbers are rounded to two decimal places for the sake of readability. At each intermediate step of the computation represented in Fig. 4, relevant information necessary for an external observer to verify correctness of that step and consequently of the whole process is provided. A visualisation of a computation similar to the one in Fig. 4 frees any examiner from putting trust in robustness of our counting rules, their correctness both in mathematical formalisation and implementation, and from fear of hardware malfunctioning that might lead to distortion of computation. This *trace* of computation acts as *evidence* independently verifiable by a third party on any other theorem-prover or machines which they have trust in. Figure 4 is a visualisation of a formal concept in our system, namely *provable judgement*. Informally speaking, a provable judgement is a judgement that is reachable (or *constructable*) from an initial stage by a sequence of counting rule applications. For example, in

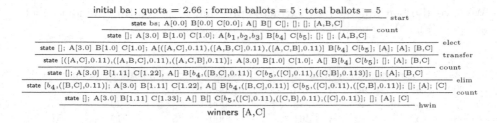

Fig. 4. Example of a certificate

Fig. 4 the last judgement is a provable judgement because it is constructed from the step before it, that is already reachable from initial stage witnessed by the proof above it, and application of the rule *ewin*. Certificates resemble the one in Fig. 4, and they are output by the extracted Haskell code upon each run of the extracted function which computes an election.

4   Extraction and Experiments

Coq has a built-in mechanism for automatic code extraction into some functional languages such as Haskell. The extraction is essentially a *syntactic* translation of the encoded Coq types and non-propositional declarations into Haskell types, as their semantics differ. While this may (rarely) be a possible source of divergence of counting process happening in Coq with its counterpart proceeding in Haskell, we alleviate this risk by producing a certificate that can be verified independently. As a consequence, simply checking the certificate (using hardware and software that is trusted by the verifier) eliminates the need of trust in the entire tool chain that has been used to generate election results. We have tested our approach against some of the past Australian Legislative Assembly elections in ACT for years 2008 and 2012 (Fig. 5). Our program returns the winners exactly as the outcome of the elections have been (despite the fact that the protocol for counting votes is slightly different). We have not benchmarked our verified and certificate-producing implementation against other, publicly available implementations as neither of them are sufficiently specified for a meaningful comparison.

electoral	ballots	vacancies	candidates	time (sec)	certificate size (MB)	year
Brindabella	63334	5	19	212	84.0	2008
Ginninderra	60049	5	27	502	124.8	2008
Molonglo	88266	7	40	1915	324.0	2008
Brindabella	63562	5	20	638	95.8	2012
Ginninderra	66076	5	28	412	131.5	2012
Molonglo	91534	7	27	2409	213.7	2012

Fig. 5. ACT Legislative Assembly 2008 and 2012

We have also benchmarked the extracted program by generating random ballot samples (Figs. 6, 7 and 8)[1].

ballots	vacancies	candidates	time (sec)
160000	5	40	2076
80000	5	40	938
40000	5	40	461

ballots	vacancies	candidates	time (sec)
80000	5	40	938
80000	5	20	213
80000	5	10	51

Fig. 6. Varying list of ballots size   **Fig. 7.** Varying number of candidates

It appears that the complexity in list of initial ballots and number of candidates is linear and quadratic, respectively. However, the program behaves differently with respect to the vacancies. As Fig. 8 shows, termination of the program does not show a necessary relation with increase or decrease in the number of vacancies. The reason is due to a complex combination of factors such as the *difference* of the number of candidates and vacancies, the overall length of each of the initial ballots, the number of *elim* rules that occur in the execution tree, and the amount of the transfer values as the result of *elim* applications.

ballots	vacancies	candidates	time (sec)
80000	1	40	982
80000	5	40	938
80000	10	40	798
80000	20	40	977

Fig. 8. Varying vacancies

To elaborate more, randomly generated ballots are almost uniformly distributed among candidates. Therefore, all of the candidates receive, more or less, the same preferences. As a result, when testing the program on random ballots since they are uniformly allocating preferences, the rule *elect* almost never applies. So only *count*, *transfer*, and *elim* apply along with *hwin*. None of these rules introduces fractional values. The only rule that creates fractional values is *elect*. The arithmetic behind our computation is that of Coq for rational numbers. Its operations perform calculations such as addition and multiplication and are not implemented tail-recursive in Coq. As a result, computations proceed slower compared to the case were values are just integers. This situation becomes worse when number of *elect* rules applied in a execution increases, because both of nominator and denominator of fractions become larger thus increasing the amount of time for these function to do the computation. Unlike randomly generated

---

[1] Results have been produced on an Intel i7 3.60 GHz Linux desktop computer with 16 GB of RAM.

elections, in real-world elections there could be many instances of the *elect* rule applications. This explains why the real elections often take longer to tally than randomly generated ballots. Also this same reason tells us why the ACT Legislative Assembly of Molonglo 2012 terminates slower than its counterpart in 2008, despite the fact that the former has fewer candidates than the later. In the Molonglo 2012, instances of the *elect* application happen for candidates with larger numbers of votes. Hence, the fractional numbers created as the result of computation of the new transfer values to be distributed according to the *transfer* rule are lager than the ones which occur in Molonglo 2008. This costs us almost ten more minutes to terminate.

Moreover, in case of varying vacancies, as the number of empty seats increases, the length of each of the initial ballots would increase too. This is because people would list more number of candidates if there are 20 seats to fill as compared to when there are merely 5 seat. Length of ballots to be counted plays a crucial role in termination time, because two of the functions which do costly computations are called by the *count* rule. These two functions are used to find the first continuing candidates of each ballot and place it into the pile of the appropriate candidate. If the length of ballots increase, cost of performing the counting increases as well. This explains why in Fig. 8, we see an increase in termination time. In Fig. 8, as the number of vacancies grow larger, the cost of counting increases as well. However, at the same time, the number of *elim* rule applications decreases which means that computationally we pay less from this aspect. Therefore, it happens that the cost of more number of *elim* rule applications outweighs the cost of counting as we increase the number of vacancies up to 15. However, when we reach 20 vacancies, scenario reverses in such a way that we experience a different balance between the two factors mentioned above.

Consequently, for the role which number of vacancies plays in termination time, one has to consider all of the aforementioned factors two of which were discussed above. Since combination of the factor is complicated, prediction of the program behaviour becomes challenging with respect to variation of vacancies.

5   Discussion

Our work represents the counting of an election as a formal process, where every component of the election count is represented syntactically. Here, we refer not to the specification (which is inherently non-deterministic) but to any implementation (including ours that we have extracted form the formal Coq development). In terms of the meta-theory, we can think about this in at least three distinct ways. The first approach is to take the process as a finite state machine (FSM). Given the initial list of candidates, $\mathcal{M} = < \Sigma, \mathcal{S}, \mathcal{I}, \delta, \mathcal{F} >$ is the mathematical characterisation of the machine where

$$\Sigma := \text{the name of rules as the input alphabet}$$
$$\mathcal{S} := \text{the set of all possible stages}$$
$$\mathcal{I} := \text{the set of all possible initial stages}$$
$$\mathcal{F} := \text{the set of all possible final stages}$$
$$\delta := \text{the state transition function: } \delta : \mathcal{S} \times \Sigma \to \mathcal{S}$$

The content of rule application theorem and termination theorem, respectively, show that the FSM is deterministic, and that for every initial stage of the machine, the execution of the machine terminates in (exactly) one of the unambiguous final stages. Therefore, the certificate produced upon each execution of the machine can be thought of as a trace of the states which the machine goes through to terminate the execution.

A different interpretation is to understand the initial ballots as a *program* and the counting rules as its (small step) operational semantics. In this way, every valid program (initial list of ballots) is interpreted as a sequence of the computational small-steps taken in an execution. Therefore, the final step reached upon the execution of the program (initial list of ballots) is the value computed by the program. The termination theorem tells us that (1) every program has a meaning, (2) this meaning is unambiguous, and (3) there is a value for it. The certificate, then, plays the role of an instruction trace of a classical program execution.

Finally, one can preferably think of ANU-Union STV as similar to a typed lambda-calculus. This perspective advocates considering the concept of computation as *constructive manipulation of syntactic entities*, everything is taken as mere symbols without any meaning. To be more concrete, given the *names* of candidates and the number of seats, one can perceive the initial ballots as a combination of symbols constituted of names of candidates, symbol representing a rational number and some symbols for characterising lists (such as brackets). Then one can construct other symbols such as initial stages by simply putting together an already constructed list of ballots and the name initial to obtain a new syntactic entity. This process can proceed so that all of the concepts, like judgement and provable judgement, with the hierarchy between them are captured as pure symbols. The rules of the count would play the role of reduction rules in the calculus. Therefore, the termination theorem can be rephrased as stipulation of the strong normalisation property of the calculus so that beginning from a symbol initial (ba), for some ba, we always reach to a single normal form such as winners (w) for some symbol w. Every instance of a certificate output would be a visualisation of an instance of a provable judgement along with all of the reduction steps taken to reach a normal form for the judgement.

6   Future Work

Protocols of STV schemes are sometimes vague with respect to tie breaking between candidates. Consequently, the legislation remains open to interpretation and therefore divergent formalisations. ANU-Union, in particular, only stipulates that when a tie occurs between two candidates one of which is to be removed, "the Returning Officer" should determine how to break the tie. This sentence does not specify as to how the officer decides the matter exactly. For this reason, we chose to *avoid dealing in depth* with tie breaking at the moment (see Remark 1). The program extracted from the proof of Theorem 2 *is* deterministic and simply breaks ties by removing the candidate whose name precedes the other candidates who are tied with them. So one way of tie breaking rather fairly would be to list the initial list of candidates in the conclusion of the rule *start* randomly. Even though the authors do not favour the proposal, it could be a naive, yet fair, solution so that when a tie is broken no one would feel disadvantaged. Alternatively, one can additionally stipulate that the program takes a sequence of random integers as additional inputs that are then used to break ties.

Moreover, there are other STV schemes which differ from ANU-Union's in one way or another. For example, some versions STV diverge from ANU-Union only in the way they transfer surplus votes. In those versions, all of the surplus must be dealt with before any other rule can apply. Modularity of the formalisation makes it considerably easier to adjust the system to such contrasts and discharge the proof burdens with smaller workload. Also it would help in establishing the strong normalisation property for STV scheme, in general, *as a class of typed lambda-calculi* by proving the same three theorems given for ANU-Union.

Also we have ideas for speeding the program up. Increase in number of candidates costs our program more than any other factor as Fig. 5 shows. But we can improve our encoding to compute faster. When some candidate is elected or eliminated, their name is not removed from ballots. Instead the program checks, each time, if a candidate whose name appears in the ballot, is in the continuing list and proceeds until it finds the first one who actually is. However, we can separate the list component of a ballot into two parts; one of which includes already elected or eliminated candidates and the other part for continuing candidates in the ballot so that we reduce excessive computations.

Most importantly, currently we are trying to write a checker for the certificate and verify the checker inside the theorem prover HOL4. Then by the built-in mechanisms of the CakeML, extract SML code which would be provably-correct down to the machine level. This provides us with the highest guarantee possible in verifying a certificate.

References

1. Bertot, Y., Castéran, P., Huet, G., Paulin-Mohrin, C.: Interactive Theorem Proving and Program Development - Coq'Art: The Calculus of Inductive Constructions. Texts in Theoretical Computer Science. An EATCS Series, pp. 1–472. Springer, Heidelberg (2004). doi:10.1007/978-3-662-07964-5, ISBN 978-3-642-05880-6
2. Cordover, M.: LS4883 outcome of internal review of the decision to refuse your FOI request no. LS4849. http://www.aec.gov.au/information-access/foi/2014/files/ls4912-1.pdf
3. Dawson, J.E., Goré, R., Meumann, T.: Machine-checked reasoning about complex voting schemes using higher-order logic. In: Haenni, R., Koenig, R.E., Wikström, D. (eds.) VOTELID 2015. LNCS, vol. 9269, pp. 142–158. Springer, Cham (2015). doi:10.1007/978-3-319-22270-7_9
4. DeYoung, H., Schürmann, C.: Linear logical voting protocols. In: Kiayias, A., Lipmaa, H. (eds.) Vote-ID 2011. LNCS, vol. 7187, pp. 53–70. Springer, Heidelberg (2012). doi:10.1007/978-3-642-32747-6_4
5. Girard, J.: Linear logic. Theor. Comput. Sci. **50**, 1–102 (1987)
6. Hales, T.C.: Formal proof. Notices AMS **55**(11), 1370–1380 (2008)

7. Kremer, S., Ryan, M., Smyth, B.: Election verifiability in electronic voting protocols. In: Gritzalis, D., Preneel, B., Theoharidou, M. (eds.) ESORICS 2010. LNCS, vol. 6345, pp. 389–404. Springer, Heidelberg (2010). doi:10.1007/978-3-642-15497-3_24

8. Letouzey, P.: Extraction in coq: an overview. In: Beckmann, A., Dimitracopoulos, C., Löwe, B. (eds.) CiE 2008. LNCS, vol. 5028, pp. 359–369. Springer, Heidelberg (2008). doi:10.1007/978-3-540-69407-6_39

9. Lundie, R.: The disputed 2013 WA Senate election. http://www.aph.gov.au/About_Parliament/Parliamentary_Departments/Parliamentary_Library/FlagPost/2013/November/The_disputed_2013_WA_Senate_election

10. Gerck, E., Neff, C.A., Rivest, R.L., Rubin, A.D., Yung, M.: The business of electronic voting. In: Syverson, P. (ed.) FC 2001. LNCS, vol. 2339, pp. 243–268. Springer, Heidelberg (2002). doi:10.1007/3-540-46088-8_21

11. Schack-Nielsen, A., Schürmann, C.: Celf – a logical framework for deductive and concurrent systems (system description). In: Armando, A., Baumgartner, P., Dowek, G. (eds.) IJCAR 2008. LNCS, vol. 5195, pp. 320–326. Springer, Heidelberg (2008). doi:10.1007/978-3-540-71070-7_28

12. The ANU-Union: The ANU-Union Constitution. http://www.anuunion.com.au/wp-content/uploads/2013/10/UnionConstitution-3.pdf

13. Verity, F., Pattinson, D.: Formally verified invariants of vote counting schemes. In: ACSW, pp. 31:1–31:10 (2017)

Reverse Bayesian Poisoning: How to Use Spam Filters to Manipulate Online Elections

Hugo Jonker[1,2]([✉]), Sjouke Mauw[3], and Tom Schmitz[3]

[1] Department of Computer Science,
Open University of the Netherlands, Heerlen, Netherlands
hugo.jonker@ou.nl
[2] Digital Security Group, Radboud University, Nijmegen, Netherlands
[3] CSC/SnT, University of Luxembourg, Luxembourg, Luxembourg
sjouke.mauw@uni.lu
http://www.open.ou.nl/hjo/
http://satoss.uni.lu/sjouke/

Abstract. E-voting literature has long recognised the threat of denial-of-service attacks: as attacks that (partially) disrupt the services needed to run the voting system. Such attacks violate availability. Thankfully, they are typically easily detected. We identify and investigate a denial-of-service attack on a voter's spam filters, which is not so easily detected: *reverse Bayesian poisoning*, an attack that lets the attacker silently suppress mails from the voting system. Reverse Bayesian poisoning can disenfranchise voters in voting systems which rely on emails for essential communication (such as voter invitation or credential distribution). The attacker stealthily trains the voter's spam filter by sending spam mails crafted to include keywords from genuine mails from the voting system.

To test the potential effect of reverse Bayesian poisoning, we took keywords from the Helios voting system's email templates and poisoned the Bogofilter spam filter using these keywords. Then we tested how genuine Helios mails are classified. Our experiments show that reverse Bayesian poisoning can easily suppress genuine emails from the Helios voting system.

1   Introduction

System security is typically divided into Confidentiality, Integrity and Availability. Voting systems present an interesting research challenge where confidentiality of the vote (privacy) and verification of integrity of the vote (verifiability) must be combined in one system. As these two requirements cannot be fully satisfied simultaneously [CFS+06], their interplay thus poses an interesting topic for research. Much research attention has been invested in addressing the interplay of confidentiality and integrity in voting. This has led to the development of various notions of verifiability, e.g. [Cha04, JCJ05, CRS05], and privacy [Cha81, BT94, JCJ05]. The efforts towards formalising verifiability culminated in the concept of *end-to-end verifiability*. The name derives from the fact that the voter can verify every step from the input of her choice up to and

© Springer International Publishing AG 2017
R. Krimmer et al. (Eds.): E-Vote-ID 2017, LNCS 10615, pp. 183–197, 2017.
DOI: 10.1007/978-3-319-68687-5_11

including the counting of her ballot. As such, end-to-end verifiability ensures verifiability for a voter who casts a vote.

Availability requirements have also been considered: for more than a decade, denial-of-service (DoS) attacks have been considered a serious threat to e-voting systems. Various authors have argued including this class of attacks in the security analysis of e-voting systems [GNR+02, Rub02, JRSW04, Agg16]. Until now, however, DoS attacks have mainly been considered from a generic point of view: a DoS attack is seen as disrupting (some of) the services that are necessary for an e-voting system to operate. The occurrence of such attacks can relatively easily be detected by one or more of the involved parties. It can be expected that the goal of such a DoS attacker is mainly to disrupt the election process and not to directly influence its outcome. Hence, literature views DoS attacks as attacking *availability* of the system and not *integrity* of the election.

In this view on availability, either an attack on availability is noted (and action is taken to rectify this), or every voter who wants to vote, is not impeded by the system from doing so. In the latter case, end-to-end verifiability ensures that the result of the election process matches the collective intent of the voters.

In this paper, we will explore one DoS-related vulnerability that will influence the result without disrupting general availability of the system: using spam filters to suppress voter invitation, thereby impeding voters to vote.

Though various sources have different estimates for the current global amount of spam email, they agree that it is above 50%. As such, spam filters have become a necessity – most incoming emails will be filtered for spam. We investigate the extent to which an attacker can exploit this. We find a novel attack on voting systems: the attacker trains a voter's spam filter to ensure that legitimate emails from the voting system are marked as spam and thus likely remain unseen by the voter. This borrows from the notion of *Bayesian poisoning*, in which an attacker sends emails to ensure that his spam is not detected by the target's filter. Since our attacker seeks the reverse, we call this type of attack *reverse Bayesian poisoning*.

In contrast to DoS attacks as considered in e-voting literature, a reverse Bayesian poisoning attack is stealthy and targeted. It is stealthy in the sense that it is not obvious that the system is under attack, and after the attack it may not even be possible to prove the system has been attacked. It is targeted in the sense that it does not attempt to exceed system capacity, but it is an attack on a particular essential service that maliciously alters that service's behaviour. As this change of behaviour is under the control of the attacker, he can manipulate the outcome of the elections. Thus, this type of DoS attacker focusses on the *integrity* of the elections.

Consequently, the question whether this type of stealthy and targeted attacks are possible in e-voting systems becomes a concern that goes beyond the generic problem of service availability and influences the integrity of the election process.

For the purposes of this paper, we investigate whether the well-known Helios voting system [Adi08] is susceptible to reverse Bayesian poisoning. Helios is an online election system that provides end-to-end verifiability. It offers email facilities for communicating election particulars to voters. The Helios voting system was used in a number of elections, such as by the International Association for Cryptologic Research for electing board members and directors.

Contributions. In this paper:

- We argue that e-voting security also depends on availability of supporting procedures and systems. We identify and investigate one example of a vulnerability in such a supporting system: email interaction between the voting system and the voter.
- We demonstrate that it is possible and even fairly easy to suppress relevant emails from a voting system by means of a reverse Bayesian poisoning attack. In particular, we are able to manipulate the BogoFilter spam filter such that it suppresses emails from the Helios voting system.
- Finally, we discuss several possible solution directions.

2 Notions of Election Security

An election has to satisfy a wide range of security and privacy requirements. In literature and in practical systems, the focus tends to be on preventing misuse of the system. As such, there are requirements to prevent double voting and to allow a voter to verify that her vote counts in favor of the candidate for whom she submitted a ballot. Little attention is paid to the setup of the election: determining who is eligible, and distributing voting credentials to authorized voters.

This lack of attention to election setup is natural for voting systems targeting supervised voting (i.e. a setup with a polling station). In supervised voting, such security requirements are supposed to be guaranteed by the supervision. However, online voting systems have no such infrastructure to fall back upon and must therefore address security and privacy aspects of this part as well.

To determine the limits of the scope of end-to-end verifiability, we divide the election into the below administrative processes. These processes are placed into the first election phase where they can be executed. Remark that some processes can be postponed. For example, voter eligibility can be checked before, during or after the election.

- **Pre-election phase.** Processes typically executed in this phase are:
  - **Voter registration.** For some elections, voters need to register themselves. For other elections (e.g. in associations), the register is pre-existing (e.g. the membership list). This process establishes the voter register.
  - **Voter eligibility.** Not all those who are registered are eligible. For example, general elections typically only allow people above a certain age to vote. This process eliminates all people from the register who are found to not satisfy the rules of eligibility.

- **Announcement and credential distribution.** To cast a vote, voters typically have to show some form of voter credentials. This process distributes the announcement of the election and voting credentials to all voters.
- Election phase. Processes typically executed in this phase are:
  - **Vote casting.** In this process, the voters communicate the expression of their choice to the voting system.
  - **Vote eligibility.** The votes received by the system are checked for eligibility, to ensure that only those votes that should be taken into account are considered.
- Post-election phase. Processes typically executed in this phase are:
  - **Vote aggregation.** In some elections, the encoded ballots are aggregated before opening them (e.g. systems using homomorphic encryption). In other elections, this process is omitted.
  - **Result determination.** In this process, the result of the election is determined. This can be an exact count per candidate (or option), or a simple determination of which candidate(s) (or options) won.
  - **Result announcement.** In this process, the election result is communicated to the voters and (when applicable) the world at large.

Over the last two decades, research in e-voting security has steadily worked towards designing practically usable voting systems that satisfy privacy and security requirements. Since elections have already been organised before, researchers sought to update parts of the existing process with new techniques. In particular, research was focused primarily confidentiality and integrity of the election and post-election phases. This was highly successful and led to a better understanding of the security and privacy principles involved as well as the design and development of systems that safeguard most if not all of those principles.

Availability concerns are recognised as generic concerns, but so far not as a specific risk for online election systems. However, online election systems also depend on the internet for the pre-election phase. Availability attacks on online election systems may also target the pre-election phase. To highlight the necessity for considering this part of the election process, we explore one stealthy attack upon the announcement and credential distribution process: abusing spam filtering to suppress emails sent by the voting system.

3 Spam, Filtering and Poisoning

3.1 Spam Filtering

A significant fraction of mail traffic is spam – over half, by most reports[1]. Therefore, a thorough spam filter is a necessity for any email address.

Spam filters are filters that distinguish between non-spam emails and spam emails. The output of the filter typically is a classification (*non-spam*, *spam*, or

---

[1] E.g. Kaspersky's quarterly spam reports, https://securelist.com/all/?category=442, pegs the amount of spam in email traffic in the first three months of 2017 at 55.19%.

unknown) plus a score specifying the extent to which the evaluated mail satisfied filter rules for spam. This output is then used to (automatically or not) delete mails classified as spam or divert such mails to a dedicated spam folder. Mails that end up in the category *unknown* can be flagged as such and presented to the user for further processing.

Spam filters use various tests to arrive at their result. Each test evaluates the mail and arrives at its own estimate for the probability of the examined mail being spam. These probabilities are then aggregated by the spam filter to classify the mail.

Spam filters classify emails using two thresholds: a non-spam and a spam threshold. A probability below the non-spam threshold ensures a mail is classified as non-spam. A probability above the (higher) spam threshold ensures that a mail is classified as spam. Probabilities in between are not classified – tagging the message as potential spam, while letting the mail through to the user's inbox.

There is a wide variety in tests spam filters use to determine the probability that a mail is spam, and any given spam filter will use its own subset of tests. Some of these tests focus on the body of the email, others on the header. One test, for example, checks URLs found in the mail body against a database of URLs associated with spam mail. Other tests check if the formatting of the MIME parts in the mail body is suspicious or if the mail body contains obfuscated HTML or HTML trackers. Some header tests check whether the mail was received via known open relays or if the subject refers to a specific medicine (such as viagra).

Remark that the tests are not perfect: some spam mails will not be marked as spam (*false negatives*), while some normal mails will be marked as spam (*false positives*). A false positive is worse than a false negative: a mail that is automatically directed to a spam mailbox might escape the user's notice completely, while a spam mail in a user's inbox will be easily and swiftly dealt with.

3.2   Bayesian Classification of Spam

One type of test to help reduce false positives is to determine how similar an incoming message is to known spam mails, and how similar it is to known non-spam mails. In effect, this allows the spam filter to learn from previously encountered mails and become "smarter" in separating spam from non-spam.

Such tests are based on Bayes' theorem. Bayes theorem is used to "flip" conditional probabilities: if we know $P(B \mid A)$, the probability that event B occurs if event A has occurred, and we know the probabilities $P(A)$ and $P(B)$, we can derive the "flipped" probability $P(A \mid B)$, the probability that event A would occur if event B occurred. Formally, Bayes theorem is stated as:

$$P(A \mid B) = \frac{P(B \mid A) \cdot P(A)}{P(B \mid A) \cdot P(A) + P(B \mid \neg A) \cdot P(\neg A)}$$

In terms of spam filters, Bayes theorem can be used to determine the probability that a mail is spam given that it contains a certain word, $P(spam \mid word)$, if we know the probability that word occurs in spam mails, $P(word \mid spam)$. Given a corpus of already-classified mails (either spam or non-spam), the probabilities necessary to compute the "flipped" probability can be estimated.

For example, consider the question of whether a mail containing the word "viagra" is spam. The probability that it is, is denoted $P(spam \mid \text{viagra})$. If we have an existing corpus of mails already classified as spam or non-spam, we can estimate how often this word occurs in spam messages, $P(\text{viagra} \mid spam)$, and in non-spam mails, $P(\text{viagra} \mid \neg spam)$. We also know the percentage of incoming messages that is spam, $P(spam)$. The probability that an unclassified message containing "viagra" is spam is then computed as:

$$P(spam \mid \text{viagra}) = \frac{P(\text{viagra} \mid spam) \cdot P(spam)}{P(\text{viagra} \mid spam) \cdot P(spam) + P(\text{viagra} \mid \neg spam) \cdot P(\neg spam)}$$

In actual use, the result is refined further to prevent the filter from acting on insufficient information. For example, if only one email has ever been received with the word "viagra", then the classification of that one email determines how a new mail with that word will be classified. To prevent this, the resulting probability is scaled with the number of received emails (spam and non-spam) and averaged with an assumed probability of any mail being spam (e.g. set at 50%).

3.3   Bayesian Poisoning

Bayesian spam filtering is effective, and therefore widely used. Its ubiquity raises the question if the Bayesian filtering could be deliberately exploited by one or more carefully crafted messages to fool the filter in letting through a spam message – a deliberately triggered false negative. This type of attacks on Bayesian spam filtering is known as *Bayesian poisoning*, as effectively, the spam filter is poisoned to not recognise the offending messages as spam. To achieve this, the spam mail must include a sufficient amount of sufficiently "non-spammy" words, such that in aggregate, the spam mail is marked as non-spam.

In 2004, Graham-Cumming presented the first study [GC04] into Bayesian poisoning. His experiment found that randomly adding words was not successful. He was able to devise a different attack which probes the spam filter to determine words which help ensure a non-spam classification.

To their surprise, Wittel and Wu had contradictory findings: adding random words did influence certain spam filters [WW04]. They suspected this contradiction with Graham-Cummings may be due to differences in used spam corpora or filters tested. Stern et al. [SMS04] showed that Bayesian poisoning can affect filter performance, skewing results to generate more false positives. Lowd and Meek [LM05] find that adding about 150 well-chosen words is effective in getting the average spam message through a filter. They also find that frequent retraining the spam filter is effective against this type of attack. This finding matches the intuition that retraining is important: when the spam filter fails to block spam, it should be retrained.

From existing research, we see that it is possible to masquerade spam as non-spam by using Bayesian poisoning. The concept we explore is turning this around: is it possible to masquerade non-spam as spam by using Bayesian poisoning? That is: instead of using Bayesian poisoning to increase the false positive rate, can it be used to increase the spam filter's false negative rate? In particular, can Bayesian poisoning be used to suppress mails from an online voting system? We call this *reverse Bayesian poisoning*.

Remark that the mails that the attacker sends to poison the filter *are* spam mails. The only aim of these spam mails is to associate words that are likely used in mails of the voting system with spam. Recall that spam filter retraining is important, especially when a false negative occurs, that is: when a spam message is not filtered. Therefore, reverse Bayesian poisoning is a stealthy attack: sending emails is trivial, and the emails sent by the attacker can easily be made to look like spam (since they *are* spam). A regular user who retrains her spam filter when spam gets through (as is normal) is thus aiding the attacker.

4 Experiment Setup

In order to investigate the possibility of using reverse Bayesian poisoning to suppress legitimate mails, we set up an experiment with a local spam filter and attempted to suppress emails by poisoning the filter.

The goal of this experiment was to test the feasibility of this attack, not to perform a thorough evaluation of spam filters and their susceptibility to this attack. As the attack relies on the victim training her spam filter on the attacker's poisoning mails, a thorough evaluation must also take into account the human factor.

Our feasibility experiment analyses whether, for one particular system setup in a fully-controlled and minimal environment, using one or more realistic parameter settings, it is possible to construct a limited number of *attack mails* that, when fed to the spam filter lead to the suppression of a particular administrative message.

In particular we will use the Bogofilter, trained with (a part of) the Enron spam corpus, aiming to suppress emails formatted according to the templates used by the Helios [Adi08] online voting system, such as the template depicted in Fig. 1.

As the experiment focuses on the feasibility of poisoning a Bayesian spam filter, we did not set up an email infrastructure (procmail, mailclient, postfix), but applied Bogofilter directly to the emails. We also assume the worst case for victim actions: the victim will always mark attack mails as spam.

4.1 Bogofilter

Bogofilter[2], originally written by Eric S. Raymond, was based on the ideas of Paul Graham [Gra04]. Graham proposed to apply Bayesian filtering of spam messages based on combining the probabilities for spam of the 15 words with the

---

[2] http://bogofilter.sourceforge.net/

strongest probabilities: the 15 words for which the absolute value of the difference between that word's spam probability and the neutral spam probability (50%) is the largest. Bogofilter applies Bayesian filtering in the classification of spam/non-spam mails.

The program can be trained on a given corpus of spam and non-spam mail. Moreover, explicit user input on the classification of individual emails can be used to fine-tune or correct the system's decision logic. Furthermore, the user (or system administrator) can fine-tune the statistical algorithms by modifying certain configuration parameters of the Bogofilter system. Examples are the earlier mentioned thresholds: *spam-cutoff* for spam and *ham-cutoff* for non-spam.

An interesting and relevant feature of Bogofilter is the *auto-update* feature. When this feature is used and Bogofilter classifies a message as spam or non-spam, the message will be automatically added to the wordlist for recognizing spam or non-spam, respectively. Bogofilter documentation warns that this behaviour may cause classification errors to propagate.

Retraining a Bayesian spam filter is important and can be done without user intervention – for Bogofilter by using the auto-update feature, for other spam filters by using similar automated updating features or publicly available scripts.

As the Bogofilter documentation warns, automatic retraining may cause classification errors to be exacerbated. This is exactly the goal of our attack: to exacerbate misclassification. To understand the risk that auto-update features pose with respect to this attack, we will conduct two types of experiments: one in which the user will have to classify the attack mails as spam, and one in which the auto-update feature is used to automatically classify the attack mails as spam. In the first case, the number of attack mails should be rather limited, as it involves user interaction. In the second case, we could use a larger number of attack mails.

4.2   Enron Mail Corpus

The Enron [KY04] corpus[3] is a widely-used dataset consisting of e-mail communication among executives from the (now-defunct) Enron corporation. It contains over 600.000 emails generated by 158 employees. For the experiments, we used the corpus that was enriched by Metsis et al. with spam from various sources [MAP06].

4.3   Helios

Helios [Adi08] is an end-to-end verifiable online voting system with strong privacy guarantees (receipt-free but not coercion-resistant). Its strong security features apply to the election phase and the post-election phase. However, our attack is upon the announcement and credential distribution process, which is out of scope of Helios' security features – and therefore not protected.

---

[3] http://www-2.cs.cmu.edu/~enron/

For the purpose of this paper, we omit all technical details of Helios and only focus on the features it offers to support announcement and credential distribution.

Helios is initialized by the voting officials by providing the relevant information, the register of voters and their email addresses, and customizing various emails to be sent out (announcement, credential distribution, etc.).

All voters receive an automatically generated voting invitation from Helios (see Fig. 1). To vote, the voter visits the emailed election URL and authenticates using the credentials from the email. After having voted, the voter receives an email confirmation that her ballot has been received and stored. After the elections close, the stored votes are tallied and the voter receives an email that the tally has been released. The voter can inspect the tally page through the URL provided in the tally email and she can verify that her vote is correctly counted through the provided administrative information.

Dear <*voter.name*>,

<*custom_message*>

Election URL: <*election_vote_url*>
Election Fingerprint: <*voter.election.hash*>

Your voter ID: <*voter.voter_login_id*>
Your password: <*voter.voter_password*>

Log in with your <*voter.voter_type*> account.

We have recorded your vote with smart tracker: <*voter.vote_hash*>
You may re-vote if you wish: only your last vote counts.

In order to protect your privacy, this election is configured
to never display your voter login ID, name, or email address to the public.
Instead, the ballot tracking center will only display your alias.

Your voter alias is <*voter.alias*>.

IMPORTANTLY, when you are prompted to log in to vote,
please use your *voter ID*, not your alias.

–

Helios

Fig. 1. Template of a Helios invitation.

Remark that if a particular voter does not vote (e.g. because she did not receive the invitation), this does not lead to any further action from the Helios system. Further, notice that it is impossible to vote without the email containing the authentication credentials.

4.4 Generating Attack Mails

The essence of the reverse poisoning attack is in generating the poison. To generate the attack emails, we alternated words from the genuine Helios administrative mails with words from typical spam messages. An example of an attack mail is shown in Fig. 2. Each attack mail contains 115 words, which is equal to the average size of a genuine Helios mail. Regular users will probably mark such emails as spam, even if they are expecting a communication from Helios.

We readily acknowledge that this is a rather rudimentary approach to generating attack emails. However, this experiment aims only to test feasibility of Bayesian poisoning attacks, for which purpose the thusly generated attack emails seem sufficient. Thus, we keep in mind that an attacker can likely generate stronger attack emails.

From: Luxury@experience.com
Subject: Lower monthly payment passwords
Remuneration <u>Election</u> Subsidiary <u>Link</u>: payment <u>Dear</u>
Usury <u>–</u> Reapportionment <u>Helios</u> Reply <u>How</u> Syndicate
<u>to</u> Wholesale <u>Vote</u> Return ======== Computer
<u>Election</u> roots <u>URL</u>: Coattail <u>Your</u> Challenger <u>voter</u>
Believe <u>ID:</u> Decide <u>Your</u> Permit <u>password</u>: Advertisement
<u>Log</u> Pamphlets <u>in</u> Broadcast <u>with</u> Downsize <u>your</u>
. . .

Fig. 2. Fragment of an example attack mail. The underlined words are from genuine Helios mails.

5 Experiments and Analysis

5.1 Experiments

To execute our experiments, we used a standard laptop and installed Bogofilter. Bogofilter's initial database was cleared and trained with part of the Enron corpus. We conducted the experiments with various sizes of the training set.

To test the susceptibility of Bogofilter to reverse Bayesian poisoning, we constructed 50 attack emails. We then iterated over these mails. Each iteration trained Bogofilter on one attack mail and then tested Bogofilter's classification of Helios emails. We used four fictional elections, each of which generated three genuine emails. In total, each time the classifier was tested on 12 genuine emails from Helios, see Fig. 3.

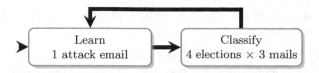

Fig. 3. The process of the experiments.

5.2   Analysis of Results

The results of the experiments are depicted in Fig. 4. The figure shows, per election, the averaged probability of genuine Helios mails being marked as spam against the number of attack emails processed by Bogofilter.

Figure 4 shows the results when training the spamfilter with 11000 messages from the Enron corpus. Each line represents the average probability of emails being spam for one of the four hypothetical elections. For each election we average the results of the three administrative Helios messages. The vertical axis shows the classification of the Helios messages as a number between 0 (non-spam) and 1 (spam). The horizontal axis shows the number of attack messages sent before feeding the genuine Helios messages to the spam filter.

As can be seen in the figure, classification of mails from every test election reacted strongly to the presence of only a few attack emails. Bogofilter has a default spam threshold of 99%. We found that it was possible to rate the official emails above this threshold. We also found that the efficacy depended on the size of the training corpus. Nevertheless, even when using the full Enron corpus for training, we found cases where less than 50 attack emails sufficed to have a genuine election email have a spam probability over 99%. When Bogofilter's

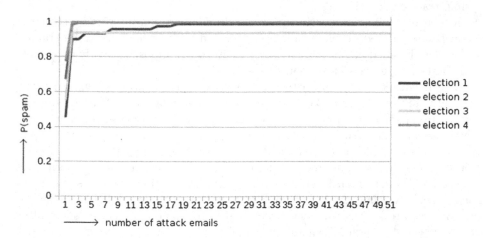

Fig. 4. Average classification of the three genuine Helios emails for each of the four hypothetical elections.

auto-update feature is switched on, this number of attack emails will be processed without any user interaction.

In other words, notwithstanding the crudeness of our attack, fifty attack emails can be sufficient to reverse Bayesian poison a spam filter to suppress official election emails.

6   Conclusions

Our simple experiments show that reverse Bayesian poisoning is indeed a feasible attack on the administrative processes surrounding a voting system. We expect that the attack mails can be further optimized as to achieve the attacker's goal with fewer attack mails.

Discussion. As the experiments were aimed at testing feasibility, we only tested one particular spam filter (Bogofilter) and made various assumptions: the attacker knows whom to target, the attacker's guess of the format of the genuine emails is sufficiently close to the actually sent emails, and the victims will mark the attack emails all as spam. Moreover, for reverse Bayesian poisoning to constitute an actual attack upon online elections a few more assumptions are made: victims ignore the fact that they did not receive voting credentials, election officials are not alerting voters to check their spam filters, and elections are not repeated if a voter finds an election email in her spam mailbox.

Remark the stealthy nature of this attack. The attack could be executed slowly, over time. The attacker would send attack emails that recipients use to train the spam filter and possibly even discard afterwards. This means that it is possible for a reverse Bayesian poisoning attack to occur without leaving a visible trace on the victim's side.

Moreover, while our experiments focused on local spam filtering by the user, spam is also filtered at the email service provider. Such filters may be trained upon user-classified mails from all users. Such a set is almost perfectly classified[4] and therefore used to classify mails for *all* users.

The downside is that an attacker can sign up for a popular email service and carry out the reverse Bayesian poisoning attack by himself, poisoning the service's spam filter without sending mails to anyone but his own mail account. The consequences of such an attack can affect many or all users of the service. It is for this reason that we did not dare to execute our experiments on GMail: Helios is used in elections (e.g. by the IACR), and even our crude experiments may train GMail's spam filters to classify genuine election emails as spam. As such, we believe that any experiment with reverse Bayesian poisoning must be done in a controlled environment. If not, others relying on the shared spam filter will be affected without adequate means of reversing the experiment's effects.

Note that reverse Bayesian poisoning of shared spam filters allows an attacker to target groups of voters that share the same spam filter, such as all voters from

---

[4] https://www.quora.com/What-does-the-Report-Spam-feature-really-do-in-Gmail

one institute. As large institutes typically have a generic, shared spam filter, an attacker could thus prevent any voters from a given institute from voting.

Mitigation Approaches. Mitigation approaches against reverse Bayesian poisoning can be classified by who should implement the measure:

- User-side mitigation measures (e.g. whitelisting),
- Centrally taken mitigation measures (e.g. multi-channel communication).

Users can mitigate the effects of reverse Bayesian poisoning in various ways. On a filter level, they could whitelist the election email address. This trumps any other spam test, and so would prevent the emails from being suppressed. Another option is to use a reminder service (e.g. a calendar service) to remind them of when credentials are to arrive, and contact election authorities if the credentials did not arrive.

Election officials can also mitigate this attack on different levels. On a technical level, they can use alternative channels (e.g. SMS messages) to notify the users that credentials have been mailed. Remark that these other channels might be attacked as well – for example, the SMS channel in the Norwegian voting system was subverted [KLH13]. They can also address this on a social level, by effectively campaigning that credentials have been sent out and spam filters should be checked.

Future Directions. In this work, we investigated a practical attack on the pre-election phase of the Helios voting system. We have not formalised this type of attack, though we see several approaches to doing so. In particular, our attack touches upon the interaction between humans and computers in voting. The security implications of such interactions have been considered before, e.g. Ryan for Prêt á Voter [Rya11], and Kiayias et al. for Helios [KZZ17]. Both these works consider the privacy and verifiability requirements on voting. In terms of the work by Kiayias et al., the reverse Bayesian poisoning attack constitutes an attack upon the setup ceremony. It is possible to formally define a requirement in their framework which would catch any shenanigans with voter credential distribution. Such a requirement could ascertain that credentials were not correctly received, but not whether this is due to lossy communication channels or due to an active attack such as reverse Bayesian poisoning. To formalise a requirement such that active attacks can be distinguished from regularly occurring circumstances requires further work.

References

[Adi08] Adida, B.: Helios: web-based open-audit voting. In: Proceedings of 17th USENIX Security Symposium, pp. 335–348. USENIX Association (2008)

[Agg16] Aggarwal, K.: Denial of service attack on online voting system. J. Eng. Sci. Comput. **6**(5), 5585–5587 (2016)

[BT94]   Benaloh, J., Tuinstra, D.: Receipt-free secret-ballot elections (extended abstract). In: Proceedings of 26th ACM Symposium on Theory of Computing (STOC), pp. 544–553. ACM (1994)

[CFS+06]   Chevallier-Mames, B., Fouque, P., Stern, J., Pointcheval, D., Traoré, J.: On some incompatible properties of voting schemes. In: Proceedings of the IAVoSS Workshop On Trustworthy Elections (2006)

[Cha81]   Chaum, D.: Untraceable electronic mail, return addresses, and digital pseudonyms. Commun. ACM **24**(2), 84–88 (1981)

[Cha04]   Chaum D.: Secret-ballot receipts: true voter-verifiable elections. In: Proceedings of 25th IEEE Symposium on Security and Privacy (S&P), vol. 2(1), pp. 38–47 (2004)

[CRS05]   Chaum, D., Ryan, P.Y.A., Schneider, S.: A practical voter-verifiable election scheme. In: di Vimercati, S.C., Syverson, P., Gollmann, D. (eds.) ESORICS 2005. LNCS, vol. 3679, pp. 118–139. Springer, Heidelberg (2005). doi:10.1007/11555827_8

[GC04]   Graham-Cumming, J.: How to beat an adaptive spam filter. In: Presentation at the MIT Spam Conference (2004)

[GNR+02]   Gerck, E., Neff, C.A., Rivest, R.L., Rubin, A.D., Yung, M.: The business of electronic voting. In: Syverson, P. (ed.) FC 2001. LNCS, vol. 2339, pp. 243–268. Springer, Heidelberg (2002). doi:10.1007/3-540-46088-8_21

[Gra04]   Graham, P., Hackers, P.: A plan for spam. In: Big Ideas from the Computer Age, pp. 121–129. O'Reilly (2004)

[JCJ05]   Juels, A., Catalano, D., Jakobsson, M.: Coercion-resistant electronic elections. In: Proceedings of the ACM Workshop on Privacy in the Electronic Society (WPES), pp. 61–70. ACM (2005)

[JRSW04]   Jefferson, D., Rubin, A.D., Simons, B., Wagner, D.: A security analysis of the secure electronic registration and voting experiment (serve). Technical report (2004)

[KLH13]   Koenig, R.E., Locher, P., Haenni, R.: Attacking the verification code mechanism in the Norwegian internet voting system. In: Heather, J., Schneider, S., Teague, V. (eds.) Vote-ID 2013. LNCS, vol. 7985, pp. 76–92. Springer, Heidelberg (2013). doi:10.1007/978-3-642-39185-9_5

[KY04]   Klimt, B., Yang, Y., Corpus, T.E.: A new dataset for email classification research. In: Proceedings of 15th European Conference on Machine Learning, pp. 217–226 (2004)

[KZZ17]   Kiayias, A., Zacharias, T., Zhang, B.: Ceremonies for end-to-end verifiable elections. In: Fehr, S. (ed.) PKC 2017. LNCS, vol. 10175, pp. 305–334. Springer, Heidelberg (2017). doi:10.1007/978-3-662-54388-7_11

[LM05]   Lowd, D., Meek, C.: Good word attacks on statistical spam filters. In: Proceedings of the Second Conference on Email and Anti-Spam (CEAS 2005) (2005)

[MAP06]   Metsis, V., Androutsopoulos, I., Paliouras G.: Spam filtering with naive Bayes - which naive Bayes? In: Proceedings of the 3rd Conference on Email and Anti-Spam (CEAS 2006) (2006)

[Rub02]   Rubin, A.D.: Security considerations for remote electronic voting. Commun. ACM **45**(12), 39–44 (2002)

[Rya11]   Ryan, P.Y.A.: Prêt à voter with confirmation codes. In: Proceedings of the 2011 Conference on Electronic Voting Technology/Workshop on Trustworthy Elections (EVT/WOTE 2011). USENIX Association (2011)

[SMS04] Stern, H., Mason, J., Shepherd, M.: A linguistics-based attack on personalised statistical e-mail classifiers. Technical report, Dalhousie University (2004)

[WW04] Wittel, G.L., Wu, S.F.: On attacking statistical spam filters. In: Proceedings of the First Conference on Email and Anti-Spam (CEAS 2004) (2004)

Return Code Schemes for Electronic Voting Systems

Shahram Khazaei[1] and Douglas Wikström[2(✉)]

[1] Sharif University of Technology, Tehran, Iran
shahram.khazaei@sharif.ir
[2] KTH Royal Institute of Technology, Stockholm, Sweden
dog@kth.se

Abstract. We describe several return code schemes for secure vote submission in electronic voting systems. We consider a unified treatment where a return code is generated as a multiparty computation of a secure MAC tag applied on an encrypted message submitted by a voter. Our proposals enjoy a great level of flexibility with respect to various usability, security, and performance tradeoffs.

1 Introduction

Electronic voting systems have the potential of achieving *end-to-end verifiability*. This is obtained through different verification mechanisms throughout all the stages of the entire voting process, known as *cast-as-intended*, *recorded-as-cast* and *counted-as-recorded* [2].

Cast-as-intended verification assures each individual voter that his vote has been cast according to his intention. Mechanisms that ensures the cast votes have been correctly received and stored are called recorded-as-cast. Counted-as-recorded verification allows any third party observer, such as voters and auditors, to verify that the result of the tally corresponds to the received votes.

In some electronic voting systems, the voter casts his encrypted vote using some voting device which might either belong to the election authorities, e.g., a computer with a touch screen in a furnished voting booth, or to the voter himself, when the risk of coercion is limited. A malicious voting device (due to malware or hostile hardware) may change a voter's intended choice. Cast-as-intended verifiability detects such attacks on voting devices.

There are two basic approaches to verifying that a vote was cast as intended: (a) verify that the right choice was encrypted and that the ciphertext was recorded, and (b) verify that the ciphertext decrypts to the intended choice.

The most straightforward solution to the first problem is to simply perform the encryption independently on a different device and compare the results as is done in Estonia [17].

Another approach is continuous blackbox testing as proposed by Benaloh [5], and adopted in Helios [1], Wombat [23], and VoteBox [25]. Here the device provides a ciphertext and the voter can choose to either use it, or to challenge the device to prove that it was formed correctly. Note that the latter choice amounts to normal blackbox testing. The key insight of Benaloh is that we can not only interlace testing with normal use (which is often done in safety critical software), we can let the *voters control when and where testing takes place* to provide maximum individual assurance. The importance of this observation lies in part in that concerned voters can run more tests, so the testing seamlessly aligns with the level of assurance needed by individual voters.

Depending on trust assumptions, i.e., who performs the verification of outputs that have been challenged (an electronic device, jointly with a human, or third parties), Benaloh's approach is more or less practical and gives different types of assurances.

The reader may object that the encryption device must commit to its output before the choice to verify it is made or not, but this is no different from many other types of testing done on software. Benaloh's approach is often confused with cut-and-choose zero knowledge proofs due to the choice given to the voter between two choices, but is better described as a *have-or-eat* protocol: you can't have your cake and eat it too (to see that the cake is not poisonous).

So called *return codes* have received a considerable amount of attention particularly due to their usability properties. We refer the reader to [3,4,12,14,18, 19,22] for several proposals. This approach has been used in nation-wide elections in Norway [12,13,22] and Switzerland [10].

The idea of return codes is that each possible choice of the voter is associated with a random code that is returned upon submission of the encrypted vote as an acknowledgement that the ciphertext received encrypts the intended choice. To ensure privacy, the random codes of different voters are chosen independently. In other words, individual codes reveal nothing about the vote itself.

Note that at its core this is classical code book encryption, i.e., the parties receiving a vote in encrypted form send back the vote in encoded form to the voter. However, we only use the return codes for acknowledgement, so there is no need for the codes to uniquely identify the choices. Thus, for each voter we need a fairly regular random map from the set of choices to a set of codes, i.e., a message authentication code (MAC) with a guaranteed privacy property.

For coherent integration with electronic voting systems, the following properties must be taken into account:

1. **Secure printing.** It must be possible to generate and secretly transmit return codes for all voting options to a trusted printer.
2. **Distributed evaluation.** It must be possible to compute the return codes in a distributed way such that no knowledge is leaked about the selected voting option by the voter.

The first property can be achieved as follows. Let $E_{pk}(m)$ be a ciphertext encrypted using a homomorphic cryptosystem. The secret key, unknown to printer, is verifiably secret shared among some parties. For printing m, the trusted printer, chooses a random one-time pad α and hands $E_{pk}(\alpha)$ to the parties who will then execute a distributed decryption protocol for $E_{pk}(\alpha)E_{pk}(m) =$

$E_{pk}(\alpha m)$. When αm is received back, the random pad is removed and m is printed.

Remark 1 (Code voting). One potentially serious privacy drawback with any system where votes are encrypted even in a relatively well protected environment is that it is hard to guarantee that no information about votes is leaked through malicious hardware, software, or any form of side channel.

Chaum's *code voting* idea [7] addresses this problem by letting the voters use code book encryption to submit their votes, i.e., each voter is given a list of codes along with their plaintext meanings who will then enter the code as is into a device. The Prêt à Voter [8,24] system can be viewed as a code voting scheme that uses a public key cryptosystem to prepare the code book and decode in a distributed way using a mix-net.

Motivation and contribution. We provide several proposals achieving the second property with different trust assumptions and trade-offs. Some allow a single vote to be submitted and some do not have such a restriction. Some are safe to use with write-ins and some are not. In some schemes, for each individual voter some value must be verifiably secret shared (making them less practical); whereas in other schemes, the verifiably secret shared values are not voter dependent. Some schemes demand that the tallying servers be online during the vote collecting phase, which is not desirable from a security point of view; some others allow online servers to collect the votes without any help from the tallying servers. The latter property is highly desirable since the tallying servers can decrypt the votes off-line behind an airwall.

We think it is important to provide a tool box to practitioners that allow them to choose the best trade-off between security properties, how trust is distributed, and practical and cost considerations for the given setting, since the requirements differ substantially in different election schemes and cultural contexts.

Most of our schemes work with any homomorphic public key cryptosystem, however, we concentrate on the El Gamal cryptosystem for concreteness.

2   Notation

We assume that the reader is familiar with standard definitions of public key cryptosystems, message authentication codes (MAC), zero-knowledge proofs and the random oracle model. The reader is referred to [15,16] for the required background.

El Gamal cryptosystem. Recall that the El Gamal public key cryptosystem is defined over a group G_q of prime order q with generator g over which the Decisional Diffie-Hellman assumption holds. The secret key is a random $x \in \mathbb{Z}_q$ and the corresponding public key is $y = g^x$. The encryption of a message $m \in G_q$ is $E_y(m) = E_y(m, r) = (g^r, my^r)$, where the randomness $r \in \mathbb{Z}_q$ is chosen randomly.

The encryption of a ciphertext $(u, v) \in G_q \times G_q$ is then defined by $\mathsf{D}_x(u, v) = vu^{-x}$. El Gamal is *homomorphic*, which means that for every two encryptions $(u_1, v_1) = \mathsf{E}_y(m_1, r_1)$ and $(u_2, v_2) = \mathsf{E}_y(m_2, r_2)$, the product ciphertext $(u_1 u_1, v_1 v_2)$ is an encryption of $m_1 m_2$ with randomness $r_1 + r_2$. Consequently, a ciphertext $(u, v) = \mathsf{E}_y(m)$ can be *re-encrypted* to produce a fresh *re-encryption* of m. This can be done without knowing the secret key, by simply multiplying the ciphertext with an encryption of identity to compute $\mathsf{RE}_y(u, v) = (ug^r, vh^r)$, for some randomness r.

Verifiable secret sharing and distributed key generation of El Gamal. Sometimes we require that a number of M parties jointly generate a public key. The corresponding secret key is *verifiably secret shared* among them such that it can be recovered by any subset of size at least λ of the parties, but it remains hidden to any coalition of size at most $\lambda - 1$. Feldman's verifiable secret sharing protocol [9] is an efficient way for distributed key generation for El Gamal. In Feldman's method, parties jointly produce a random tuple $(y_0, \ldots, y_{\lambda-1}) = (g^{x_0}, \ldots, g^{x_{\lambda-1}})$ where $x_j \in \mathbb{Z}_q$, $j \in [\lambda]$. The parties do not know x_j's; rather, each party $\ell \in [M]$ receives a share $s_\ell = f(\ell)$, where $f(z) = \sum_{i=0}^{\lambda-1} x_i z^i$. This can be viewed as sharing a secret key $x = x_0$ using the Shamir's [26] method, but parties also compute a public key $y = y_0$ and receive the Feldman commitment g^{s_ℓ} to the share of ℓth party. The same idea can be extended to Pedersen's perfectly-hiding commitment scheme [21], when verifiably sharing a secret is a preliminary goal; details are omitted.

Distributed exponentiation. Suppose an El Gamal secret key x is shared among the M parties and, given $u \in G_q$, they wish to jointly compute u^x. This can be done using the following procedure [11]. Each party ℓ, publishes $f_\ell = u^{s_\ell}$ along with a zero-knowledge proof of discrete logarithm equality. From any subset $\Delta \subseteq [M]$ of size λ of published shares, parties then compute $u^x = \prod_{\ell \in \Delta} f_\ell^{c_\ell}$, where c_ℓ's are Lagrange coefficients defined as $c_\ell = \prod_{i \in \Delta - \{\ell\}} i/(i-\ell)$. The method can be modified to work with Pedersen's verifiable secret sharing [21] as well.

Distributed decryption of El Gamal ciphertexts. When an El Gamal secret key is shared among some parties, distributed decryption of a given ciphertext (u, v) is also possible, without recovering the secret key itself. The parties first go through a distributed exponentiation protocol and compute u^x. The plaintext is then simply recovered as $m = v/u^x$.

Mix-nets. Mix-net, first introduced by Chaum [6], is an important cryptographic protocol which lies at the heart of several electronic voting systems and has other applications as well. It is executed by N voters and M mix-servers. In a re-encryption mix-net [20], mix-servers jointly generate a public key for a homomorphic cryptosystem and keep shares of the corresponding secret key. Each voter $i \in [N]$ submits a ciphertext along with a zero-knowledge proof of knowledge. When write-ins is not allowed, we assume that the voters have to choose among a set $\{m_j\}_{j \in [s]}$ of pre-defined voting options. In this case, a zero-knowledge proof must guarantee that the submitted ciphertext decrypts to one of the pre-defined choices.

When all encrypted votes have been received, the mix-net takes the list of all valid submitted ciphertexts and produces a mixed list of the decrypted plaintexts. More precisely, mix-servers take turns and re-encrypt each ciphertext. A permuted list of ciphertexts is then published along with a so called zero-knowledge *proof of shuffle*. The output list of the last mix-server is then jointly decrypted to determine the permuted list of submitted plaintexts. Any coalition of size less than λ mix-servers cannot obtain any knowledge about the correspondence between input ciphertexts and output plaintexts.

3   Online Tallying Servers

In this section we consider four return code schemes, including a few variations. All are practical but the drawback is that the tallying servers must be online during the online voting stage. The main differences between the proposed schemes come from the choice of the underlying MAC scheme Mac. Tallying servers run the mixnet and in a setup phase they jointly generate a public key y while shares of the corresponding secret key are kept private.

We assume that each voter is allowed to vote for one of a pre-defined set of choices $\{m_j\}_{j\in[s]}$. In all schemes, the ith voter submits a ciphertext $\mathsf{E}_y(m)$, where m is either one of the pre-defined choices or some random (known or unknown) representation of the designated choice. A corresponding zero-knowledge proof will also be submitted. The voter then receives a MAC tag $\mathsf{Mac}_{k_i}(m)$ as his return code, through the execution of a secure multiparty computation. Here, k_i is some (possibly) voter-dependent symmetric key shared between online vote collecting parties. Computation of such return codes are only possible by online participation of tallying servers.

In some schemes, we need to assign to each voter i a secret random value β_i and/or choice-dependent secret random values $\beta_{i,j}$ for every $j \in [s]$. This is done by assigning random encryptions $\mathsf{E}_y(\beta_i)$ and $\mathsf{E}_{pk}(\beta_{i,j})$ to the corresponding voter. In practice the ciphertexts can be defined as the output of a random oracle applied to the voter's identifier (along with that of voting alternative, if required, and other session identifiers). Thus, there is no need for the mix-servers to generate and communicate the ciphertexts to the voter.

Remark 2. We use the term "message authentication code" loosely in the sense that the schemes may not satisfy the standard definition of MACs for general purpose and the security level may also be much lower, since this suffices in our context.

3.1   Universal Hash Functions Used as MACs

Consider the ensemble of functions $F = \{f_{a,b}\}_{(a,b)\in\mathbb{Z}_q^2}$, where $f_{a,b}(x) = ax + b \bmod q$. This is the canonical example of a universal$_2$ hash function. It is well known that this is an unconditionally secure one-time MAC scheme if q is prime and large enough.

The function $f_{a,b}$ is linear, so it can be computed over homomorphic encryptions, i.e., given a ciphertext $\mathsf{E}_y(g^x)$ we can compute $\mathsf{E}_y(g^x)^a \mathsf{E}_y(g^b) = \mathsf{E}_y(g^{f_{a,b}(x)})$, which can then be decrypted in a distributed way. Any element $m \in G_q$ can be represented as g^x for a unique $x \in \mathbb{Z}_q$ since G_q is cyclic, so we can express the same relation as $\mathsf{E}_y(m)^a \mathsf{E}_y(\beta) = \mathsf{E}_y(g^{f_{a,b}(x)})$, where $m = g^x$ and $\beta = g^b$.

Thus, we can trivially compute a MAC tag for any individual party that submits a ciphertext as long as we do not do it more than once. More precisely, in a voting system we generate for the ith voter a verifiably secret shared $a_i \in \mathbb{Z}_q$ and an encryption $\mathsf{E}_y(\beta_i)$ for a randomly chosen $\beta_i \in G_q$. When the voter submits a ciphertext $\mathsf{E}_y(m_j)$ along with a zero-knowledge proof indicating that indeed one the pre-defined choices has been encrypted, he receives back the return code $m_j^{a_i} \beta_i$. Therefore, the underline MAC function is $\mathsf{Mac}_{a_i,\beta_i}(m) = m^{a_i}\beta_i$ for the ith voter. Return codes can be computed online using protocols for distributed exponentiation and decryption as explained in Sect. 2. In the setup phase, only distributed exponentiation is performed for every pre-defined voting option. The resulting ciphertexts are then communicated to a trusted third party to be securely printed, e.g., using the method described in the introduction. Furthermore, by construction the MAC tag is randomly distributed, so it can be truncated directly.

The security follows directly from the underlying MAC scheme. In addition to the danger of tallying servers being online, the drawback is that it only allows a single vote to be submitted and we need to generate a verifiably secret shared value for each voter.

3.2 One-Time Pad and Random Choice Representatives

Consider the MAC function $\mathsf{Mac}_\beta(m) = \beta m$ where key and message spaces are both G_q. The tag is a one-time pad symmetric encryption of the message and clearly not a secure MAC scheme. Indeed, an adversary can guess m and compute $\beta m'/m$ for another message m' to attempt to construct a valid MAC tag for m'. However, it *is* a one-time secure MAC for a random choice of plaintext unknown to the adversary.

A simple way to make sure that this is the case is to assign unique representatives of the choices for each voter, i.e., for the ith voter we generate random elements $\beta_{i,j} \in G_q$ for $j \in [s]$, but in encrypted form as ciphertexts $w_{i,j} = \mathsf{E}_y(\beta_{i,j})$. We can now provide the ciphertexts $w_{i,1}, \ldots, w_{i,s}$ to the ith voter. The voter then chooses the encryption of its choice, re-encrypts it, and proves in zero-knowledge that it is a re-encryption of one of its designated ciphertexts. This is a small constant factor more expensive than the corresponding proof for public choice representatives.

In the setup phase, for each voting option all representatives are shuffled, but they are published in *encrypted* form. More precisely, for each $j \in [s]$, the ciphertext list $w_{1,j}, \ldots, w_{N,j}$ is shuffled without decrypting and the re-encrypted list is made public.

The return code corresponding to the jth alternative of ith voter is then $\beta_{i,j}\beta_i$ where again β_i is a random secret value known in encrypted form $\mathsf{E}_y(\beta_i)$.

When all votes have been submitted and return codes have been received, the ciphertexts are mixed and the random elements encrypted by voters are published in permuted order. To be able to decode the actual voters' choices, the shuffled lists of representatives are also decrypted for every voting option. It is of course important that the shuffled random representatives are only decrypted *after* all votes have been collected.

The advantage of this system is that there is no need for verifiably secret shared exponents and re-voting is allowed. But zero-knowledge proofs are slightly more costly.

3.3   One-Time Pad and Standard MAC Schemes

Another way to resolve the problem encountered by solely using one-time pad is to construct a MAC scheme Mac' by combining it with a standard MAC scheme Mac [27]. More precisely, a key consists of a pair (β, k), where $\beta \in G_q$ is chosen randomly, and k is a randomly chosen key for Mac. The combined scheme Mac' is then defined by $\mathsf{Mac}'_{\beta,k}(m) = \mathsf{Mac}_k(\beta m)$.

This can be distributed in the generic way between M servers, each holding a secret key k_ℓ, by replacing the application of Mac_k by an array that is compressed with a collision resistant hash function H, i.e., we can define

$$\mathsf{Mac}_{\beta,K}(m) = \mathsf{H}\big((\mathsf{Mac}_{k_\ell}(\beta m))_{\ell \in [M]}\big),$$

where $K = (k_1, \ldots, k_M)$. It may seem that this does not suffice to satisfy our requirements for secure printing in electronic voting systems, since apparently the printer must send βm to the servers. However, the MAC keys $k_1, \ldots, k_M$ can be shared with the trusted party to print the pre-computed return codes without loss of security.

In an electronic voting system a ciphertext $\mathsf{E}_y(\beta_i)$ is generated for the ith voter and the MAC key for that voter is $(\beta_i, K) = (\beta_i, k_1, \ldots, k_M)$. The mix-servers simply take an input ciphertext $\mathsf{E}_y(m)$ submitted by the ith voter, decrypt $\mathsf{E}_y(\beta_i)\mathsf{E}_y(m) = \mathsf{E}_y(\beta_i m)$, and output $\mathsf{H}\big((\mathsf{Mac}_{k_\ell}(\beta_i m))_{\ell \in [M]}\big)$.

The advantage of this system is that there is no need for mix-servers to generate a secret shared value for each individual voter and re-voting is also allowed. The disadvantage is that it is not robust. If a server is down, the return code cannot be computed. One way to resolve this problem is to let each server verifiably secret share his symmetric key between other servers. But this guarantees security only against semi-honest adversaries and malicious servers cannot be detected.

3.4   Diffie-Hellman MAC Schemes

Recall that the Diffie-Hellman assumption states that no efficient algorithm can compute g^{ab} given g^a and g^b as input, where $a, b \in \mathbb{Z}_q$ are randomly chosen.

Furthermore, a standard hybrid argument shows that it is also hard to compute any $g^{a_i b_j}$ given g^{a_i} and g^{b_j} for $i \in [N]$ and $j \in [s]$ for some N and s, where $a_i, b_j \in \mathbb{Z}_q$ are randomly chosen. If we accept the decisional Diffie-Hellman assumption, then this is strengthened to the claim that $g^{a_i b_j}$ is indistinguishable from a randomly chosen element in G_q.

This immediately gives two MAC schemes that are compatible with mix-nets based on the El Gamal cryptosystem. Both schemes use random representations of voting options. The first variant is voter independent while the second is not. In both cases hashing the MAC tag allows truncation for any underlying group.

3.5   First Variant

We encode the jth choice by a randomly chosen element $\gamma_j \in G_q$, where in contrast to Sect. 3.2, $\gamma_1, \ldots, \gamma_s$ may be public and known at the beginning. Let the mix-servers generate a verifiably secret shared MAC key a_i for the ith voter. Then, computing the MAC of the plaintext γ_j provided in encrypted form $\mathsf{E}_y(\gamma_j)$ is done by simply computing $\gamma_j^{a_i}$ by distributed exponentiation and decryption. Note that $\gamma_j = g^{b_j}$ for some $b_j \in \mathbb{Z}_q$, so the result is $g^{a_i b_j}$. To summarize, the underlying MAC scheme is defined by $\mathsf{Mac}_{a_i}(m) = m^{a_i}$ for the ith voter. This can be computed under encryption, which means that we can also provide the result in one-time pad encrypted form to a third party. This system remains secure when re-voting is allowed.

3.6   Second Variant

The first variant is somewhat impractical in that the mix-servers must generate a secret shared exponent $a_i \in \mathbb{Z}_q$ for each individual voter. We can switch the roles of randomly chosen representatives of choices and verifiably distributed secret exponents. More precisely, random elements $\beta_{i,j}$ in encrypted form as ciphertexts $\mathsf{E}_y(\beta_{i,j})$ are generated for every $i \in [N]$ and $j \in [s]$. The preparation phase and encryption procedure is exactly like that of Sect. 3.2, but now a single verifiably secret shared value a is generated and the same function $\mathsf{Mac}_a(m) = m^a$ is used for all voters.

The advantage of this scheme is that the MAC function can be evaluated in batches on submitted ciphertexts and in contrast to the construction in Sect. 3.2 the representatives may be shuffled and decrypted before all ciphertexts have been received. Re-voting is still allowed.

4   Offline Tallying Servers

In this section, we propose two schemes to resolve the online-server danger of presented schemes of Sect. 3. This is achieved without a considerable amount of performance loss or organizational overhead. The main idea is to use two independent public keys with shared secret keys. More precisely, in the setup phase, the tallying servers generate a public key y and keep shares of the corresponding secret key. Additionally, the vote collecting servers produce a public key z in the same manner.

In the online voting phase, ith voter submits a pair of ciphertexts (v_i, w_i), along with some scheme-dependent zero-knowledge proof. Here, v_i and w_i are ciphertexts encrypted under public keys y and z, respectively. The first ciphertext, v_i, is used to decode voter's choice after mixing. The second ciphertext, w_i, is an encryption of a random value, so it basically contains no information about the voter's choice. To compute the return code, w_i is simply decrypted by online servers who collect the encrypted votes. Therefore, the shares of y are never exposed during the online voting phase. Even if the secret key of z is revealed, no knowledge is leaked about the voter's choice which is encrypted under y.

When all ciphertexts have been collected, the ciphertexts list $v_1, \ldots, v_N$ is shuffled. Then, they are decrypted, and if necessary decoded, to obtain the cast votes. Since tallying can be performed behind an airwall, this approach ensures a high level of privacy for the voters.

As an alternative approach to print the pre-computed return codes, the online servers can simply share their secret key with the trusted party without loss of security.

The main requirement to be satisfied is that the two submitted ciphertexts are constructed such that they cannot be split. Below, we propose two such constructions. In addition to enhanced privacy due to airwalling, the advantage of these systems is that there is no need for voter-dependent verifiably secret shared values and re-voting is also allowed. The drawback is that the zero-knowledge proofs are more costly compared with the schemes of Sect. 3.

4.1   First Variant

In setup phase, for every $i \in [N]$ and $j \in [s]$, servers generate secret random pairs of elements $(\alpha_{i,j}, \beta_{i,j})$ in encrypted form as random ciphertext pairs $(v_{i,j}, w_{i,j}) = (\mathsf{E}_y(\alpha_{i,j}), \mathsf{E}_z(\beta_{i,j}))$ As it was explained in Sect. 3, such ciphertexts can be simply interpreted as the output of a random oracle. To vote for jth choice, the ith voter computes v_i and w_i as respective re-encryptions of $v_{i,j}$ and $w_{i,j}$. The pair (v_i, w_i) is then submitted along with a zero-knowledge proof.

In the setup phase, for each voting option j all representatives $v_{1,j}, \ldots, v_{N,j}$ are mixed and a permutation of the decrypted list $\alpha_{1,j}, \ldots, \alpha_{N,j}$ is published. When every voter i has submitted a ciphertext pair (v_i, w_i), the first elements are shuffled, decrypted and decoded.

4.2   Second Variant

In the second variant, for every $i \in [N]$ and $j \in [s]$, the pre-computed random values $w_{i,j} = \mathsf{E}_z(\beta_{i,j})$ are prepared as before. To vote for jth choice, the ith voter computes v_i as an encryption $\mathsf{E}_y(m_j)$ and w_i as a re-encryptions of $w_{i,j}$. The pair (v_i, w_i) is then submitted along with a zero-knowledge proof. Computation of return codes and tallying is straightforward. Zero-knowledge proofs are slightly less costly compared with the first variant.

5   About Write-In Candidates

Some of the systems can be adapted to allow write-ins in the sense that voters simply encrypt a representation of one of the pre-determined choices, or an arbitrary message. The zero knowledge proof of knowledge would then not impose any additional structure. Naturally, return codes can not be provided in printed form for a relatively small number of messages, so to have a chance to verify a return code for an arbitrary message the voter needs the shared MAC key.

The scheme of Sect. 3.1 is based on an unconditionally secure one-time MAC scheme, so it remains as secure for any message. The scheme of Sect. 3.2 does provide some security, but for reasons discussed in that section only if write-in votes are rare and unpredictable. Finally, the scheme of Sect. 3.5 also works for write-ins, but under a strong non-standard DDH-assumption with some care. We must assume that δ^{a_i} is indistinguishable from a random element even when the message δ strictly speaking is not randomly chosen. One way to make this a more plausible assumption is to pad a message with random bits before interpreting it as a group element, but it remains a non-standard assumption that is fragile in a complex system where slight changes may render it difficult to defend.

6   Conclusion

We present several return code systems for electronic voting applications, some of which overlaps or encompasses schemes previously proposed as separate schemes. We are unable to single out one scheme that is superior to all the other schemes in every way.

Table 1. Summary of: what is pre-computed by the tallying servers, the form of ciphertexts submitted by the ith voter to vote for the jth choice, the form of the corresponding return codes for different features of proposed schemes. Furthermore, for each scheme it is indicated if: a single global MAC key is used or if a separate key must be secret shared for each individual voter, if multiple votes can be submitted, and if the scheme matches well with write-in votes (for which the voter can not receive any pre-computed return codes in advance of course).

Section	Pre-computed	Submitted	Return code	Global MAC key	Re-voting	Write-ins
Section 3.1	$\mathsf{E}_y(\beta_i)$	$\mathsf{E}_y(m_j)$	$m_j^{a_i}\beta_i$	–	–	✓
Section 3.2	$\mathsf{E}_y(\beta_i)w_{i,j} = \mathsf{E}_y(\beta_{i,j})$	$\mathsf{RE}_y(w_{i,j})$	$\beta_{i,j}\beta_i$	✓	✓	Partly
Section 3.3	$\mathsf{E}_y(\beta_i)$	$\mathsf{E}_y(m_j)$	$\mathsf{Mac}_{\beta_i,K}(m_j)$	–	✓	–
Section 3.5	γ_j	$\mathsf{E}_y(\gamma_j)$	$\gamma_j^{a_i}$	–	✓	Partly
Section 3.6	$w_{i,j} = \mathsf{E}_y(\beta_{i,j})$	$\mathsf{RE}_y(w_{i,j})$	$\beta_{i,j}^a$	✓	✓	–
Section 4.1	$v_{i,j} = \mathsf{E}_z(\alpha_{i,j})$ $w_{i,j} = \mathsf{E}_y(\beta_{i,j})$	$\mathsf{RE}_y(v_{i,j})$ $\mathsf{RE}_z(w_{i,j})$	$\beta_{i,j}$	✓	✓	–
Section 4.2	$w_{i,j} = \mathsf{E}_z(\beta_{i,j})$	$\mathsf{E}_y(m_j)$ $\mathsf{RE}_z(w_{i,j})$	$\beta_{i,j}$	✓	✓	–

Instead our view is that all the schemes are simple combinations of cryptographic constructions that are well understood and that they together give a powerful toolbox to construct return codes for many types of elections. Table 1 summarizes different features of proposed schemes.

References

1. Adida, B.: Helios: web-based open-audit voting. In: Proceedings of the 17th USENIX Security Symposium, 28 July–1 August 2008, San Jose, pp. 335–348 (2008)
2. Adida, B., Neff, C.A.: Ballot casting assurance. In: 2006 USENIX/ACCURATE Electronic Voting Technology Workshop (EVT 2006), Vancouver, 1 August 2006
3. Allepuz, J.P., Castelló, S.G.: Internet voting system with cast as intended verification. In: Kiayias, A., Lipmaa, H. (eds.) Vote-ID 2011. LNCS, vol. 7187, pp. 36–52. Springer, Heidelberg (2012). doi:10.1007/978-3-642-32747-6_3
4. Ansper, A., Heiberg, S., Lipmaa, H., Øverland, T.A., van Laenen, F.: Security and trust for the Norwegian E-voting pilot project E-valg 2011. In: Jøsang, A., Maseng, T., Knapskog, S.J. (eds.) NordSec 2009. LNCS, vol. 5838, pp. 207–222. Springer, Heidelberg (2009). doi:10.1007/978-3-642-04766-4_15
5. Benaloh, J.: Simple verifiable elections. In: 2006 USENIX/ACCURATE Electronic Voting Technology Workshop (EVT 2006), Vancouver, 1 August 2006
6. Chaum, D.: Untraceable electronic mail, return addresses, and digital pseudonyms. Commun. ACM 24(2), 84–88 (1981)
7. Chaum, D.: Surevote: technical overview. In: Proceedings of the Workshop on Trustworthy Elections (WOTE 2001) (2001)
8. Chaum, D., Ryan, P.Y.A., Schneider, S.: A practical voter-verifiable election scheme. In: di Vimercati, S.C., Syverson, P., Gollmann, D. (eds.) ESORICS 2005. LNCS, vol. 3679, pp. 118–139. Springer, Heidelberg (2005). doi:10.1007/11555827_8
9. Feldman, P.: A practical scheme for non-interactive verifiable secret sharing. In: 28th Annual Symposium on Foundations of Computer Science, Los Angeles, 27–29 October 1987, pp. 427–437 (1987)
10. Galindo, D., Guasch, S., Puiggalí, J.: 2015 Neuchâtel's cast-as-intended verification mechanism. In: Haenni, R., Koenig, R.E., Wikström, D. (eds.) VOTELID 2015. LNCS, vol. 9269, pp. 3–18. Springer, Cham (2015). doi:10.1007/978-3-319-22270-7_1
11. Gennaro, R., Jarecki, S., Krawczyk, H., Rabin, T.: Secure distributed key generation for discrete-log based cryptosystems. J. Cryptol. 20(1), 51–83 (2007)
12. Gjøsteen, K.: Analysis of an internet voting protocol. IACR Cryptology ePrint Archive, 2010:380 (2010)
13. Gjøsteen, K.: The Norwegian internet voting protocol. IACR Cryptology ePrint Archive, 2013:473 (2013)
14. Gjøsteen, K., Lund, A.S.: The Norwegian internet voting protocol: a new instantiation. IACR Cryptology ePrint Archive 2015:503 (2015)
15. Goldreich, O.: The Foundations of Cryptography. Basic Techniques, vol. 1. Cambridge University Press, Cambridge (2001)
16. Goldreich, O.: The Foundations of Cryptography. Basic Applications, vol. 2. Cambridge University Press, Cambridge (2004)

17. Heiberg, S., Laud, P., Willemson, J.: The application of I-voting for Estonian parliamentary elections of 2011. In: Kiayias, A., Lipmaa, H. (eds.) Vote-ID 2011. LNCS, vol. 7187, pp. 208–223. Springer, Heidelberg (2012). doi:10.1007/978-3-642-32747-6_13

18. Heiberg, S., Lipmaa, H., van Laenen, F.: On E-vote integrity in the case of malicious voter computers. In: Gritzalis, D., Preneel, B., Theoharidou, M. (eds.) ESORICS 2010. LNCS, vol. 6345, pp. 373–388. Springer, Heidelberg (2010). doi:10.1007/978-3-642-15497-3_23

19. Lipmaa, H.: Two simple code-verification voting protocols. IACR Cryptology ePrint Archive, 2011:317 (2011)

20. Park, C., Itoh, K., Kurosawa, K.: Efficient anonymous channel and all/nothing election scheme. In: Helleseth, T. (ed.) EUROCRYPT 1993. LNCS, vol. 765, pp. 248–259. Springer, Heidelberg (1994). doi:10.1007/3-540-48285-7_21

21. Pedersen, T.P.: Non-interactive and information-theoretic secure verifiable secret sharing. In: Feigenbaum, J. (ed.) CRYPTO 1991. LNCS, vol. 576, pp. 129–140. Springer, Heidelberg (1992). doi:10.1007/3-540-46766-1_9

22. Puigalli, J., Guasch, S.: Cast-as-intended verification in Norway. In: 5th International Conference on Electronic Voting 201 (eVOTE 2012), Co-organized by the Council of Europe, Gesellschaft für Informatik and E-voting.CC, 11–14 July 2012, Castle Hofen, Bregenz, Austria, pp. 49–63 (2012)

23. Rosen, A., Ta-shma, A., Riva, B.: Jonathan (Yoni) Ben-Nun. Wombat voting system (2012)

24. Ryan, P.Y.A., Schneider, S.A.: Prêt à voter with re-encryption mixes. In: Gollmann, D., Meier, J., Sabelfeld, A. (eds.) ESORICS 2006. LNCS, vol. 4189, pp. 313–326. Springer, Heidelberg (2006). doi:10.1007/11863908_20

25. Sandler, D., Derr, K., Wallach, D.S.: Votebox: a tamper-evident, verifiable electronic voting system. In: Proceedings of the 17th USENIX Security Symposium, 28 July–1 August 2008, San Jose, pp. 349–364 (2008)

26. Shamir, A.: How to share a secret. Commun. ACM **22**(11), 612–613 (1979)

27. Wikström, D.: Proposed during rump session of evote 2015 (2015)

Eos a Universal Verifiable and Coercion Resistant Voting Protocol

Ştefan Patachi and Carsten Schürmann[✉]

DemTech, IT University of Copenhagen,
Copenhagen, Denmark
{stpa,carsten}@itu.dk

Abstract. We present the voting protocol Eos that is based on a conditional linkable ring signatures scheme. Voters are organized in rings allowing them to sign votes anonymously. Voters may assume multiple pseudo identities, one of which is legitimate. We use the others to signal coercion to the Election Authority. Eos uses two mixing phases with the goal to break the connection between the voter and vote, not to preserve vote privacy (which is given already) but to guarantee coercion resistance by making it (nearly) impossible for a coercer to follow their vote through the bulletin board. Eos is universally verifiable.

1 Introduction

Most well-known voting protocols use a form of mixing to break the connection between vote and voter. Prêt-à-Voter [19], Helios [1], JCJ [12], Civitas [14], encrypt the votes at the time of casting, and then mix them before decrypting them for tabulation. Under the assumptions that at least one mixer is honest, so the argument, it is impossible to link a decrypted vote back to the identity of its voter. BeliniosRF [5] uses randomizable cipher-texts instead. Selene [20] follows a different approach. It uses tracker numbers and assigns them to voters, who eventually will be able to identify their votes on a bulletin board but only after the election authority has shared cryptographic information with the voter. In Selene, voters can fool a coercer into believing that *any* and not just *one* vote on the bulletin board was theirs. Both JCJ and Selene are receipt-free and coercion-resistant.

To our knowledge not much work has been done to leverage the power of ring signatures [18] to the design of voting protocols, besides perhaps the mention in [7,13,22]. Here, a ring refers to a group of participants who have the ability to sign messages anonymously by hiding their respective identities within the group. Assuming that the message is sent over an anonymous channel, the receiver of

---

C. Schurmann—This work was funded in part through the Danish Council for Strategic Research, Programme Comission on Strategic Growth Technologies under grant 10-092309. This publication was also made possible by NPRP grant NPRP 7-988-1-178 from the Qatar National Research Fund (a member of Qatar Foundation). The statements made herein are solely the responsibility of the authors.

© Springer International Publishing AG 2017
R. Krimmer et al. (Eds.): E-Vote-ID 2017, LNCS 10615, pp. 210–227, 2017.
DOI: 10.1007/978-3-319-68687-5_13

the message will not be able to trace the signature back to the signer. Ring signatures bring also other advantages. For example, an election authority will be able to publish all ballots and their signatures on a public bulletin board for public scrutiny without revealing the voters' identities. Every voter can check their vote by accessing the bulletin board. But there are also challenges: First, the administration of the voter's identities, i.e. private keys, and second the protection of such identities from misuse, for example, for the purpose of vote-selling or voter coercion.

For the first challenge, we do not provide a solution in this paper, we merely assume that an effective, trusted identity infrastructure is in place that allows a voter to access a private key on a secure platform, for example, by means of a trusted Hardware Security Module (HSM), such as for example, a Bitcoin wallet called Trezor. This may seem like a controversial assumption, but it really is not: Our experiments have shown that suitable HSMs exist. They may not be totally secure, but they are reasonable well designed to protect private keys against malicious agents and against malicious firmware. Hacking such an HSM is possible and requires fiddling with firmware and hardware, but we argue that this is difficult to do on a large scale in practice.

In this paper, we tackle a second challenge. We devise a ring signature scheme that allows voters to assume different pseudo identities, and that provides mechanisms for linking such identities from the point of view of the signature verifier. This scheme is a generalization of the so called linkable spontaneous anonymous group (LSAG) signatures [13], where all signatures from the same signer are linked. Correspondingly, we refer to this scheme as a *conditional-linking ring* (CLR) signature scheme. Using CLR signatures it is up to the voter to allow linking or not. Linking does not break anonymity. Compared to BeliniosRF [5], which is not based on conditional linkability but on signatures based on randomizable cipher-texts [3], anonymity follows directly from the definition of ring signatures and does not have to be added by another mechanism.

Based on CLR signatures, we develop the Eos voting protocol. Every voter is assumed to have physical access to an HSM and a way to authenticate. The HSM guards the voter's private key. The authentication method yields additional entropy, such as, for example, a PIN number, a picture, or a fingerprint. When casting a vote, before submission, it is either put into a "green envelope" marking it as valid, or a "red envelope" marking it as invalid or possibly coerced.

The entropy collected during the authentication procedure determines which pseudo-identity is used. We encrypt the color of the envelope and the electoral identity of the voter (which is unique), alongside the vote itself. All envelopes together with their corresponding CLR signatures are recorded and shared on a public bulletin board. Pseudo identities are malleable, which means that from the point of view of the voter or the coercer, it will be "discrete logarithm hard" to link any two ballots from the bulletin board. Voters and coercers will be able to check whether the ballot was recorded as cast but neither the voter nor the coercer will be able to link their ballots.

The protocol proceeds and executes two verifiable decryption mixes. The first mix-net shuffles the ballots and decrypts color and the electoral identity, but leaves the votes encrypted. All information is posted on a public bulletin board accompanied by zero-knowledge proofs of correct shuffle and correct decryption. Red envelopes are discarded and green envelopes are opened. The encrypted votes contained within (and only those) are passed to the second and last mixing stage. If two green envelopes are cast from two different pseudo-identities that correspond to the same electoral identity, this indicates a malicious attempt to double vote. In this case we discard all votes associated with this electoral identity. In the second and final mixing stage, we use a verifiable decryption mix to shuffle and decrypt votes. Also here, the resulting bulletin board is published including zero-knowledge proofs for public scrutiny.

For the subsequent security analysis of Eos, we consider an adversarial environment where only voters and their respective HSM devices have to be trusted. Election authorities, mixing nodes, and tellers may be assumed to be under the adversary's control. The adversary is assumed to have the usual adversarial capabilities, which includes deletion, addition or modification of any kind of information, including votes, logs entries, or messages. We show that Eos is universally verifiable.

Closely related to the adversary is the coercer, an agent that aims to exert undue influence onto the voter, for example by forcing the voter to vote in a particular way. In addition also election authorities, mix nodes and tellers, may be under the coercer's control. A coercer may be physically present in the room when voting takes place, or he may observe the voting procedure remotely. We consider a coercion attempt successful, if the coercer succeeds to force voter to vote a particular way and the coerced vote is then included in the final tally, in a way that is observable by the coercer. For the analysis of coercion resistance to make sense, we must assume that the coercer and the voter are different principals, and we do this by assuming that only the voter can authenticate successfully to the HSM device. In this paper we consider three different attacks against the coercion-freeness: (1) A coercer steals a voter's identity, (2) a coercer obtains a receipt by tracking a vote through the system and (3) a coercer steals the HSM and impersonates the voter.

Eos is constructed to be resistant against all three kinds of coercion attacks: Because of the use of CLR signatures, a coercer can always be assigned an alternate valid identity (1). Under a commonly accepted assumption, it is always possible to guarantee that not all mixing nodes are under the coercer's control, which means that neither voter nor coercer will be able to track the votes, but will have to revert to checking zero-knowledge proofs of knowledge (2). And finally, the authentication mechanisms provided by an HSM can be made arbitrarily complex, making it increasingly hard for a coercer to brute-force his way in (3).

Contributions. The contributions of this paper are (1) a Conditional Linkable Ring (CLR) signature scheme, described in Sect. 3, (2) an efficient mixer that satisfies special soundness but still produces a proof of correct shuffle ($2n$ modexp operations to generate and $4n$ modexp operations to verify shuffle proofs), described in Sect. 4, (3) the Eos voting protocol, described in Sect. 5, and (4) proofs that the Eos is vote secrecy and integrity preserving, universally verifiable, receipt-free and coercion resistant, discussed in Sect. 6.

2   Basic Notations

We define the following notations that we will use throughout our paper. We work with an ElGamal cryptosystem that is defined over a cyclic group $\mathbb{G}$ of prime p order q generated by g. All mathematical operations presented in this paper are done modulo p.

We use standard notation and write $\{m\}_y^r = (g^r, y^r m)$ for the ElGamal tuple that one obtains by encrypting message m with randomness r and a public key y. We use r to denote randomness, and write $r \in_R \mathbb{Z}_q$ to express that we choose r from $\mathbb{Z}$ modulo q at random using a uniform distribution. We will also use sequences of n elements over $\mathbb{Z}_q$, written as $\langle x_1, ..., x_n \rangle \in \mathbb{Z}_q^n$. We define $[n]$ to denote the index set of natural numbers up to n as $\{1, ..., n\}$. Furthermore, we use Greek letters σ for signatures and π to denote permutations. We write $\mathbb{P}_n$ as the set of all permutation of n elements. Concatenation of two elements $a, b \in \{0, 1\}^*$ is written as $a \| b$.

3   Conditional-Linkable Ring Signatures

We begin the technical exposition of this paper by defining the concept of Conditional Linkable Ring (CLR) signatures. In a linkable ring (LR) signature scheme [13], a verifier can learn which signatures originate from the same signer. Note that this does not mean that the verifier learns something about the identity of the signer — ring signatures always guarantee the anonymity of the signer. For our application however, linkability is overly restrictive – if we were to use LR signatures naively, we could not achieve coercion-resistance. Therefore, we relax the notion of linkability, and introduce *conditional linkability* giving the signer the ability to link (revealing that the signatures originate from the same signer) or not to link (making it look like as if two signatures were produced by two different signers) and *claimability* allowing the signer to claim the authenticity of a signature by proving his position in the ring in zero knowledge. When a signature is claimed, the signer reveals his position in the ring an looses anonymity.

Preparation Phase: Every prospective member of the ring creates a secret key $x_i \in \mathbb{Z}_q$, and shares the public key $y_i = g^{x_i}$ with a designated election authority.

Set-Up Phase: The election authority produces the set of ring members $L = \langle y_1, ..., y_n \rangle$, which represents eligible voters.

Identity Selection Phase: Assume that the signer is the member of the ring at position α. The signer selects a pseudo-identity by choosing $\phi \in_R \mathbb{G}$ and by forming the pair (ϕ, θ) where $\theta = \phi^{x_\alpha}$. The pair (ϕ, θ) is called a pseudo identity. If the signer wishes his signature to be linkable, he will always choose the same value of ϕ, otherwise, he will choose a different value for ϕ for every signature.

CLR signatures give us quite a lot of freedom to choose ϕ. To see that LR signatures proposed in [13] are simply an instance of CLR signatures, choose ϕ to be the cryptographic hash value of L (written as $h = H_2(L)$ in their paper) and compute $\theta = h^{x_\alpha}$. Liu et al. denote this value as $\tilde{y}$. The security of linkability reduces therefore to a secure choice of ϕ, for which it is sufficient to require that finding $\log_g \phi$ is a hard problem.

Signing Algorithm. We begin now with the presentation of the signing algorithm. Our algorithm follows closely the original LR signing algorithm described in [13], the most notable difference being that we use ϕ and θ instead of h and $\tilde{y}$, respectively. Given the message to be signed $m \in \{0,1\}^*$, for each element in the ring L, a cipher text is computed, starting from the position of the signer in the ring, α, to the end of the list and from the beginning of the list back to α. The first computed cipher text is therefore

$$c_{\alpha+1} = \mathcal{H}\left(m\|g^u\|\phi^u\right)$$

where, $\mathcal{H}$ is a cryptographic hash function that returns a number from $\mathbb{Z}_q$ (referred to as H_1 in [13]) and $u \in_R \mathbb{Z}_q$. Next, for each element in L from $i = \alpha + 1$ to n and from $i = 1$ to $\alpha - 1$, the signer computes:

$$c_{i+1} = \mathcal{H}\left(m\|g^{s_i} \cdot y_i^{c_i}\|\phi^{s_i} \cdot \theta^{c_i}\right)$$

where each $s_i \in_R \mathbb{Z}_q$ is a random number assigned for each entity in L. Note that at step $i = n$, we generate $c_1 = c_{i+1}$. The signer computes:

$$s_\alpha = u - x_\alpha \cdot c_\alpha \bmod q$$

Finally, the output of the CLR signing algorithm is the signature σ on message m with the pseudo-identity (ϕ, θ) that has the following structure:

$$\sigma(m) = (c_1, \langle s_1, ..., s_n \rangle)$$

Verification Algorithm. After having received a message m and the corresponding signature, $\sigma(m) = (c_1, \langle s_1, .., s_n \rangle)$ from the pseudo-identity (ϕ, θ), anybody can now verify the signature by executing the following steps of the verification algorithm, which is computationally linear in terms of size of L, that should output either the signature is valid or not, i.e. it was generated by a ring member or not. For each element in L starting from $i = 1$ to n compute:

$$c_{i+1} = \mathcal{H}\left(m\|g^{s_i} \cdot y_i^{c_i}\|\phi^{s_i} \cdot \theta^{c_i}\right)$$

The algorithm validates the signature if and only if the last $c_{n+1} = c_1$, where c_1 is contained as the first argument in the signature.

Discussion. The idea to consider other ways to compute ϕ was already discussed in [13]. What is new in our work is to allow ϕ to be drawn at random from $\mathbb{G}$. We shall see in Sect. 5 how to choose ϕ to encode pseudo-identities.

The definition, properties and proofs of the signature scheme presented in [13], such as existential unforgability and signer ambiguity, and the rewind-on-success lemma, carry over verbatim to the CLR signature scheme. CLR signatures are conditionally linkable and claimable. Once generated, the signer and only the signer can claim responsibility of a signature generated by him by providing in zero knowledge a discrete logarithm equality proof between $\log_\phi \theta = \log_g y_\alpha$.

4   Mix-Net

Next, we describe the mix-net the we will be using. The goal of the mixing is to shuffle ballots in such a way that it is impossible to correlate outputs to inputs.

The mixing task is standard, the literature on mix-nets that emit proofs of correct (parallel) shuffle is mature. In essence, any state-of-the-art mix-net could be used as long as it supports parallel shuffle, for example, Bayer [2], Groth [10,11], Wikström [23], or more recently Fauzi and Lempaa [8] whose security proof no longer relies on the Random Oracle Model.

While analyzing the different mix-net protocols, in particular [9,15,16,21], we observed simplifications to Neff's protocol that we describe next. These make the proof of parallel shuffle more efficient while still satisfying special soundness, justifying why we have included a description of the *simplified Neff's protocol* in this paper. The protocol is mathematically elegant, intuitive, and easier to understand than Neff's original protocol as it follows closely the classic discrete logarithm equality zero knowledge proof.

Our proof of shuffle also relies on the Random Oracle Model. In comparison with Groth's work, our proof has only three rounds and requires only $2n$ modexps for generating a proof and $4n$ modexps for verifying a proof. On the other hand, Bayer's [2] protocol requires only sub-linear operations but needs 9 rounds to finish.

Below, we provide a semi-formal analysis that our proposed protocol is a zero-knowledge proof of correct shuffle.

4.1   Proof of Correct Shuffle

Our mix-net consists of several mixing servers, each of which receives as input a bulletin board of n ElGamal tuples (a_i, b_i) and produces an output bulletin board, where all tuples are re-encrypted and shuffled:

$$(c_i, d_i) = \left(a_{\pi(i)} \cdot g^{s_{\pi(i)}}, b_{\pi(i)} \cdot y^{s_{\pi(i)}} \right) \text{ for } i \in [n]$$

where y is the encryption key, $\langle s_1, ..., s_n \rangle \in_R \mathbb{Z}_q^n$ the randomness used for re-encryption, and $\pi \in_R \mathbb{P}_n$ the permutation underlying the shuffle.

The challenge when defining a mix-net is how each mixing server can prove the correctness of the shuffle to a public verifier, without revealing information about the permutation π or the randomness $\langle s_1, ...s_n \rangle$ used for re-encryption.

The following proof of correct shuffle is inspired by the protocol developed by Sako and Kilian [21], where they say that the proof should show that the

$\mathcal{P}$ secretly generates: $k \in_R \mathbb{Z}_q$ and $\langle m_1, ..., m_n \rangle \in_R \mathbb{Z}_q^n$ and publishes commitment:

$$A = g^k \cdot \prod_{i \in [n]} a_i{}^{m_i} \qquad\qquad B = y^k \cdot \prod_{i \in [n]} b_i{}^{m_i}$$

$\mathcal{V}$ sends challenge: $\langle e_1, ..., e_n \rangle \in_R \mathbb{Z}_q^n$
$\mathcal{P}$ publishes response:

$$r_i = m_i + e_{\pi^{-1}(i)} \bmod q \text{ for } i \in [n]$$

$$t = k + \sum_{i \subset [n]} \left(e_i \cdot s_{\pi(i)} \right) \bmod q$$

$\mathcal{V}$ accepts the proof if the following verification calculations match:

$$g^t \cdot \prod_{i \in [n]} a_i{}^{r_i} = A \cdot \prod_{i \in [n]} c_i{}^{e_i} \qquad\qquad y^t \cdot \prod_{i \in [n]} b_i{}^{r_i} = B \cdot \prod_{i \in [n]} d_i{}^{e_i}$$

Fig. 1. Protocol: proof of correct shuffle

output of the mixer could be generated in some manner from the input. Finally, the aggregation of the entire set of ElGamal pairs, is inspired by Ramchen's work [17]. Our proof follows the natural flow of a classic discrete logarithm equality zero knowledge proof depicted in Fig. 1, i.e. the mix server publishes a commitment of the input, a verifier challenges the output of the mixer and then mixer generates a response, which convinces the verifier that the shuffle was correct.

Let (a_i, b_i) be the n ElGamal tuples that form the input for the mix server. Let (c_i, d_i) be n ElGamal tuples, computed as above, be the output of the mix server. To prove the correctness of the shuffle, the mix server $\mathcal{P}$ and a public verifier $\mathcal{V}$ have to follow the protocol that is described in Fig. 1.

Theorem 1. *The protocol described in Fig. 1 is complete.*

Proof. To show that our protocol is correct, we have to prove that the equations that $\mathcal{V}$ verifies hold when the response $(\langle r_1, ..., r_n \rangle, t)$ is computed correctly.

$$g^t \cdot \prod_{i \in [n]} a_i{}^{r_i} = A \cdot \prod_{i \in [n]} c_i{}^{e_i}$$

$$g^{k + \sum_{i \in [n]} e_i \cdot s_{\pi(i)}} \cdot \prod_{i \in [n]} a_i{}^{m_i + e_{\pi^{-1}(i)}} = g^k \cdot \prod_{i \in [n]} a_i{}^{m_i} \cdot \prod_{i \in [n]} \left(a_{\pi(i)} \cdot g^{s_{\pi(i)}} \right)^{e_i}$$

$$g^k \cdot g^{\sum_{i \in [n]} e_i \cdot s_{\pi(i)}} \cdot \prod_{i \in [n]} a_i{}^{m_i} \cdot \prod_{i \in [n]} a_i{}^{e_{\pi^{-1}(i)}} = g^k \cdot \prod_{i \in [n]} a_i{}^{m_i} \cdot \prod_{i \in [n]} \left(a_{\pi(i)}{}^{e_i} \cdot g^{s_{\pi(i)} \cdot e_i} \right)$$

$$\prod_{i \in [n]} g^{e_i \cdot s_{\pi(i)}} \cdot \prod_{i \in [n]} a_i{}^{e_{\pi^{-1}(i)}} = \prod_{i \in [n]} a_{\pi(i)}{}^{e_i} \cdot \prod_{i \in [n]} g^{s_{\pi(i)} \cdot e_i}$$

$$\prod_{i \in [n]} a_i{}^{e_{\pi^{-1}(i)}} = \prod_{i \in [n]} a_{\pi(i)}{}^{e_i}$$

The last equation in the proof is true because the product aggregation happens through the entire set of n elements. This means we can compute the product aggregation of $a_i^{e_{\pi^{-1}(i)}}$ in a permuted way, namely $a_{\pi(i)}^{e_{\pi(\pi^{-1}(i))}} = a_{\pi(i)}^{e_i}$.

In the same way, the second equations that $\mathcal{V}$ has to verify can be proven to hold if the response $(\langle r_1, ..., r_n \rangle, t)$ is computed correctly.   □

Theorem 2. *The protocol described in Fig. 1 satisfies special soundness.*

Proof. Each transcript of our protocol has the following form:

$$\text{View}\,[\mathcal{P} \leftrightarrow \mathcal{V}] = (A, B, \langle e_1, ...e_n \rangle, \langle r_1, ..., r_n \rangle, t)$$

where A and B represent the initial commitment, sequence $\langle e_1, ...e_n \rangle$ is the random challenge picked by the verifier, and the sequence $\langle r_1, ..., r_n \rangle$ together with the value t represent the response to the challenge.

For any cheating prover $\mathcal{P}^*$ (that does not know the permutation $\pi(i)$ and the re-encryption coefficients $\langle s_1, ..., s_n \rangle$), given two valid conversations between $\mathcal{P}$ and the verifier $\mathcal{V}$, $(A, B, \langle e_1, ...e_n \rangle, \langle r_1, ..., r_n \rangle, t)$ and $(A, B, \langle e'_1, ...e'_n \rangle, \langle r'_1, ..., r'_n \rangle, t')$ that have the same commitment but different challenge $e_i \neq e'_i$, the permutation $\pi(i)$ used for shuffling the board can be computed in polynomial time in the following way:

$$\forall i \in [n], \exists p \text{ such that } \pi(i) = p, \text{ where } r_p - r'_p = e_i - e'_i$$

The permutation $\pi(i)$ is the actual secret the mixing server has to hide. The re-encryption coefficients $\langle s_1, ..., s_n \rangle$ are also assumed to be kept secret.

This is precisely what our choice of re-encryption mechanism guarantees.   □

Theorem 3. *The protocol described in Fig. 1 is honest verifier zero knowledge.*

Proof. We prove that for any cheating verifier $\mathcal{V}^*$, there exists a simulator $\mathcal{S}$ that can produce a computationally indistinguishable transcript of the protocol that would take place between $\mathcal{P}$ and $\mathcal{V}^*$ if it knew the challenge in advance.

Our simulator $\mathcal{S}$ gets as input: the initial set of n ElGamal tuples (a_i, b_i), the mixed set of ElGamal tuples (c_i, d_i) and a challenge in the form of a random sequence $\langle e_1, ..., e_n \rangle$. $\mathcal{S}$ proceeds by picking a random response of the transcript:

$$\langle r_1, ..., r_n \rangle \in_{\mathrm{R}} \mathbb{Z}_q^n$$

$$t \in_{\mathrm{R}} \mathbb{Z}_q$$

$\mathcal{S}$ computes the initial commitment:

$$A = g^t \cdot \prod_{i \in [n]} \left(a_i^{r_i} \cdot c_i^{-e_i} \right) \qquad B = y^t \cdot \prod_{i \in [n]} \left(b_i^{r_i} \cdot d_i^{-e_i} \right)$$

$\mathcal{S}$ outputs the transcript: $(A, B, \langle e_1, ..., e_n \rangle, \langle r_1, ..., r_n \rangle, t)$.

It is obvious that the transcript $\mathcal{S}$ outputs will always pass the equations that $\mathcal{V}$ has to verify. Note that this transcript was generated independently of the permutation $\pi(i)$ and the re-encryption coefficients $\langle s_1, ...s_n \rangle$ used for mixing, thus is zero knowledge.   □

4.2 Proof of Correct Parallel Shuffle

The proof of shuffle for mixing individual cipher texts can be extended to a proof of correct parallel shuffle for sequences of ElGamal tuples. Such a parallel mixer expects as input a matrix over ElGamal tuples with n rows and ℓ columns: $(a_{i,j}, b_{i,j})$, where $i \in [n]$ and $j \in [\ell]$, the Mixer then outputs a mixed and re-encrypted matrix where only the rows are shuffled. This matrix is defined as

$$(c_{i,j}, d_{i,j}) = \left(a_{\pi(i),j} \cdot g^{s_{\pi(i),j}}, b_{\pi(i),j} \cdot y^{s_{\pi(i),j}} \right)$$

where y is the encryption key, $\langle s_{1,1}, ..., s_{n,\ell} \rangle \in_R \mathbb{Z}_q^{n \times \ell}$ are the re-encryption coefficients and $\pi \in_R \mathbb{P}_n$ is a permutation.

The proof of correct parallel shuffle depicted in Fig. 2 is designed to convince a public verifier that the same permutation $\pi(i)$ was applied to each column. The proof, inspired by [17], deviates slightly from the construction that we have presented for the simple case in the previous section. By applying the same challenge e_i to all columns in the matrix, the verifier will be assured that the same permutation $\pi(i)$ was applied consistently across all columns.

$\mathcal{P}$ secretly generates: $\langle k_1, ..., k_\ell \rangle \in_R \mathbb{Z}_q^\ell$ and $\langle m_1, ..., m_n \rangle \in_R \mathbb{Z}_q^n$ and publishes commitment:

$$A_j = g^{k_j} \cdot \prod_{i \in [n]} a_{i,j}{}^{m_i} \text{ for } j \in [\ell] \qquad\qquad B_j = y^{k_j} \cdot \prod_{i \in [n]} b_{i,j}{}^{m_i} \text{ for } j \in [\ell]$$

$\mathcal{V}$ sends challenge: $\langle e_1, ..., e_n \rangle \in_R \mathbb{Z}_q^n$
$\mathcal{P}$ publishes response:

$$r_i = m_i + e_{\pi^{-1}(i)} \bmod q \text{ for } i \in [n]$$

$$t_j = k_j + \sum_{i \in [n]} \left(e_i \cdot s_{\pi(i),j} \right) \bmod q \text{ for } j \in [\ell]$$

$\mathcal{V}$ verifies for each $j \in [\ell]$ and accepts the proof if all calculations match:

$$g^{t_j} \cdot \prod_{i \in [n]} a_{i,j}{}^{r_i} = A_j \cdot \prod_{i \in [n]} c_{i,j}{}^{e_i} \qquad\qquad y^{t_j} \cdot \prod_{i \in [n]} b_{i,j}{}^{r_i} = B_j \cdot \prod_{i \in [n]} d_{i,j}{}^{e_i}$$

Fig. 2. Protocol: proof of correct parallel shuffle

Our proof has the same security properties as the simple proof presented in the previous section. Completeness holds as it follows a slightly more generalized version of the calculation done in the proof of Theorem 1, as now we need to take into account index j for each ElGamal tuple in a sequence. Special soundness follows exactly the same arguments as in the proof of Theorem 2. The proof of honest verifier zero knowledge is an elegant generalization of the proof of

Theorem 3: The simulator $\mathcal{S}$ is modified in such a way that it outputs a sequence of initial commitments for each $j \in [\ell]$:

$$A_j = g^{t_j} \cdot \prod_{i \in [n]} \left(a_{i,j}^{r_i} \cdot c_{i,j}^{-e_i} \right) \qquad B_j = y^{t_j} \cdot \prod_{i \in [n]} \left(b_{i,j}^{r_i} \cdot d_{i,j}^{-e_i} \right)$$

where $\langle r_1, ..., r_n \rangle \in_R \mathbb{Z}_q^n$ and $\langle t_1, ..., t_\ell \rangle \in_R \mathbb{Z}_q^\ell$ represent the response of the challenge $\langle e_1, ..., e_n \rangle$.

This proof might be seen as an ℓ-run of the simple protocol, to which we feed the same challenge sequence $\langle e_1, ..., e_n \rangle$. Note that our proof of correct parallel shuffle does not break the honest verifier zero knowledge property because in each run, the prover picks a different value k_j. Moreover, each run of the protocol is applied on a different partial board $(a_{i,j}, b_{i,j})$, for $i \in [n]$. We summarize these findings in form of a theorem.

Theorem 4. *The proof of correct shuffle satisfies completeness, special soundness, and honest verifier zero knowledge.*

As for complexity, the computation cost for the proof of correct parallel shuffle is summarized as follows. To generate a proof of correct shuffle of the entire matrix, a prover will require $2n\ell + 2\ell$ exponentiations and $3n\ell$ multiplications. In contrast, the verifier will be more expensive, because it requires $4n\ell + 2\ell$ exponentiations and $4n\ell$ multiplications.

5   Eos Protocol

CLR signatures and mix-nets are the building blocks of the Eos Voting protocol that we define next. The hallmark characteristics of the protocol is that voters are organized in rings and they can sign their ballots anonymously. The use of mix-nets make it impossible for coercers to trace the coerced ballot. Each voter has the possibility to assume one out of many pseudo identities. This mechanism can be used, as least in theory, to signal to the election authority that the ballot was submitted as coerced. More research is necessary to study how to do this in practice. For the purpose of this paper, we can assume that voter has access to green and red envelopes. A green envelope means that the vote contained within reflects the voter's intention while a red envelope signals coercion. The color of the envelope will be encrypted.

A *voter* is a person that can participate legitimately in the election process. All voters together generate a set of CLR signed ballots as input. Every ballot cast must be signed by an eligible voter, but not every eligible voter is required to cast a ballot. A voter may be under the influence of a *coercer*, who may be colluding with the election authorities, mix nodes, or tellers, to steal a voter's identity, tries to track the vote, or steals the voter's HSM.

The *election authority* administrates the election. Its role is to initialize the election, form the ring for CLR signing and collect the signed ballots cast by the voters. Each ballot is recorded on a public bulletin board allowing the voter to check that it was recorded as cast. The election authority is responsible for starting and supervising the mixing phase. Eos assumes that all bulletin boards are append-only, but other variants are possible (although not discussed here). Votes are cast for one *candidate* only. The result of Eos is a public bulletin board with all votes recorded in clear text. Eos supports distributed and threshold decryption schemes, which entails that shares of the decryption key are distributed among different tellers.

Election Set-Up Phase. The election authority prepares $L = \langle y_1, ..., y_n \rangle$, the list of all eligible voter public keys that will form the ring. In addition, the election authority prepares the set of candidates as vote choices $\mathbb{V} \subset \mathbb{Z}_p^*$. We assume that there are several mixing servers maintained by different non-colluding principals, each with access to a good source of entropy. We call a mixing server *honest*, if it is correct and not controlled by either the adversary or the coercer. An honest mixing server does not reveal the permutation used for mixing.

As it is common practice, we use a (t, e)-threshold cryptosystem, as described in [6], to encrypt and decrypt ballots. All ballots will be encrypted with a public key Y, while the corresponding private key is split and shared among e tellers. Recall that in threshold encryption, it takes the shares of at least t tellers in order to decrypt successfully. Decryption will fail, if less than t shares are available.

Voting Phase. The voter commits to the color of the envelope, using the respective private key $x_i \in \mathbb{Z}_q$ associated with a public key $y_i = g^{x_i} \in L$ and some entropy generated during the authentication process. We use both, private key and entropy to derive (deterministically) using a secure hashing function, the randomness needed in the ElGamal encryption. Once the ballot is generated and signed, it is sent to the election authority that publishes it on the (append only) public bulletin board.

Ballot Generation. A ballot consists of three ElGamal tuples: an encryption of the color of the envelope, an encryption of the electoral identity of the signer and an encryption of the vote. *Encryption of the color:* Recall from Sect. 3 the definition of h and $\tilde{y}$. A green envelope is formed as an encryption of h, whereas the red envelope is an encryption of 1. *Encryption of the electoral identity:* In the case of a green envelope, there will be an encryption of $\tilde{y}$, while in the case of a red envelope, there will be again an encryption of 1. *Encryption of the vote:* The vote, to be encrypted, will be represented as value $v \in \mathbb{V}$.

The ballot generation algorithm is depicted in Fig. 3. Formally, the ballot generation algorithm for voter α depends on the following inputs, the authentication entropy $\mathcal{E}$ (such as PIN, a picture, a fingerprint), the private key x_α, and an election specific generator h. The first two ElGamal tuples (F, ϕ) and (T, θ) of the generated ballot play an important role in forming the pseudo identity. Let ϕ be the second projection (trap door commitment) of the encryption of the color of the envelope, and θ is the second projection of the encryption of the electoral identity. Together, (ϕ, θ) form the pseudo identity of the signer.

Due to the deterministic nature of the randomness used for ElGamal encryption, a voter is able to generate the same pseudo identity deterministically multiple times. If an implementation of Eos uses, for example, a PIN code as entropy

The algorithm of Ballot Generation starts by the device computing:

$$f = \mathcal{H}\left(\mathcal{E}\|x_\alpha\|h\right)$$

$$t = f \cdot x_\alpha \bmod q$$

$$d \in_R \mathbb{Z}_q$$

$$(D,\delta) = \{v\}_Y^d = \left(g^d, Y^d \cdot v\right)$$

If authentication was successful:

$$(F,\phi) = \{h\}_Y^f = \left(g^f, Y^f \cdot h\right) \qquad\qquad (T,\theta) = \{\tilde{y}\}_Y^t = \left(g^t, Y^t \cdot \tilde{y}\right)$$

If authentication was unsuccessful:

$$(F,\phi) = \{1\}_Y^f = \left(g^f, Y^f\right) \qquad\qquad (T,\theta) = \{1\}_Y^t = \left(g^t, Y^t\right)$$

The generated ballot is: $\big((F,\phi),(T,\theta),(D,\delta)\big)$.

Fig. 3. Algorithm: ballot generation

for authentication, the pseudo identity of the voter is uniquely defined by the choice of PIN. The valid pseudo identity is selected locally on the voting device by correct authentication, i.e. by using the correct PIN. If the same coercer forces the same voter to vote multiple times, Eos will do so, as it computes the same coerced pseudo identity.

In addition, to guarantee the internal consistency of an encrypted ballot, the signer proves in zero knowledge that the encryptions of the color of the envelope and of the electoral identity are correct by providing a proof of the discrete logarithm equality between $log_F T = log_\phi \theta$. This means that there will be only one pseudo identity per device, for each value of f. Note that $\log_\phi \theta = x_\alpha$ (i.e. private key of an eligible voter) is enforced by the CLR signature verification algorithm. Together with the encrypted vote, one must include also a proof of knowledge of the discrete logarithm of $\log_g D$. This will protect against vote copying.

A malicious user might also try to cast multiple countable votes by encrypting his electoral identity with different values of f. Obviously, this could happen in theory, but practically this attack would require the malicious voter to tamper with software or hardware to trick the protocol. This however, would be noticed as we discuss later in the description of the Ballot Verification Phase Sect. 5 where the value of $\tilde{y}$ will be decrypted and duplicates will be visible. We suggest, in this case, to discard the multiple votes from the same electoral identity.

Note that only during the Tallying Phase (Sect. 5), the vote v will be visible in plain text. There the public can scrutinize and validate each plain text and if it represents a valid candidate v, such that $v \in \mathbb{V}$. Otherwise, the vote should be disregarded.

Signing a Ballot. The CLR signature of a ballot is computed as described in Sect. 3. Concretely, the pseudo-identity (ϕ, θ) is embedded in the ballot and the message to be signed is publicly computable.

$$m = \mathcal{H}\left(D \| \delta\right)$$

The CLR signature will then be computed as:

$$\sigma\left(m\right) = \left(c_1, \langle s_1, ..., s_n \rangle\right).$$

Beside the ballot and the signature, a voter has to send also the two zero knowledge proofs described above: one for proving the correct encryptions and the second for proving the knowledge of the vote.

Public Bulletin Board. The public bulletin board is a public file, to which only the election authority is allowed to append to. Each entry on the board contains a ballot, its corresponding CLR signature and two zero knowledge proofs. Note that no ballots will ever be removed from the public bulletin board, only added. Each voter and coercer is able to check that their respective vote have been appended on the bulletin board after submission, hence individually verifiable. Ballots from the same pseudo identity can be related on the board as they have pseudo identity (ϕ, θ). Assuming that voter and coercer use different pseudo identities, their votes can only be related with a negligible probability.

Ballot Verification Phase. Once the Voting Phase finished and all votes have been collected, the election authority no longer accepts signed ballots and seals the public bulletin board cryptographically. The election authority performs a cleansing operation on the public bulletin board and only copies those ballots (without signatures and zero knowledge proofs) to a new board, for which both zero knowledge proofs are checked and the CLR signature is validated. In the case multiple ballots were cast from the same pseudo identity, only the most recent ballot is copied. The cleansing operation is publicly verifiable. This procedure is visible in Fig. 4, as some of the ballots get crossed out and disregarded.

Parallel Mixing. Before the election authority commences with decrypting the ballots, it first uses the parallel shuffle described in Sect. 4.2 to shuffle the entire bulletin board by re-encrypting all three ElGamal tuples of each entry. We assume that there are multiple mixing servers, at least one of which is honest, which protects confidentiality and prevents a coercer to follow a vote through the protocol. Each mixing server performs a mixing operation on the output of the previous mix server and constructs a mixed board together with a Proof of Correct Parallel Shuffle, which is subsequently validated by the election authority. In case a proof fails, an error has occurred, and the output of this particular server is disregarded and another mixing server is used. After the shuffle is complete neither voters nor coercers will be able to identify their ballots on the mixed board, unless all mixing servers collude.

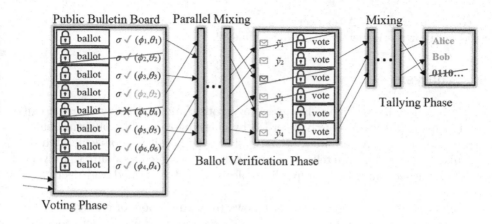

Fig. 4. Protocol overview

Pseudo Identity Decryption. To decrypt the pseudo identities for each entry, t tellers out of e must come together and decrypt the contents of the mixed board using the threshold decryption scheme. At this stage, only the first two ElGamal tuples will be decrypted, i.e. the color of the envelope and the electoral identity of each entry. The vote itself will not be decrypted and this is guaranteed assuming that strictly more than $e-t$ tellers are honest. All ballots whose color of envelope do not decrypt to the value of h or 1 will be disregarded as they are not well-formed. All ballots whose color decrypts to 1 will be discarded because they are coerced. The remaining ballots should all have unique values for the electoral identity. In case there are multiple ballots whose electoral identity decrypts to the same value $\tilde{y}$, these ballots should be disregarded as they represent an attempt to cast multiple votes. This scenario might happen in case of a malicious voter misusing the Eos protocol. These examples can be seen in Fig. 4 as some ballots are crossed out in the Ballot Verification Phase.

Tallying Phase. The remaining ballots are those that encrypt valid votes that must be counted. To extract the votes from these ballots, we drop the encryptions of the color and electoral identity and create a new bulletin board to undergo another round of mixing before decryption. The bulletin board only contains encrypted votes of the form (D, δ). This way, we assure that the link between an electoral identity and the vote is broken.

Mixing. Recall that CLR signatures are claimable as the voter can prove in zero knowledge the discrete logarithm equality between $log_g y_i = log_h \tilde{y}$. By mixing the list of encrypted votes once more, a voter might only prove to a potential coercer, that he voted but not who he voted for. For this phase, the simple mixing protocol described in Sect. 4.1 is used.

Vote Decryption. Finally, the tellers get together once more and perform a threshold decryption of the board of remaining encrypted votes and produce a proof of correct decryption. After decryption, each value of v should be counted as a valid vote for the respective candidate if $v \in \mathbb{V}$.

6   Analysis

Eos is individually verifiable, because every voter (and also every coercer) can check if his ballot was correctly recorded by checking the public bulletin board. Eos is also universally verifiable, because all zero knowledge proofs generated by the mixing servers and the tellers are public. Eos is designed to assure that every ballot published on any of the public bulletin boards is mixed and decrypted correctly.

The integrity of the Eos protocol follows from the proofs of correct decryptions for each of the two bulletin boards. Mixing and decryption operations are applied to the entire bulletin board and can be challenged by any public verifier. The removal of invalid and coerced votes from any of the bulletin boards is verifiable, because it can also be challenged by a public verifier as the color (red or green) of the envelopes will be made visible during the Ballot Verification Phase.

The secrecy of the vote is guaranteed by the ElGamal cryptosystem and the use of a cryptographically secure hashing function. The anonymity of the voter is guaranteed by the CLR signature scheme, which protects the voter's true identity. At the same time, we have to assume that there will be at least one honest mixing server that will not disclose its choice of permutation. This assures that a coercer is not able to trace his ballot all the way to the decrypted board and learn if the coerced vote was cast in a green or red envelope. Last but not least, we assume that there will be at least $e - t + 1$ honest tellers to participate in the threshold decryption. This means that we assume that t dishonest tellers will never collude to decrypt the ballots from the bulletin board before the final step of the protocol as this will represent an attack to the fairness of the election.

In terms of receipt-freeness, Eos guarantees that neither a voter nor a coercer can identify his ballot on the decrypted board. This is achieved through two mixing phases which break the connection between the ballot on the public bulletin board and the one on the decrypted board. In addition, a coercer may force a voter to cast a particular vote. In this case, the voter will use one of the alternate pseudo identities to sign the ballot, which will subsequently be discarded during the Ballot Verification Phase.

Eos is constructed in such a way that the pseudo identity used for a coerced vote is computationally indistinguishable from the real pseudo identity of the voter. Even if the coercer had stolen the voter's identity, he would not be able to use it to identify the signer of the CLR signature, because this identity is encrypted and will only be decrypted after the first round of mixing. As Eos is receipt-free, the coercer will not be able to track a coerced vote through the system. And lastly, if a coercer steals the voter's HSM, he might in principle be able to cast a vote for each pseudo-identity. However, clever authentication schemes, possibly even using a combination of pin numbers and biometrics, can be devised to make the space of pseudo identities prohibitively large. We conclude that Eos is resistant against the three coercion attacks we have outlined in the introduction of this paper.

One bit of power that the coercer has over the voter is that of an abstention attack, to force a vote for a particular candidate for which he knows will receive only this one vote, something like an invalid write-in vote. All the coercer has to do is to check that this vote appears on the final decrypted board of votes. If it does, this would mean that the coercer forced the voter to cast an invalid vote, spoiling the ballot. This situation can be mitigated by the voter proving that his vote is part of the valid set of votes V without revealing what the vote is, for example using a disjunctive zero knowledge proof protocol as described in [4]. These votes could be cleansed earlier, and would therefore never appear on the final board.

7   Conclusion and Future Work

We have described in this paper a verifiable, privacy preserving coercion-resistant voting protocol that was inspired by Conditional-Linkable Ring (CLR) signatures. Furthermore, we argued for why this protocol protects the integrity of the election, how it guarantees the secrecy of the vote, receipt freeness and is coercion resistant as long as one of the mixing servers is honest. In future work, we plan to reduce the size of CLR signatures from linear to constant size, for example using "accumulators" such as described in [7]. These constant sized signatures can also be made linkable [22].

Our protocol is different from other coercion mitigating protocols, such as Selene [20] or JCJ [12]. In Selene tracker numbers are generated prior to the election, and once a vote is cast, only the trap-door commitment is shared with the voter. After the election is over, the randomness necessary to decrypt the tracker number is shared, allowing each voter to gain confidence in that his or her vote was recorded correctly. Moreover, this protocol allows every voter to trick a potential coercer into believing that he or she voted for the coercer's choice. In JCJ, every voter has access to different kinds of credentials. One credential is there to be used to cast a valid vote, whereas as the other credentials are there to cast a vote that from the outset looks like a valid vote, but really is not. The election authority will be able to weed out coerced votes. A detailed comparison to Selene and JCJ is left to future work.

References

1. Adida, B.: Helios: web-based open-audit voting. In: Conference on Security Symposium, pp. 335–348. USENIX Association (2008)
2. Bayer, S., Groth, J.: Efficient zero-knowledge argument for correctness of a shuffle. In: Pointcheval, D., Johansson, T. (eds.) EUROCRYPT 2012. LNCS, vol. 7237, pp. 263–280. Springer, Heidelberg (2012). doi:10.1007/978-3-642-29011-4_17
3. Blazy, O., Fuchsbauer, G., Pointcheval, D., Vergnaud, D.: Signatures on randomizable ciphertexts. In: Catalano, D., Fazio, N., Gennaro, R., Nicolosi, A. (eds.) PKC 2011. LNCS, vol. 6571, pp. 403–422. Springer, Heidelberg (2011). doi:10.1007/978-3-642-19379-8_25

4. Camenisch, J., Stadler, M.: Proof systems for general statements about discrete logarithms. Technical report, ETH Zurich (1997)
5. Chaidos, P., Cortier, V., Fuchsbauer, G., Galindo, D.: BeleniosRF: a non-interactive receipt-free electronic voting scheme. In: Proceedings of the 2016 ACM SIGSAC Conference on Computer and Communications Security (CCS 2016), pp. 1614–1625. ACM, New York (2016)
6. Cramer, R., Gennaro, R., Schoenmakers, B.: A secure and optimally efficient multi-authority election scheme. In: Fumy, W. (ed.) EUROCRYPT 1997. LNCS, vol. 1233, pp. 103–118. Springer, Heidelberg (1997). doi:10.1007/3-540-69053-0_9
7. Dodis, Y., Kiayias, A., Nicolosi, A., Shoup, V.: Anonymous identification in *Ad Hoc* groups. In: Cachin, C., Camenisch, J.L. (eds.) EUROCRYPT 2004. LNCS, vol. 3027, pp. 609–626. Springer, Heidelberg (2004). doi:10.1007/978-3-540-24676-3_36
8. Fauzi, P., Lipmaa, H., Zając, M.: A shuffle argument secure in the generic model. In: Cheon, J.H., Takagi, T. (eds.) ASIACRYPT 2016. LNCS, vol. 10032, pp. 841–872. Springer, Heidelberg (2016). doi:10.1007/978-3-662-53890-6_28
9. Furukawa, J., Sako, K.: An efficient scheme for proving a shuffle. In: Kilian, J. (ed.) CRYPTO 2001. LNCS, vol. 2139, pp. 368–387. Springer, Heidelberg (2001). doi:10.1007/3-540-44647-8_22
10. Groth, J.: A verifiable secret shuffle of homomorphic encryptions. J. Cryptol. **23**(4), 546–579 (2010)
11. Groth, J., Ishai, Y.: Sub-linear zero-knowledge argument for correctness of a shuffle. In: Smart, N. (ed.) EUROCRYPT 2008. LNCS, vol. 4965, pp. 379–396. Springer, Heidelberg (2008). doi:10.1007/978-3-540-78967-3_22
12. Juels, A., Catalano, D., Jakobsson, M.: Coercion-resistant electronic elections. In: Workshop on Privacy in the Electronic Society, pp. 61–70. ACM (2005)
13. Liu, J.K., Wei, V.K., Wong, D.S.: Linkable spontaneous anonymous group signature for ad hoc groups. In: Wang, H., Pieprzyk, J., Varadharajan, V. (eds.) ACISP 2004. LNCS, vol. 3108, pp. 325–335. Springer, Heidelberg (2004). doi:10.1007/978-3-540-27800-9_28
14. Myers, A.C., Clarkson, M., Chong, S.: Civitas: toward a secure voting system. In: Symposium on Security and Privacy, pp. 354–368. IEEE (2008)
15. Neff, C.A.: A verifiable secret shuffle and its application to E-voting. In: Proceedings of the 8th ACM Conference on Computer and Communications Security (CCS 2001), pp. 116–125. ACM, New York (2001)
16. Neff, C.A.: Verifiable mixing (shuffling) of elgamal pairs (2003). http://www.votehere.org/vhti/documentation/egshuf.pdf
17. Ramchen, K., Teague, V.: Parallel shuffling and its application to prêt à voter. In: Proceedings of the 2010 International Conference on Electronic Voting Technology/Workshop on Trustworthy Elections (EVT/WOTE 2010), pp. 1–8. USENIX Association, Berkeley (2010)
18. Rivest, R.L., Shamir, A., Tauman, Y.: How to leak a secret. In: Boyd, C. (ed.) ASIACRYPT 2001. LNCS, vol. 2248, pp. 552–565. Springer, Heidelberg (2001). doi:10.1007/3-540-45682-1_32
19. Ryan, P.Y., Bismark, D., Heather, J., Schneider, S., Xia, Z.: The Prêt á Voter verifiable election system. IEEE Trans. Inf. Forensics Secur. **4**(4), 662–673 (2009)
20. Ryan, P.Y.A., Rønne, P.B., Iovino, V.: Selene: voting with transparent verifiability and coercion-mitigation. In: Clark, J., Meiklejohn, S., Ryan, P.Y.A., Wallach, D., Brenner, M., Rohloff, K. (eds.) FC 2016. LNCS, vol. 9604, pp. 176–192. Springer, Heidelberg (2016). doi:10.1007/978-3-662-53357-4_12

21. Sako, K., Kilian, J.: Receipt-free mix-type voting scheme. In: Guillou, L.C., Quisquater, J.-J. (eds.) EUROCRYPT 1995. LNCS, vol. 921, pp. 393–403. Springer, Heidelberg (1995). doi:10.1007/3-540-49264-X_32
22. Tsang, P.P., Wei, V.K.: Short linkable ring signatures for E-voting, E-cash and attestation. In: Deng, R.H., Bao, F., Pang, H.H., Zhou, J. (eds.) ISPEC 2005. LNCS, vol. 3439, pp. 48–60. Springer, Heidelberg (2005). doi:10.1007/978-3-540-31979-5_5
23. Wikström, D.: A commitment-consistent proof of a shuffle. In: IACR Cryptology ePrint Archive: Report 2011/168 (2011)

Clash Attacks and the STAR-Vote System

Olivier Pereira[1,2]([✉]) and Dan S. Wallach[2]

[1] Université catholique de Louvain, Louvain-la-Neuve, Belgium
olivier.pereira@uclouvain.be
[2] Rice University, Houston, USA
dwallach@cs.rice.edu

Abstract. STAR-Vote is an end-to-end cryptographic voting system that produces both plaintext paper ballots and encrypted electronic records of each ballot. We describe how clash attacks against STAR-Vote could weaken its security guarantees: corrupt voting terminals could identify voters with identical ballot preferences and print identical receipts for them, while generating electronic ballot ciphertexts for other candidates. Each voter would then be able to "verify" their ballot on the public bulletin board, but the electronic tally would include alternative ciphertexts corresponding to the duplicate voters. We describe how this threat can be exploited and mitigated with existing STAR-Vote mechanisms, including STAR-Vote's use of Benaloh challenges and a cryptographic hash chain. We also describe how this threat can be mitigated through statistical sampling of the printed paper ballots as an extension to the risk-limiting audits that STAR-Vote already requires.

1   Introduction

Clash attacks, a term coined by Küsters, Truderung and Vogt [12], are a family of attacks on verifiable voting systems in which corrupted voting machines manage to provide the same vote receipt to multiple voters, so that the verification procedure succeeds for each voter individually, while corrupted voting machines are able to cast whatever vote they like for each of the voters who were given a duplicate receipt. Examples of clash attacks have been proposed against ThreeBallot [15], Wombat [3], and a variant of the Helios voting system [1].

Clash attacks happen when voting machines can prepare ballots in such a way that a voter cannot verify that they contain an element that is unique to them. This is the case for STAR-Vote [2], since a voter will not have seen any other ballots, and thus won't know that ballot ID numbers are reused.

How would a clash attack on STAR-Vote appear in practice? Under the assumption that the software running inside one or more STAR-Vote voting stations was corrupt, the voting station could detect when a voter casts an *identical* ballot to a previous voter. At this point, the voting station would print a paper ballot corresponding to the previous voter while potentially having the freedom to generate a ciphertext ballot completely unrelated to the voter's intent.

Each of these voters now has a receipt that includes the hash of a completely valid vote for exactly each voter's intent. Unfortunately, the two receipts are

© Springer International Publishing AG 2017
R. Krimmer et al. (Eds.): E-Vote-ID 2017, LNCS 10615, pp. 228–247, 2017.
DOI: 10.1007/978-3-319-68687-5_14

pointing to same exact ballot, which neither voter would necessarily discover, while meanwhile a fraudulent ballot would be counted as part of the electronic tally. STAR-Vote provides evidence to auditors both while the election is ongoing and after it has completed that could *potentially* detect clash attacks like this, but suitable procedures were not part of the original STAR-Vote design. In this paper, we describe several variants on clash attacks and present a number of countermeasures to discover or rule out the presence of clash attacks.

2   STAR-Vote

We describe the key elements of STAR-Vote, omitting in various places details that are not relevant for our analysis in this paper.

Entities. Running a STAR-Vote election requires the participation of four groups of persons: (1) *Voters*, who submit votes and are invited to participate in various optional auditing operations as part of the end-to-end (E2E) verifiable component of STAR-Vote; (2) *Internal auditors*, who run the risk limiting audit (RLA) part of STAR-Vote; (3) *Trustees*, who are responsible of holding and using the decryption keys responsible for the confidentiality of the votes; and (4) *Election managers*, who are responsible of setting-up and supervise the election operations.

As part of their role, the election managers need to setup in each voting station a locally networked set of devices: (1) *Voting stations*, to be used by the voters to produce ballots, under electronic and paper format; (2) *Ballot boxes* that receive the paper ballots; (3) a *Ballot control station* (BCS) that orchestrates the various devices in a voting precinct.

Setup. Before an election starts, the trustees jointly produce an election public key k_T for a threshold commitment consistent encryption scheme [9], and two unique hash chain seeds are chosen: zp_0 and zi_0, one for the public audit chain, and one for the internal audit chain. The internal audit chain logs, and replicates on all machines connected to the local network, all the events happening in each voting station, ballot box and on the BCS, with a fine-grained modularity, with the intent of collecting as much evidence as possible in case of a disaster (while making sure to encrypt all potentially sensitive data). The public audit chain logs all the elements that are needed in order to run the end-to-end verification of the election, and is designed so that it can be used and verified while only using data that hide the content of the ballots in an information theoretic sense (in particular, this hash chain does not include any encrypted vote). Every time a ballot is printed, the current state of the public chain is printed on the take-home receipt prepared for the voter.

The BCS also selects a public key k_C for an internal use and, through the BCS, all voting stations and ballot boxes are initialized with k_T, k_C, zp_0, zi_0. The final step of the setup is to initialize both chains with a unique identifier of the precinct in which the machines are located.

Casting a Ballot. When signing-in, a voter receives a unique token t associated to his ballot style bst. When entering the booth, the voter enters his token and the voting station displays an empty ballot of style bst, so that the voter can make his selection v.

The voting station processes these choices as follows, based on the current values zi_{i-1} and zp_{i-1} of the hash chains:

1. It broadcasts the information that the token t introduced by the user is consumed.
2. It computes the number of pages that the printed ballot will take and, for each page, selects an unpredictable ballot page identifier $bpid$. This identifier is not intended to become public or listed anywhere in digital form, for vote privacy reasons that will be explained later, and is used as part of the RLA.
3. It computes an encryption of the vote $c_v = \mathsf{Enc}_{k_T}(v\|zi_{i-1})$ and a vector c_{bpid} of ciphertexts that encrypt $\mathcal{H}(bpid\|r_i)$ with k_T for each race r_i printed on page $bpid$ of the ballot.
4. It selects a unique ballot casting identifier $bcid$ and computes $c^C_{bcid} = \mathsf{Enc}_{k_C}(bcid)$, which will be used by the BCS to detect when a paper ballot corresponding to a given electronic record is cast in a ballot box.
5. It broadcasts a message containing the time t, bst, c^C_{bcid}, c_{bpid}, c_v and computes a hash $zi_i := \mathcal{H}(zi_{i-1}\|t\|bst\|c^C_{bcid}\|c_{bpid}\|c_v)$ for inclusion in the internal audit trail.
6. It prints each page of the ballot, the last page being made of two pieces that can be easily taken apart. The first part contains a human readable summary of v and a machine readable version of $bpid$, $bcid$ and the ballot style bst. The second part is a take home receipt that contains a human readable version of the election description, the time t and $zp_i := \mathcal{H}(zp_{i-1}\|bst\|t\|\mathsf{CExt}(c_v))$. The $\mathsf{CExt}()$ function extracts, from a ciphertext, a component that is a perfectly hiding commitment on the encrypted plaintext. This commitment is expected to include ZK proofs of knowledge on an opening to a valid vote.

When receiving this, the controller decrypts c^C_{bcid} and appends the pair $(bcid, zp_i)$ into a local table, until a ballot with that $bcid$ is scanned by a ballot box.

Challenging a Voting Station. When a voter, or a local auditor, wants to challenge the voting station, she brings the printed ballot to a pollworker. The pollworker: (1) stamps the ballot to mark it as spoiled; (2) scans the $bcid$ so that the ballot is recorded in the internal and external hash chains to be treated as part of the spoiled ballot box.

Later, at tallying time, the spoiled ballots are all decrypted (or their randomness is disclosed by the voting station that produced them) and they are posted on the election bulletin board for public verification (including by the voter).

Casting a Ballot. If the voter is happy with the ballot printed by the voting station, it brings it to a ballot box. There, the two pieces of the last ballot page are split, the take-home receipt is kept by the voter, and all the pages are put into the ballot box, which scans the *bcid* printed on each page, and both hash chains are then appended with the information that these pages have been cast and that the corresponding encrypted votes need to be included in the tally. If the scanned *bcid* is unknown to the BCS, the ballot is rejected by the ballot box and an error signal is triggered.

Electronic Tallying. At the end of the day, all the encrypted votes c_v's that have been marked as to be included for the tally are checked for validity and aggregated into an encryption $\mathbf{c_v}$ of the tally. This tally is then jointly decrypted by the trustees and published. (This is done as needed for the different races, ballot styles, ...)

Then, CExt() is applied to all the c_v's, the result is published with all the information needed to check the zp hash chain, and the trustees publish a proof that the tally is consistent with zp. Eventually, the trustees jointly and verifiably decrypt and publish the content of the spoiled ballots.

Audit of the Electronic Process. Anyone can perform a number of verifications from the published information: (1) check the validity of the published $\mathsf{CExt}(c_v)$'s; (2) check that the tally is consistent with the published $\mathsf{CExt}(c_v)$'s; (3) check the validity of the zp hash chain; (4) check the number of ballots against the number of voters if the information is public; (5) check that the scanned spoiled ballots were correctly built.

Furthermore, voters are invited to check whether the zp_i value printed on their receipt appears in the list of ballots included in the tally and, if they spoiled a ballot, to check that their spoiled ballot really appears in the list of spoiled ballots. If any of these verification steps fails, complaints should be filed.

Audit of the Paper Ballots. After having checked the validity of all the encrypted votes, the trustees supervise (or perform), contest by contest, a shuffle of all (c_{bpid}, c_v) pairs corresponding to valid ballots (after splitting the c_v's into race components), yielding a list of (c'_{bpid}, c'_v) pairs. This shuffle needs to be made verifiable, at least with respect to the privacy properties that it offers, either by using a fully verifiable mix-net [11,17], or possibly by using a lighter solution like a marked mix-net [13].

After completion of this shuffle, the trustees decrypt all c'_v and c'_{bpid} tuples. This decryption yields, for each race r_i, a list that contains $\mathcal{H}(bpid\|r_i)$ and the cleartext choices that should be those on the ballot page *bpid* for race r_i. This table is made available to all the people who are taking part to the risk-limiting audit. The use of the hash function and high entropy *bpid*'s guarantees that noone is able to decide which race results belong to the same ballot page, which helps defeating pattern voting attacks.

From this table, a ballot-comparison risk limiting audit (RLA) can take place. The gist of the process is to start by verifying that all the hashes in the above-computed table are unique, that the number of such hashes is consistent with the number of ballots and their ballot styles as reported for the ballot boxes, then repeat, a number of times that is a function of the election margins computed from the results of the electronic tally, a process that consists in: (1) selecting a random ballot page (2) read its $bpid$ and search for $\mathcal{H}(bpid\|r_i)$ values in the table for all races r_i present on the ballot; (3) compare the corresponding plaintexts to the paper ballot.

3   Clash Attacks on STAR-Vote

We now present a threat model for how a clash attacker might be able to operate and discuss how clash attacks might be detected.

3.1   Threat Model

Clash attacks require a fairly sophisticated attacker, capable of running malicious code on every computer in a given STAR-Vote precinct: the controller, every ballot terminal, and the ballot box as well. Under normal circumstances, we might hope that this is not feasible, but certainly many commercial voting systems have suffered from vulnerabilities that allowed for the viral spread of malware (see, e.g., the results of California's "Top to Bottom Review" [7] and Ohio's "EVEREST" [14] studies in 2007). Consequently, under such an attack, many of STAR-Vote's security protections become weaker, but others remain strong.

- STAR-Vote specifies human-readable paper ballots, printed by its voting stations, and deposited in a ballot box. It remains possible to ignore the electronic results entirely and tally the paper ballots independently, whether by hand or by scanning into another computer.
- STAR-Vote specifies the use of Benaloh challenges [5,6] to catch a voting machine in the act if it tries to substitute a ciphertext that doesn't correspond to the voter's intent, as printed on the plaintext ballot. Our attacker will try to tamper with unchallenged ballots, and will try to take advantage of the end-of-day distribution of STAR-Vote's encrypted ballot records.
- STAR-Vote specifies a SOBA risk-limiting audit [4], which selects electronic ballots at random and requires the audit to identify the corresponding paper ballots. If this audit selects a printed ballot for which there is no corresponding electronic record, then the audit will discover this absence.
- STAR-Vote encrypted ballots are constructed from homomorphically encrypted counters which include non-interactive zero knowledge (NIZK) proofs that they are well-formed (e.g., no counter indicates anything other than one or zero votes for a given candidate). Our attacker does not have the power to forge these proofs.
- STAR-Vote specifies the use of a cryptographic hash chain to preserve the integrity of the encrypted ballots. Every voter is also given a printed receipt containing the hash of the record of their vote, which in turn includes the hash of the previous record. While we cannot guarantee that voters will verify every

single receipt, any voter receipt protects the integrity of every vote cast before it in the same precinct. Our attacker does not have the power to find hash collisions and thus cannot create alternative histories consistent with each voter's hash.

Consequently, it's within the scope of our threat model for a STAR-Vote voting terminal, when given a voter who expresses selections identical with a previous voter, to print a duplicate copy of the prior voter's ballot and receipt, while publishing an encrypted vote for other candidates STAR-Vote's hash chain. This paper analyzes the ways in which such a powerful adversary might attempt to operate and how it might later be discovered.

Our threat model does not empower an attacker to tamper with *every computer in the world*, merely every computer in the control of a given local election authority. External computers might still be considered trustworthy. As an example, a smartphone app that scans ballot receipts and posts them to an independent cloud service for analysis could be considered beyond the reach of our attacker.

3.2   How Could This Work on STAR-Vote?

A clash attack on STAR-Vote could happen in different ways, based on the following approach:

1. Alice comes and expresses a vote v, encrypted as c_v^A, and included in the hash chain, leading to a public hash zp^A, which is printed on the ballot with v, *bpid* and *bcid*. The paper ballot is split and cast.
2. Bob comes and happens to express the same vote v, something that is noticed by the malicious voting station. The voting station then produces a ciphertext c_v^B, encrypting a different vote v^* (of the same style), and encrypts *bcid**'s and *bpid**.
3. When printing Bob's paper ballot, the voting station prints a ballot with v written on it, the hash zp^A that was printed for Alice, and *bcid**'s and *bpid**.

The expectation is that, when Alice and Bob read their paper ballot, they see their vote intent correctly reflected and, at the end of the day, they will both find a ballot containing the expected hash in the public hash chain: they will both look at the same place. However, the cheating machines manage to replace Bob's vote v with a different vote, while not modifying the total number of votes.

Several variants of this attack can be considered, depending on whether $bcid = bcid^*$ and $bpid = bpid^*$. Various strategies can also be adopted when voting stations want to scale the attack: they can create many pairs of clashing ballots, each pair having a distinct hash, or create one large clash, in which many ballots would have the same hash, or adopt any strategy in between.

3.3   Can We Detect It?

The high-level description of STAR-Vote, as reflected above and in the STAR-Vote documentation [2,16], does not seem to provide obvious ways of spotting the attack that we just described. We split our analysis according to the two parts of the verification of a STAR-Vote election: the end-to-end electronic verification part, and the RLA part.

End-to-end Verification. On the side of the electronic process, all the mandatory verification steps succeed: the trustees tally the expected number of ballots with the expected races, the hash chains looks legitimate, and the voters find their zp_i on the election bulletin board. However, if the verification is pushed further and ballots are challenged, then discrepancies can be detected.

If Bob decides to challenge its voting station, the voting station can offer a decryption of c_v^A, which will be consistent with the printed voter intent and be included in the hash chains. Inspections can also be made regarding the *bcid* and *bpid* (though they do not seem to be explicitly prescribed in the original documentation).

The internal hash chain contains an encryption c_{bcid}^C of the ballot casting identifier *bcid* that is printed on the ballot. Here, the attacker has two options:

1. It can generate a fresh *bcid* for Bob's ballot. In this case, the printed ballots will have distinct *bcid*'s, as expected, and a possibly honest ballot box or BCS has no way of detecting a potential duplicate. But, if Bob's ballot is spoiled, there will be a discrepancy between the *bcid* printed on the ballot, and the one pointed by the hash printed on the receipt, which will be Alice's *bcid*. So, if the voting station bets that Bob's ballot will not be spoiled, no evidence is left (at the *bcid* level, at least).
2. It can resuse Alice's *bcid* on Bob's ballot. In this case, the decryption of the encrypted *bcid* pointed by the hash printed on the receipt will be consistent with the *bcid* printed on the paper ballot. But the ballot box will contain two ballots with identical *bcid*'s. So, by adopting this strategy, the voting station can pass an inspection of the *bcid* at spoiling time, but it will leave (potentially hard to find) evidences in the ballot box. Also, if the BCS happens to be honest, it may happen that it notices the same *bcid* coming twice.

With the current description of STAR-Vote, and given the above threat model, the second strategy seems likely to be a successful one, at the electronic level at least.

A deeper inspection of the hash chains will show other discrepancies, though: every time a ballot is cast or spoiled, this event must be recorded in both hash chains. There are again two attack strategies that can be followed here, as depicted in Figs. 1 and 2.

1. As depicted in Fig. 1, the BCS may mark Alice's ballot as cast in both chains as soon as it is notified of Alice's dropping of her ballot in the ballot box. If Bob cast's his ballot, then the BCS marks the malicious ciphertexts prepared on Bob's behave as cast too, and nothing is visible. However, if Bob decides to spoil his ballot, then the machines are facing a difficulty: the public hash chain should have Alice's ballot marked as spoiled, but this creates an inconsistency

in the chain since this ballot has already been marked as cast. So, a public evidence is left, and this one is easy to notice.

2. As depicted in Fig. 2, the BCS can record that Alice cast her ballot, but not append that information in the hash chains, and wait to see what Bob will do with his ballot. Now, if Bob casts or spoils his ballot, the BCS can simply append that instruction in the chain (and always mark Bob's ciphertext as cast, in order to preserve a consitency in the number of ballots cast and spoiled). However, if Bob spoils his ballot, Alice's ballot will be shown as spoiled on the bulletin board, and Alice may file on complaint on the ground that she cast her ballot.

Still, this last strategy seems to be the "safest" for malicious machines: a discrepancy will only become visible if Bob challenges his ballot and if Alice checks her ballot on the election board, notices the problem, and files a complaint.

To conclude, it appears that all clash attack variants can be detected by the audit trail left by the end-to-end verifiable part of STAR-Vote. Our analysis sheds a new light on the importance of the "cast" and "spoil" marks that are included in the hash chains, and stresses that the system should provide easy mechanisms to detect that no single ballot appears as cast or spoiled in the bulletin board. (If the cast and spoiled ballots appear separately, as it is done in many end-to-end verifiable voting system prototypes, this may be easily overlooked.)

Taking a look back, a countermeasure against clash attacks proposed by Küsters et al. [12] consists in asking voters to type a random number and to print that number on the receipt, for verification. This would be feasible with STAR-Vote and would render duplicate ballots very difficult to produce, as duplicates could only happen between voters with identical vote intents and picking choosing the same random number. However, we would prefer to avoid extra interaction with the user. As a variant, we imagine that receipts could add a sequence number, synchronized across every voting station, printed in large type so it's visible to poll workers and watchers. Any repeats of recent numbers or incidences of numbers wildly out of sequence would be suspicious.

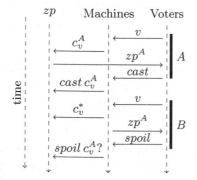

Fig. 1. Clash attack with immediate recording of ballot casting.

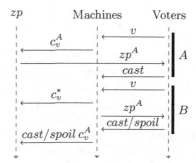

Fig. 2. Clash attack with recording of cast ballots delayed.

Risk Limiting Audit. The risk limiting audit component of STAR-Vote is expected to offer confidence in the election results, independently of the effectiveness of the end-to-end verifiable component. The inputs of the RLA are:

1. Ballot manifests, that list all ballot boxes, as well as the number of ballots contained in each box, and the style of these ballots.
2. An electronic vote record, that contains, race by race, a list of hashes of the form $\mathcal{H}(bpid\|r_i)$, and associated to each of these hashes, the choices made for race r_i that must be printed on the ballot page $bpid$.
3. Paper ballots in boxes, as per the ballot manifests.

For the sake of our discussion, we assume that the manifests are correct, and that the election outcome resulting from the electronic record is consistent with the one announced from the end-to-end verifiable tally.

The $bcid$'s are not part of the electronic records, and are therefore not used in the RLA. The $bpid$'s, though, offer the crucial link that is expected to define the bijection between paper ballots and electronic records. Again, there are two possible strategies for malicious machines running a clash attack:

1. A malicious voting station can print different $bpid$'s on the ballots with clashing receipts. In this case, if Bob's ballot is selected as part of the RLA, the $bpid$ printed there won't point to the electronic record of Alice's ballot, which is precisely the kind of discrepancy that the RLA is designed to efficiently detect.
2. A malicious voting station can print identical $bpid$'s on Alice's and Bob's ballots. Assuming that both ballots are cast, the boxes now contains two ballots with the same $bpid$. And, even if one of the two ballots is picked as part of the RLA, no discrepancy will appear: Alice's electronic record will be picked in both cases, and will match the paper ballot content.

This second strategy seems to be a successful one: the RLA assumes that there is a bijection between the paper and electronic ballots, and does not attempt at verifying that there is a bijection indeed. In order to solve this issue, we investigate the possibility of a bijection audit.

4   Bijection Audit

We want to determine whether there is a bijection (i.e., a one-to-one correspondence) from the paper ballots to the electronic ballots. Paper ballots that do not have a match in the electronic records are easy to detect. However, bijection failures resulting from clashing ballots can only be detected if we pick duplicate paper ballots. Of course, as described earlier, two voters might well have identical voting selections, but every ballot page is *supposed* to have a unique $bpid$, which is a randomly selected 128-bit number, and thus highly unlikely to repeat (from the birthday paradox, this will only become likely after casting around 2^{64} ballots in the same box). The discovery of two identical $bpid$ numbers on two separate pages would imply election fraud. For the remainder of this section, we will assume that we want an auditing procedure that's completely independent of the end-to-end verifiable side of STAR-Vote. We don't want to rely on the hash chains, the cryptographic receipts, or the Benaloh challenges. We wish to design a process for validating the bijection by considering the paper ballots and the cleartext electronic vote records, alone. We assume that the shuffle and audit data are kept at the precinct level, so that inter-precinct clashes would be equivalent to missing ballots.

4.1 Why Not Sort?

A seemingly attractive solution is to sort the ballots by *bpid*, after which detecting duplicates would be a simple linear scan. The problem is that we're dealing with as many as $N = 1000$ paper ballots in a given precinct. We need a completely manual process that a small set of poll workers can accomplish quickly. Manual sorting doesn't scale well.

A merge sort, wherein the pile of ballots is partitioned into smaller piles, each of which is sorted, and then the sorted piles are merged, might seem attractive. The initial partition happens quickly, giving a hypothetical sixteen poll workers 1/16 of the ballots. If our workers sorted their initial piles using an insertion sort, taking 10 s per ballot, then the initial phase would only take ten minutes. The merging phase, however, would be more cumbersome. If we followed a tree-like binary merging process, each merge phase must consider twice as many ballots and would use half as many poll workers. Again, assuming ten seconds per ballot, the first phase would reduce 16 to 8 piles in 21 min. The second phase would reduce 8 to 4 piles in 42 min, then 4 to 2 piles in 84 min, with the final merge taking 168 min. The whole process totals up to almost 5.5 h. Even if our poll workers can insert a ballot every 5 s instead of 10 s, this process might still take 3 h.

Of course, there are many variations, but they all suffer from expensive phases. A bucket sort, for example, requires a linear scan to begin, partitioning the ballots based on their prefixes, but it makes the merging process trivial, since the sorted buckets can simply be stacked rather than painstakingly merged.

If we lived in the 1960's, we might suggest the use of a *sorting machine*, such as were used with punchcard decks [8]. Alas, such devices now only exist in museums, with any modern need to sort pieces of paper being handled digitally after the use of a high-speed scanner. We need a procedure that can be accomplished without the use of computers, and this procedure must only take a few minutes, not hours. In return, we're willing to trade off a *guarantee* of finding a duplicate for a chosen *probability* of that detection.

4.2 Audit Methodology

The SOBA risk limiting audit [4] is designed to provide a required degree of confidence in its outcome, regardless of the number of ballots. We will now specify a simple sampling procedure that can audit a pile of ballots for uniqueness of the *bpid* numbers, assuming that the *bpid*'s are actually random and that at most one duplicate is made of any given *bpid*. (We will relax this assumption in Sect. 4.3.).

Variable	Definition	Example value
m	margin of victory (fraction)	0.05
d	duplicated ballots (fraction)	0.03
n	number of ballots sampled	100
N	total number of ballots in the box	1000
P_d	probability of discovering duplicates	0.95
T	number of trials (e.g., precincts sampled)	5

Subsampling the Ballots. We will start with N ballots (perhaps as many as 1000 in a box) and need an efficient procedure for subsampling a more reasonable number n (perhaps 50, perhaps 100), with the added concern that our adversary will be aware of our subsampling methodology. We imagine that our poll workers can roll dice to select specific digits for use in a search. (Since digits are printed in hexadecimal, a 16-sided dice would be most convenient.) We have a variety of options for how to proceed. For example, to sample $\frac{1}{16} \cdot \frac{1}{16} = \frac{1}{256}$, we can roll dice to select specific values for the first and second digit of the $bpid$. To sample $\frac{1}{128}$ of the ballots, we could pick two possible values for one of the digits (i.e., $\frac{1}{16} \cdot \frac{2}{16} = \frac{1}{128}$).

In this fashion, we can design samples to get close to any ratio that we might want. For example, if we truly want to sample exactly 10% of the ballots, we might select three possible values for the first digit and nine possible values for the second digit, yielding roughly $\frac{3}{16} \cdot \frac{9}{16} = 0.1055$. So long as the resulting fraction is slightly larger than the target ratio of $\frac{n}{N}$, we will have the number of samples that we want. It doesn't matter if the adversary knows the digit locations we will consider (e.g., most-significant vs. least-significant). If there exists duplicate $bpid$ numbers anywhere in the pile, then they have a chance of being selected by the sample (i.e., we are not making n random draws from the pile of ballots; we are making queries against $bpid$ digits). Conversely, and anticipating on our further discussion, it's important that we roll dice for the specific values of the digits. Otherwise, the adversary could guarantee that the $bpid$ values on duplicate ballots were never selected for an audit.

Discovering Duplicates. Once we have our sample of ballots, we then must discover duplicates in the sample. If the sample is small enough, sorting is going to be much more feasible. For example, ballots could be split into piles based on the most-significant-digit of $bpid$ and then each pile could be sorted by hand. This process would take minutes, not hours. But what are the odds of discovering a duplicate? We can solve for the probability of discovery and then rearrange the equation to solve for the fraction f of the $bpid$'s to be sampled. The first line below expresses that the probability of detection P_d equals one minus the probability that all Nd $bpid$'s which are duplicates are not picked, which will happen with probability $1 - f$ every time.

$$P_d = 1 - (1 - f)^{Nd}$$
$$f = 1 - (1 - P_d)^{1/Nd}$$

Of these, it's helpful to use the equation for f and plug in values we might expect for d, P_d and N. For example, if $d = 0.03$, $N = 1000$, and we want $P_d = 0.95$, then $n = 95$. With a sample of 95 ballots, we can thus have a 95% chance of discovering a duplicate. Here are some other solutions:

d	P_d	f	n
0.010	0.95	0.259	259
0.030	0.95	0.095	95
0.050	0.95	0.058	58
0.100	0.95	0.03	30

If the duplication rate d is high, we can detect it with a fairly small number of samples n and a very high probability of success P_d. However, we can see that we need more than 250 samples when d is only 1%. So when might poll workers be required to conduct such a large sample? Consider that every process like this occurs after the election is complete, which means that we know the margin of victory m. We can simply specify that $d = m$, i.e., we're looking for enough ballot duplication to change the election outcome. Consequently, as the margin of victory shrinks, only then do we need to sample a large number of ballots.

Repeated Trials. Consider what might happen if we repeated the above process across multiple precincts, selected at random. It's entirely possible, from the attacker's perspective, that they could just as well attack one precinct or attack every precinct, so as an auditor, we should look at more precincts. Or, if we simply want to avoid the non-linear costs of manually sorting large numbers of paper ballots, we could conduct multiple trials in the same precinct. The resulting $AggregateP_d = 1 - (1 - P_d)^T$, simply multiplying together the odds that the attacker gets away with it in each trial.

d	P_d	n	T	$AggregateP_d$
0.010	0.60	88	1	0.60
0.005	0.40	97	1	0.40
0.010	0.60	88	5	0.99
0.010	0.50	67	5	0.97
0.005	0.40	97	5	0.92

Now, even with very small duplicate rates like $d = 0.01$, we can conduct five trials, perhaps across five precincts or perhaps within the same precinct, of only

67 ballots per trial. While each trial has only a 50% chance of discovering a duplicate, all five together have a 97% chance. (Sorting 67 ballots, five times, is significantly easier than sorting 259 ballots, even once.).

4.3   Non-random Duplicates

Next, we will consider the possibility that an attacker arranges for every duplicate ballot in the box to share the same *bpid*. In this case, the odds of detection are only the odds that the dice match the attacker's *bpid*. If we match, then we get every duplicate. If we fail to match, then we get no duplicates.

Furthermore, in our threat model, the attacker can control the *bpid* number distributions, making sure that any biases introduced through the duplicates is evened out over the other ballots. For example, if the duplicates were more likely to have a "3" in the first digit, the attacker could arrange for other ballots to never start with a "3", and could go further and arrange for "9" to occur most often. Consequently, we cannot rely on relatively simple procedures, like splitting on digits and counting each pile, as a statistic to detect duplicates.

Instead, we will propose a sampling methodology with a relatively low success rate, in any given precinct, but which will gain its power in aggregate when repeated across many precincts. We will only assume that we can make a random draw of n ballots from any given ballot box. Rather than this process involving dice, we instead imagine a process similar to "cutting" a deck of cards, whereby each draw involves splitting a pile of ballots and selecting the next ballot from the location of the cut.

Given this sample, we can then manually sort it and look for duplicates. If n is, for example, 100 ballots, this process will only take a few minutes. The odds of successfully detecting duplicates are a function of the size of the sample n and of the fraction of duplicates d. We compute this by measuring the probability of selecting *only* from the non-duplicates and the probability of selecting *exactly one* of the duplicates: $P_d = 1 - (1 - d)^n - n \cdot (1 - d)^{n-1} \cdot d$.

If $d = 0.01$ and $n = 100$, then P_d is approximately 26%[1]. If this is repeated for T trials, we can compute $AggregateP_d$ in the same fashion. For example, with $T = 10$ trials, we again can find a precinct with duplicates with a 95% probability. This represents significantly more work than we needed in the case with randomly distributed duplicates, but it's still feasible to conduct this without requiring hours of effort.

(We note that *sampling without replacement* would be preferable, both because it would slightly increase the odds of success, and because we wish to physically demonstrate the existence two separate ballots with the same *bpid*. The equation above, however, assumes *sampling with replacement*, which is only an approximation that becomes less accurate when N gets smaller. An accurate combinatorial expression of P_d is not particularly necessary for our discussion.).

---

[1] If we select values for n and d where $n \cdot d = 1$, then the expression for P_d tends to $1 - 2/e$.

4.4   Non-random Precinct Corruption

We first considered uniformly distributed duplicates within a precinct. We next considered how every duplicate in a precinct could share the same *bpid*, making them harder to find via sampling. Here, We apply the same consideration to the election as a whole. We now assume that our attacker wants to do all of the corruption in a very small number of precincts rather than spreading it uniformly out across every precinct.

Let's revisit P_d and *AggregateP$_d$* from above. In the limiting case where *every* ballot in a precinct is a duplicate, then *any* audit that touches more than one ballot will detect the duplication. This means that P_d is either trivially 1 or 0. A similarly process we can conduct in every precinct might be to draw a handful of ballots and eyeball them for duplicate *bpid* numbers. This would guarantee the detection of a precinct with 100% duplicates.

4.5   Linear Auditing with Buckets

The subsampling methods described above all begin with a linear pass to select ballots having IDs with a desired pattern. This section presents an alternative method for detecting duplicates that requires only two linear passes over the ballots.

This method requires some basic record-keeping that can be accomplished with pencil and paper. In the first pass, we will be mapping from ballot IDs to *buckets*. Let's say we use the first two hex digits of the *bpid*, which we can map to a 16×16 grid, pre-printed on a single sheet of paper; a poll worker would then write down the third (and maybe fourth) hex digit in the bucket. At the end of the pass, the buckets are searched for duplicates. If the number of ballots and buckets are well chosen, the number of ballots per bucket will be small, and this search will be easy. If a collision is found, the bucket is marked as suspicious: this may come from a collision on the first hex digits that will stop after a few more digits, or be the result of a clash. The purpose of the second pass is to inspect the suspicious buckets: during that pass, the ballots belonging to these buckets are further inspected, in order to make sure that no clash happens.

An exact estimation of the expected number of ballots per buckets is challenging to express: these are non-trivial variations around the "birthday paradox" problem. However, fairly accurate approximations based on the Poisson distribution can be obtained (see, e.g., DasGupta [10]).

Let us say that we want to estimate the probability $P(b, n, k, m)$ that, in a setting with b buckets and n ballots, there are k buckets containing m ballots. We first compute the probability that m ballots with randomly selected *bpid* would go into the same bucket: that probability is b^{1-m}. Now, we consider the process of selecting n ballots as actually picking $\binom{n}{m}$ m-tuples of ballots. This is of course an approximation, since the independence between these m-tuples is not obtained when we just have a pile of n ballots, but it turns out that it is accurate enough for our purpose (it over-estimates the number of collisions, while being asymptotically exact). The last step consists in estimating the probability

Table 1. Estimation of bucket fillings. The last two columns indicate bounds on the number of buckets containing at least "multiplicity" ballots, bounds that are satisfied with probability 50% and 95% respectively.

Ballots	Buckets	Multiplicity	50%	95%
100	256	2	19	27
100	256	3	2	5
100	256	4	0	1
100	256×16^3	2	0	0
1000	1024	5	7	12
1000	1024	6	1	3
1000	1024	7	0	1
1000	1024×16	2	30	40
1000	1024×16	3	0	2

$P(b, n, k, m)$ as the probability that an event happening with probability $\lambda = \binom{n}{m}/b^{1-m}$ happens k times, as given by the Poisson probability mass function: $P(b, n, k, m) = e^{-\lambda}\frac{\lambda^k}{k!}$.

Let us consider two examples: one in which we apply this approach to around 100 ballots, as would occur in the non-random duplicate search mechanism of Sect. 4.3 for instance, and one in which we apply this approach to a full box of around 1000 ballots.

Linear Search of Duplicates Among 100 Ballots. Let us consider that we have a 16×16 grid on a single tabloid format page, providing 256 buckets, and that each bucket is split into 3 blocks in which 3 hex characters can be written (the page would be large enough to offer blocks of 8×15 mm, which is comfortable).

Based on the expression above, there is a probability 0.5 that at most 19 buckets will contain two (or more) ballots, and 0.95 that at most 27 buckets contain two (or more) ballots (see Table 1). A small number (less than 5) buckets will contain 3 ballots, and it is most likely (80% probability) that no bucket would take 4 ballots. If this happens, then a separate note could be created at the bottom of the page, in order to compensate for the lack of space. So, all the ballots are expected to fit easily on the grid that we just described.

Now, we can estimate the probability that a collision happens inside a bucket, that is, that two ballots share identical 5 first digits. Here, there is a 0.995 probability that no such collision would happen. In the unlikely case that one happens, then a second linear search is performed in order to determine whether a clash has been detected. As we can see, this procedure is extremely effective.

Linear Search of Duplicates Among 1000 Ballots. Let us now consider that we have four tabloid format pages, each having a 16×16 grid providing

256 buckets, and that each bucket is split into 6 blocks in which 1 hex character can be written. Let us also consider that the first character of the *bpid* is chosen among 4 values instead of 16 (this could be just by prefixing the *bpid* with an extra random symbol).

Now, during the linear pass, four poll workers hold one page each. An other audit officer (possibly under surveillance) makes a linear pass on the ballots, reads the first digit of the *bpid* in order to point to one of the four poll workers holding the grids, then reads the next two hex digit in order to point to one bucket, and finally read the next hex digit to be written in that bucket.

Based on the Poisson estimate, it is fairly unlikely that a single bucket will need to contain more than 6 ballots: this would happen with probability 0.16, and just one or two buckets will contain exactly 6 ballots (again, see Table 1). If we turn to the number of collisions that will be found on the single hex digit written on the bucket, we can expect that around 30 buckets will contain a single collision, and that it is quite unlikely to observe more than a 2-collision in a single bucket.

In order to sort these collisions out, we make a second linear pass on all the ballots, but only focusing on the collisions. The four officers take a fresh grid, mark the colliding buckets and the prefixes that need to be examined, and now write 3 more hex digits in the bucket when a suspected ballot is read (there will be enough space, since we only write something down for the few colliding ballots). Any collision repeating on these extra digits would be an overwhelming indication of a clash.

4.6   Other Potential Uses of Bijection Audits

The assumption of a bijection is at the core of comparison audit processes like SOBA. Our work raises the question of whether bijection audits would be useful to detect clash attacks in other circumstances that could be completely independent of STAR-Vote or even of end-to-end verifiable systems. For instance, in locations where paper ballots have a serial number and paper ballots are scanned in order to perform an electronic tally, ballots with clashing serial numbers could be distributed to voters who are known to vote in the same way (e.g., straight party), and a malicious scanner could replace the images of those paper ballots with clashing serial numbers with fresh ballots of its choice. This would break the bijection from the paper and electronic records, and potentially make a risk limiting audit ineffective, unless a bijection audit is run first.

5   Recommendations and Conclusions

STAR-Vote has a variety of security mechanisms and we've described a number of different auditing and testing procedures. This section considers how these individual procedures and tests might best be combined to defeat clash attacks.

Real-Time Receipt Auditing. The bijection-audit procedures described in the previous section are feasible, but are considerably more expensive than a SOBA audit, so it would be helpful to have a cheaper alternative.

Recall that a clash attack would cause the receipts of a significant number of voters to be exactly the same. As such, we propose that independent poll watchers, or perhaps the official poll workers themselves, use an independent electronic tool to sample these receipts as they go by. This could be implemented with a smartphone app that scans a printed QRcode, provided that a comparison between the result of the scan and the printed value is made. If the same value is ever scanned twice, then either a ballot receipt was accidentally scanned twice or a duplicate was produced.

One nice aspect of this procedure is that we can rely on independent computers, outside the influence of our attacker, to simplify the process. The odds of successfully detecting a duplicate are the same as with the audit procedure we described in Sect. 4.3, only without the requirement for sorting the sampled ballots. This makes the procedure easy to perform. And because the ballot receipts are safe to share with the world, this procedure can be performed by anybody. Of course, if a duplicate is ever discovered, suitable alarms should be raised and a more invasive audit conducted.

We note that this process would be easy to perform across every precinct in an election, making it particularly valuable for detecting focused attacks on a small number of precincts as described in Sect. 4.4. Also, as described in Sect. 3.3, Benaloh challenges may discover clash attacks in real-time, provided that the public hash chain is inspected on the fly, and an attackers that aims for multiple clashes on a single receipt will be more easily spotted than an adversary focusing on mere duplicates, since a single challenged ballot among $n+1$ clashing receipts will make it possible for n voters to see their ballot unduly marked as spoiled on the bulletin board. We discuss how to resolve these issues below.

Post-election Ballot Auditing. In Sect. 4.2, we described a subsampling audit process based on digits selected by rolling dice. This is a relatively efficient procedure, but local poll workers might be unwilling to perform it, or might introduce errors by performing it poorly. Also, it's preferable to know the margin of victory for the election, which can be used to select an appropriate number of samples to achieve a desired level of confidence. This won't be possible until the election is complete, so it's probably better to wait until all the ballots are brought back from the local precincts to the election headquarters. The bijection audit procedure could then be performed centrally, on a subset of precincts, alongside the SOBA audits that STAR-Vote already requires.

SOBA risk-limiting audits will sample ballots from across an entire election, while our bijection audits happen at the level of a local precinct. This suggests that the two audits could be conducted concurrently, although it might be procedurally simpler to first conduct the SOBA audit, since it's fast. The bijection audit will be slower, although it's amenable to parallelization in that each precinct can be audited independently.

If the bijection audit fails, this invalidates one of the assumptions behind SOBA, which assumes there is a bijection. Similarly, if post-election verification of the hash chains on the public bulletin board turn up discrepancies (see Sect. 3.3), we must again resolve these discrepancies.

What if a Duplicate Is Found? If a precinct *fails* its bijection audit or if independent auditors discover duplicate receipts, we now have compelling evidence that a clash attack has occurred. Now, the local election official will be under pressure from all sides. Lawsuits will be filed. Reporters will be asking hard questions. It's essential to have clear procedures to resolve the conflict. Under our definition of a clash attack, duplicates appear in the paper ballots, but the paper ballots still reflect the intent of the voters, while the ciphertexts are more likely than not fraudulent.

Consequently, faced with this attack, we might discard the encrypted ballots in their entirety and do a manual tally from the paper ballot boxes. This would be slow and would also face the risk that our attacker introduced a small clash attack for precisely the purpose of triggering the fallback to paper ballots, which might as well have been tampered in a coordinated effort. Consequently, we believe an appropriate procedure is to render a judgment on a precinct-by-precinct basis as to whether the paper ballots or electronic ballots are more trustworthy. This judgment would be informed by:

- Conducting a bijection audit and SOBA audit on *every* precinct.
- Considering the available physical evidence (e.g., tamper-evident seals on voting terminals and ballot boxes).
- Auditing the voting terminals for software and/or hardware tampering.
- Auditing the hash chain copies, which should be copied identically across all voting terminals in a precinct.
- Considering other factors outside of the voting system itself (e.g., correlations between different delivery trucks and the confirmed incidences of clash attacks or other election attacks).

STAR-Vote provides multiple forms of evidence of the voters' intent. It's entirely possible, for example, that only a fraction of the voting terminals in a given precinct were tampered, and their hash chains may store a different version of the history of the election. That version of history, for the non-tampered terminals, may be judged worthwhile for the votes cast on those terminals, and then the electronic records might only need to be discarded for the tampered voting terminals. Ultimately, the power of STAR-Vote's design is that it provides election officials with redundant evidence of what happened during the election. We might never anticipate every possible attack, but with STAR-Vote's evidence, we can support a variety of auditing and resolution procedures, enabling the detective work necessary to identify and, if possible, remediate issues.

Concluding Thoughts. Clash attacks present a tricky challenge for an election auditor, faced with the possibility of systematic computer tampering. We have shown a number of auditing techniques that can be conducted by poll workers, in a post-election setting, in a tolerable amount of time, mitigating the risk of clash attacks.

Acknowledgements. This work is supported in part by NSF grants CNS-1409401 and CNS-1314492 and by the F.R.S.-FNRS project SeVote. Part of this work was performed when the first author was a Fulbright Scholar at Rice University.

References

1. Adida, B., de Marneffe, O., Pereira, O., Quisquater, J.J.: Electing a university president using open-audit voting: analysis of real-world use of Helios. In: EVT/WOTE 2009, Montreal, August 2009
2. Bell, S., Benaloh, J., Byrne, M., DeBeauvoir, D., Eakin, B., Fischer, G., Kortum, P., McBurnett, N., Montoya, J., Parker, M., Pereira, O., Stark, P., Wallach, D., Winn, M.: STAR-Vote: a secure, transparent, auditable, and reliable voting system. USENIX JETS **1**, 18–37 (2013)
3. Ben-Nun, J., Farhi, N., Llewellyn, M., Riva, B., Rosen, A., Ta-Shma, A., Wikström, D.: A new implementation of a dual (paper and cryptographic) voting system. In: EVOTE 2012, July 2012
4. Benaloh, J., Jones, D., Lazarus, E., Lindeman, M., Stark, P.: SOBA: secrecy-preserving observable ballot-level audits. In: EVT/WOTE 2011. USENIX (2011)
5. Benaloh, J.: Simple verifiable elections. In: EVT 2006, Vancouver, B.C., June 2006
6. Benaloh, J.: Ballot casting assurance via voter-initiated poll station auditing. In: EVT 2007, Boston, MA, August 2007
7. Bishop, M.: UC Red Team Report of California Secretary of State Top-to-Bottom Voting Systems Review, July 2007
8. da Cruz, F.: IBM card sorters. Columbia University Computing History. http://www.columbia.edu/cu/computinghistory/sorter.html
9. Cuvelier, É., Pereira, O., Peters, T.: Election verifiability or ballot privacy: do we need to choose? In: Crampton, J., Jajodia, S., Mayes, K. (eds.) ESORICS 2013. LNCS, vol. 8134, pp. 481–498. Springer, Heidelberg (2013). doi:10.1007/978-3-642-40203-6_27
10. DasGupta, A.: The matching, birthday and the strong birthday problem: a contemporary review. J. Stat. Infer. Plann. **130**, 377–389 (2004)
11. Jakobsson, M., Juels, A., Rivest, R.L.: Making mix nets robust for electronic voting by randomized partial checking. In: 11th USENIX Security Symposium (2002)
12. Küsters, R., Truderung, T., Vogt, A.: Clash attacks on the verifiability of e-voting systems. In: IEEE Symposium on Security and Privacy (2012)
13. Pereira, O., Rivest, R.: Marked mix-nets. In: Workshop on Advances in Secure Electronic Voting - Voting 2017 (2017)
14. Project EVEREST (Evaluation, Validation of Election-Related Equipment, Standards, Testing): Risk Assessment Study of Ohio Voting Systems. http://www.sos.state.oh.us/sos/info/everest.aspx
15. Rivest, R.L., Smith, W.D.: Three voting protocols: ThreeBallot, VAV, and Twin. In: EVT 2007, Boston, MA, August 2007

16. Travis County Purchasing Office: STAR-Vote: Request for Information for a New Voting System. http://traviscountyclerk.org/eclerk/content/images/pdf_STARVote_2015.06.03_RFI.pdf
17. Wikström, D.: A commitment-consistent proof of a shuffle. In: Boyd, C., González Nieto, J. (eds.) ACISP 2009. LNCS, vol. 5594, pp. 407–421. Springer, Heidelberg (2009). doi:10.1007/978-3-642-02620-1_28

Verifiability Experiences in Government Online Voting Systems

Jordi Puiggalí[1]([✉]), Jordi Cucurull[1], Sandra Guasch[1], and Robert Krimmer[2]

[1] Research and Security Department, Scytl Secure Electronic Voting,
08008 Barcelona, Spain
{jordi.puiggali,jordi.cucurull}@scytl.com
[2] Ragnar Nurkse Department for Innovation and Governance,
Tallinn University of Technology, 12618 Tallinn, Estonia
robert.krimmer@ttu.ee

Abstract. Since the introduction of verifiability in the online government elections of Norway in 2011, different governments have followed similar steps and have implemented these properties in their voting systems. However, not all the systems have adopted the same levels of verifiability nor the same range of cryptographic mechanisms. For instance, Estonia (2013) and New South Wales (Australia, 2015) started by adopting individual verifiability to their systems. Switzerland updated its regulation in 2014 to include individual and universal verifiability in order to by-pass the previous limitation of voting online up to 30% of the electorate. Geneva and Swiss Post voting systems are adapting their systems to this regulation and currently provide individual verifiability (and universal in the case of Swiss Post). In this exploratory paper, we study the different approaches followed by the election organizers that offer online voting, their current status and derived future tendencies.

Keywords: Electronic voting protocols · Election verifiability

1 Introduction

Whenever an election process is carried out using traditional or electronic means, transparency and auditability are the basis to ensure the accuracy of the results. In traditional elections, audit processes can be easily implemented since they are based on physical tangible elements: paper ballots, physical ballot boxes, manual recount, etc. These items can be supervised by both, voters and external auditors or international election observers (see, amongst others, [7]).

However, in electronic environments, the same elements are not tangible and most of the processes are performed through computers and communication networks, making human audits almost impossible [35]. While security measures such as vote encryption or digital signatures can protect the secrecy and integrity of votes, it is also important to verify that these mechanisms are behaving properly: i.e., they are certainly encrypting, decrypting and digitally signing the selection made by the voter. Some governments publish the source code of

© Springer International Publishing AG 2017
R. Krimmer et al. (Eds.): E-Vote-ID 2017, LNCS 10615, pp. 248–263, 2017.
DOI: 10.1007/978-3-319-68687-5_15

their voting systems to ensure that these security mechanisms have been correctly implemented (for a discussion of its relevance see [19]), like Norway in 2011 (fully disclosure), Estonia in 2013 (partial disclosure) or Geneva (Switzerland) in 2017 (partial disclosure). Nevertheless, while this measure provides certain transparency as it allows to auditing the implementation of the system, it does not provide any proof of accuracy in the election process. For instance, it does not avoid an undiscovered bug in the source code to be exploited during the election, neither it guarantees that the source code used in the voting system is the one published. For this reason, it is essential to provide means to audit the proper behavior of the systems during the election, regardless of the correctness of the software source code neither its proper execution. Apart from the evaluation and certification (for a discussion see [13]) the solution suggested would be the implementation of mechanisms that allow both voters and external auditors to verify the proper behavior of the voting system: verifiable voting.

1.1 Verifiability Concepts

Verifiable voting systems are those that implement mechanisms, based either on physical means (e.g., paper trails [36]) or cryptographic ones (e.g., cryptographic proofs [21]), that can be used to audit the proper execution of computer-based electronic processes. Generally, these mechanisms are classified in the electronic voting literature [5, 10, 23] in two types, based on who performs the verification: individual verifiability and universal verifiability.

- **Individual verifiability:** It is related to the verification mechanisms that can be used by the voter during the voting process. These can be subdivided in two complementary mechanisms [23]: cast-as-intended and recorded-as cast verifiability. Cast-as-intended verifiability enables the voter to verify if the electronic vote registered in the system really contains the selections made. In other words, it allows the voter to detect if any error or attack manipulated the vote contents when it was recorded (i.e., encrypted) by the voting system. Recorded-as-cast enables the voter to verify that her verified vote has been successfully stored in the electronic Ballot Box that will be used in the tallying phase. Like in any audit process, the number of verified votes is important to have a more accurate audit. So, the larger amount of voters able to verify their votes, the higher is the probability to detect even small inconsistencies. For instance, in an election with 10.000 votes, if there is a manipulation of 100 votes (1%) the verification of 1% of the voters (100 votes) has a probability of 64% of being detected (see General Recount Formula in [39]). Whether the manipulation is larger the chances are closer to 100% (e.g., a manipulation of 200 votes will be detected with a probability of 87% by the same amount of verifier voters). Therefore, it is important that these mechanisms facilitate the participation of the voters in the verification process.
- **Universal verifiability:** It refers to the verification mechanisms [23] that can be performed by anyone regardless of the level of privileges of the actor of the system (i.e., a voter or election manager of the voting system). In this sense,

universal verification does not include cast-as-intended and recorded-as-cast verifiability mechanisms because they are processes that can be only used by voters. However, it includes the so called counted-as-recorded verifiability mechanisms, whose purpose is allowing anyone the verification of accurate results in both vote opening (decryption) and counting.

In both cases, individual and universal verifiability should not compromise any of the other security requirements of an election, specially voter privacy. When individual and universal verifiability are given, it is said that systems provide end-to-end verifiability.

Another significant aspect related to verifiability is to prove that the verifiable mechanism implements this property in a sound way. Therefore, it is possible to discern if the verification mechanism is weak or strong against attackers, or even if it just a fake claim. To this end, provable security [14] is used to make a formal statement of the security properties of the verification mechanism (security proof) and the assumptions under which these properties must be evaluated, so the academic community or experts can validate the correctness or robustness of the verifiability claims. Security proofs can be complemented with formal proofs (i.e., formal languages) to facilitate the security proof automatic validation.

1.2   Methodology

To date, verifiability is an understudied phenomenon in electronic voting, and elections in general. Hence there is a need for an empirical study within its real-life context, ideally by means of a case study [44]. The present topic at hand is ideal for an exploration of the matter in deep. For this study, election systems in countries, where verifiability has been introduced in a recent legally-binding election on regional or federal level, are analyzed.

1.3   Government Adoption

Since the first government experiences in early 2000 [33], the security of internet voting systems has improved notably. One of the main enhancements was the adoption of audit processes based on verifiability mechanisms, which provided more transparency to electronic voting elections. The relevancy of verifiability in elections was already present in the first version of the e-voting standards of the Council of Europe [6]. Being this concept further developed in the new revision of these standards [5] and related implementation guidelines [4]. Following the recommendations of the Council of Europe, verifiability mechanisms were initially introduced by the Norwegian government in 2011 [8], and later by Estonia (2013) [9], Switzerland (2015) [11] and Australia (2015). However, the approach followed in each of the four contexts differs on the verifiability **scope** (individual and/or universal) and the verifiability **mechanism** implemented. Despite there are other well-known government online voting experiences, such as Canada or other Swiss voting systems, they are not considered because they have not adopted yet any type of verifiability (e.g., Zurich that currently lost its authorization).

Scope: Norway adopted in 2011 individual and universal verifiability, with the particularity that universal verifiability was only publicly accessible on demand (i.e., auditors needed to apply for an audit). Estonia adopted in 2013 individual verifiability, and it is planing to include universal verifiability in the near future. Switzerland changed in 2014 its Federal regulation to request individual and universal verifiability in their voting systems. In addition to it, Swiss regulation has a particular interpretation of universal verifiability as the publication of information is not required for verification. Neuchâtel and Geneva adopted individual verifiability in 2015. Finally, Australia adopted individual verifiability in 2015 but without universal verifiability like the Estonian case.

Mechanism: Both Norway and Switzerland follow the approach based on Return Codes as the way voters can verify the content of their vote (see Sect. 2). The main difference within both countries is that while Norway allowed voters to vote multiple times and therefore, in case of discrepancy, voters could vote again, in Switzerland, voters are only allowed to cast one vote. In this scenario then, voters need to introduce a Confirmation Code to confirm or reject the vote after verification. On the other hand, Estonia and Australia use the approach of decrypting votes after casting them. In Estonia verification requires the installation of an application to the mobile phone and the verification period is only possible during a limited period after casting the vote (between 30 min and 1 h). In Australia (New South Wales State), the verification is done by contacting a specific call center that decrypts the vote and describes the content to the voter. In this case, the verification process was open until the end of the election.

   This paper is focused on the verifiable internet voting systems implemented by different governments in the last years, their advances regarding verifiability and future plans. Section 2 includes an explanation of the individual verification mechanisms introduced by the governments who are or have been providing internet voting. Section 3 is focused on universal verification mechanisms, while in Sect. 4 there is a comparative analysis together with some conclusions.

2   Individual Verifiability in Government Implementations

There are multiple proposals in academia of cryptographic protocols implementing individual verifiability and more concretely cast-as-intended verifiability. However, current government implementations can be classified in two main groups:

- Return Codes mechanisms: In this case, voters cast their votes and receive from the voting system a set of numeric codes that are calculated over the encrypted vote (e.g., four numbers sent though SMS or shown in the same screen). By using a Voting Card sent during the election setup, voters can check whether the received codes are related to their selected voting options. The main references of this mechanism are the Norwegian [37] and Neuchâtel (Switzerland) [22] voting systems. Geneva implements Return Codes over unencrypted votes.

– Cast and decrypt: In this approach, voters cast their votes, latterly, they have the option of recovering and decrypting them to see the contents. Recovery can be done through a trusted device (e.g., mobile phone) or a trusted third party (e.g., a verification server). Reference implementations are Estonia [28] and Australia [16].

Despite that one of the most well known open source voting system is Helios, none of the government voting systems implement its "cast or verify" method [12]. That is why it is not considered for this analysis.

In addition to cast-as-intended, the recorded-as-cast verifiability is also implemented by some government electronic voting solutions. The most common approach consists in providing the voter with a Receipt that can be used to check whether the vote was recorded (stored) in the Ballot Box. The Receipt contains a fingerprint of the encrypted vote and whenever the vote is cast and recorded into the Ballot Box, a fingerprint of this encrypted vote is published in a Bulletin Board. A Bulletin Board is an append-only public repository (e.g., website) accessible to voters for them to search for the fingerprint contained within their Receipts. The presence of the fingerprint ensures voters that their votes are stored in the Ballot Box. The fingerprints in the Bulletin Board can also be used by auditors to crosscheck them with the actual votes, guaranteeing this way the integrity of the Ballot Box and adding the universal verifiability value to the process. The main reference of this mechanism is the Norwegian voting system [37].

Finally, some of the individual verifiable propososals also included a vote correctness property [15]. Vote correctness allows the voting systems to check if the encrypted votes contain a valid vote without decryption. Hence, in case of a potential mistake or attack in the client side that could invalidate the vote casting, it will be detected in the server before storing the vote in the Ballot Box. This way, the voter can be notified and can try to cast the vote again. For instance, the system will detect whether the content of an encrypted vote has either an invalid option or an invalid combination of options without learning the vote contents (i.e., repeated candidates or an invalid combination of them). It is not a specific requirement for individual verifiability but a property used in Norway and Switzerland inherit from their verification mechanism.

2.1   Individual Verifiability in Norway

Norway introduced individual verifiability in the voting system requirements of the public process started in 2009 [29]. Among different proposals, the government finally chose a solution based on using Return Codes for individual verifiability. The voting system was used by 10 municipalities during the 2011 Municipal Elections, and 13 municipalities during the 2013 General Elections. After 2013 elections, there was a change of government and the new winning party (contrary to internet voting) stopped using the voting system [31]. However, online voting is currently still in use in Norway by municipalities, especially for referendums and consultations.

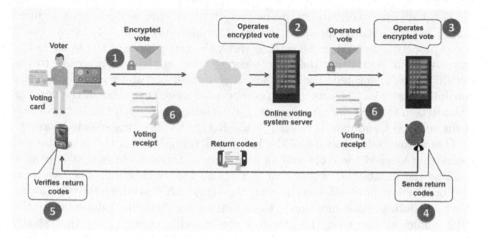

Fig. 1. Norwegian voting system

The Norwegian voting system (Fig. 1) is based on Return Codes, i.e. generation of specific Voting Cards for voters containing 4 digits code for each possible voting option. The 4 digits codes of each Voting Card are different for each voter, so it is not possible to deduce the Return Code without having the Voting Card. When the voter casts a vote, this is encrypted and digitally signed in the voter device, and it is also sent to the voting servers. One first server (Vote Collector Server) performs a cryptographic operation over the encrypted vote and sends the result of this operation to a second server (Return Code Generator). The Return Code Generator performs a second cryptographic operation, uses the result of this operation to obtain the 4 digits of the Return Code and sends it to the voter through SMS. Using their voting card, voters can verify if the received Return Code corresponds to their selection, ensuring that the encrypted vote received by the server contains the correct selections. If the contents of the encrypted vote are different, the operation will not return the correct Return Code. However, as the Norwegian voting system permits multiple voting, the voter can cast another vote if does not agree with the previous one. This cast-as-intended mechanism is responsible of the individual verifiability of the system, but does not include recorded-as-cast verification. For a detailed description of this voting system the following references are recommended [30, 37].

In the 2013 National Elections, the Norwegian voting system included recorded-as-cast to individual verifiability by means of Voting Receipts. The Voting Receipt was provided to the voter once the vote was accepted and stored in the Ballot Box. This receipt contains a fingerprint of the encrypted and digitally signed vote cast by the voter.

In addition to the receipt, the fingerprints of all the votes stored in the Ballot Box were also published, so voters were able to check the presence of their votes by searching the fingerprint of the Voting Receipt in a public Bulletin Board.

The individual verifiability properties of the voting system were security proven using a security proof of the cryptographic protocol [24]. As an additional property, the system allowed to check the correctness of the votes in the server without decrypting them (vote correctness) applying some rules to the Return Codes generated. For instance, it detects if one Return Code appears multiple times (i.e., the same option is encrypted more than once in the vote) or if the Return Code is the expected one for the selection (e.g., if the Return Code of the selected Candidate is related to the Return Code of the selected Party).

One of the main concerns of the individual verifiability is the percentage of voters that verified their votes. The limitation of this system is that it cannot monitor the number of voters that performed the verification, since verification does not require interaction with the server after sending Return Codes. However, during some small-scale test elections (referendums) done before the 2011 municipal elections, the Ministry conducted a voter survey that shown that almost 90% of the voters admitted the Return Codes verification [40]. Furthermore, during these elections an error in the printing process made 1% of the voters of some municipalities to receive a wrong Voting Card. Based on the number of calls received from voters claiming that the Return Code was incorrect, the election manager was able to infer the percentage of voters that verified the votes. The verification was carried out by more than 70% of the affected voters. However, this number cannot be considered representative of the whole participants since in both cases was obtained from an small sample of voters (hundreds).

Finally, the source code of the voting system was also made publicly available before the election [30].

2.2 Individual Verifiability in Estonia

The Estonia voting system individual verifiability was introduced in 2013 Municipal Elections [28]. The individual verifiability cast-as-intended mechanism is based on using a mobile phone application for the voter verification process. In the Estonian example (Fig. 2), the votes are encrypted and digitally signed in the voting terminal (computer) and sent to the server. If the vote is accepted, the voting terminal displays a 2D barcode containing the ballot identity and the secret padding used for encrypting the vote. By using this application, voters can scan the 2D barcode, obtain the ballot identifier and used it to download the encrypted vote from the voting server. Once the encrypted vote is downloaded, the mobile application uses the secret padding to recover the contents of the encrypted vote and present it to the voter. Since the Estonian voting system allows multiple voting, voters can cast another vote if they do not agree with the contents shown in the mobile phone application. To avoid coercion or vote buying, the voter has a predefined limited verification period (between 30 min and 1 h). More details about the voting systems can be found in the following reference [28].

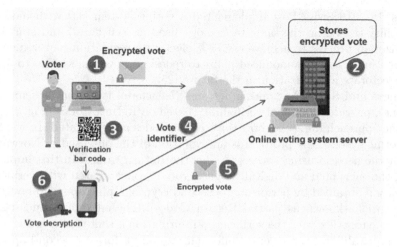

Fig. 2. Estonian voting system

Since the voter downloads the encrypted vote from the voting system, it can be assumed that the verification process also involves recorded-as-cast verifiability. However, the limitation of verification time does not ensure that the vote remains in the Ballot Box or reaches the counting process.

This system allows monitoring the number of voters that performs the verification process, since voters need to be connected to the server to download the ballot. Current verification percentage is about 4% of the voters [27].

Regarding provable security, there is no proof yet published that demonstrates the security of the individual verifiable protocol properties of the system. Additionally, it does not support server vote correctness verification of the encrypted vote. In 2013, the Estonia government published the source code of the system, but just the server and mobile application part [3]. The source code of the voting client was not published to avoid the creation of fake voting clients.

2.3 Individual Verifiability in Switzerland

Switzerland updated its Internet Voting regulation in 2014 including both individual and universal verifiability [18]. The main aim was to authorize Swiss Cantons to increase up to 50% and 100% the percentage of the electorate that could use online voting (Originally, authorization was restricted to 30% of the Canton electorate). In order to authorize to increase the electorate up to 50%, systems needed to include individual verifiability and must be certified by an entity accredited by the Federal Chancellery. The certification process includes the provision of security and formal proofs of the individual verifiability protocol, as well as passing a Common Criteria certification with assurance level 2. Geneva [2] and Neuchâtel [22] cantons updated their voting systems to achieve individual verifiability in 2015, but they did not start the 50% electorate authorization process. In 2016 Swiss Post implemented a voting system [41] with individual verifiability (based on the same technology used in Neuchâtel) and started the authorization process to achieve the 50% electorate regulation requirements. In the meantime, Geneva announced plans to redesign its voting system to achieve 100% electorate authorization in the future [25].

Geneva and Swiss Post voting systems (Neuchâtel is currently using Swiss Post one), provide individual verifiability based on Return Codes (Fig. 3). However, the approach differs on how the Return Codes are generated. In the Swiss Post voting system, the protocol is an evolution of the one used in Norway but without the need of using two servers for the Return Codes. In this implementation, the encrypted and digitally signed vote is concatenated with verification information obtained by performing a second cryptographic operation over each voting option (known as partial Return Codes). The encrypted and digitally signed vote together with the verification information is sent to the voting server. This server validates the received information and performs a second operation over the verification information, obtaining the information that allows to recover the 4-digit Return Code of the selected voting options. These Return Codes are sent back to the voter and displayed in the same voting device. If the voter agrees, then a Confirmation Code is sent, which is required for the acceptance of the vote in the counting process and the update of the voting status in the electoral roll. If the voter disagrees, the vote remains unconfirmed and the Internet voting channel cannot be used again, but the voter can still use another voting channel for contingency (postal or pollsite) because her vote casting status in

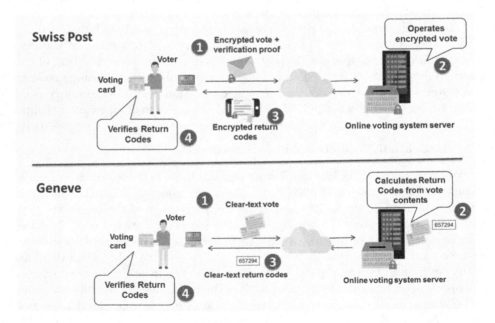

Fig. 3. Swiss voting systems

the electoral roll has not been updated. More detailed information of the voting system can be found in [41, 42].

In the Geneva voting system, the cast vote is not encrypted in the voter device but sent though an encrypted communication channel (SSL) to the voting server. The voting server can see the selected voting options, calculates the 4-digit Return Codes and sends the codes back to the voter. The vote is then encrypted by the server and stored waiting for voter confirmation. Voter confirmation is also based on a Confirmation Code that must be sent by the voter after verification. Without confirmation, the vote will not be used in the counting phase. Detailed information about the voting system can be found in [2].

Both voting systems provide cast-as-intended verifiability, nevertheless Geneva checking the presence of the vote in the counting phase (recorded-as-cast) is not possible in the Genevan model. Only in the case of Swiss Post voting system a Voting Receipt is provided together with a fingerprint of the encrypted and digitally signed vote (as in Norway). Apart from that, the list of the fingerprints of the votes present in the Ballot Box is published after the voting period ends. Both voting systems provide vote correctness properties as in Norway, but only the Swiss Post model has security and formal proofs of the individual verifiability protocol. Geneva published in 2017 the source code of its voting system, but only the administration offline components [1]. In none of the cases, there are numbers of the percentage of voters that verified their votes, since the verification is offline.

2.4   Individual Verifiability in Australia

Australia introduced individual verifiability in 2015 through the New South Wales (NSW) State election [16]. The year before, the State of Victoria implemented a pollsite voting system that provided also individual verifiability (vVote [17]). However, this voting system was designed to be deployed in local and remote polling stations (e.g., consulates), so it has not been considered as an online voting system for this study.

The individual verifiability mechanism implemented by the NSW voting system (Fig. 4), known as iVote, was based on phone calls that voters had to make to verify the content of their cast votes (i.e., cast-and-decrypt approach). During the voting process, votes were encrypted and digitally signed in the voter device and after casting, the voter received a Receipt with a unique Receipt Number. Votes were encrypted with a double encryption mechanism, to allow both the decryption by the Electoral Board and the decryption by a Verification Server with the help of the voter (using the Receipt Number). The voter was able then to call before the voting period expired to validate her vote. When calling, the voter needed to introduce her voting credentials and the voter Receipt Number. The Verification Server used the voter credentials to retrieve the encrypted vote, and used its private key and Receipt Number to decrypt it. Through the phone, the voter was able to listen the vote contents. To make the phone voting process more user friendly, the voter credentials and Receipt Number were numerical. In case voters did not agree with the voting options, they had to contact the

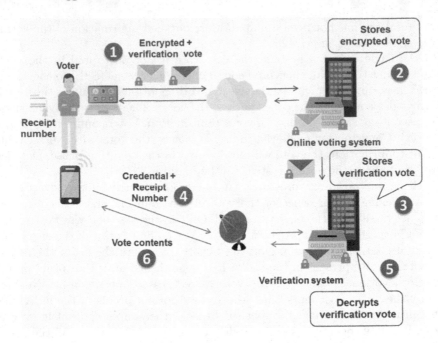

Fig. 4. New South Wales voting system

election authorities. Multiple voting was not allowed, but election officers were able to cancel the vote and provide new credentials to the voter when necessary.

The NSW individual verification approach, provided cast-as-intended and recorded-as-cast verifiability, since the validation process allowed to check that the vote was present in the Ballot Box until the voting period ended. Since the verification required to be connect to a server, it was possible to monitor the number of voters that verified their votes. In this case the verification ratio was 1,7% in 2015 election [16]. Regarding the availability of the source code and security proofs, the source code is not available and no security proofs of the voting protocol were generated. The verification mechanism did not provide vote correctness either.

3   Universal Verifiability in Government Implementations

Currently, universal verifiability is only implemented the Norwegian and the Swiss Post voting systems. In both cases, this is mainly achieved by means of a universal verifiable mixnet and decryption components.

In the case of Norway, in 2011 a universal verifiable mixnet designed by Scytl [38] was used, while in 2013 the Verificatum Mixnet [43] was also used. In both cases, instead of publishing the verification data, the Norwegian government made a public call for participating in the universal verification of the results. However, the source code of the system was made publicly available.

In Switzerland, the Swiss Post voting system has been using a verifiable Mixnet since 2015 (Geneva only implements a standard Mixnet without verifiability). However, the Federal Chancellery regulation requires a specific universal verifiability approach to certify a voting system and achieve the 100% electorate authorization process [18]. This model requires that the universal and individual verification processes use specific and independent trusted components for the audit proofs generation, known as Control Components. According to the regulation [18], these Control Components can be implemented in two different ways: (i) as two Hardware Security Modules (HSM) from two different vendors, or (ii) as 4 standard computers using different operating systems. These Control Components should be deployed completely isolated one from the other and operated by different teams. With these conditions, the Federal Chancellery considers that universal verifiability can be implemented without publishing the verification information.

Swiss Post and Geneva are working on adapting their voting system architecture to achieve these requirements (Geneva announced in 2016 a new redesign of the voting protocol to accomplish these requirements).

Estonia does not implement universal verifiability (it does not implement any Mixing process), but announced plans to incorporate it in a short-mid term [26]. In Australia, the NSW voting system does not implement any Mixing process and it has not announced any plans for universal verifiability yet. However, it implements a mechanism to match the decrypted votes with the ones present in the Verification Server (performing a reencryption of the decrypted votes).

4   Comparison

Table 1 summarizes the different verifiability properties compiled from the information of the online voting systems studied in this paper.

Despite the Norwegian voting system was the first in introducing verifiability to online voting systems, it can be still considered one of the most complete ones in the sector.

Switzerland (and more concretely the Swiss Post voting system) has a similar level of verifiability, which is explained by the fact the Chancellery used the Norwegian government experience as a reference for its regulation.

The other voting systems (except for Australia) have already started incorporating individual verifiability and have even announced plans to incorporate universal verifiability in a near future. Therefore, it is clear that verifiability is becoming essential for any online voting system.

Regarding the percentage of voters that participate in the verification process, it is easier to monitor it on the systems that perform vote decryption for verification (i.e. Cast and decrypt). Numbers in these cases seem to be low, but they are a good reference to calculate the probability in issues detection. In the case of Return Codes, the only reference comes from Norway and it seems extraordinarily high. However, further analysis should be done in this mechanism because numbers are based on small samples.

Table 1. Properties of evaluated systems

	Norway	Estonia	Switzerland (Swiss Post)	Switzerland (Geneva)	Australia (NSW)
Cast-as-intended	Return codes	Decryption in device	Return codes	Return codes	Decryption in server
Recorded-as-cast	At any time with receipts	Up to 1 h	After counting with receipts	None	N
Counted-as-recorded	Verifiable mixnet	None	Verifiable mixnet	None	Yes, through vote re-encryption
Voter verification	90–70% (small sample)	4% (large sample)	No data	No data	1% (large sample)
Public source code	All the system	Only server side	None	Only counting side	None
Vote correctness	Yes	None	Yes	Yes	None
Provable security	Yes (Individual and Universal)	None	Yes (Individual and Universal)	None	None

Regarding the publication of the source code, only Norway had a full disclosure. The other voting systems that published the source code did it partially. This can be in part justified based on the fact that these other voting systems do not provide end-to-end verifiability and therefore, the risk of an undetected attack is higher. In any case, Estonia and Geneva announced plans of full disclosure in the future, which indicates a general tendency among online voting systems. In the meantime, the Swiss Federal Chancellery is not demanding source code disclosure yet for systems that are under the 100% electorate authorization.

Vote correctness was present in the Norwegian voting system and latterly adopted by the Swiss voting system as well. It is still uncertain whether other voting systems will also adopt this trend, which was initially provided by homomorphic tally voting systems [20] and currently by those using Return Codes.

Finally, from the point of view of provable security, only Norway and Switzerland used security proofs to demonstrate the security properties of their verification mechanisms. In fact, Switzerland is even more exigent as also formal proofs for authorization of the voting systems are required. Proving the security of the voting systems using cryptographic and formal proofs is a recommended practice that it is expected to be extended, since it allows security experts to verify whether the claimed verifiability properties are certainly present in the voting system and whether they are robust (i.e., under which assumptions these properties are present). This way the governments can certify the verifiability of the voting systems and discard those that are not providding these guarantees or are poorly implemented.

As a general conclusion, the assumption is that verifiability in elections will be implemented in the future, in particular due to transparency needs and to the inherent general distrust in not visible or tangible processes. Still, none approach can be identified as "best-practice". However, Norway and Switzerland can be identified as the ones that have made so far more efforts towards verifiability implementation. It can be certainly stated that election operators start implementing individual verifiability before the universal one due to the mentioned additional advantage for the individual voter. Nevertheless, while universal verifiability brings a significant security gain, its implementation is less frequent mainly due to trusted arguments defended by governments (audit environments considered secure because they are under the control of election authorities) and due to its mathematical complexity hard to understand for most.

Acknowledgments. The contributions of R. Krimmer to this article are partially supported by Estonian Research Council Project PUT1361 and Tallinn University of Technology Project B42.
Disclaimer. The authors of the paper affiliated to Scytl Secure Online Voting have been involved in some of the electronic voting systems described.

References

1. E-voting system chvote 1.0. source code offline administration application. https://github.com/republique-et-canton-de-geneve/chvote-1-0
2. E-voting system chvote 1.0. system overview. https://github.com/republique-et-canton-de-geneve/chvote-1-0/blob/master/docs/system-overview.md
3. Estonia voting system source code repository. https://github.com/vvk-ehk
4. Guidelines on the implementation of the provisions of Recommendation CM/Rec(2017)5 on standards for e-voting. https://search.coe.int/cm/Pages/result_details.aspx?ObjectID=0900001680726c0b
5. Recommendation CM/Rec(2017)5[1] of the Committee of Ministers to member States on standards for e-voting. https://search.coe.int/cm/Pages/result_details.aspx?ObjectID=0900001680726f6f
6. Recommendation Rec(2004)11 adopted by the Committee of Ministers of the Council of Europe on 30 September 2004 and explanatory memorandum. http://publiweb104.coe.int/t/dgap/goodgovernance/Activities/GGIS/E-voting/Key_Documents/Default_en.asp
7. Election Observation Handbook: Sixth Edition. OSCE/ODIHR, Warsaw (2010)
8. Final Report of the Election Assessment to Norway. OSCE/ODIHR, Warsaw (2011)
9. Final Report of the Election Assessment Mission to Estonia. OSCE/ODIHR, Warsaw (2013)
10. Handbook for the Observation of New Voting Technologies. OSCE/ODIHR, Warsaw (2013)
11. Final Report of the Election Assessment Mission to Switzerland. OSCE/ODIHR, Warsaw (2015)

12. Adida, B.: Helios: web-based open-audit voting. In: van Oorschot, P.C. (ed.) USENIX Security Symposium, pp. 335–348. USENIX Association (2008)
13. Barrat, J., Bolo, E., Bravo, A., Krimmer, R., Neumann, S., Parreño, A.A., Schürmann, C., Volkamer, M., Wolf, P.: Certification of ICTs in Elections. International IDEA, Stockholm (2015)
14. Bellare, M.: Practice-oriented provable-security. In: Damgård, I.B. (ed.) EEF School 1998. LNCS, vol. 1561, pp. 1–15. Springer, Heidelberg (1999). doi:10.1007/3-540-48969-X_1
15. Bibiloni, P., Escala, A., Morillo, P.: Vote validatability in mix-net-based eVoting. In: Haenni, R., Koenig, R.E., Wikström, D. (eds.) VOTELID 2015. LNCS, vol. 9269, pp. 92–109. Springer, Cham (2015). doi:10.1007/978-3-319-22270-7_6
16. Brightwell, I., Cucurull, J., Galindo, D., Guasch, S.: An overview of the iVote 2015 voting system (2015). https://www.elections.nsw.gov.au/about_us/plans_and_reports/ivote_reports
17. Burton, C., Culnane, C., Schneider, S.: Secure and Verifiable Electronic Voting in Practice: the use of vVote in the Victorian State Election. CoRR abs/1504.07098 (2015). http://arxiv.org/abs/1504.07098
18. The Swiss Federal Chancellery: Federal chancellery ordinance on electronic voting (2013). http://www.bk.admin.ch/themen/pore/evoting/07979
19. Clouser, M., Krimmer, R., Nore, H., Schürmann, C., Wolf, P.: The Use of Open Source Technology in Election Administration. International IDEA, Stockholm (2014)
20. Cramer, R., Gennaro, R., Schoenmakers, B.: A secure and optimally efficient multi-authority election scheme. In: Fumy, W. (ed.) EUROCRYPT 1997. LNCS, vol. 1233, pp. 103–118. Springer, Heidelberg (1997). doi:10.1007/3-540-69053-0_9
21. Damgård, I.: On sigma-protocols. http://www.cs.au.dk/ivan/Sigma.pdf
22. Galindo, D., Guasch, S., Puiggalí, J.: 2015 Neuchâtel's cast-as-intended verification mechanism. In: Haenni, R., Koenig, R.E., Wikström, D. (eds.) VOTELID 2015. LNCS, vol. 9269, pp. 3–18. Springer, Cham (2015). doi:10.1007/978-3-319-22270-7_1
23. Gharadaghy, R., Volkamer, M.: Verifiability in electronic voting - explanations for non security experts. In: Krimmer and Grimm [32], pp. 151–162
24. Gjøsteen, K.: Analysis of an internet voting protocol. Cryptology ePrint Archive, Report 2010/380 (2010)
25. Haenni, R., Koenig, R.E., Dubuis, E.: Cast-as-intended verification in electronic elections based on oblivious transfer. In: Krimmer, R., Volkamer, M., Barrat, J., Benaloh, J., Goodman, N., Ryan, P.Y.A., Teague, V. (eds.) E-Vote-ID 2016. LNCS, vol. 10141, pp. 73–91. Springer, Cham (2017). doi:10.1007/978-3-319-52240-1_5
26. Heiberg, S., Martens, T., Vinkel, P., Willemson, J.: Improving the verifiability of the estonian internet voting scheme. In: Krimmer, R., Volkamer, M., Barrat, J., Benaloh, J., Goodman, N., Ryan, P.Y.A., Teague, V. (eds.) E-Vote-ID 2016. LNCS, vol. 10141, pp. 92–107. Springer, Cham (2017). doi:10.1007/978-3-319-52240-1_6
27. Heiberg, S., Parsovs, A., Willemson, J.: Log analysis of Estonian internet voting 2013–2014. In: Haenni, R., Koenig, R.E., Wikström, D. (eds.) VOTELID 2015. LNCS, vol. 9269, pp. 19–34. Springer, Cham (2015). doi:10.1007/978-3-319-22270-7_2
28. Heiberg, S., Willemson, J.: Verifiable internet voting in Estonia. In: 6th International Conference on Electronic Voting: Verifying the Vote (EVOTE 2014), Lochau/Bregenz, 29–31 October 2014. pp. 1–8 (2014). http://dx.doi.org/10.1109/EVOTE.2014.7001135

29. KRD: Specification, tenders, evaluation and contract (2009). https://www.regjeringen.no/en/dep/kmd/prosjekter/e-vote-trial/source-code/specification-tenders-evaluation-and-con/id612121/
30. KRD: evalg2011 system architecture (2011). https://web.archive.org/web/20120309072858/http://www.regjeringen.no/en/dep/krd/prosjekter/e-vote-2011-project/source-code/the-system-architecture-.html?id=645240
31. KRD: Internet voting pilot to be discontinued - KRD press release (2014). https://www.regjeringen.no/en/aktuelt/Internet-voting-pilot-to-be-discontinued/id764300/
32. Krimmer, R., Grimm, R. (eds.): Electronic Voting 2010 (EVOTE 2010), 4th International Conference, Co-organized by Council of Europe, Gesellschaft für Informatik and E-voting.CC, 21st–24th July 2010, in Castle Hofen, Bregenz, Austria. LNI, vol. 167. GI (2010)
33. Krimmer, R., Triessnig, S., Volkamer, M.: The development of remote E-voting around the world: a review of roads and directions. In: Alkassar, A., Volkamer, M. (eds.) Vote-ID 2007. LNCS, vol. 4896, pp. 1–15. Springer, Heidelberg (2007). doi:10.1007/978-3-540-77493-8_1
34. Kripp, M.J., Volkamer, M., Grimm, R. (eds.): 5th International Conference on Electronic Voting 2012, (EVOTE 2012), Co-organized by the Council of Europe, Gesellschaft für Informatik and E-voting.CC, 11–14 July 2012, Castle Hofen, Bregenz, Austria, LNI, vol. 205. GI (2012)
35. Lenarcic, J.: Opening Address on 16 September 2010 at the OSCE Chairmanship Expert Seminar on the Present State and Prospects of Application of Electronic Voting in the OSCE Participating States, Vienna (2010)
36. Mercury, R.: A better ballot box? IEEE Spectr. **39**, 46–50 (2002)
37. Puigalli, J., Guasch, S.: Cast-as-intended verification in Norway. In: Kripp et al. [34], pp. 49–63
38. Puiggalí, J., Guasch, S.: Universally verifiable efficient re-encryption mixnet. In: Krimmer and Grimm [32], pp. 241–254. http://subs.emis.de/LNI/Proceedings/Proceedings167/article5682.html
39. Saltman, R.G.: Effective Use of Computing Technology in Vote-Tallying. Technical report, NIST (1975)
40. Stenerud, I.S.G., Bull, C.: When reality comes knocking norwegian experiences with verifiable electronic voting. In: Kripp et al. [34], pp. 21–33, http://subs.emis.de/LNI/Proceedings/Proceedings205/article6754.html
41. Swiss Post: Individual Verifiability, Swiss Post Online Voting Protocol Explained. https://www.post.ch/-/media/post/evoting/dokumentc/swiss-post-online-voting-protocol-explained.pdf?la=en&vs=3
42. Swiss Post: Swiss Post Online Voting Protocol. https://www.post.ch/-/media/post/evoting/dokumente/swiss-post-online-voting-protocol.pdf?la=en&vs=2
43. Wikström, D.: A sender verifiable mix-net and a new proof of a shuffle. In: Roy, B. (ed.) ASIACRYPT 2005. LNCS, vol. 3788, pp. 273–292. Springer, Heidelberg (2005). doi:10.1007/11593447_15
44. Yin, R.: Case Study Research: Design and Methods. Applied Social Research Methods. Sage Publications, London (2003). https://books.google.es/books?id=BWea_9ZGQMwC

Cast-as-Intended Mechanism with Return Codes Based on PETs

Achim Brelle and Tomasz Truderung[(✉)]

Polyas GmbH, Berlin, Germany
{a.brelle,t.truderung}@polyas.de

Abstract. We propose a method providing cast-as-intended verifiability for remote electronic voting. The method is based on plaintext equivalence tests (PETs), used to match the cast ballots against the pre-generated encrypted code tables.

Our solution provides an attractive balance of security and functional properties. It is based on well-known cryptographic building blocks and relies on standard cryptographic assumptions, which allows for relatively simple security analysis. Our scheme is designed with a built-in fine-grained distributed trust mechanism based on threshold decryption. It, finally, imposes only very little additional computational burden on the voting platform, which is especially important when voters use devices of restricted computational power such as mobile phones. At the same time, the computational cost on the server side is very reasonable and scales well with the increasing ballot size.

1 Introduction

Modern electronic voting systems are expected to provide a combination of security guarantees which includes, most importantly, ballot secrecy and end-to-end verifiability. For the latter, one crucial part is so-called *cast-as-intended* verifiability which means that a voter has means to make sure that the ballot cast on his or her behalf by the voting client application and recorded by the voting server contains the intended voting option, as chosen by the voter. This property must be guaranteed without assuming that the voter platform is honest. Indeed, such assumption would be unjustified especially in the context of remote voting, where voting client programs (typically HTML/JS applications) run on voters' devices. One cannot reasonably assume that such devices are properly maintained, patched and free of malware. Moreover, as often the code of the voting client application is served by the voting server, such trust assumption would have to be extended to such servers as well.

The problem of providing adequate and usable solutions for cast-as-intended verifiability has recently attracted significant attention. In particular, various solutions based on the idea of *return codes* have been proposed [2,6,8–11,14], where different solutions provide different balance of security and usability features. Notably, solutions based on return codes [8,9,16] were used in Norway in legally binding municipal and county council elections in 2011 and 2013, [6] was

© Springer International Publishing AG 2017
R. Krimmer et al. (Eds.): E-Vote-ID 2017, LNCS 10615, pp. 264–279, 2017.
DOI: 10.1007/978-3-319-68687-5_16

used in 2015 in binding elections in the Swiss canton of Neuchâtel, while [10], as stated in the paper, is planned to be used as a part of the electronic voting system for the State of Geneva (Switzerland) [11].

The above mentioned solutions share the following underlying idea. In the registration phase, each voter obtains over a trusted channel a ballot sheet, where pre-generated return codes (typically short random alpha-numeric sequences) are printed next to each voting choice. Then, in the voting phase, after the voter has selected her voting choices and the voting client application has submitted an encrypted vote to the remote voting server, the voting authorities compute/retrieve (in some way dependent on the specific solution) return codes which are meant to correspond to the choices made by the voter. These codes are sent back to the voter (possibly using an independent channel) who compares them with the codes printed on her ballot sheet next to the selected choices. The idea here is that when this match succeeds, the voter can be sure that the submitted (encrypted) vote indeed contains her intended choices (as otherwise the voter would not have obtained the matching codes). The voter may then finalize the ballot casting process (by, for instance, submitting some kind of finalization code) or, if the match does not succeed, she may undertake different steps (for instance, vote from another device or use a completely different voting method).

Our Contribution. In this paper we propose a new cast-as-intended mechanism based on return codes. Our solution provides an attractive balance of security and functional properties:

1. It is based on well-known cryptographic building blocks and relies on standard cryptographic assumptions, which allows for relatively simple security analysis. In fact, our analysis is modular in that it does not depend on the details of the underlying voting protocol to which our return code scheme is added.
2. Our scheme is designed with distributed trust in mind: the computations carried out to retrieve/compute return codes are distributed in their nature, such that a threshold of trustees must be corrupted in order to carry out a successful attack and fool the voter.
3. Our solution imposes only very little additional computational burden on the voting platform, which is especially important if voters use devices of restricted computational power such as mobile phones. The computational cost on the server side is very reasonable and scales well with the increasing ballot size (it is, up to ballots of fairly big size, essentially constant).

Our scheme is meant to provide *cast as intended* verifiability even if the voting platform is controlled by the adversary under the following assumptions. First, we assume that not more than $t - 1$ tellers are corrupted (i.e. controlled by the adversary), where t is the threshold of the used threshold-decryption scheme. Second, we assume that the printing facility and the ballot delivery channel are not corrupted. Under these assumptions, if the voter, during the voting process, obtains the expected return codes (that is the codes printed on her ballot sheet next to her intended choices), then the cast ballot is guaranteed to contain the intended voter's choice.

We note that the second assumption is shared with other return code solutions. It is a strong assumption and requires special measures in order to be justified in specific deployments. The same assumption (in addition to the standard assumptions that the voter platform is honest and that at most $t-1$ tellers are corrupted) is necessary for *voters' privacy*. Finally, note that our scheme (similarly to most of the return code solutions; see below for more discussion) is not meant to provide *receipt freeness*.

On the technical level, our scheme is inspired by the PGD system [12,15] which however does not implement the idea of returns codes, but instead the one of *voting codes* (where a voter *submits codes* corresponding to her choice). Sharing some similarities with this construction, our system differs substantially from PGD in many aspects.

As an additional contribution of this paper, we demonstrate an attack on a return code scheme recently proposed in [10,11] which was planned to be used in the context of the Geneva Internet voting project (see below for more details).

Related Work. As already mentioned, our scheme is inspired by the PGD system [12,15] and, on the technical level, uses some similar ideas: it uses distributed PETs (plaintext equivalence tests) to match the submitted ballots against a pre-published encrypted code table. Our scheme, however, differs from PGD in some significant ways. Our scheme scales better with increasing ballot complexity (PGP performs one PET for every entry in the voter's code table; we perform only one PET per voter even for relatively complex ballots). On the technical level we avoid the use of encrypted permutations (onions). Finally, PGD uses the idea of voting codes, where a voter submits codes corresponding to the chosen candidates (although the authors also suggest the possibility of using return codes). We note here that the use of voting codes (as in PGD) results in stronger ballot secrecy (the voting client does not get to learn how the voter's choice and hence it does not have to be trusted for ballot secrecy). As a trade-off, using voting codes tends to be less convenient for the voters.

In a series of results including [2,8,9,14], related to the Norwegian Internet voting projects (*eValg2011* and *eValg2013*) [16], the underlying, shared idea is as follows. The code for a voting option v (which is cast in an encrypted form $\mathsf{Enc}_{pk}(v)$) is deterministically derived from v using a per-voter secret s (it typically is v^s). This derivation process is carried out by two servers (playing fixed, specific roles) in such a way that if only one of them is corrupted, the security goal of the return codes is not subverted. In order to make this idea work for more complex ballots, [8,9] uses a technique of combining codes, which however requires some non-standard cryptographic assumption (hardness of the SGSP problem, where SGSP stands for *Subgroup Generated by Small Primes*). These schemes (as opposed to ours) do not allow for more fine-grained distribution of trust: there are exactly two parties with specific roles, one of which must be honest.

The above idea was further transformed in a scheme proposed for the voting system in the canton of Neuchâtel in Switzerland [6], with the main technical difference that in this system a voter holds one part of the secret used for code generation (which causes some usability issues which were addressed by introducing of a so-called usability layer, which unfortunately weakens security guarantees). Security of this construction relies on the same non-standard security assumption as [8, 9] do and, similarly, there is no built-in fine grained mechanism for distributed trust. Compared to our system, this system requires much more complex computations on the voting platform, but less computations for the election authorities (although in both cases the ballot processing time on the server side is essentially constant independently of the number of voting options).

Recently, an interesting solution has been proposed in the context of the Geneva Internet voting project [10, 11]. This solution is based on oblivious transfer, where, intuitively, the security of the mechanism is provided by the fact that the authorities (even although they may know all the codes) do not know which codes are actually transfered to the voter. This provides some level of protection against vote buying schemes which otherwise could be very easily mounted by a dishonest authority (if a voter was willing to disclose her ballot sheet). To our knowledge, this is the only return-codes scheme with this property.

As a downside, in this protocol, codes cannot be transfered using an independent channel (they must be transfered via the voter's platform), which rules out the use of this protocol in elections where re-voting is allowed. Furthermore, this protocol, again, uses the same non-standard cryptographic assumption as [8, 9].

Finally, as already mentioned, we have discovered a serious flaw in this construction, described in detail in Appendix A. Our attack violates the cast-as-intended property of the scheme (the voter cannot be sure that the cast ballot represents her intended choice even if she receives the expected return codes) and can be mounted by an attacker who only controls the voting platform. In short, we show that such an attacker (which is exactly the kind of attacker the system is meant to defend against) *can cast invalid ballots* and still provide the voters with valid return codes. These invalid ballots are accepted by the voting server, tallied, and only discovered and rejected after tallying, when the link between the ballot and the voter has been hidden. Note that even if the protocol could be augmented with a mechanism enabling us to trace the malformed decrypted ballots back to the voters, it would only point to dishonest voters' devices which cannot be held accountable.

While there is a natural countermeasure for this attack (adding appropriate zero-knowledge proofs of well-formedness of the ballot), it comes with significant degradation of performance: it works, roughly, in quadratic time with respect to the number of voting options, which renders this solution impractical for bigger ballots.[1]

Structure of the Paper. After introducing some preliminary definitions (Sect. 2) and providing an overview of the election process (Sect. 3), we describe in Sect. 4 a simple variant our scheme, applicable only for ballots with one binary choice. The general variant is described in Sect. 5, after which the security analysis

---

[1] We contacted the authors who confirmed the flaw and are working on a more efficient countermeasure for the attack which is described in [11].

is presented in Sect. 6. The mentioned attack on [10] is described in the appendix. More details are available in the extended version of this paper [4].

2   Preliminaries

Our return code scheme uses the well-known ElGamal cryptosystem over a cyclic group G of quadratic residues modulo a safe prime $p = 2q + 1$. This cryptosystem is multiplicatively homomorphic (that is $\mathsf{Enc}_{pk}(m) \cdot \mathsf{Enc}_{pk}(m')$ results in an encryption $\mathsf{Enc}_{pk}(m \cdot m')$ if m and m' are elements of the underlying group). A distributed key generation protocol for the ElGamal cryptosystem (where n tellers jointly generate a secret key and the corresponding public key, and pre-determined threshold $t < n$ out of n tellers is necessary for decryption) is proposed, for instance, in [7].

A plaintext-equivalence test [13] is a zero-knowledge protocol that allows the (threshold of) tellers to verifiably check if two ciphertexts c and c' contain the same plaintext, i.e. to check if $\mathsf{Dec}_{sk}(c) = \mathsf{Dec}_{sk}(c')$, but nothing more about the plaintexts of c and c'.

Our return codes solution can be added to any voting system with encrypted ballot of a form which is compatible with our scheme in the following sense: (1) ElGamal cryptosystem with threshold decryption, as introduced above, is used to encrypt voters' choices and (2) ballots contain zero-knowledge proofs of knowledge of the encrypted choices (which is a very common case); additionally, for the general case, we require that (3) voters' choices are encoded in a specific way (see Sect. 5) before encryption. We do not fix details of the authentication mechanism nor those of the tallying process. In fact, our security analysis works independently of these details. Examples of voting systems compatible with our scheme are Helios [1] and Belenios [5] with mix-net-based tallying and, for the simple variant, also with homomorphic tallying (so our cast-as-intended mechanism can be used in addition to or instead of the ballot audit procedure used in Helios and Belenios).

3   Overview of the Election Process

In this section we present an overview of the voting process. Because our scheme (like other return codes solutions) is aimed at providing cast-as-intended verifiability even when the voting platform is potentially corrupted, we make the distinction between *voters* and their *voting platform*, that is devices, including the software potentially served by the voting server, voters use to cast ballots.

The election process is run by the set of **authorities** including:

- *Tellers* who jointly generate the public election key pk_e key and share the corresponding decryption key in a threshold manner. They also, similarly, jointly generate the *public code key* pk_c which will be used to encrypt codes in code tables and an auxiliary public key pk_a for which the corresponding secret key is known to every teller (here we do not need threshold decryption and use any CCA2-secure cryptosystem). The tellers take part in code table generation and generation of additional codes for voters (authentication, finalisation and confirmation codes). They may also carry out additional steps (such as ballots shuffling), as specified by the underlying protocol.

- *Secure bulletin boards* which, traditionally for e-voting systems, are used by voting authorities to publish results of various steps of the election procedure, including the final election result. Secure bulletin boards provide append-only storage, where records can be published (appended) but never changed or removed.
- *Voting server* which is responsible for voters' authentication and ballot recording (where a ballot is published on a designated secure bulletin board).
- *Printing facility*, including the ballot sheets delivery, used to print ballot sheets in a trusted way and to deliver ballot sheets to eligible voters. The printing facility, in the setup phase generates its private/public encryption key pair and publishes the public key pk_p.

Our return code schemes supports the following, general **ballot structure**: a ballot may contain a number of voting options (candidates), where a voter can independently select each of these options (or, put differently, provide 'yes'/'no' choice independently for each voting option). Further restrictions can be imposed (such as for example, that exactly k or at most k options are selected) and checked after the ballots are decrypted. Note that with this ballot structure we can encode different types of ballots, such as for instance, ballots where each candidate can get more than one vote.

The election process consists of the following **voting phases**:

In the *setup phase* the tellers and the printing facility generate keys and codes, as described above. In the *registration phase* every eligible voter obtains (via a trusted channel) a ballot sheet. The ballot sheet contains an *authentication code* (used as a authentication measure; we abstract here from the details of the authentication mechanism and simply assume that a mechanism with sufficient security level is used), a *finalization code*, a *confirmation code*, and a list of voting options (candidates) with printed next to each of them two return codes: one for the 'no' choice and one for the 'yes' choice.

In the *voting phase*, the voter, using her voting platform and the authentication code, authenticates to the voting server and selects her choices. The voting platform creates a ballot with the selected choices and submits it to the voting server. The ballot is then processed by the voting authorities who send back to the voter (via the voting platform or via some other, independent channel) sequence of return codes that correspond to the cast (encrypted) choices. The voter compares the obtained codes with the ones printed on her ballot sheet to make sure that they indeed correspond to her intended choices. If this is the case, the voter provides the voting platform with the finalization code which is forwarded to the voting server. Given this finalization code, the voting server sends the confirmation code to the voter and completes the ballot casting process by adding the ballot to the ballot box. If something does not work as expected (the voter does not get the expected return codes or does not obtain the confirmation code after providing her finalisation code), the voter can undertake special steps, as prescribed by the election procedure (use, for instance, another device or the conventional voting method).

Finally, in the *tallying phase*, the ballots published on the ballot box are tallied and the result is computed.

4 The Variant with One Binary Choice

In this section, we present a simple variant of our scheme, where the ballot contains only one binary choice (two candidate races or 'yes'/'no' elections). This variant, while avoiding the technical details of the general variant, demonstrates the main ideas of the scheme.

Code Table and Ballot Sheet. As shortly mentioned before, in the setup phase, the voting authorities generate for every voter an encrypted *code table*. We will now only describe the expected result of the code generation procedure, without going into the detail. Such details will be given in Sect. 5.2, where the general case is covered (which subsumes the simple case discussed in this section). We only mention here that code tables are generated in fully verifiable way.

The code generation procedure generates, for every voter, two random codes c_0 and c_1, corresponding to the 'no' and 'yes' choice, and a random bit b, called a *flip bit*. It also generates for every voter a random *finalization code* and a *confirmation code*. Additionally, we assume that some kind of *authentication codes* for voters may be generated by this procedure as well, but we abstract away from the details of the authentication mechanism, as the presented construction does not depend on them.

The *ballot sheet* (delivered to the voter over a trusted channel) contains the authentication, finalization, and confirmation codes, the return codes c_0 and c_1 printed in clear next to, respectively, the 'no' and the 'yes' voting choice, and the flip bit b. For usability reasons, the flip bit can be integrated into the authentication code, so that the voter does not have to enter it separately.

The *code table* associated with the voter, published on a bulletin board, is of the form

$$c_{fin}, \; e_{conf}, \; (e_0, d_0), (e_1, d_1)$$

where c_{fin} is a commitment to the finalization code, e_{conf} is encryption of the confirmation code under pk_c and

$$e_0 = \mathsf{Enc}_{pk_e}(b), \quad d_0 = \mathsf{Enc}_{pk_c}(c_b), \quad e_1 = \mathsf{Enc}_{pk_e}(1 - b), \quad d_0 = \mathsf{Enc}_{pk_c}(c_{1-b}).$$

Note that the this record contains the pair of ciphertexts corresponding to the 'no' choice (encrypted 0 and encrypted code c_0) and the pair of ciphertexts corresponding to the 'yes' choice (encrypted 1 and encrypted code c_1). The order in which these two pairs are placed depends on the flip bit (if the flip bit is 1 the order is flipped).[2]

---

[2] Note that the plaintext are first mapped into G before being encrypted; for an appropriate choice of the mapping, we obtain a system which coincides with the general variant with $k = 1$ and, furthermore, allows for homomorphic tallying.

Ballot Casting. The voter provides her voting application with her authentication code, the flip bit b, and her voting choice $v \in \{0, 1\}$. The voting application produces a ballot containing

$$w = \mathsf{Enc}_{pk_e}(v), \quad \mathsf{Enc}_{pk_a}(\tilde{b}), \quad \pi$$

where $\tilde{b} = v \oplus b$ and π is a zero-knowledge proof of knowledge of the plaintext in the ciphertext w ($\tilde{b}$ is encrypted in order to hide it from an external observer; the tellers will decrypt this value in the next step).

The voting authorities check the zero-knowledge proof π, decrypt $\tilde{b}$, select $e_{\tilde{b}}$ from the voter's table and perform the PET of this ciphertext with the ciphertext w submitted by the voter's platform. It is expected that this PET succeeds (which is the case if the voting platform follows the protocol and the ballot sheet and the code table are correctly generated). If this is the case, the corresponding encrypted code $d_{\tilde{b}}$ is decrypted (which should result in c_v) and delivered to the voter. The voter makes sure that, indeed, the return code is c_v, i.e. it corresponds to the voting choice v, before she provides her finalization code (in order to finalize the ballot casting process). The voting authorities check that the provided finalization code is a valid opening for the commitment c_{fin}. If this is the case, they finalise the ballot casting process: they jointly decrypt the confirmation code, send it to the voter, and add the voter's ballot to the ballot box.

Tallying. Finally, after the voting phase is over, ballots collected in the ballot box are tallied. We abstract here from the details of the tallying procedure. Importantly, our security results work regardless of the details of this procedure.

The intuition behind security of this scheme is as follows. Because, of the correctness of the code table and PET operations (which is ensured by zero-knowledge proofs), if the PET succeeds, then the decrypted code must be the return code corresponding to the *actual* plaintext in the encrypted ballot. To fool the voter, an adversary would have to send him the code contained in the second ciphertext which has not been decrypted. But the best the adversary can do—not being able to break the used encryption scheme—is blindly guess this code, which gives him very small probability of success.

Remark 1. For this simple variant, we do not really need to include the flip bit in the ballot sheet: the ciphertext w could be matched, using the PET protocol, against both e_0 and e_1, one of which should succeed, which would determine $\tilde{b}$. Including the flip bits in the ballot sheets is however crucial for efficiency of the general variant.

We can note that the additional computational cost of this scheme added to the voting platform is only one encryption. The computational cost incurred by this scheme on the server side (per one voter) is one additional decryption to decrypt $\tilde{b}$, one verifiable PET, and one distributed decryption to decrypt the return code.

As we will see in a moment, the general variant of our scheme (with k independent choices) can be seen as a combination of k simple cases as described here with some optimisations. Interestingly, with these optimisations, the additional computational cost incurred by our scheme—if the size of the ballot does not grow too much—remains essentially the same.

5   The General Variant

In this section we present the general variant of our code voting scheme, where ballots can contain some number k of independent binary choices, one for each voting option. This variant is expressive enough to handle wide variety of complex ballots. Despite some technical details used for optimisation, this variant shares the same underlying idea, illustrated by the simple variant.

We assume some encoding γ of the voting options $1, \ldots, k$ as elements of the group G such that the voter's choice, which is now a subset of individual voting options, can be encoded as the multiplication of the encodings of these individual options. Of course, we assume that the individual voting options can be later efficiently retrieved from such an encoding. As an example of such encoding we can use the technique used for instance in [6,10], where the voting options are encodes as small prime numbers which belong to the group G.

Similarly, we assume a family of efficient encodings δ_i ($i \in \{1, \ldots, k\}$) from the set of return codes to the group G, such that individual codes $c_1, \ldots, c_k$ can be efficiently extracted from the product $\delta_1(c_1) \cdot \ldots \cdot \delta_k(c_k)$. An example of such an encoding is given in the full version of this paper [4].

5.1   Ballot Structure and Voting Procedure

Code Table and Ballot Sheets. The code generation procedure is described in details in Sect. 5.2. In addition to finalisation and confirmation codes which are generated as previously, this procedure generates, for every voter and every voting option $i \in \{1, \ldots, k\}$, two random codes c_i^0 and c_i^1 corresponding to, respectively, the 'no' and 'yes' choice. It then generates a random sequence of flip bits $\boldsymbol{b} = b_1, \ldots, b_k$, where $b_i \in \{0, 1\}$.

The ballot sheet sent to the voter contains now, besides the authentication, finalisation, and confirmation codes, return codes $(c_1^0, c_1^1), \ldots, (c_k^0, c_k^1)$ printed in clear next to corresponding voting options and marked as, respectively the 'no' and the 'yes' choice. It also contains the flip bits $\boldsymbol{b}$ (as before, this vector can be integrated in the authentication code).

The published code table associated with the voter contains, as before c_{fin}, e_{conf} and

$$\left(u_i^0, u_i^1\right)_{i=0}^k = \left(t_i^{b_i}, \ t_i^{1-b_i}\right)_{i=0}^k$$

where

$$t_i^0 = (\mathsf{Enc}_{pk_e}(1)), \ \mathsf{Enc}_{pk_c}(\delta_i(c_i^0)) \quad \text{and} \quad t_i^1 = (\mathsf{Enc}_{pk_e}(\gamma(i))), \ \mathsf{Enc}_{pk_c}(\delta_i(c_i^1)).$$

Note that t_i^0 corresponds to the 'no' choice (it contains an encryption of 1 and the encoded code for 'no') and t_i^1 corresponds to the 'yes' choice (it contains an encryption of the encoded option i and the encoded code for 'yes'). Note also that $u_i^{b_i} = t_i^0$ and $u_i^{1-b_i} = t_i^1$.

Ballot Casting. The voter provides her voting application with her voting choice $v_1, \ldots, v_k \in \{0, 1\}$ and the bit sequence $\boldsymbol{b}$. The voting application computes $v = \prod_{i \in V} \gamma(i)$, where we define V as the set $\{j : 1 \leq j \leq k, \ v_j = 1\}$, and produces a ballot containing

$$w = \mathsf{Enc}_{pk_e}(v), \quad \mathsf{Enc}_{pk_a}(\tilde{\boldsymbol{b}}), \quad \pi$$

where π is, as before, a zero-knowledge proof of knowledge of the plaintext of w and $\tilde{\boldsymbol{b}} = \tilde{b}_1, \ldots, \tilde{b}_k$ with $\tilde{b}_i = b_i \oplus v_i$.

The voting authorities decrypt $\tilde{\boldsymbol{b}}$ and select the values $w_i = u_i^{\tilde{b}_i}$, for $i \in \{1, \ldots, k\}$. Note that if the voter has *not* chosen the i-th election option, then $w_i = u_i^{b_i} = t_i^0$, by the definition of u. Otherwise, $w_i = u_i^{1-b_i} = t_i^1$.

The voting authorities multiply $w_1, \ldots, w_k$ (component-wise) obtaining the pair (e^*, c^*), where e^* should be (if the voter platform followed the protocol) encryption of $v = \prod_{i \in V} \gamma(i)$. The voting authorities perform the PET of e^* with the encrypted choice w from the ballot. If this PET fails, the casting procedure is canceled. Otherwise, the decryption tellers jointly decrypt c^*. Observe that, by the properties of the published code table, this decrypted value is the product of $\delta_j(c_j^{v_j})$, i.e. it is the product of the codes corresponding to the choices made by the voter. This value is decomposed into individual codes $c_1^{v_1}, \ldots c_k^{v_k}$ and sent to the voter (via the voting platform or an independent channel). As before, the voter makes sure that the received codes correspond to her choices before providing the finalisation code.

Note that the ballot processing on the server side only requires one verifiable PET, one decryption and one threshold decryption, independently of the number k of the voting options, plus some number of multiplications and divisions (which depends on k), as long as k codes can be efficiently represented as one element of the group G which is in detail discussed in the full version of this paper [4].

5.2 Code Table Generation

The code table generation presented below is fully verifiable. Note that we could also consider a version without zero-knowledge proofs, but with partial checking instead, where a bigger number of records is produced and the some of them (randomly selected) are open for audit.

We will assume that the code generation procedure is carried out by the tellers, but it can by carried out by any set of independent parties, as it does not require possession of any secret keys. We will present here a version, where, for the same voting option, distinct voters obtain distinct codes, although different variants are also possible (and may be useful if the number of voters is very big).

The set of codes is $\mathsf{Codes} = \{1, \ldots, m\}$ with $m > 2n$, where n is the number of voters (reasonable values for m, that is values corresponding to desired security levels, can be determined using the result below).

For simplicity of presentation, in the following, we will leave out handling of the authentication, finalization and confirmation codes. The procedure consists of the following steps.

1. For every voting option j, the tellers deterministically compute

$$\mathsf{Enc}_{pk_c}(\delta_j(1)), \mathsf{Enc}_{pk_p}(1), \ldots, \mathsf{Enc}_{pk_c}(\delta_j(m)), \mathsf{Enc}_{pk_p}(m).$$

   where all the ciphertext are obtained using the pre-agreed randomness 1.

2. The tellers shuffle the above sequence of ciphertexts using a verifiable mix net obtaining a sequence of the form

$$\mathsf{Enc}_{pk_c}(\delta_j(c_1)), \mathsf{Enc}_{pk_p}(c_1), \ldots, \mathsf{Enc}_{pk_c}(\delta_j(c_m)), \mathsf{Enc}_{pk_p}(c_m),$$

   where $c_i = \pi(i)$ for some permutation π and the ciphertext are re-randomized. Note that for this we need to use a version of verifiable mixing which applies the same permutation (but independent re-randomization factors) to pairs of ciphertexts. Such generalizations of know verifiable shuffling algorithms are possible.[3]

3. The tellers take the consecutive encrypted codes produced in the previous step and organize them into the records of the following form, one for each voter i:

$$\big\{ \mathsf{Enc}_{pk_p}(0), \mathsf{Enc}_{pk_p}(c_j'), \mathsf{Enc}_{pk_p}(1), \mathsf{Enc}_{pk_p}(c_j''),$$
$$\mathsf{Enc}_{pk_e}(1), \mathsf{Enc}_{pk_c}(\delta_j(c_j')), \mathsf{Enc}_{pk_e}(\gamma(j)), \mathsf{Enc}_{pk_c}(\delta_j(c_j'')) \big\}_{j \in \{1, \ldots, k\}}$$

   where the ciphertext with (encoded) choices are generated deterministically with the randomness 1.

4. The tellers perform, one after another, series of micro-mixes for every such a record: Each teller, for the input record $R = (a_1, b_1, a_2, b_2, a_1', b_1', a_2', b_2')$ (which is the output of the previous teller or, for the first teller, the record produced in the previous step) picks a random bit. If this bit is 0, then it only re-encrypts all the elements R. If the flip bit is 1, then, in addition, it accordingly flips the elements of the record and outputs a re-encryption of $R' = (a_2, b_2, a_1, b_1, a_2', b_2', a_1', b_1')$. The teller produces a zero-knowledge proof of correctness of this operation (such step can be implemented as a verifiable mixing operation; it can be also realized using disjunctive Chaum-Pedersen zero-knowledge proofs of the fact that the resulting record is either a re-encryption of R or R').

5. The parts of the records encrypted with pk_c and pk_e are published in voters' code tables. The parts encrypted with pk_p are given to the printing facility which decrypts the records. The decrypted content contains the return codes and (implicitly, via the order of plaintexts) the flip bit sequence b.

---

[3] In particular, it is straightforward to generalize the shuffle protocol of [3] to provide such functionality.

Note that, in the above procedure, all the steps are fully deterministic or come with appropriate zero-knowledge proofs. This design is meant to provide the following correctness guarantees:

> The code generation procedure produces correctly linked ballot sheets and encrypted code tables with overwhelming probability. Moreover, unless the threshold of trustees are dishonest, only the printing facility learns how codes are distributed amongst voters.

6   Security Analysis

As noted in the introduction, coercion resistance and receipt-freeness are not the goals of our scheme. In fact, the use of return codes, as in many similar solutions, specifically makes the scheme prone to vote selling *if dishonest authorities are involved in the malicious behaviour.*

The results presented in this section are stated for the case where re-voting is not allowed. For the case with re-voting (casting multiple ballots, of which, say, the last is counted), we expect that the privacy result holds, while only a weaker form of cast-as-intended verifiability than the one presented in Sect. 6.2 can be guaranteed: namely, we have to assume that an independent channel is used to send return codes to voters and that both the tellers (who see the sent return codes) and this channel are honest.

6.1   Ballot Secrecy

Ballot secrecy means, informally, that it is impossible (for an adversary) to obtain more information about the choices of individual *honest* voters (that is voters following the protocol), than can be inferred from the explicit election result. Our code voting scheme is designed to provide voters privacy under the following assumptions:

P1. The voting platform is not corrupted.
P2. At most $t - 1$ tellers are corrupted, where t is the threshold for decryption.
P3. The printing facility and the ballot sheet delivery channel are not corrupted.

The first two assumptions are standard and for voters' privacy and shared by many e-voting protocols (using and not using return codes). The third assumption is also shared by any code voting scheme (where codes need to be printed and delivered to the voter). Therefore, in this sense, these are the minimal assumptions for electronic voting with return codes.

Note also, that the informal definition of privacy given above only protect honest voters who, in particular, do not reveal their ballot sheet to another parties, excluding voters who want to sell their ballots.

We formalize the above notion of privacy using the following game between the adversary and the system P representing the honest components of the e-voting system, where the adversary gets to control all but two (honest) voters.

For simplicity of presentation, we consider here the simple case where voters have only one yes/no choice. We will consider two variants of P: variant P_0, where the first of the honest voters votes for the 'no' option and the second honest voters chooses the 'yes' option, and variant P_1, where the choices of the honest voters are swapped. With these definitions, we express the notion of privacy by requiring that there is no polynomially bounded adversary A which can detect if he is interacting with P_0 or P_1 (up to some negligible probability), that is:

$$\mathsf{Prob}[P_0 \parallel A \mapsto 1] \equiv_{\mathsf{negl}} \mathsf{Prob}[P_1 \parallel A \mapsto 1] \tag{1}$$

where $P_i \parallel A \mapsto 1$ denotes the event that in the run of the system composed of P_i and A, the adversary outputs 1 (accepts the run). We assume that the adversary can interact with the system in the following way: it interacts with the honest tellers playing the role of the dishonest tellers (in all the protocol stages). It also casts ballots of the dishonest voters and, at some chosen time, triggers the honest voters to cast their ballots.

We will now formulate our privacy result in a modular way, independently of many details of the underlying voting system to which our return code scheme is added. We only assume that the system has the structure which allows for the described above game and which uses ballot encoding 'compatible' with our construction, as described in Sect. 2. Under these assumptions, our code voting scheme is meant to satisfy the following property:

Let U be the underlying voting protocol and let P denote the protocol obtained from U by adding our return code scheme. If U provides ballot secrecy, as expressed by (1), then P provides secrecy as well.

A sketch of the proof of this statement is given in the full version of the paper [4] where we show that all the additional elements of P (related to codes) can be simulated by a simulator which has only black-box access to U.

6.2 Cast-as-Intended Verifiability

Cast-as-intended verifiability means that an honest voter can, with high probability, make sure that the ballot cast on her behalf by her voting platform and recorded in the ballot box by the voting server contains her intended choice. Our scheme provides cast-as-intended verifiability under one of the following cases: (1) The voter client is honest. (2) The following trust assumptions are satisfied:

V1. At most $t - 1$ tellers are corrupted.
V2. The printing facility and the ballot sheet delivery channel are not corrupted.

The first case is trivial (note that the very purpose of code voting is to provide cast-as-intended verifiability in the case the voter client is *not* honest). We only need to assume that the voting client has means to check that the cast ballot has been in fact added to the ballot box and that there is a mechanism preventing any party from removing or modifying this ballot (which is the case if we assume that the ballot box is an instance of a secure bulletin board).

In the following, we analyse the second case. We claim that the following result holds for our system.

Under the assumption V1 and V2, for any given honest voter (possibly using a dishonest voting platform) and for any of the k voting options, the probability that the voter obtains the expected code (that is the code printed next to voter's choices), while the recorded ballot contains different choices for this voting option is not bigger than $\frac{1}{m-n-n'}$ (plus a negligible value), where m is the number of generated codes, n is the total number of voters, and $n' < n$ is the number of corrupted voters.

This result, similarly to the privacy result, does not depend on the details of the authentication mechanism nor on the details of the tallying phase.

The intuition behind this statement is that everything that the adversary can learn about code distribution is, essentially (up to cases of a negligible probability), what is explicitly given to him, that is (a) n codes that have been decrypted by the tellers (b) n' remaining codes of dishonest voters (because the adversary gets to see all the codes of these voters). So, if the adversary wants to come up with the code corresponding to the opposite choice (for the considered voting option) of the honest voter in order to fool her, the best he can do is pick one of the remaining $m - n - n'$ codes at random.

In order to prove this statement, similarly to the privacy result, one can use the ideal (honest) code generation procedure and replace PETs by the appropriate ideal functionality. In this setting we argue that the following is true.

Because the code table is correct (correctly corresponds to the printed ballot sheets) and the results of PETs is correct too (as we are using the ideal functionality), it follows that the decrypted codes correspond to the actual voting options in the encrypted ballots. One can then show that, if the adversary had a strategy of guessing an unencrypted code of an honest voter with better probability than given by the blind guess as described above (where the adversary picks one of the possible codes at random), this would break the IND-CPA property of the underlying encryption scheme.

A   Attack on [10]

In order to understand the attack presented below, it may be useful for the reader to first consult the original paper [10]. It is worth noting that this attack scenario does not undermine the underlying (k out of n)-OT scheme. It only utilizes the fact that a dishonest receiver in this scheme can obtain up to k (but not more) values even if it does not follow the protocol. We describe here an attack for the case with $n = k = 2$.

The *intended run* of the protocol is as follows. For the voter's choice $s = (s_1, s_2)$, the voting platform (VP) prepares an OT query

$$\boldsymbol{a} = (a_1, a_2), \quad \text{where} \quad a_j = \Gamma(s_j) \cdot y^{r_j},$$

for random r_j, where y is the public election key. It also computes $b = g^{r_1+r_2}$. Let a denote the product of elements of $\boldsymbol{a}$ that is $a_1 \cdot a_2$. Note that $c = (b, a)$ is an ElGamal ciphertext (which, although not explicitly sent, will be considered to be the ciphertext cast by the voter) encrypting the plaintext $p = \Gamma(s_1) \cdot \Gamma(s_2)$ with randomness $r = r_1 + r_2$. The VP sends $\boldsymbol{a}$ and b along with a ZKP of knowledge of r and p.

From the OT response, the VP can now compute the codes for s_1 and s_2 which are shown to the voter who provides the confirmation code and the protocol goes on. Here are the details of how the codes are retrieved. The OT response contains:

$$a_1^\alpha, \ a_2^\alpha, \ y^\alpha,$$
$$c_1 \oplus H(\Gamma(s_1)^\alpha), \ c_2 \oplus H(\Gamma(s_2)^\alpha), \ \dots$$

for some random α, where c_1 and c_2 are the codes corresponding to choices s_1 and s_2. Knowing r_1 and r_2, the VP can compute $\Gamma(s_1)^\alpha$ and $\Gamma(s_2)^\alpha$ and, in turn, the codes c_1, c_2.

The *dishonest run* goes, for example, like this: For the voter's choice $s = (s_1, s_2)$ as before, the VP prepares the OT query

$$\tilde{\boldsymbol{a}} = (a_1, \tilde{a}_2), \quad \text{where} \quad \tilde{a}_2 = \Gamma(s_1)^7 \cdot \Gamma(s_2) \cdot y^{r_2}$$

and sends $\tilde{\boldsymbol{a}}$ along with b and a ZKP of knowledge of r and the plaintext $\tilde{p}$, which is now $\Gamma(s_1)^8 \cdot \Gamma(s_2)$. Jumping ahead, this plaintext will be rejected as invalid, but only after (mixing) and final decryption, when there is no visible link between the decrypted ballot and the voter.

Nevertheless, from the OT response, the VT can easily compute the codes for s_1 and s_2 and make the protocol proceed as if the intended, valid ballot was cast. To see this, we can notice that, given the OT response, the VT can compute values $\Gamma(s_1)^\alpha$ and $(\Gamma(s_1)^7 \cdot \Gamma(s_2))^\alpha$, from which it is easy to compute $\Gamma(s_2)^\alpha$ and the same codes c_1 and c_2 as in the honest run. These codes are delivered to the voter who then continues the procedure.

A straightforward countermeasure for this attack would be adding appropriate zero-knowledge proofs of correctness of each a_j, which however adds a significant computational overhead (it works in time $O(k \cdot n)$).

References

1. Adida, B.: Helios: web-based open-audit voting. In: van Oorschot, P.C. (ed.) Proceedings of the 17th USENIX Security Symposium, pp. 335–348. USENIX Association (2008)
2. Allepuz, J.P., Castelló, S.G.: Internet voting system with cast as intended verification. In: Kiayias, A., Lipmaa, H. (eds.) Vote-ID 2011. LNCS, vol. 7187, pp. 36–52. Springer, Heidelberg (2012). doi:10.1007/978-3-642-32747-6_3
3. Bayer, S., Groth, J.: Efficient zero-knowledge argument for correctness of a shuffle. In: Pointcheval, D., Johansson, T. (eds.) EUROCRYPT 2012. LNCS, vol. 7237, pp. 263–280. Springer, Heidelberg (2012). doi:10.1007/978-3-642-29011-4_17

4. Brelle, A., Truderung, T.: Cast-as-intended mechanism with return codes based on PETs. Extended Version. Technical report arXiv:1707.03632 (2017)
5. Cortier, V., Galindo, D., Glondu, S., Izabachène, M.: Election verifiability for Helios under weaker trust assumptions. In: Kutyłowski, M., Vaidya, J. (eds.) ESORICS 2014. LNCS, vol. 8713, pp. 327–344. Springer, Cham (2014). doi:10. 1007/978-3-319-11212-1_19
6. Galindo, D., Guasch, S., Puiggalí, J.: 2015 Neuchâtel's cast-as-intended verification mechanism. In: Haenni, R., Koenig, R.E., Wikström, D. (eds.) VOTELID 2015. LNCS, vol. 9269, pp. 3–18. Springer, Cham (2015). doi:10.1007/ 978-3-319-22270-7_1
7. Gennaro, R., Jarecki, S., Krawczyk, H., Rabin, T.: Secure distributed key generation for discrete-log based cryptosystems. J. Cryptol. **20**(1), 51–83 (2007)
8. Gjøsteen, K.: The Norwegian internet voting protocol. In: Kiayias, A., Lipmaa, H. (eds.) Vote-ID 2011. LNCS, vol. 7187, pp. 1–18. Springer, Heidelberg (2012). doi:10.1007/978-3-642-32747-6_1
9. Gjøsteen, K.: The Norwegian internet voting protocol. IACR Cryptology ePrint Archive, 2013:473 (2013)
10. Haenni, R., Koenig, R.E., Dubuis, E.: Cast-as-intended verification in electronic elections based on oblivious transfer. In: Krimmer, R., Volkamer, M., Barrat, J., Benaloh, J., Goodman, N., Ryan, P.Y.A., Teague, V. (eds.) E-Vote-ID 2016. LNCS, vol. 10141, pp. 73–91. Springer, Cham (2017). doi:10.1007/978-3-319-52240-1_5
11. Haenni, R., Koenig, R.E., Locher, P., Dubuis, E.: CHVote System Specification. Cryptology ePrint Archive, Report 2017/325 (2017). http://eprint.iacr.org/2017/ 325
12. Heather, J., Ryan, P.Y.A., Teague, V.: Pretty good democracy for more expressive voting schemes. In: Gritzalis, D., Preneel, B., Theoharidou, M. (eds.) ESORICS 2010. LNCS, vol. 6345, pp. 405–423. Springer, Heidelberg (2010). doi:10.1007/ 978-3-642-15497-3_25
13. Jakobsson, M., Juels, A.: Mix and match: secure function evaluation via ciphertexts. In: Okamoto, T. (ed.) ASIACRYPT 2000. LNCS, vol. 1976, pp. 162–177. Springer, Heidelberg (2000). doi:10.1007/3-540-44448-3_13
14. Puigalli, J., Guasch, S.: Cast-as-intended verification in Norway. In: 5th International Conference on Electronic Voting 201. (eVOTE 2012), Co-organized by the Council of Europe, Gesellschaft für Informatik and E-voting.CC, 11–14 July 2012, Castle Hofen, Bregenz, Austria, pp. 49–63 (2012)
15. Ryan, P.Y.A., Teague, V.: Pretty good democracy. In: Christianson, B., Malcolm, J.A., Matyáš, V., Roe, M. (eds.) Security Protocols 2009. LNCS, vol. 7028, pp. 111–130. Springer, Heidelberg (2013). doi:10.1007/978-3-642-36213-2_15
16. Stenerud, I.S.G., Bull, C.: When reality comes knocking Norwegian experiences with verifiable electronic voting. In: 5th International Conference on Electronic Voting 201 (eVOTE 2012), Co-organized by the Council of Europe, Gesellschaft für Informatik and E-voting.CC, 11–14 July 2012, Castle Hofen, Bregenz, Austria, pp. 21–33 (2012)

How Could Snowden Attack an Election?

Douglas Wikström[1]([✉]), Jordi Barrat[2], Sven Heiberg[3], Robert Krimmer[4], and Carsten Schürmann[5]

[1] KTH Royal Institute of Technology, Stockholm, Sweden
dog@kth.se
[2] University of Catalonia, Barcelona, Spain
jordi.barrat@urv.cat
[3] Smartmatic-Cybernetica Centre of Excellence for Internet Voting, London, UK
sven@ivotingcentre.ee
[4] Tallinn University of Technology, Tallinn, Estonia
robert.krimmer@ttu.ee
[5] IT University of Copenhagen, Copenhagen, Denmark
carsten@demtech.dk

Abstract. We discuss a new type of attack on voting systems that in contrast to attacks described in the literature does not disrupt the expected behavior of the voting system itself. Instead the attack abuses the normal functionality to link the tallying of the election to disclosing sensitive information assumed to be held by the adversary. Thus the attack forces election officials to choose between two undesirable options: Not to publish the election result or to play into the adversary's hand and to publicize sensitive information. We stress that the attack is different from extortion and not restricted to electronic voting systems.

1 Introduction

Existing paper-based voting systems are often considered to be the gold standard against which any other voting system is measured, despite that the classic systems have security weaknesses.

For example, a certain degree of errors when voters fill in ballots is sometimes accepted as long as the voters' intent can still be determined. Similarly, blank ballots may be allowed to give the possibility to vote for unlisted candidates, or as a last resort to counter attacks where ballot papers are stolen from a polling station.

Another example is how the results are reported, e.g., in Norway the results for voting districts that are deemed too small are reported at an aggregate level

---

We use "Snowden" as a placeholder for somebody in possession of sensitive information and do not in any way suggest that he has any intention to attack any elections. The recent presidential election in USA 2016 show that there may be other parties in possession of similar information with the intent to disrupt elections.

R. Krimmer—Work supported in part by the Estonian Research Council project PUT1361.

© Springer International Publishing AG 2017
R. Krimmer et al. (Eds.): E-Vote-ID 2017, LNCS 10615, pp. 280–291, 2017.
DOI: 10.1007/978-3-319-68687-5_17

to preserve the privacy of voters. Even when a result for a given voting district is not needed to compute the distribution of seats, the result is often considered an important channel of information of the broader democratic system.

However, such weaknesses are typically well known and due to a careful tradeoff between several conflicting goals such as security, availability, cultural values and traditions, and economy.

In this paper we introduce a previously unknown type of attack that should be added to the list of threats to be considered in such tradeoffs. How serious the attack is depends strongly on the strategic value of the election and how well the election management body is prepared to handle it. Important factors include legal, procedural, and the strategic value of causing confusion or a delay in the tabulation of an election. The vulnerability to the attack of an election depends both on how ballot papers are designed and marked, and how the election is tallied.

2 Contribution

We first present a novel attack that can be executed on numerous existing voting systems with potentially far-reaching and serious implications. Then we identify the most important parameters of the attack and discuss how and to what extent the attack can be mitigated.

We hope that this paper will raise the awareness among researchers, governments, and other stakeholders. Short term, election owners must prepare plans and procedures to handle an attack. Modest improvements may also be applied to existing voting systems within current laws. Long term, each voting system should be studied carefully to see if it is possible to mitigate the attack in a way that is acceptable from a democratic point of view and election laws should be changed if needed. Due to the diversity of the details of voting systems, election schemes, legal frameworks, and democratic cultures, this is out of scope of this paper.

In this paper we focus on the mechanics of the attack at a high level. We do not consider the details of specific elections and voting systems to determine how vulnerable they are to the attack, assess the strategic value of carrying out the attack, and the threat model. Legal and political aspects are also out of scope of this paper, but we hope to inspire such research.

In an appendix we consider to what extent the attack can be applied to the particular voting systems of a handful of countries and informally propose a number of modest changes that could be deployed quickly to raise the cost to execute the attack and improve the chance to identify the perpetrator.

3 The Attack

We first observe that most voting systems provide a channel to voters that not only allow them to express their voting intents, but also to send arbitrary information through the voting system. More precisely, given a piece of information, one or more voters can use their right to vote to encode the information into the output of the voting system. In this context, the *output consists not only of the tally of the election, but also of all auxiliary information that is published or otherwise available*, e.g., the number of invalid votes and in what way they are invalid. Depending on how restricted the access to different parts of the output is, the attack is more or less feasible. In Sect. 4 we discuss several examples of how the information can be encoded depending on the specifics of the voting system.

Then we assume that the adversary has access to sensitive information that must not be published by the election authority. Secret information is clearly sensitive such as information published by WikiLeaks, but other information which is not particularly secret may also be sensitive. In Sect. 3.1 we consider different types of sensitive information.

We also assume that the adversary is able to publish information on "the Internet" in the sense that the data is made broadly available and can not be deleted. Today this is a very mild assumption due to the plethora of forums and servers that store information for free without deep authentication of the users.

Throughout we write $\mathsf{Enc}(k, m)$ to denote the encryption of a message m with a secret key k, and we denote by m the sensitive data. An example of a suitable cryptosystem is AES. We denote by H a cryptographic hash function such as SHA-3 that compresses an arbitrarily long input to a short digest. The basic attack proceeds as follows:

1. The adversary forms a ciphertext $c = \mathsf{Enc}(k, m)$ using the sensitive information m and a randomly chosen secret key k, and publishes it on the Internet anonymously.
2. She uses corrupted voters to submit votes that encode the secret key k in such a way that it can be easily derived from the output of the election after tallying.
3. She anonymously informs the relevant authorities, and possibly media or other parties, that if the result is tallied, then the sensitive data m will be published by the election authority.
4. She makes sure that her claim is credible, e.g., by revealing parts of the sensitive information to the owner of the election and chosen government agencies and media.

Example 1. Suppose that the attacker has access to Snowden's complete information m and consider an election that allows write-in votes, and that the contents of all votes are reported in the final result. Here the adversary picks a random party name p, hashes it to form the key $k = \mathsf{H}(p)$, encrypts the sensitive data to form the ciphertext $c = \mathsf{Enc}(k, m)$ which is published on the Internet. Then it submits p using a write-in vote. Then it informs the election authority and chosen media. If the election is tallied, then p appears in the result, $k = \mathsf{H}(p)$ can be computed, and the sensitive information $m = \mathsf{Dec}(k, c)$ is disclosed.

We stress that the attack is easy to execute completely anonymously, since the ciphertext c can be published through any electronic channel and the voting system itself provides privacy to the attacker when k is encoded into the votes.

The attack puts the owner of the election, e.g., a national election authority, in a situation where they de-facto become fully responsible for publishing the sensitive information and this is known by a wide audience. This immediately spawns a number of questions that demands answers such as:

- How vulnerable is a given system to the attack?
- What can we do to counter the attack?
- Is it legal to tally, or conversely refuse to tally, and can tallying be delayed?
- Should the election authority tally unconditionally?
- Who is politically and legally responsible for publishing the information?
- Can individuals or organizations demand damages for disclosed information?

3.1   Types of Sensitive Information

Before we consider how the attack differs from extortion we give a number of examples of sensitive information and discuss how the type of information influences the characteristics of the attack.

State Secrets. Imagine that a disgruntled officer in the military, or arms industry, decides to execute the attack. The obvious real world example is somebody like Edward Snowden, but with a more sinister agenda. The sensitive data may be worth billions and threaten the lives of many people if it is leaked.

The motivation may be political to punish the establishment, or at a national level to punish a foreign state. In the latter case, it may be clear that the attacker has no intention to leak the information, i.e., the goal is specifically to stop or delay the election.

We can even imagine an attack that is intended to look like an attack by an insider, but which in reality is an attack by a corrupt state. It is not far-fetched that elements of a country like USA or Russia sacrifices a measured amount of sensitive information and manufactures an insider attack on their own, or a foreign country, for political purposes. Consider the political pressure these countries can exert on small states to delay an election if needed.

The motive could also be economical. We would expect that the stock market reacts quickly if the tallying of the election is delayed. Trading on movements on the stock market in a covert way is not difficult and could result in huge revenues. A single individual with access to sensitive information and plausible deniability could today with little risk of detection execute this attack in several countries.

Private Information About Voters in the Election. Suppose that the election, or part of it, is performed using an electronic voting system. Due to lack of analysis and poor understanding of cryptography and computer security, several such systems have been broken [3,4,6].

Consider a political activist that has repeatedly pointed out vulnerabilities and tried to convince the authorities to not use the electronic voting system, and that she in despair decides to grab the secret key, or the votes of many voters, and use it as the sensitive information in the attack. Note how this differs from simply proving knowledge of the secret key where the government could dismiss the complaint with various explanations. Here the election cannot be tallied (as planned) and still preserve the privacy of voters.

We stress that the attacker has no intention to leak the information and has no incitement to claim otherwise. The goal is in fact to protect the privacy of voters.

This would of course be illegal, but it is also a form of whistleblowing on an election authority that ignores valid criticism through legitimate channels. Thus, we expect that many citizens would side with the attacker.

Information about how voters cast their votes could also be collected using something as simple as covertly filming voters in the polling station. The attacker would then cast her vote among the last in the election.

Illegal Information. Recall that the key feature of the attack is not that the sensitive information is secret, but that the election authority becomes responsible for publishing it. There are several examples of information that is sometimes publicly available, but not in aggregated form that allows, e.g., searching, and such information can be very difficult to collect without detection.

One example is an attacker that holds a large catalogue of child pornography. Publishing this information would not only be illegal, it could also seriously harm many children and people emotionally and constitute defamation leading to lawsuits.

Another example is sensitive user data from, e.g., forums, social media, infidelity websites, and perhaps more seriously, medical journals. Disclosing medical journals is not only problematic because it violates the privacy of people, it can cause people to lose their jobs and insurance policies. In the case of medical journals the goal could be to force the government to take action to improve the privacy properties of systems to protect the citizens.

In both latter examples, it could be clear that the attacker has no malicious intent and no intention of publishing the data on her own.

3.2   Is This Simply a Form of Extortion?

One may object that the attack is simply a form of extortion aiming to disrupt an election, i.e., the attacker could just as well simply explain that if the election is tallied, then it will publish the sensitive information. However, there are prominent features of the attack that distinguishes it from extortion.

An extortionist must convince the victim that the threat is credible, i.e., that she is willing to publish the data unless the victim stops the election. This is not the case in our attack. As illustrated in the examples above, it can be clear that the attacker has no intention to publish the data.

An extortionist can also change its mind. Thus, it is meaningful to negotiate with her and if she is captured in time, then the attack can be stopped. In our attack on the other hand, not even the attacker can stop the attack after it has been set in motion.

We believe that the distinction is of fundamental importance and changes the way governments can, and should, respond.

4   Encoding Data into the Output of the Election

A closer look at a typical voting system reveals that the bandwidth from the attacker to the output of the election is large. Below we give a non-exhaustive list of ways to encode information, but note that these may be combined if available. An additional factor is who is given access to the information and this is discussed in the next section.

4.1   Write-In Votes

There are two types of votes that are sometimes called write-in, but are quite different in our setting. Both assume that the voter can use a blank ballot and simply write on it the name of their favorite candidate.

Type I assumes that the candidate has been registered in advance, so in the election result such a write-in vote would be indistinguishable from votes cast using pre-printed ballots. A narrow channel of information is given by such ballots if available to the observers, since the candidate name may, e.g., be positioned differently on the ballot paper to encode information, but the ballot is difficult to spot even given access to the tallying.

Type II allows the voter to write anything on a blank ballot, and as long as it can be interpreted as something meaningful when it appears in the election result. This can be used directly to execute the attack if the vote is available to the observers, since the voter can simply write the secret key k used to encrypt the sensitive information as the candidate name. To make sure that the key seems meaningful the attacker can first come up with a randomly chosen name p and hash it to derive the actual secret key k as explained in Example 1.

4.2   Invalid Votes

In our setting invalid votes can be viewed as a form of write-in votes, but with limited information capacity. There are numerous ways to make a vote invalid and how they are processed depends on the type of election, so we can only give some examples to illustrate the problem. In all variations the observers must of course be able to record information about invalid votes.

In countries where detailed statistics about different types of invalid votes are disclosed they are truly a form of write-in votes of Type II in the eyes of the attacker.

In countries where envelopes are used and the observers may witness the counting, the attacker can simply put, or not put, post-it notes of different colors to encode a sequence of bits. Post-it notes stand out in the counting and are easy to spot.

4.3   Bundled Races

Countries that artificially bundle together multiple races create ballots that can be exploited by encoding the key as a list of components of a few bits, where each such component represents a choice in a race. For example, a bundled ballot with three races containing two candidates each can encode three bits. To be of use a larger number of races and/or multiple candidates is needed, but it is not merely the number of possible votes that is important. It is the size of the space of possibilities expected to remain unused by legitimate voters that determines the feasibility of the attack.

4.4   Ranked Elections

In ranked elections a single ballot is used with a large number of different possible votes corresponding to the possible permutations of the available candidates. Variable-basis representations of integers are easily converted to and from more natural representations of permutations and a key may be viewed as an integer, so an arbitrary key can be cast as a vote. These ballots cannot in general be tallied except by revealing a large part of each vote.

4.5   Supporting Evidence

Most voting systems have embedded features for auditing. The auxiliary information provided for auditing can provide a channel for the attacker even if the rest of the election output does not. Thus, the election output must be understood as consisting of all information and all physical artifacts resulting from the tallying of an election. A concrete example could be images of the ballots scanned by ballot scanning machines that could embed information using tiny markings, placement of text, or steganography.

4.6   Elections with a Fixed Set of Candidates

Even in single-seat elections where the election output consists only of the reported election results, the attack may be feasible, but at a higher cost to the adversary in terms of the needed number of corrupted voters. This is best explained by an example.

Example 2. Consider an election with three fixed candidates where the election result is reported per voting district among a large number of voting districts. Assume that the first two candidates get almost all of the votes so that the third candidates get zero votes in most voting districts.

Here an adversary that controls n voters throughout the voting districts that typically receives zero votes for the third candidates can encode bits by simply casting, or abstaining to cast, votes for the third candidate in those districts. A somewhat more expensive encoding with more cast votes can add error correction. A randomized encoding where zero and one are instead encoded as, say more or less than two votes, respectively, gives plausible denial for every individual vote. This may protect the attacker against sanitation of the result under governing laws, since votes of legitimate votes cannot be eliminated.

Note that the example does not require the attacker to register new candidates, but the attack is of course facilitated if this is possible, since it almost guarantees the existence of a candidate that can be expected to get very few votes. In some countries this is unlikely to be the case due to requirements for registering new parties or candidates.

The critical weakness of the election is how the result is reported. If there are only a few large voting districts, then the attack is infeasible.

4.7   Multiple Elections

It is important to understand that the above encodings can not only be combined with each other, but also for multiple elections. If the adversary is unable to encode the needed number of bits into one election, then she may still be able to encode a fraction of the bits in each election. The semantics are changed slightly with this approach since when a key is partially disclosed outside parties may be able to recover the remainder of the key using algorithmic methods.

4.8   Preventing Sanitation

An attacker may worry that authorities sanitize the output of the election in a controlled environment to mitigate the attack. This may be possible apriori depending on who has immediate access and governing laws. To circumvent any such procedures the attacker can use a proof of work to make sure that nobody can recover the key except after a certain suitable amount of time. A trivial way to accomplish this is to only encode part of the secret key k used for encryption. This means that a brute force search for the missing bits of the key is needed to decrypt. This variation shows that there is little value in attempting to sanitize the output of the election by trying to identify the encoding of k, since this can only be done long after the result must be published.

4.9   Access to the Output of the Election

A necessary condition for the attack to succeed is that the sensitive information is revealed to parties that must not have access to it. However, this is a not a black or white property. For example, national security and military secrets *should not* be disclosed to anybody, but it *must not* be disclosed to unfriendly foreign states. Similarly, child pornography can safely, and should be, disclosed to the Police, but must not fall into the hands of the general public.

Thus, to properly analyze the value of the attack and capabilities of the adversary in a given election, we need a comprehensive and detailed understanding of the voting system. This is important, since it is likely to be infeasible to unconditionally mitigate the attack for many election schemes.

The attack relies on the transfer of responsibility. Suppose election workers perform their duties in a closed room and the encoded key only appears in the room. Then if the key is disclosed we can argue that the election workers are culpable and not the election authority or government. This way of looking at the attack may be more or less realistic depending on the nature of the sensitive information.

5   Mitigating the Attack

The best we can hope to achieve may seem to be a voting system that outputs who won the election in a single seat race, or correspondly the distribution of seats in a multi-seat election, but a closer look at democratic systems shows that this is view is naive. The role of an election is not only to distribute seats, but also to communicate the voice of the voters in a broader sense such as fringe opinions and the geographic distribution of supporters of different candidates.

Thus, a more modest goal is that the voting system outputs the election result in the form it is currently output in most voting systems. This can clearly not be achieved if write-in votes are reported as part of the result without prior registration. The number of bundled races and cardinality of ranked elections combined with the number of candidates must also remain small. Furthermore, the result can only be reported for subsets of voters such that the number of votes for each candidate is large enough to hide encoded information in statistical noise provided by the votes of honest voters.

In addition to the above requirements, it must be ensured that no additional part of the output is leaked to the wrong parties. The specifics of this is inherently tied to particular elections, but we can make some general observations.

In elections with a voting envelope we can not allow the counting to be done in public. It is far too simple to insert arbitrary paper content into an envelope. However, it is probably fine to randomly select people from the general population to audit the counting and inform them to not leak any information except that they can dispute the counting.

Statistics about invalid votes should be kept to a minimum and reported in aggregate form and not per voting district or other small regions. The detailed statistics and information should be considered secret.

6   Variations

The attack could possibly be combined with a deliberate manipulation of the election result, and used to dissuade the authorities from publishing information that would indicate the manipulation. The key may be encoded not in the outcome, but in the evidence of the correctness of the outcome leading to a situation where the government is unable to allow a normal audit. Examples in an electronic voting system includes logging information such as timing of various events, flawed inputs, etc.

7   Future Work

There are two natural directions for future work. Firstly, understanding vulnerabilities and developing techniques and procedures that increase the cost of executing the attack is certainly possible, both for traditional and electronic voting systems.

There are also natural theoretical questions to be investigated. A function for which the adversary provides some of the inputs may be viewed as a channel in an information theoretical sense and we could demand that its capacity is low in the worst case, or average case, over the choice of the other inputs. Similarly to the discussion above, in a multiparty computation of the function, we must consider the output to be the complete view of the parties interested in the communicated information.

Acknowledgments. We thank a number of researchers that took part in our early discussions. We also thank civil servants and politicians in government organizations in several countries for their valuable feedback.

A   Situation in Selected Countries

To make things more concrete we briefly discuss how serious the attack is in a handful of countries.

A.1   Australia

Many Australian elections allow each voter to rank many candidates, so each ballot may have about 100! different possibilities. Furthermore, tallying by Single Transferable Vote (STV) generally needs knowledge of most of each permutation—there is no easy way to split up the vote when tallying. Many Australian electoral authorities make complete voting data available on the web, for the very good reason that third parties may independently redo the count.

These sorts of voting systems are also vulnerable to a coercion attack sometimes called the "Italian attack", in which voters are coerced into casting a particular voting pattern. The attack presented in this paper uses a similar feature, namely the large number of possible votes, but in a different way. Hence there is already some literature on how to compute a verifiable STV tally using cryptographic methods without revealing individual votes [2]. These mechanisms would also address the attack described in this paper, though they remain computationally intensive and not integrated into the Australian electoral process.

A.2   A.2 Estonia

A discussion related to the attack took place in Estonia in 2011 when an invalid i-vote was experienced for the first time in the history of Estonian i-voting system. The discussion is presented in [5] 3.1 Case: Invalid I-vote. Executive summary follows. One of the i-votes was registered invalid by the system during the tabulation phase of the Parliamentary Elections on March 6th, 2011.

The analysis of the system error logs showed that the invalid i-vote appeared to be correctly encrypted with the election public key. The reason behind the invalid i-vote could have been a bug in some of the components of the i-voting system, human mistake in the system setup or somebody could have intentionally cast an invalid i-vote (by implementing their own voting client or interfering with the existing one).

Only human mistake in the setup procedures could be excluded without decrypting the i-vote, so the National Electoral Committee (NEC) decided to decrypt the invalid i-vote and examine its contents in hopes to find out the root cause of the problem. The time window between the decision and the planned action gave an opportunity to consider invalid i-vote as a possible attack. If the attacker was aiming for publicity, then the simple scenario allowing manipulation would be used by the attacker himself to decoy the election officials to show whether the NEC – contrary to their claims – can find out who did cast the vote from the contents of the ballot.

If some more sophisticated technique to invalidate the ballot would have been applied, then the contents of the ballot could have been anything from the personal identification of the attacker or personal identification of someone not involved at all to a well formed ballot with an invalid candidate number.

After considering the matter of ballot secrecy and the possibility of an attack against i-voting as such, the NEC reached the conclusion that it would be better not to create a precedent of decrypting one i-vote separately from others. The decision from April 1st was reverted on April 8th.

A.3   A.3 Sweden

In Sweden the elections for parliament, county councils, and municipalities all take place at the same time, but using three distinct ballots and envelopes. Thus, it is not a bundled election. A voter picks a ballot paper with a pre-printed party name and a list of persons. He may make a single mark in front of one of the persons to increase her chances of getting a seat. This is called a "personröst" (person vote).

Votes are then counted and sieved for invalid votes at several levels and all counting is open for the public. The ballot papers are first taken out of their envelopes in the polling station by the election workers. Ballots that are deemed invalid are put back into their envelopes and put in a separate stack. There are exceptions, but broadly speaking a ballot is invalid if it is not formed as described above. The votes are then recounted by another authority before the final result is announced. During the first counting only party votes are counted and the person votes are ignored.

The voting system in Sweden has been reformed in several ways in preparation for the 2018 elections. Fortunately, a side effect of these changes is that the attack presented in this paper is harder to execute. Before the reform a voter could cast a write-in vote for a party or person. As of 2018 all parties and persons must be registered and acknowledge that they are willing to serve if they are elected.

We remark that parties such as "Kalleankapartiet" (Donald Duck party) would always receive a couple of votes and the results from the 2014 election are available at [1]. Although there are no longer any write-in votes (of Type II as defined in Sect. 4.1), an attacker can demand to see invalid votes and she could use post-it notes of multiple colors, corrupt a handful of voters and execute the attack in this way. There is also a fair number of fringe parties that only get a handful of votes and even more individuals listed for the parties that get even fewer votes. Thus, there is plenty of room to encode a key.

The system could be substantially hardened by replacing the public counting with counting in the presence of a randomly selected set of citizens and by not reporting results for parties that receive a small number of votes, or reporting them in aggregated form at a national level if the number of votes increases notably by doing this. Furthermore, a threshold could be introduced to register a party whereby it must be made plausible that it will receive, e.g., a few thousand votes. Such thresholds are already in place in several countries. A similar approach could be used for person votes.

References

1. Swedish Election Authority: Election results 2014. http://www.val.se
2. Benaloh, J., Moran, T., Naish, L., Ramchen, K., Teague, V.: Shuffle-sum: coercion-resistant verifiable tallying for STV voting. IEEE Trans. Inf. Forensics Secur. 4(4), 685–698 (2009)
3. Halderman, J.A., Pereira, O. (eds.): 2012 Electronic Voting Technology Workshop/Workshop on Trustworthy Elections (EVT/WOTE 2012), Bellevue, WA, USA, 6–7 August 2012. USENIX Association (2012)
4. Halderman, J.A., Teague, V.: The New South Wales iVote system: security failures and verification flaws in a live online election. In: Haenni, R., Koenig, R.E., Wikström, D. (eds.) VOTELID 2015. LNCS, vol. 9269, pp. 35–53. Springer, Cham (2015). doi:10.1007/978-3-319-22270-7_3
5. Heiberg, S., Laud, P., Willemson, J.: The application of i-voting for Estonian parliamentary elections of 2011. In: Kiayias, A., Lipmaa, H. (eds.) Vote-ID 2011. LNCS, vol. 7187, pp. 208–223. Springer, Heidelberg (2012). doi:10.1007/978-3-642-32747-6_13
6. Khazaei, S., Terelius, B., Wikström, D.: Cryptanalysis of a universally verifiable efficient re-encryption mixnet. In Halderman and Pereira [3]

Bits or Paper: Which Should Get to Carry Your Vote?

Jan Willemson[1,2](✉)

[1] Cybernetica AS, Ülikooli 2, 51003 Tartu, Estonia
janwil@cyber.ee
[2] Software Technology and Applications Competence Center,
Ülikooli 2, 51003 Tartu, Estonia

Abstract. This paper reviews several aspects where electronic/Internet and paper voting can be compared (vote secrecy, verifiability, ballot box integrity, transparency and trust base). We conclude that for many vulnerabilities of Internet voting systems, there exist related weakness in paper systems as well. The main reason why paper-based elections are perceived as more secure is historical experience. We argue that recent criticism about Internet voting has unfairly concentrated on the associated risks and neglected the benefits. Remote electronic voting lowers the cost of election participation and provides the most secure means for absentee voting. The latter is something that is more and more needed in the contemporary, increasingly mobile world. Hence, we need to give Internet voting a chance, even if it means risking with unknown threats.

1 Introduction

The idea of using electronic means to assist in elections is as old as human use of electricity itself. On June 1, 1869 Thomas A. Edison received U.S. Patent 90,646 for an "electrographic vote-recorder" to be used in Congress elections. The system was never used, and the reason is very instructive – politicians felt that machine-assisted elections would speed up the voting process so much that they would lose their familiar way of verbal discussions about the political matters [8].

The history has shown that, contrary to the fear of the 19th century politicians, advances in technology have provided their modern colleagues with a much wider choice of discussion platforms including radio, TV and Internet. However, a certain amount of conservativism seems to be built into a human nature, and hence many innovations have been met with opposition ranging from caution to active objections.

The idea of casting a vote via electronic means or even via Internet is no exception. Internet voting for example has a potential to change the whole election process so drastically that it must be threatening for at least someone. Improved absentee voting could mobilise many expatriates, a younger generation otherwise indifferent towards paper-based alternatives could start participating in democratic processes more actively, etc. All of these factors have a chance to

© Springer International Publishing AG 2017
R. Krimmer et al. (Eds.): E-Vote-ID 2017, LNCS 10615, pp. 292–305, 2017.
DOI: 10.1007/978-3-319-68687-5_18

bias the unstable political balance that many of the modern democracies seem to have trouble with.

Hence, there are a lot of reasons to retain the *status quo* of the election mechanism. However, the accessibility improvements provided by electronic voting are significant enough that they must at least be considered. The problem from the e-voting opponent's point of view is that the argument of introducing a new bias into the electorate is not a valid counter-argument, at least in front of the public.

Luckily, there are other arguments, with security of the new technologies being on top of the list. Since almost any means of communication can in principle be used for vote transmission, any problem with any of these almost automatically translates into an argument against electronic voting. There is an extensive body of research revealing potential weaknesses in many of the proposed systems and even whole communities devoted to criticising electronic voting[1].

Majority of these e-voting-sceptic initiatives seem to rely on the implicit assumption that the conventional paper-based voting systems are somehow inherently more secure, so that mankind can always fall back to them once all the electronic alternatives are banned. Of course, the history of paper-based election fraud is as old as such systems themselves. Still, the mere fact that life goes on and societies have learnt to limit this fraud on a somewhat reasonable level seems to confirm that paper voting is at least secure enough.

Of course, the *feeling of security* based on historical experience is an important argument when seeking continued acceptance for legacy systems in the society. However, we argue that apart from a longer history, there is little in the paper-based technology itself that ensures its superiority over electronic solutions. Sure, the two have different characteristics and hence possess different strengths and weaknesses, but only comparing strengths of one system to the weaknesses of another is presenting a biased view.

The current paper aims at balancing this discussion. The author argues that even though paper voting seems to limit the fraud on a reasonable level, this level was not pre-set before paper voting systems were designed, but rather adjusted *post factum* to what such systems were capable of providing. There is no reason why we could not do the same thing with electronic voting.

This paper reviews some of the acclaimed security features of the paper-based voting systems, matching them to the criticism against electronic ones. We also point out some (often unfairly neglected) benefits that Internet voting provides over paper elections.

The current paper was partly motivated by the recent report of Springall *et al.* [18] criticising the Estonian Internet voting system. The following discussion can be regarded as one possible reply to that report.

---

[1] Examples of such communities include http://verifiedvoting.org/, http://www.handcountedpaperballots.org/, http://thevotingnews.com/, http://www.votersunite.org/, etc.

2 Vote Secrecy

Vote secrecy is one of the fundamental requirements in contemporary electoral systems with the main aim of limiting manipulation and assuring the freedom of choice for the voter. This requirement has even been considered important enough to mention it in Article 21.3 of the Universal Declaration of Human Rights.[2]

Estonian Internet voting has been criticised for its potential to break vote secrecy if sufficiently many server-side actors collaborate either maliciously or due to an attack [18].

In a typical paper-based voting system, vote secrecy is implemented via anonymous ballot paper. What is typically not advertised while setting up such a system is that on a physical level, fully unidentifiable paper is very difficult to achieve. Real sheets of paper can be fingerprinted based on slight variations in colour or 3D surface texture of paper, requiring only a commodity desktop scanner and custom software [5]. This requires malicious access to the ballot sheets both before and after the vote casting, but isn't malicious activity also what is assumed by Springall *et al.* [18]?

Of course, digital attacks scale better than the physical ones. However, in case of harming vote secrecy the attacker is not necessarily after the scaling effect anyway. Recall that the requirement of secret ballots is established to guarantee voting freedom and non-coercion. On the other hand, coercion is an inherently personal thing. This means that in order to fully utilise a large-scale vote secrecy violation, the attacker would need to additionally take a number of non-scaling real-life steps. This makes paper fingerprinting attacks comparable to digital vote disclosure in terms of effort/effect ratio.

Even if perfectly unidentifiable paper would be possible, paper elections are still susceptible to various types of fraud. Ballot box stuffing is the most well-known example here, but voter impersonation may also lead to problems if an impersonator manages to cast a vote (unfortunately, voter authentication is not always as strong as we would like it to be). In this case a legitimate voter may later discover that a vote has already been submitted on her behalf. If the ballots are completely anonymous, there is no way of recovering from this attack.

With such problems in mind, several countries have made trade-offs between vote secrecy and fraud-resistance. UK, Singapore and Nigeria use serial numbers printed directly on ballots, whereas some others like Canada and Pakistan print serial numbers on the counterfoil.[3]

Ballot numbering in UK has been criticised several times by OSCE/ODIHR [1,2,4], because election officials have the capability of breaching vote secrecy. However, the system is still perceived as secure in the society "because of the high levels of public trust in the integrity of the electoral process" [1].

---

[2] http://www.un.org/en/universal-declaration-human-rights/.

[3] http://aceproject.org/electoral-advice/archive/questions/replies/912993749.

In the author's view, this is an excellent example of the *feeling of security* being based on historical experience rather than rational risk analysis. From the latter point of view, the trusted operational base is much larger, including almost all the election officials, whereas for example the Estonian flavour of Internet voting has only a single point of failure for a large scale vote secrecy violation attack. Sure, a single point of failure makes the stakes higher, but on the other hand it is also much easier to secure, if done properly.

Unfortunately, convincing the public that everything is done properly, is hard. In case of UK, the legislation specifying ballot numbering has been in force since 1872 [1], whereas Internet voting in Estonia has only taken place since 2005. So the difference really comes from generations-long experience which Estonian Internet voting system can not yet possibly have.

For even a clearer comparison, let's go through the following mental argument: If we would take all the requirements that we currently have about paper voting and apply them to early elections, could we call those elections secure? The answer would probably be no, since for example pre-19th century elections did not typically feature vote privacy nor equal suffrage for all the citizens.

Does this mean that all the early elections should be called void and all their results should be disqualified retrospectively? Of course not. It is impossible to build a practical system by first imagining all the restrictions possible. A real working system has to go through its evolution with trial and error.

One may argue that the stakes are too high and that the result may be an election being "hijacked" by a wrong party. In this case, please look at history again. We as mankind have come to where we are through a long series of experiments, including failed ones. This is the nature of development.

3 Individual Verifiability and Ballot Box Integrity

When designing and evaluating Internet voting systems, two properties often required are individual and universal verifiability. Individual verifiability essentially means that any voter can verify that her own vote ended up in the ballot box the way she intended to. Universal verifiability, on the other hand, refers to the situation where anyone is able to check that the ballots in the box(es) have been counted correctly.

In fact, these are reasonable requirements for any kind of a voting system, and paper-based systems should comply with them as well. But how far does this compliance go?

Indeed, everything can be made fine with individual verifiability of paper voting up to the point where the voter drops her ballot into the box. It is possible for a voter to take care marking the ballot the way that it would get counted correctly with high probability. You can even use your own pen that you trust not to have come with self-erasing ink (you never use pens provided in the voting booth, do you?).

Contemporary Internet voting systems also possess the means to get a confirmation from the vote storage server about the safe and sound arrival of the vote. To get around possible vote manipulating malware living on the voter's computer, this confirmation must come via an independent channel. For example, Norwegian Internet voting experiment used SMS as the second channel, whereas the Estonian system uses a mobile device to download and verify the vote [11].

Of course, independence of the voter's PC and mobile device is the crucial assumption here. As mentioned by Springall *et al.*, the strength of the verification claim is decreased if this assumption gets violated [18]. They also point out a way of infecting both devices with coordinated malware when the user connects them for, say, regular data transfer.

What Springall *et al.* do not say is that this attack is something the voter can avoid by informed activity. Just like you should take care when marking the ballot in a readable way, you can choose a verification device that is definitely independent from your PC. The main reason why voters do not do it already is insufficient understanding of the associated risks. Again, we may expect this situation to improve in time when people gather more experience with vulnerabilities of digital communication devices.

The first real difficulty with both paper and electronic ballots manifests itself in the storage stage as the ballot box integrity problem. In case of Estonian Internet voting, integrity of the vote storage server is maintained using organisational measures. One may argue that cryptographic techniques would give a higher level of assurance, and since organisational and cryptographic measures do not exclude each other, this would apparently be true.

But let's look at the ballot box integrity assurance problem in case of paper voting. If a voter wants to make sure that her vote is counted, she must check that her vote was not maliciously removed before counting. The ballot box may be sealed and stamped and the voter may even believe that the seal is checked before counting, but if it was sealed once, there is a technical way to do it again if someone would like to break it in the meantime.

Hence, the only way to be sure that the ballot is still intact is to stay next to the ballot box during the time period between vote casting and counting. The author had a discussion with professor Melanie Volkamer from Darmstadt University, Germany, and she claimed to do exactly that. To make the time frame manageable, she would go to the polling station 5 min before closing and then follow the box to the counting area.

In this way, anyone can in principle observe the polling station workers counting the ballots and later perform the recount him/herself. Can the observer now be 100% sure that his/her vote was included in the final tally? No, unfortunately not.

Human attention is limited and no single person can not observe all the poll workers all the time. So it is still possible for a malicious official to silently put some of the ballots aside and not count them.

Of course, the number of ballots in the box would then be smaller than the number of issued empty ballot sheets, but what do you do? It is legal for a voter to obtain an empty ballot and not to cast a vote, so there is a plausible explanation to this discrepancy.

Hence, if the observer really wants to be sure that his/her vote ended up in the counted-pile, he/she should mark her ballot. However, this introduces another problem – ballot marking can be used as a proof in the act of vote selling. It is possible for a vote buyer to act as a legal observer during the counting and demand to see a ballot with a prearranged sign on it. In Netherlands, for example, a ballot sheet with a mark making it uniquely identifiable may be considered invalid for that reason.

Thus, being sure that your vote safely reaches the counting stage only goes as far as another requirement – vote anonymity for coercion resistance – allows it to. Even if marked ballots are not declared void in some jurisdictions, the mere need for such a measure to check ballot box integrity is a deviation from clean voting practices paper-based elections supposedly provide.

The next problem of universal verifiability, in turn, translates to the question how transparently the vote counting procedure of paper voting can be managed.

4 Transparency and Accuracy of Counting

One of the fundamental properties of paper-based voting is the possibility of independent recount. Ideally, written marks on paper ballots should be the *lingua franca* that every human auditor perceives the same way, so that it will be easy for a group of people to agree on the counting result (even if some of them have a political motivation to bias the result).

However, reality is not that simple. A recent study by Goggin *et al.* [9] has shown that, depending on the paper vote counting method used, the human error rate is roughly between 1–2%. This is more than enough to raise reasonable doubt in close cases, of which the history of democratic elections is very rich. (Just recall the 2000 US presidential elections where the outcome was depending on the convention to be used when counting ambiguous ballots.)

Even if the count is not close, an independent observer may still claim distrust in the accuracy of the result and demand recounting. This opens up opportunities of attacks against the paper vote counting procedure. Namely, the auditor demanding the recount and possibly even performing it may be an attacker himself. Having access to the first result, he knows exactly by how much the second count has to differ to provide a different end result [21]. It is also possible for a dishonest auditor to create havoc just by claiming that his count does not match the previous count(s), and keep doing so for numerous times.

Of course, in practical systems there must be safeguards protecting against such misuses. For example, the guidelines given to the returning officers in UK [3] state:

6.35 You must consider any recount request but by law may refuse if, in your opinion, the request is unreasonable. [...]

This introduces an interesting dilemma between the transparency advertised by the paper-voting advocates, and practical resilience against system misuse. Ultimately, a simple official will decide whether someone is allowed to exercise his/her legal right to become convinced in correct vote counting, or whether such a request is considered erroneous.

One way or another, we can argue that such a guideline is written for a reason. Quite probably once upon a time there was someone who tried to abuse the system by over-exaggerated references to his/her right of vote recount. That person may have been forgotten long ago, but the regulation is still there, expressing the current social agreement about the reasonable limitations to the transparency enforcement. Again, there is no reason why a similar agreement could not be achieved in case of electronic voting. It's just that this medium for vote transmission is yet too young for such a settlement.

Even though the error rates of hand counting and the implied disputes can be decreased by adopting more error resistant practices [9], the errors and disputes will never come down to zero. The root cause of this problem is the fact that a paper vote (unlike its electronic counterpart) has no strictly defined semantics. There will always be people with poor handwriting or intentionally willing to spoil their ballot (and one may even argue that it is their legal right to do so). This in turn means that until we stick with paper voting, there will always be an option for a dispute.

Of course, electronic voting is not free from related problems either, but they have a different nature. Namely, humans are very poor at perceiving bits directly, so they need a mediating device, which may then become a target of attack on its own. For example, a proof-of-concept malware was presented during 2011 Estonian Parliamentary elections changing the visual image displayed to the user on the computer screen, allowing for undetected vote manipulation [10].

Ultimately, the problems with both paper and electronic votes come down to agreeing on a single interpretation by all the parties. As already seen above, with paper votes this is in principle not achievable, since an analogue medium can not have a strict formal meaning. With electronic votes this is at least theoretically possible. However, the problem of agreeing that everyone has the same view on the bits still remains.

This is generally known as a secure bulletin board problem, and despite its simple statement, it turns out to be highly non-trivial to implement. What seems to be the difficult point is achieving consensus about the state of a digital system in a distributed manner.

One interesting option for solving this problem is provided by a public hash block chain in the style of BitCoin [15]. There are properties of vanilla BitCoin protocol that make it less appealing from the viewpoint of voting, like involved financial incentives. But at least as a proof-of-concept it shows that community-wide agreement on a digital asset is possible in practice.

Of course, using a block chain does not prevent all integrity attacks on its own. For example, BitCoin's block chain "history" can be rewritten if more than 50% of the participating peers decide to collaborate. However, even the deprecated/rewritten branches have still been made public, and hence such attacks can easily be detected.

There have already been first attempts of using block chain technology as a part of a voting system. One of the most prominent players is NASDAQ that has offered shareholders a remote voting opportunity, using BitCoin as a public log integrity provider.[4] Another interesting initiative was taken by a minor Danish political party (the Liberal Alliance) that reported using block chain based voting technology during their meeting.[5]

Of course, the problem of shareholder voting is an easier one compared to, say, parliamentary elections, since in the former case the vote secrecy requirement is not that strict. BitCoin provides a privacy layer in the form of pseudonymous public keys, but unfortunately it is not directly usable for real elections, since one user may establish many pseudonyms, hence breaking the one-man-one-vote requirement. Another block chain voting initiative, BitCongress[6], acknowledges this problem and admits that some collaboration with a central voter registration service is still necessary. Other new implementations of block chain based voting systems are being constantly developed, too.[7,8]

There has also been a resent proposal by Culnane and Schneider for a bulletin board implementation targeted specifically for use in e-voting systems not using block chain technology [6]. For correct operations, it relies on a threshold of (a relatively few) computing peers to behave honestly. However, integrity violations can always be detected by means of verifiable receipts, and this is the most important property we expect any voting system to have.

All in all, it seems that the secure bulletin board problem is solvable in practice, allowing at least in principle higher accuracy of counting than the paper voting can ever provide.

5   Trust Base

Elections are an inherently social thing, involving millions of people, registration lists, ballots, logistics, counting, etc. This means that no single person can do it all, we have to rely on someone.

Relying implicitly assumes trust and this in turn makes attacking elections really simple. You tell me what/whom you trust, I tell you I manipulate that entity and my attack is complete.

This is the essence of the most severe claims that Springall *et al.* make about Estonian Internet voting [18]. So you say that you use some computer to write server installation disks? Good, then we say we can attack that one. Or you say that you rely on SHA-256 hashes to prove integrity of these images? Excellent,

---

[4] http://www.coindesk.com/nasdaq-shareholder-voting-estonia-blockchain/.
[5] https://www.cryptocoinsnews.com/blockchain-voting-used-by-danish-political-party/.
[6] http://www.bitcongress.org/.
[7] https://followmyvote.com/.
[8] http://www.unchain.voting/.

then we can implement our own phony hash application. It does not matter if you record all the server installation on the video and put it up on YouTube for everyone to watch, there will always be something happening behind the scenes before you start filming, and that's what we are claiming to attack.

So all in all, the struggle goes over the trust base. What you do not usually read in the papers such as [18] is that the trust base of paper voting has a much more complex structure than the one of, say, voting over Internet. You implicitly trust all the people who count the votes to do their job correctly, you trust the paper manufacturers that they have not included tiny identifying marks on the ballots, you trust the storage facility owner that some of the packages with ballots do not mysteriously disappear, etc.

It is true that Internet voting concentrates a lot of trust around relatively few components (like central servers and their administrators). Hence the attackers have clear targets and can expect relatively larger effects if their attacks succeed [13].

On the other hand, such a trust concentration makes the crucial components of Internet voting also easier to guard. For example background checks of server administrators have to be very thorough, but there is only a rather limited number of them.

At the same time, the number of people involved in hand counting easily reaches tens of thousands of individuals for large elections. There is some redundancy in the form of recounting, but there is a limit to that, too. Hence, in order to manipulate the election result, an attacker has to bribe far less than 10,000 people. Even worse, the number of subsets of counting officials that may give rise to undetected fraud is huge, and no-one is able to check all of them for honesty.

Stating it otherwise, the problem of one person being unable to check the count of millions of ballots does not go away that easily. As a solution, risk-limiting audits proposed by Philip Stark have recently become very popular [19]. The underlying idea is simple – using a predefined correctness threshold, a statistical sample of ballots is selected and manually recounted. If the threshold is not met, more ballots are selected, etc. In the worst case, this method may end up selecting all the ballots, but hopefully it will finish much earlier. For example, after EU Parliament elections in Denmark, risk-limiting auditing was used and only 1903 ballots were required to be studied to obtain 99.9% confidence level [20].

Does this mean that risk-limiting audits reduce our trust assumptions? Not really. In order to perform the statistical test, a random sample needs to be generated. This means that we need to trust (=can attack) the random number generator and manipulate it to give us the seed that the attacker needs to prove that his version of the count is correct.

People preparing the Danish 2014 audit actually thought about this problem and established a dice-throwing ceremony that determined the seed. The ceremony was also recorded and the video was made publicly available.

However, the "I claim to attack what's behind the scenes" approach still applies. We do not know how many attempts of filming this video were made until a suitable random seed was generated. We do not know where the dice came from and whether they were fair or not. So all of a sudden, the dice manufacturer and supplier are added to the trust base. Is this really what people had in mind when introducing post-election statistical auditing? Not necessarily.

When comparing the trust bases of paper and Internet voting, the comparison ultimately boils down to the questions like which one is harder to manipulate without detection – dice or SHA-256 hash implementation? The answer is far from being straightforward or clear.

6   Cost vs. Benefit

Even though many of the risks of Internet voting are not new and have accepted analogues in paper-based systems, this is not true universally. The two are fundamentally different as a horse and a train, even though they serve the same purpose.

However, when emphasising threats posed by remote electronic voting, many esteemed researchers including Rivest *et al.* [8] and Springall, Halderman *et al.* [18] present the situation in a biased light.

Namely, they concentrate on *cost* (in terms of potential problems) instead of a more balanced *cost-benefit* analysis. Following similar reasoning, it would never make sense to invest any money, take a plane or even go outside, since these actions involve risks. However, in reality we do all of those things, because we estimate the gains exceeding the potential losses.

When taking such decisions, we can rarely rely on precise scientific measurement. Often the scale for such a measure can not even be properly defined. Is it riskier to starve to death or catch a flu while shopping for food? Is it worse to leave more people without a convenient voting method or to risk that a hostile neighbouring country hacks its way into your government? There is no single answer. In fact, the answer depends on subjective risk estimation, and this differs from country to county, from person to person.

Coming back to the Estonian context, there definitely is a big neighbouring country with its clear geopolitical agenda. However, would hacking the Internet voting system be the easiest way to achieve its goals? Again, there is no clear answer. But the author argues that bribing local politicians or using overwhelming military power (and hoping that NATO is willing to give up Estonia, avoiding World War III) are still good alternatives to consider.

More importantly, as said above, we also need to look at the potential benefits. One of the clearest gains of Internet voting is solving the absentee problem. In 2001, Ron Rivest wrote:

> In my opinion, however, by allowing such an increase in absentee voting we have sacrificed too much security for the sake of voter convenience. While voters should certainly be allowed to vote by absentee ballot in cases of need, allowing voting by absentee ballot merely for convenience seems wrongheaded. I would prefer seeing "Voting Day" instituted as a national holiday to seeing the widespread adoption of unsupervised absentee or remote electronic voting [16].

These words nicely illustrate the way people lived just 15 years ago. However, the world has changed a lot since then. Moving abroad is not a matter of convenience, but for many of us it is a need to find a job. For instance, according to Eurostat, on January 1st 2016, in EU there were 19.3 million persons who had been born in a different EU Member State from the one where they were resident.[9] It is unrealistic to assume that all those people would move back to their country of origin just for the voting day. The question that the above-cited researchers [8,16,18] conveniently ignore is how should these people vote.

One way or another, overseas voters must be given the means to exercise their civil right and duty. In US, this is done under the Uniformed and Overseas Citizens Absentee Voting Act. As of 2016, 32 states out of 50 states allow some form of electronic transmission of ballots over the Internet [12] like downloading, filling and submitting PDF forms via fax or e-mail.[10]

Security of this method is, on the other hand, still comparable to 19-century postal voting. Strength of authentication is questionable, transmission lines are vulnerable to tampering and voter coercion is insufficiently addressed.

As long as absentee voting is marginal, these problems may be ignored, but this is no more the case. Despite its researcher-backed rhetoric, even US is doing vote transmission over the Internet, and there is in fact no real alternative (see [14] for a further discussion on the comparison of Internet and postal voting).

There are also benefits in Internet voting for the people who have not migrated, but have stayed. In many parts of the world (including Estonia), a strong drive towards urbanisation can be observed. A lot of people move to bigger cities, because the infrastructure is much better there, the salaries are higher, etc. The remaining population in rural areas is no more sufficient to justify running the schools, cultural centres, shops, post offices, etc. As a result, many of these institutions have been closed down recently in rural Estonia.

An unfortunate side effect for elections is that in such places, there is no more location to put the polling station into. Also, there are no more school teachers who used to act as polling station workers. The only alternative is to travel a relatively long distance to a county capital to cast a vote, and the cost of this is the higher, the further away the voters live.

A recent study by Solvak and Vassil [17] has shown that in Estonia, the probability of being an Internet voter reaches over 50% as soon as the round trip duration to the polling station increases over 30 min. Following Rivest, we can declare all the people who do not undertake this trip as being too convenience-oriented, but the sad fact is that decrease in rural population has also made public transportation considerably less available in those areas, making participation in paper elections simply too costly.

All in all, we see that compared to the conventional alternative, casting votes over Internet increases availability and (if done properly) also security of absentee

---

[9] http://ec.europa.eu/eurostat/statistics-explained/index.php/Migration_and_migra nt_population_statistics.

[10] https://www.sec.state.ma.us/ele/elemil/milidx.htm.

voting. Additionally, it decreases the cost of participation in elections, allowing to make the whole process more accessible for example in rural areas.

7   Conclusions

Voting on paper and by using the assistance of machines are two very different things. Hence, their risk and trust models differ also by a fair margin; in fact to an extent where comparing them becomes very complicated.

With paper voting, security assumptions are largely social (a person is able to mark the ballot correctly, another person is able/willing to count it the intended way, a third person verifies the counting fairly, a fourth one keeps a good guard of the key for a ballot storage facility, etc.). In case of machine (and especially Internet) voting, digital threats become prominent. The more a voting system relies on electronic means, the more an attacker is able to utilise scalability of digital attacks.

Mankind has been relying on voting with paper medium for centuries. Its properties and potential vulnerabilities are considered to be known and threats are considered as mitigated to an acceptable level by the current legislation.

Electronic means of communications and data processing are only a few decades old. We have not yet seen all the evil that can be done with them, and hence we tend to over-estimate the risks compared to what we feel comfortable with.

Unfortunately, there is no *a priory* measure for the margin of this over-estimation. The only reliable way to see which problems occur in practice and how severe they are is to try the whole system out live.

Yes, there are risks involved, but these are inevitable if we want to move the state of the art forward. Recall the loss of two British Overseas Airways Corporation Comet airliners in 1954 [7]. These planes were revolutionary in their own time, having some of the first commercial jet engines, pressurised cabins, etc. Yet, they came crashing down. The reason established after a long series of tests was that microscopic production defects were amplified in the corners of the rectangular doors and windows. Thanks to that study, airplane windows now have round corners.

Would it have been possible to predict those crashes? Theoretically, yes – mathematical methods required to model stresses in surfaces had been developed by that time already. But in practice there are so many aspects to consider that ultimately the deployment in a real environment is what determines what is important and what is not.

Of course, this does not mean that we should leave all the known vulnerabilities wide open for everyone to exploit. But waiting until the implementation is theoretically perfect is not an option either. Requirements set to elections in general are contradictory in nature (like vote secrecy vs full auditability), so there will always exist a security definition according to which a given system is not secure. Likewise, there will always be some parts of the setup that the voter will have to trust as given, and hence critically-minded researchers will have an eternal chance to write papers about breaking them.

But let's remember that this holds true universally and not only for electronic voting. The only aspect where paper voting is really superior to its electronic sibling is its centuries-long head start. But if we do not give electronic voting a chance, we will also miss all the opportunities of increased accessibility, lowered cost of participation and fully repeatable counting which, contrary to the paper voting, really is doable by everyone.

I'd like to conclude the paper with a thought by the creator of Helios Internet voting system Ben Adida who stated during the panel of EVT/WOTE'11 conference:

Internet Voting is terrifying, but it may be inevitable.

Indeed, the world has changed a lot in recent years. People move around freely and we can not assume any more that all of our citizens are born, live their lives and die in close proximity of the polling station. As a result, absentee voting is going from an exception to a rule.

So instead of attacking the inevitable, let's concentrate on making it as secure as possible by introducing strong cryptographic authentication tokens, improving digital ballot box integrity and developing verifiability techniques.

And last but not least – let's remember that personal security is largely a *feeling* that can be supported by voter education and positive experience. Our children will not question Internet voting the way we do, since for them it will have always been existing.

Acknowledgements. The author is grateful to Melanie Volkamer, Sven Heiberg and Arnis Paršovs for useful and inspiring discussions.

The research leading to these results has received funding from the European Regional Development Fund through Estonian Centre of Excellence in ICT Research (EXCITE) and the Estonian Research Council under Institutional Research Grant IUT27-1.

References

1. United Kingdom of Great Britain and Northern Ireland. General election 5 May 2005. OSCE/ODIHR Assessment Mission Report, May 2005. http://www.osce.org/odihr/elections/uk/16204
2. United Kingdom of Great Britain and Northern Ireland. General election 6 May 2010. OSCE/ODIHR Election Assessment Mission Report, May 2010. http://www.osce.org/odihr/elections/69072
3. Part E - Verifying and counting the votes. UK Parliamentary general election in Great Britain on 7 May 2015: guidance for (Acting) Returning Officers, May 2015. http://www.electoralcommission.org.uk/_data/assets/pdf_file/0006/175389/Part-E-Verifying-and-counting-the-votes.pdf
4. United Kingdom of Great Britain and Northern Ireland. General election 7 May 2015. OSCE/ODIHR Election Expert Team Final Report, May 2015. http://www.osce.org/odihr/elections/uk/174081

5. Calandrino, J.A., Clarkson, W., Felten, E.W.: Some consequences of paper finger-printing for elections. In: EVT/WOTE (2009)
6. Culnane, C., Schneider, S.: A peered bulletin board for robust use in verifiable voting systems. In: 2014 IEEE 27th Computer Security Foundations Symposium (CSF), pp. 169–183. IEEE (2014)
7. Fearon, P.: The growth of aviation in Britain. J. Contemp. History **20**(1), 21–40 (1985)
8. Gerck, E., Neff, C.A., Rivest, R.L., Rubin, A.D., Yung, M.: The business of electronic voting. In: Syverson, P. (ed.) FC 2001. LNCS, vol. 2339, pp. 243–268. Springer, Heidelberg (2002). doi:10.1007/3-540-46088-8_21
9. Goggin, S.N., Byrne, M.D., Gilbert, J.E.: Post-election auditing: effects of procedure and ballot type on manual counting accuracy, efficiency, and auditor satisfaction and confidence. Election Law J. **11**(1), 36–51 (2012)
10. Heiberg, S., Laud, P., Willemson, J.: The application of l-voting for estonian parliamentary elections of 2011. In: Kiayias, A., Lipmaa, H. (eds.) Vote-ID 2011. LNCS, vol. 7187, pp. 208–223. Springer, Heidelberg (2012). doi:10.1007/978-3-642-32747-6_13
11. Heiberg, S., Willemson, J.: Verifiable internet voting in Estonia. In: 2014 6th International Conference on Electronic Voting: Verifying the Vote (EVOTE), pp. 1–8. IEEE (2014)
12. Horwitz, S.: More than 30 states offer online voting, but experts warn it isn't secure. The Washington Post, May 016
13. Jefferson, D.: If i can shop and bank online, why can't i vote online? https://www.verifiedvoting.org/resources/internet-voting/vote-online/
14. Krimmer, R., Volkamer, M.: Bits or paper? Comparing remote electronic voting to postal voting. In: Electronic Government - Workshop and Poster Proceedings of the Fourth International EGOV Conference, pp. 225–232 (2005)
15. Noizat, P.: Blockchain electronic vote. In: Lee Kuo Chuen, D. (ed.) Handbook of Digital Currency. Elsevier, London (2015). Chap. 22
16. Rivest, R.L.: Electronic voting. In: Financial Cryptography, vol. 1, pp. 243–268 (2001)
17. Solvak, M., Vassil, K.: E-voting in Estonia: Technological Diffusion and Other Developments Over Ten Years (2005–2015). University of Tartu, Johan Skytte Institute of Political Studies (2016)
18. Springall, D., Finkenauer, T., Durumeric, Z., Kitcat, J., Hursti, H., MacAlpine, M., Halderman, J.A.: Security analysis of the Estonian internet voting system. In: Proceedings of the 2014 ACM SIGSAC Conference on Computer and Communications Security, pp. 703–715. ACM (2014)
19. Stark, P.B.: Conservative statistical post-election audits. Ann. Appl. Stat. **2**, 550–581 (2008)
20. Stark, P.B., Teague, V.: Verifiable european elections: risk-limiting audits for d'hondt and its relatives. USENIX J. Election Technol. Syst. (JETS) **1**, 18–39 (2014)
21. Yasinsac, A., Bishop, M.: The dynamics of counting and recounting votes. IEEE Secur. Priv. **6**(3), 22–29 (2008)

Estonian Voting Verification Mechanism Revisited Again

Ivo Kubjas[1], Tiit Pikma[1], and Jan Willemson[2,3](✉)

[1] Smartmatic-Cybernetica Centre of Excellence for Internet Voting,
Ülikooli 2, 51003 Tartu, Estonia
{ivo,tiit}@ivotingcentre.ee
[2] Cybernetica AS, Ülikooli 2, 51003 Tartu, Estonia
janwil@cyber.ee
[3] Software Technology and Applications Competence Center,
Ülikooli 2, 51003 Tartu, Estonia

Abstract. Recently, Muş, Kiraz, Cenk and Sertkaya proposed an improvement over the present Estonian Internet voting vote verification scheme [6]. This paper points to the weaknesses and questionable design choices of the new scheme. We show that the scheme does not fix the vote privacy issue it claims to. It also introduces a way for a malicious voting application to manipulate the vote without being detected by the verification mechanism, hence breaking the cast-as-intended property. As a solution, we propose modifying the protocol of Muş *et al.* slightly and argue for improvement of the security guarantees. However, there is inherent drop in usability in the protocol as proposed by Muş *et al.*, and this issue will also remain in our improved protocol.

1 Introduction

Estonia is one of the pioneers in Internet voting. First feasibility studies were conducted already in early 2000s, and the first legally binding country-wide election event with the option of casting the vote over Internet was conducted in 2005. Up to 2015, this mode of voting has been available on every one of the 8 elections. In 2014 European Parliament and 2015 Parliamentary elections, more than 30% of all the votes were cast over Internet [7].

During the period 2005–2011, the basic protocol stayed essentially the same, mimicking double envelope postal voting. The effect of the inner envelope was achieved by encrypting the vote with server's public key, and the signed outer envelope was replaced by using a national eID signing device (ID card, Mobile-ID or Digi-ID) [1].

In 2011, several potential attacks were observed against this rather simple scheme. The most significant one of them was developed by a student who implemented proof-of-concept malware that could have either changed or blocked the vote without the voter noticing it.

To counter such attacks, an individual verification mechanism was developed for the 2013 elections [5]. The mechanism makes use of an independent mobile

© Springer International Publishing AG 2017
R. Krimmer et al. (Eds.): E-Vote-ID 2017, LNCS 10615, pp. 306–317, 2017.
DOI: 10.1007/978-3-319-68687-5_19

computing device that downloads the vote cryptogram from the storage server and brute forces it using the encryption random seed, obtained from the voter's computer via a QR code. The value of the vote corresponding to the downloaded cryptogram is then displayed on the device screen, and the voter has to make the decision about its match to her intent in her head.

The complete voting and verification protocol is shown in Fig. 1.

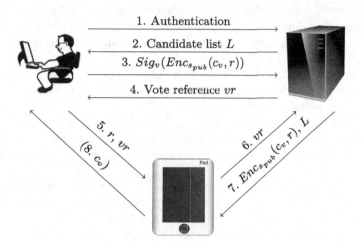

1. Authentication

2. Candidate list L

3. $Sig_v(Enc_{s_{pub}}(c_v, r))$

4. Vote reference vr

5. r, vr

(8. c_v)

6. vr

7. $Enc_{s_{pub}}(c_v, r), L$

Fig. 1. Estonian Internet voting and verification protocol

In the figure, c_v stands for the voter's choice, r is the random seed used for encryption, vr is the vote reference used to identify the vote on the server and s_{pub} is the election system's public key.

A recent report by Muş *et al.* [6] discusses the Estonian vote verification scheme and draws attention to its weak privacy properties. It also proposes an improvement over the existing system (we will give technical details of the proposal in Sect. 2.2). The first objective of this paper is to dispute the motivation of [6] and show vulnerabilities of the proposed improvement. Finally, in Sect. 3 we will also show how a relatively small modification of the protocol presented in [6] will help to remove these vulnerabilities.

2 Analysis of the Scheme by Muş *et al.*

2.1 Assumptions and Motivation of [6]

Individual vote verification was introduced to Estonian Internet voting scheme in 2013 to detect potential vote manipulation attacks in the voter's computer [1,5]. It was never designed as a privacy measure for a very simple reason.

Since the verification application needs access to the QR code displayed on the screen of the voter's computer, verification can only happen in close physical proximity of the voting action.[1] But if this is the case, the verifier can anyway observe the vote on the computer screen. For this reason we disagree that the potential privacy leak from the verification application makes vote buying attacks easier, as claimed in [6].

It is true that a malicious verification application sending the vote out of the device would be unintended behaviour. However, the authors of [6] make several debatable assessments analysing this scenario.

Firstly they claim that "all voter details including the real vote are displayed by the verification device." In fact, up to the 2015 parliamentary elections, the vote has been the *only* piece of data actually displayed. Note that following the protocol [5], the verification device only obtains the vote encrypted with the voting system's public key. The signature is being dropped before the cryptogram is sent out for verification from the server, so the verification device has no idea whose vote it is actually verifying.

The reason for this design decision was the problem that back in 2011 when the development of the new protocol started, less than half of the mobile phones used were smartphones. Hence the protocol needed to support verification device sharing.

However, such an anonymised verification procedure is vulnerable to attacks where, say, a coalition of malicious voting applications manipulates a vote and submits a vote cryptogram from another voter for verification. This way they can match the voter verification expectation, even though the actual vote to be counted has been changed.

To counter such attacks, the protocol to be used in 2017 for Estonian local municipal elections will be changed [2]. Among other modifications, the verification app will get access to the vote signature and the identity of the voter will be displayed on the screen of the verification device. Thus the privacy issue pointed out by Muş *et al.* has not been as problematic previously, but starting from 2017 its importance will rise.

Second, the authors of [6] argue that verification privacy leaks may be aggregated to obtain the partial results of the election before it has concluded. We feel that this scenario is too far-fetched. First, only about 4% of the Internet voters actually verify their votes [3]. Also, nothing is known about the preference biases the verifiers may have, so the partial results obtained would be rather low-quality. There are much easier, better-quality and completely legal methods of obtaining the result (like polls). Hence this part of the motivation is not very convincing.

Third, getting the user to accept a malicious verification application from the app store is not as trivial as the report [6] assumes. For example Google Play store displays various reliability information about the application like the number it has been installed and the average mark given by the users. When the voter sees several competing applications, a smaller number of installations

---

[1] Of course we assume here that the voter's computer is honest in the sense that it does not send the QR code anywhere else. But if it would be willing to do so in order to break the voter's privacy, it could already send away the vote itself.

should already give the first hint that this is not the officially recommended verification app.

At the time of this writing (July 2017), the official application "Valimised"[2] is the only one under that or similar name, with more than 10,000 installations and an average score of about 3.6 points out of 5. If the attacker wants to roll out his own version, he would need to beat those numbers first. Occurrence of an alternative verification app is completely acceptable *per se*, but it will be widely visible. App stores can and are being constantly monitored, and any independent verification apps would undergo an investigation. In case malicious behaviour is detected, the malicious applications can be requested to be removed from the app store.

However, it is true that at this point the protocol relies on organisational measures, not all of which (like removing a malicious app from the official app store) are under control of the election management body. Organisational aspects can probably never be fully removed from the security assumptions of elections, but decreasing the number of such assumptions is definitely a desirable goal.

All in all, we agree that privacy enhancement of the Estonian vote verification mechanism would be desirable. Hence the initiative by Muş *et al.* is welcome, but their approach needs further improvements that we will discuss in this paper.

2.2 Description of the Scheme

The scheme proposed in [6] extends the Estonian vote verification protocol by adding another parameter q to the scheme. The role of q is to serve as a random, voter-picked verification code that will be encrypted using the hash of the vote cryptogram $h = H(Enc_{s_{pub}}(c_v, r))$ as a symmetric key (see Fig. 2).

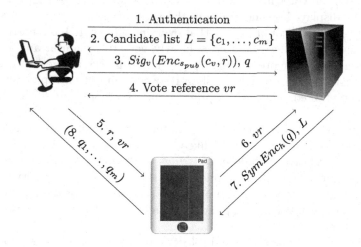

Fig. 2. Proposed update to the Estonian protocol

---

[2] "Valimised" means "Elections" in Estonian.

The verification mechanism will also be altered accordingly. In the original Estonian verification scheme, the verification application goes through the candidate list and tries to re-create vote cryptogram, using the random seed obtained from the voting application via a QR code. In the modification proposed by [6], the candidate list is also traversed in a similar manner, but the hashes of all the vote cryptogram candidates are used as symmetric keys to try to decrypt q.

The trick is that even an incorrect symmetric decryption key leads to some sort of a decrypted value q_i, so that the task of the verifier becomes recognizing the correct one in the list of decrypted values $q_1, q_2, \ldots, q_m$ (where m is the number of election candidates) displayed to her.

More formally, let us have the candidate list $L = \{c_1, c_2, \ldots, c_m\}$. The verification application computes $h_i = H(Enc_{s_{pub}}(c_i, r))$ for $i = 1, 2, \ldots, m$ and displays the list $\{q_1, q_2, \ldots, q_m\}$ where

$$q_i = SymDec_{h_i}(SymEnc_h(q)) \quad (i = 1, 2, \ldots, m) . \tag{1}$$

The voter accepts verification if $q = q_i$, where c_i was the candidate of her choice.

2.3 Analysis of the Scheme – Privacy and Usability

Even though clever conceptually, the scheme of Muş et al. fails in usability, and this will unfortunately lead to considerable weakening of the protocol.

First and foremost, humans are notoriously poor random number generators [8]. This is also acknowledged by the authors of the scheme, so they propose not to require the user to generate the entire value of q, but only 32 rightmost bits denoted as q_{right}. The remaining bits q_{left} would be generated by the voting application, so that $q = q_{\text{left}} \parallel q_{\text{right}}$. In the authors' vision, the 32 bits could be asked from the voter in the form of 4 characters, and these characters would later also be displayed on the screen of the verification device.

Such an approach would assume that every possible byte has a corresponding keyboard character. However, this is clearly not true. Capital and lower-case letters, numbers and more common punctuation marks altogether give about 70–75 symbols, which amounts to slightly over 6 bits of entropy. Hence, four-letter human entered codes can in practice have no more than 25 bits worth of randomness.

Achieving this theoretical maximum assumes that humans would select every character for every position equally likely and independently. This is clearly not the case, and a relatively small set of strings like "1234", "aaaa" or "qwer" may be expected to occur much more frequently than others. This observation gives the first simple attack against the proposed scheme – the attacker can observe the output of the verification application and look for some of these frequent codes.

Even if the voter takes care and selects a rather random-looking 4-character pattern, the attacker still has a remarkable edge. Namely, when the 32-bit parts of the decrypted values are converted into characters, some of these characters may fall out of the ~75 character set. In fact, several of the 256 possible byte values do not have a printable character assigned to them at all. Spotting such a code, the adversary can disregard that one immediately.

To give a rough quantification of the attacker's success probability, assume that the set $\mathcal{C}$ of characters used by the voter to input a code consists of 75 elements. When in the Eq. (1) we have $h \neq h_i$, the resulting values q_i (and their 4-byte code parts $q_{i,\text{right}}$) are essentially random (assuming the underlying symmetric encryption-decryption primitive behaves as a pseudorandom permutation).

This means that the probability that one single character of an incorrect $q_{i,\text{right}}$ falls outside of the set $\mathcal{C}$ is $\frac{256-75}{256} \approx 0.707$. The probability that at least one of the four characters falls outside of this set is

$$ 1 - \left(1 - \frac{256 - 75}{256} \right)^4 \approx 0.993 $$

which is very-very high. The attacker will have an excellent chance of spotting the correct code, since with very high probability there are only very few candidates $q_{i,\text{right}}$ that have all the characters belonging to the set $\mathcal{C}$. This observation completely breaks the privacy claims of [6].

Another usability problem is the need to display the list of all candidate values of q_{right} on the screen of the verification device. The list has the same number of elements as there are candidates in a given district. In case of Estonian elections, this number varies between tens and hundreds, with the most extreme cases reaching over 400. It is unrealistic to expect the voter to scroll through this amount of unintuitive values on a small screen.

Even worse – when the user really scrolls through the list until her candidate of choice has been found, we obtain a side channel attack. A malicious verification device may observe the moment when the user stops scrolling, making an educated guess that the correct candidate number must have then been displayed on the screen. This attack does not lead to full disclosure, but may still reveal the voter's party preference when the candidates of one party are listed sequentially (as they are in the Estonian case).

2.4 Vote Manipulation Attack

The core motivation of introducing an individual verifiability mechanism is to detect vote manipulation attacks by a malicious voting application. In this Section we show that with the updates proposed by Muş et al., vote manipulation attacks actually become very easy to implement.

Consider an attack model where the attacker wants to increase the number of votes for a particular candidate c_j by manipulating the voting application or its operational environment. The key to circumventing detection by the verification mechanism is to observe that the voting application has a lot of freedom when choosing two random values – r for randomizing the encryption and q_{left} for padding the voter-input code. By choosing these values specifically (even the freedom of choosing r is sufficient), a malicious voting application can make the vote it submitted for c_j to verify as a vote for almost any other candidate c_i.

To implement the attack, the attacker needs a pre-computation phase. During this phase, the attacker fixes his preferred choice c_j and the encryption randomness $r^\star \in \mathcal{R}$, and computes $h = H(Enc_{s_{pub}}(c_j, r^\star))$. The attacker can also set his own q arbitrarily, say, $q = 00\ldots0$.

For every possible pair of voter choice $c_i \in L$ and $q_{\text{right}} \in \{0, 1, \ldots, 2^{32} - 1\}$, the attacker tries to find a suitable encryption randomness $r_{i,q_{\text{right}}}$ that would give the last 32 bits of q' being equal to q_{right}, where

$$h' = H(Enc_{s_{pub}}(c_i, r_{i,q_{\text{right}}})) \quad \text{and} \quad q' = SymDec_{h'}(SymEnc_h(00\ldots0)). \quad (2)$$

If the attacker succeeds in finding such a $r_{i,q_{\text{right}}}$, then later during the voting phase he casts his vote to the server as $Enc_{s_{pub}}(c_j, r^\star)$, but sends $r_{i,q_{\text{right}}}$ to the verification application. This random seed will cause the voter picked q_{right} to occur next to the voter's choice c_i. The leftmost non–voter chosen bits of q' would not match, but they are not important, since they are not shown to the voter anyway.

The pre-computed values of encryption randomness for all candidates can be tabulated as in Table 1.

Table 1. Pre-computation dictionary

q_{right}	choice c_i	$r_{i,q_{\text{right}}}$
0	c_1	$r_{1,0}$
$\vdots$	$\vdots$	$\vdots$
$2^{32} - 1$	c_1	$r_{1,2^{32}-1}$
0	c_2	$r_{2,0}$
$\vdots$	$\vdots$	$\vdots$
$2^{32} - 1$	c_2	$r_{2,2^{32}-1}$
$\vdots$	$\vdots$	$\vdots$
0	c_m	$r_{m,0}$
$\vdots$	$\vdots$	$\vdots$
$2^{32} - 1$	c_m	$r_{m,2^{32}-1}$

Note that only the last column of this table needs to be stored. Hence the size of required storage is $2^{32} m \log_2 |\mathcal{R}|$, where $\log_2 |\mathcal{R}|$ is the number of bits required for representing elements in the randomness space $\mathcal{R}$. In practice, the length of the random value is not more than 2048 bits. This means that the size of the database is $1024m$ GB. By restricting the randomness space (for example, by fixing some bits of the random value), we can decrease the table size.

Another option of limiting the storage requirement is referring to the observations described in Sect. 2.3. Human users will not be able to make use of the whole 2^{32} element code space, but at most 2^{25}. This will bring the storage requirement down 2^7 times to only $8m$ GB. If the attacker is willing to settle only with the most common codes, the table will become really small.

Even without reducing the table size, storing it is feasible as hard drives of several TB are readily available. A malicious voting application only needs one online query per vote to this database, hence the attacker can for example set the query service up in a cloud environment.

There are several possible strategies for filling Table 1. We suggest starting from the choice and randomness columns (selecting the randomness truly randomly) and computing the corresponding q_{right} values. In the latter case the computation complexity of the pre-computation phase is $2^{32}m$ times one asymmetric encryption, one hash function application and one symmetric decryption (see Eq. (2)). This amount of computation is feasible even for an ordinary office PC.

This strategy is not guaranteed to 100% succeed, since we may hit the same value of q_{right} for different inputs $r_{i,q_{\text{right}}}$. To estimate the success probability, consider generating the table for a fixed election candidate c_i. Let us generate $N = 2^{32}$ random values and use them to compute the corresponding values q_{right} using the Eq. (2).

The probability of one specific q_{right} *not* being hit in one attempt is $\frac{N-1}{N}$. Consequently, the probability of *not* hitting it in N attempts is

$$\left(\frac{N-1}{N}\right)^N \approx \frac{1}{e}.$$

Hence, the expected probability of hitting one specific value at least once is $1 - \frac{1}{e} \approx 0.63$.

By linearity of expectation, we may conclude that using $2^{32}m$ computation rounds, about 63% of the whole table will be filled.

This percentage can be increased allowing more time for computations. For example, if we would make twice as many experiments, we would get the expected success probability

$$1 - \left(\frac{N-1}{N}\right)^{2N} \approx 1 - \frac{1}{e^2} \approx 0.86.$$

Allowing four times more computation time would give us already more than 98% of the values for q_{right} filled.

Hence we obtain a vote manipulation attack by a malicious voting application with very high success rate, essentially invalidating Theorem 2 of [6].

Note that in order to implement this attack, it is not necessary to manipulate the actual voting application. It is sufficient for the attacker to be able to only change the values of the vote, random seed and q. He can achieve this e.g. by manipulating suitable bytes in voter computer's memory, similar to the vote invalidation attack from 2015 Estonian Parliamentary elections [4]. The random value transferred from the voting application to the verification application can be manipulated by overlaying the QR code that carries it on the voter computer's screen similar to the Student's Attack of 2011 [1].

3   Improving the Protocol

Analyzing the attacks presented above we see that the major vulnerabilities of the scheme presented in [6] were enabled by the fact that the voter herself had to choose q. This allowed both privacy leakage due to format guessing of q_{right} and fooling the verification application via carefully crafting the value of q.

Fixing these flaws starts from the observation that it is actually not necessary for the voter to select q (or q_{right}). We propose a solution where q is generated by the server instead and later sent to the voter application to display. Note that the cryptogram $SymEnc_h(q)$ can be computed by the server, too. Hence the overall change required to the high-level description given in Sect. 2.2 is relatively small. On Fig. 2, q will be dropped from message 3, and will be sent from the server to the voter application in a later pass.

Selection of the exact message pass for sending q is a question of design choice, subject to trade-offs. The first obvious candidate is message number 4 of Fig. 2, where q can be added to the vote reference vr.

The next choice one has to make is when to display the code to the voter. This choice is potentially privacy critical. Displaying q on the voter screen next to the QR code enables a malicious verification application to read it. Having access to q will in turn allow the verification app to reveal the voter's choice during the verification process.

Hence the code q has to be displayed to the user after the QR code. The question now becomes at which point this should be done. From the usability point of view, displaying q should happen right after the voter has scanned the QR code. However, the problem with the current protocol is that the voter application is not informed about the moment of scanning. Thus a new message needs to be added to the protocol. Once the need for a new message is already established, it is natural to define q as its content.

This will also give rise to a cleaner cryptographic protocol design where a party (voting application) does not have access to a value (q) before it absolutely needs to. We will later see in Sect. 3.1 that such a design choice is crucial in preventing the vote manipulation attack.

Finally we observe that the voting application does not need access to the whole q, but only the part q_{right} that will be displayed to the voter. Hence, sending over only q_{right} will be sufficient.

The resulting protocol is depicted in Fig. 3.

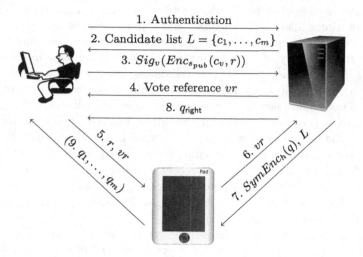

1. Authentication

2. Candidate list $L = \{c_1, \ldots, c_m\}$

3. $Sig_v(Enc_{s_{pub}}(c_v, r))$

4. Vote reference vr

8. q_{right}

5. r, vr

(9. $q_1, \ldots, q_m$)

6. vr

7. $SymEnc_h(q), L$

Pad

Fig. 3. Improved update to the Estonian protocol

3.1   Analysis of the Improved Protocol

In this Section we will analyse to which extent does the proposed update help to mitigate the vulnerabilities present in [6].

The vote manipulation attack described in Sect. 2.4 assumes access to q before selecting the encryption randomness r. On the other hand, in the updated protocol, the voter application has to commit to r before it sees q_{right}. Hence the best it can do is to guess q_{right}. Even if q_{right} is only 32 bits long, the probability of success is only 2^{-32}, assuming the choice of q is truly random.

Of course this assumption may be violated if the server behaves dishonestly. But note that even in this case we obtain a higher level of security as compared to [6], since now coordinated malicious collaboration between the voter application and the server is required to manipulate the vote in a manner undetected by verification.

Non-random choice of q can also be used to violate privacy of the vote in case of malicious collaboration between the server and the verification application. If the verification app can predict the value of q_{right}, it can trivially determine the voter preference by looking at the list of verification code candidates $q_1, \ldots, q_m$. This attack would be equivalent to leaking the value of q to the verification app, say, on step 7 of Fig. 3. Again, such an attack would only work if the server and the verification application would collaborate maliciously.

When the server generates q honestly randomly, also the guessing attack presented in Sect. 2.3 can be prevented. To achieve this, the true value of q_{right} must be (visually) indistinguishable from all the candidates obtained by decryption.

This is easy to implement for machine-generated random values. The only user interface aspect to solve is the visual representation of q_{right} and its candidates. There are standard approaches for this problem, including hexadecimal and base-64 representations, allowing to encode 4 and 6 per character, respectively. Since 6 bits allows for more entropy, we suggest using the base-64-like encoding.

As the final security observation we note that sending q_{right} instead of q on step 8 of Fig. 3 is in fact critical. If a malicious voting application would have access to the entire q, it would know all the necessary values to compute q_i ($i = 1, \ldots, m$). This would allow for a vote manipulation attack where the malicious voting app casts a vote for a different candidate, but still shows the verification code q_i that the voter sees next to her own preference on the verification device.

A malicious voting app may attempt accessing $SymEnc_h(q)$ (which would also be sufficient to restore all the values q_i) by faking a verification request. This problem should also be mitigated, possibly by using out-of-protocol measures like limiting the number of verification attempts, only allowing verifications from a different IP address compared to voting, etc.

Since our update does not change the verification experience as compared to [6], usability problems of scrolling through a long list of code candidates still remains. Consequently, the side channel determined by the moment of stopping the scrolling and leading to the hypothesis that the correct candidate number must be displayed at that moment still remains. These problems may probably be eased a little by packing as many code candidates to one screen as possible, say, in form of a 2-dimensional table. This leads to another trade-off between usability and privacy guarantees of the solution.

4   Conclusions and Further Work

Even though vote privacy was not the primary design goal of the Estonian vote verification application, it would of course be nice to have extra privacy protection capabilities. Unfortunately, the proposal made in [6] is even at the voter's best effort still completely vulnerable to a guessing attack by just looking at the characters used by the code candidates.

Also, we have demonstrated a vote manipulation attack that can be implemented with reasonable amount of pre-computation by an attacker who manages to compromise the voting application or voter's computer. As a result, the verification application does not fulfil its purpose of ensuring correct operation of the voting application.

As a possible solution, we presented an improvement to the protocol where the verification code generation is performed by the server rather than the voter. We have shown that the resulting protocol has stronger security properties, requiring at least two parties to collaborate maliciously in order to break either the verification or privacy properties.

The major drawback in both [6] and the present proposal is the drop in usability. Unfortunately, this will lead to an additional side channel attack against vote privacy in the course of verification. The question of the right balance between usability and privacy remains the subject of future research.

Acknowledgements. The research leading to these results has received funding from the European Regional Development Fund through Estonian Centre of Excellence in ICT Research (EXCITE) and the Estonian Research Council under Institutional Research Grant IUT27-1. The authors are also grateful to Arnis Paršovs for pointing out a flaw in an earlier version of the improved protocol.

References

1. Heiberg, S., Laud, P., Willemson, J.: The application of I-voting for estonian parliamentary elections of 2011. In: Kiayias, A., Lipmaa, H. (eds.) Vote-ID 2011. LNCS, vol. 7187, pp. 208–223. Springer, Heidelberg (2012). doi:10.1007/978-3-642-32747-6_13
2. Heiberg, S., Martens, T., Vinkel, P., Willemson, J.: Improving the verifiability of the Estonian internet voting scheme. In: Krimmer, R., Volkamer, M., Barrat, J., Benaloh, J., Goodman, N., Ryan, P.Y.A., Teague, V. (eds.) E-Vote-ID 2016. LNCS, vol. 10141, pp. 92–107. Springer, Cham (2017). doi:10.1007/978-3-319-52240-1_6
3. Heiberg, S., Parsovs, A., Willemson, J.: Log analysis of Estonian internet voting 2013–2014. In: Haenni, R., Koenig, R.E., Wikström, D. (eds.) VOTELID 2015. LNCS, vol. 9269, pp. 19–34. Springer, Cham (2015). doi:10.1007/978-3-319-22270-7_2
4. Heiberg, S., Parsovs, A., Willemson, J.: Log analysis of estonian internet voting 2013–2015. Cryptology ePrint Archive, Report 2015/1211 (2015). http://eprint.iacr.org/2015/1211
5. Heiberg, S., Willemson, J.: Verifiable internet voting in Estonia. In: 2014 6th International Conference on Electronic Voting: Verifying the Vote (EVOTE), pp. 1–8. IEEE (2014)
6. Muş, K., Kiraz, M.S., Cenk, M., Sertkaya, I.: Estonian voting verification mechanism revisited. Cryptology ePrint Archive, Report 2016/1125 (2016). http://eprint.iacr.org/2016/1125
7. Vinkel, P., Krimmer, R.: The how and why to internet voting an attempt to explain E-Stonia. In: Krimmer, R., Volkamer, M., Barrat, J., Benaloh, J., Goodman, N., Ryan, P.Y.A., Teague, V. (eds.) E-Vote-ID 2016. LNCS, vol. 10141, pp. 178–191. Springer, Cham (2017). doi:10.1007/978-3-319-52240-1_11
8. Wagenaar, W.A.: Generation of random sequences by human subjects: a critical survey of literature. Psychol. Bullet. **77**(1), 65 (1972)

Author Index

Printed in the United States
By Bookmasters